mance art to ruinous solipsism. It's especially good to be reminded that Wenner, in addition to being a successful media mogul and perpetual gossip item, has been a journalist of real distinction, with the ability to find talented editors like Seymour, who, I assume, did most of the actual cutting and pasting to create the book's unflagging pace from interviews with 112 sources, ranging from Jimmy Carter to Johnny Depp."   — Joe Klein, *New York Times Book Review*

"*Gonzo* is no hagiography, and it is in its unflinching look at this singular character in American letters as fearless — if not more so — as anything Thompson ever dared write. . . . The most comprehensive picture of Thompson so far, and likely the best we'll ever get."
                    — Patrick Beach, *Austin American-Statesman*

"Given Thompson's penchant for epic conversations, an oral biography is the perfect form for conveying his literary genius, on-the-edge-life, and complicated relationship with the truth. . . . This singularly well-shaped collection of candid reminiscences forms a penetrating, sharply emotional portrait of a brilliant writer. . . . Wenner and coeditor Seymour have exploded the Thompson caricature to reclaim the man in all his empathic volatility and the writer whose original and ferociously smart and funny works will forever spike the American canon."   — Donna Seaman, *Booklist* (starred review)

"Intensively researched. . . . Instructive even for those who knew Thompson slightly, *Gonzo* will positively titillate those who knew only his books and his reputation, and are entranced by the gonzo mythology. . . . *Gonzo* both entertains and illuminates. . . . A fairly candid portrait. . . . Accounts of Thompson's dead-eye sense of humor and timing spill over from page to page, as do recollections of his celebrated ability to look into the future and accurately predict changes in the political winds."   — John Colson, *Aspen Times*

"Uproarious and unpredictable, this oral biography is a fitting look at the turbulent life of gonzo journalism pioneer Hunter S. Thompson. . . . This fine, fond biography amuses, inspires, outrages, and haunts at all the right moments — and sometimes all at once."
— *Publishers Weekly* (starred review)

"As the skeletons come tumbling out of the closets, you'll be constantly amazed at the jaw-dropping, eye-popping excesses of drugs, alcohol, and emotional (and sometimes physical) violence revealed. . . . It's riveting." — Duane Davis, *Rocky Mountain News*

"A lively mosaic of American life. . . . A full, complete picture of this complex countercultural hero." — Charles C. Nash, *Library Journal*

"Engaging. It is a riotous, no-holds-barred exposé of Hunter at his provocative best. . . . Buy the ticket, it's a helluva ride."
— Mark Billingsley, *Aspen Daily News*

"Those who like their literary entertainment with a little more snarl to it might do well with *Gonzo.*" — Tim Martin, *Telegraph*

"*Gonzo* takes the reader through Hunter S. Thompson's wild ride from the eyes of those savage enough to keep up with him."
— Ron Capshaw, *Style Weekly*

"Wenner and Seymour and [110 other] insiders tell you pretty much all there is to tell about Thompson. *Gonzo* is thirteen chapters of quotes, anecdotes, tall tales, and inside info from those who knew and loved or hated him, drank with him, chapters that — as much as any bio can — bring you the real Hunter S. Thompson. It is indeed an oral biography and as such holds your interest and makes you read on."
— Bob Pepping, *Providence Journal*

"Invigorating."　　　　　　　　　　—Janet Kinosian, *AARP* Online

"Wenner and Seymour's book draws on the memories of some who knew Thompson best: childhood friends, editors, neighbors, even bartenders. They recall all sorts of things about the man who invented gonzo journalism."　　　—Karen Haymon Long, *Tampa Tribune*

"A mostly engaging attempt to account for the sudden absence of an author whose irresistible presence was always the focus of his best storytelling."　　　　　　　—Christopher Jensen, *SF Weekly*

"Offers a well-crafted insight."　　　—Sherman Smith, *Capital-Journal*

"A great, extended reminiscence by Thompson's friends and colleagues. . . . Adds more perspective to the life and times of one of our best political-cultural commentators."
　　　　　　　　—Martin Zimmerman, *San Diego Union-Tribune*

"This well-edited collection of recollections by those who knew him makes for brisk literary entertainment."
　　　　　　　　　　—Robert Wiersema, *National Post*

"A fascinating read."　　　　　　　—Rob Conery, *Cape Cod Times*

"This thorough tome presents many private elements as it touches the essential moments of this iconic author's life. . . . While many Thompson aficionados will love this book for its minutiae, newbies will no longer be referred to as such upon finishing *Gonzo*. This informative oral history turns its readers, regardless of experience, into authorities on Thompson's life."　　　　　　　—Austin L. Ray, *Paste*

GONZO

THE LIFE OF
HUNTER S. THOMPSON

An Oral Biography by

JANN S. WENNER & COREY SEYMOUR

Introduction by JOHNNY DEPP

BACK BAY BOOKS
Little, Brown and Company
New York Boston London

Back Bay Books / Little, Brown and Company
Hachette Book Group
237 Park Avenue, New York, NY 10017
Visit our Web site at www.HachetteBookGroupUSA.com

Originally published in hardcover by Little, Brown and Company, October 2007
First Back Bay paperback edition, October 2008

Back Bay Books is an imprint of Little, Brown and Company. The Back Bay Books name and logo
are trademarks of Hachette Book Group, Inc.

WENNER MEDIA

Library of Congress Cataloging-in-Publication Data
Wenner, Jann S.
Gonzo: the life of Hunter S. Thompson / by Jann S. Wenner and Corey Seymour;
introduction by Johnny Depp. — 1st ed.
p. cm.
Includes index.
ISBN 978-0-316-00527-2 (hc) / 978-0-316-00528-9 (pb)
1. Thompson, Hunter S.   2. Journalists — United States — Biography.   3. Thompson,
Hunter S. — Friends and associates.   I. Seymour, Corey.   II. Title.
PN4874.T444W38 2007
070.92 — dc22   2007011693

10 9 8 7 6 5 4 3 2 1

Interior book design by Jo Anne Metsch

RRD-IN

Printed in the United States of America

No beast so fierce but knows some touch of pity. . . .
But I know none, and therefore am no beast.

— WILLIAM SHAKESPEARE, *King Richard the Third*

CONTENTS

Editor's Note   xi

Foreword   xv

Introduction by Johnny Depp   xxi

Chapter One
Coming of Age in Louisville   3

Chapter Two
An Itinerant Professional   22

Chapter Three
**San Francisco, Hells Angels, and
Merry Pranksters**   75

Chapter Four
Freak Power in the Rockies   93

Chapter Five
The Golden Age of Gonzo   120

Chapter Six
A New Voice on the Campaign Trail   153

Chapter Seven
Failed Deadlines and a Failed Marriage   181

Chapter Eight

Wreckage in the Fast Lane   224

Chapter Nine

Circling the Wagons at Owl Farm   281

Chapter Ten

A Writer Resurgent   298

Chapter Eleven

Vegas Goes to Hollywood   330

Chapter Twelve

Where Were You When the Fun Stopped?   367

Chapter Thirteen

The End of the Road   412

Cast of Voices   439

Acknowledgments   449

Index   451

This oral history began with the memorial issue published by *Rolling Stone* immediately after Hunter S. Thompson's suicide on Sunday, February 20, 2005. The idea of creating tributes through the eyes and ears of contemporaries began early in our magazine's history. We've done it often, reaching people by phone or in person to capture their memories of the subject, and it's become a kind of ritual that starts up automatically when a hero of ours or a musical or literary giant passes.

With Hunter it was this and more. We went all out. There were a lot of people who knew and loved him, and they spoke so vividly (many of them, of course, were professional word slingers) and so fully that it was clear from the beginning (Hunter actually, for the first time, left us with a not unreasonable deadline) that we had a lot on our hands. The team effort consisted of two principal features editors, an occasional designated hitter, myself doing a final edit on everything, and the interviews and research done by two former *Rolling Stone* editorial assistants, both of whom had been tasked to Hunter on separate occasions (you'll read about that amazing perspective shortly).

I did find it amusing that once again—though for the last time—everyone at the magazine and some far-flung others were being pressed into one final, consuming deadline struggle on behalf of Dr. Thompson. It was like the old days in a curious and sweet way. We were still working for Hunter.

Corey Seymour and Tobias Perse, who were the former assistants who came in to do the grunt work, were deep in the trenches more than a decade ago, when they were each assigned at one point to be Hunter's aide-de-camp/slave when he was doing major features for the magazine. Their own stories in this volume are both eye-opening and hair-raising. In any case, they came in to show their love one last time; and Corey, because of his special devotion and doggedness, stayed on to expand that special issue fiftyfold, traveling the country and going back in person to many of the principals, visiting childhood friends, chasing down the stars, and collecting transcripts that when they were first roughly assembled came to some 500,000 words, about three times the length of this book.

For Corey, it was a labor of love, as much as anything; I feel the same.

Also, from the memorial issue, we have included as prefatory essays here my own open eulogy for a man who had been one of my closest friends and a lifelong partner in crime, as well as a tribute/memoir/ love letter written, on deadline, by Johnny Depp. Johnny and Hunter were both bad boys from Kentucky, and they admired and loved each other deeply. I saw with my own eyes how special Johnny had become to Hunter, and likewise how devoted and worshipful Johnny had been toward him.

Hunter knew an amazing number of people; he was open and friendly to most strangers; he was charismatic and compelling — to a fault, truly — and he attracted and held sway with more good, close friends than most of us have, admirers, neighbors, worshippers, politicians, groupies, fellow writers, bartenders, nut jobs, hard cases, women, and thrill seekers of all stripes. Many people who knew Hunter well over many years spoke to us but, alas, were edited out for reasons of space and duplication. Stories of Hunter's wild escapades and deadline frenzies are legendary and numerous, but after a while they can become a tedious read. Lack of inclusion here is no denial that strong and real friendships and relationships existed with many good and kind people. I'm also sorry that Hunter's second wife, Anita, would not allow her quotes to be used, but she was fully cooperative with the reporting and was forthcoming in all other aspects.

In editing this book, I learned quite a bit about Hunter that I didn't know, and I did think I nearly knew it all. He was a man of many interests, moods, quirks, and passions; more than one hundred voices start to reveal all that here. And there is the common theme of how much everyone loved him, how singular and powerful a presence he was in people's lives.

To write someone's biography — or to edit an oral history — is to sift and choose among all kinds of nuances, shadowings, points of view, and points of fact. To print any given fact is to endorse it and to give it validity; to choose any particular individual's insight or memory is to give it a historical importance.

I was glad to take on the responsibility of making those choices; it felt right, and I ask only for the reader's understanding and faith when it comes to how I portrayed my own role in Hunter's life and work. In my own mind, those decisions had to be able to stand the tests of time and a skeptical examination.

For my part, I want to thank Corey for his devotion and hard work, then and now; Paul Scanlon, a man with a fine eye and a fine pen; Lynn Nesbit, Hunter's longtime agent, and our mutual friend, who suggested and sold this book; Colonel Depp, a comrade in arms; Doug Brinkley, Juan Thompson, Sondi (Sandy always to me) Thompson, Laila Nabulsi, and Deborah Fuller, who have been friends and allies and family through many years; and Jane Wenner, "queen of the underground," whose photo was next to Hunter's phone until the day he died.

—J.S.W.
Martha's Vineyard
August 2007

My Brother in Arms by Jann S. Wenner

✠

Hunter S. Thompson was part of the DNA of *Rolling Stone,* one of those twisting strands of chemicals around which a new life is formed. He was such a big part of my life, and I loved him deeply.

He was a man of energy, physical presence, utter charm, genius talent, and genius humor. It was very hard to have to give him up and say good-bye.

When I was a young man, twenty-four years old, in the summer of 1970, I had the great fortune of meeting Hunter. He came to my office, then in San Francisco, to settle the details of writing an article about his campaign for sheriff in Aspen, Colorado. He was thirty-three, stood six-three, shaved bald, dark glasses, smoking, carrying two six-packs of beer; he sat down, slowly unpacked a leather satchel full of "travel necessities" onto my desk — mainly hardware, like flashlights, a siren, knives, boxes of cigarettes and filters, whiskey, corkscrews, flares — and didn't leave for three hours. He was hypnotic, and by the end I was deep into his campaign.

The record indicates that in 1970 we published "The Battle of Aspen"; in 1971, he wrote about the stirrings of Mexican unrest in East Los Angeles, based in part on a fiery lawyer named Oscar Zeta Acosta, who later that year emerged as Dr. Gonzo in "Fear and Loathing in Las Vegas."

In 1972, we began nonstop coverage of the Nixon-McGovern presidential campaign. Hunter took over my life then — and for many years after that, when he was reporting (long nocturnal telephone calls and frequent all-night strategy sessions) and especially when he was writing.

After "Fear and Loathing in Las Vegas," everything else he wrote was a full-out siege. Setting up the assignment was easy — Hunter was pretty much welcome everywhere and had the skills and instincts to run a presidential campaign if he had wanted. But then came the travel arrangements: hotels, tickets, researchers, rental cars. Then, later in the process, finding a place for him to hunker down and write — the Seal Rock Inn, Key West, Owl Farm, preferably somewhere isolated and with a good bar. Flying in IBM Selectric typewriters with the right typeface; booze and drugs (usually he had this part already done); arranging for a handler-assistant at his end; and then, back at *Rolling Stone,* I had to be available to read and edit copy as it came in eight-to-ten-page bursts — via the Xerox telecopier ("the mojo wire"), a primitive fax that had a stylus that printed onto treated paper (at a rate of seven minutes per page) and smelled. I had to talk to Hunter for hours, then track and organize the various scenes and sections. He usually began writing in the middle, then would back up or skip around to write what he felt good about at that moment, reporting scenes that might fit somewhere later, or spinning out total fantasies ("Insert ZZ" or "midnight screed") that would also find a place — parts that were flights of genius. Generally the lede was easy, describing the invariably dramatic weather wherever he was writing from. Then a flurry of headlines and chapter headings and the transitions he had to produce on demand to create the flow and logic, and always, sooner or later, the conclusion, which we always called "the Wisdom."

He liked to work against a crisis, and if there wasn't a legitimate one, he made one. We never had a fight about the editing. I never tried to change him or "improve" him, but since I had a pretty deep understanding of his style and his motives, I could tell where he was going and sit at his side and read the map to him. If I didn't personally supervise everything he wrote for *Rolling Stone,* he wouldn't finish. It was a bit like being the cornerman for Ali. Editing Hunter required stamina, but I was young, and this was once in a lifetime, and we were both clear on that.

Hunter's office visits and debriefings were always an event. The late arrival, the slow, long, ambling walk down the hall, the gathering commotion, and finally some kind of loud noise or shriek or siren blast as he got to my office. We had an ice-making machine installed at his insistence. He was a Pied Piper, and everyone realized how extraordinary he was — charming, flirtatious, insanely funny. And smart.

Life with Hunter was so much fun — he used to stay at my house, but that got to be a little too much. Car rides — headlights off — at three a.m. on moonless nights with a head full of acid were a pretty standard feature in those days. Later on, Hunter used to tell me that I was responsible for the drug problem in America. "Are you kidding? It's your fault, Hunter, and everyone knows it." We agreed to share the blame. (For the record, I never canceled his life insurance when he went to Saigon. And also for the record, I do not have seven thousand first editions of *Fear and Loathing in Las Vegas* secretly warehoused, to be sold upon his death.)

I am no longer pissed at him for shooting off a fire extinguisher in my elegant New York office a few years ago, which he did to remind me that he had done the same thing years earlier, very late one mellowed-out night, as I sat listening to music in front of the fireplace in my living room, deep into the lysergic.

Great stories of "bad craziness" and gonzo behavior are legendary, and they are all true. It was part of what all of us found so addictive about Hunter: It was an adrenaline rush to be with him. Walking with him, you knew you were likely to come near the edge of the cliff, to sense danger, to get as close to the edge as most of us get in our lives.

And, at the same time, so extremely funny.

Our friendship became a deep one; we were at each other's houses constantly for years; our families became close-knit. The stories of his loyalty and courage told by his many, many friends in this book convey what it was really like to be his friend.

We both were deep into politics and shared the same ambition to have a voice in where the country was going (thus, the "National Affairs Desk"). We deliberately set out to do this. We became partners in this as well, as mad as it may have seemed at the time — a rock & roll magazine and a man known for writing about motorcycle gangs, joining forces to change the country. We used to read aloud what he had just written, get to certain phrases or sentences, and just exclaim to each other, "Hot fucking damn." It was scorching, original, and it was fun. He was my brother in arms.

In my opinion, he hit his peak in humor in a piece titled "Fear and Loathing in Elko" (1992), a dark, sustained masterpiece of violence and madness. Although many people tend to neglect his later work — and he wrote much less in the last ten years — "Elko," "A Dog Took My Place" (1983), and "Polo Is My Life: Fear and Loathing in Horse Country" (1994) are among his very best, at the top of his form.

Now those days are gone. Once I had Hunter all to myself, and now I don't have him at all. He was a careful, deliberate, and calculating man, and his suicide was not careless, not an accident, and not selfish. He was in a wheelchair toward the end of his life, and he decided he would not be able to live with extreme physical disability; it just wasn't him. He had already lived longer than he, or any of us, had expected. He had lived a great life, filled with friends, his genius talent, and righteousness.

Yr. Buddy,
Jann

Woody Creek
March 11th, 1998

Dear Jann,

 Just seeing you and me and Joe [Eszterhas] mentioned in the same paragraph still gives me an atavistic rush. My memory of those days is mainly of tremendous energy and talent and rare commitment running (almost) amok, but not quite. It was like being invited into a bonfire and finding out that fire is actually your friend. Ho Ho . . .

 But just how hot can you stand it, brother, before your love will crack?

 That was the real question in those days, I think. Or maybe it was about how much money you were being paid. Or how much fun you were having. Who knows? Some people were fried to cinders, as I recall, while others used the heat to transmogrify themselves into heroes.

 (Which reminds me that you still owe me a vast amount of money — and you still refuse to even discuss payment for my recent politics memo.)

 Anyway, my central memory of that time is that everything we were doing seemed to work. Or almost everything. What the hell? Buy the ticket, take the ride, eh? Like an amusement park, or the Circus-Circus casino: It depended on your personal definition of "acceptable loss."

 I know Joe considers his days at Rolling Stone *to be an utter waste of time and talent, or maybe he just says that for his own vengeful reasons. Some people are too weird for their own good.*

 But not me, Jann. I say thanx for the rush.

Yr. Buddy,
Hunter

A Pair of Deviant Bookends by Johnny Depp

"Buy the ticket, take the ride." These are the words that echo in my skull, the words that our Good Doctor lived by and, by God, died by. He dictated, created, commanded, demanded, manipulated, manhandled, and snatched life up by the short hairs, and only relinquished his powerful grasp when he was ready. There's the rub. When HE was ready. And so it seems he was.

We are here, without him. But in no way are we left with nothing, far from it. For the multitudes of die-hard gonzo admirers out there, of which I too am one, we have his words, his books, his insights, his humor, and his truth. For those of us lucky enough to have been close to him, which most often meant rather lengthy and dangerous occasions that would invariably lead to doubling over with uncontrollable fits of laughter, we have his gift of the experiences and memories to fill us and send our thoughts forever toward that image of his Cheshire grin leading us wherever he felt we needed to go. Which, by the way, was always the right direction, however insane it may have seemed. Yes, the doctor always knew best.

I have, seared onto my brain, millions of these hideous little adventures that I was blessed enough to have lived through with him and, frankly, in certain instances, blessed to have simply lived through. He was/is a brother, a friend, a hero, a father, a son, a teacher, a partner in crime. Our crime, fun. Always, fun.

Hunter and I met in December of 1995 through a mutual friend while I was vacationing in Aspen, Colorado. I had long been a huge fan of not only "the Vegas book," as Hunter always referred to it, but basically every single word the man had spewed onto pages. Somewhere around eleven one night, while I was nursing a drink at the deep back of the Woody Creek Tavern, an unusually loud noise stole my attention and then demanded the room's attention — a hush on one side, fearful murmurings on the other, were replaced by mounting screams, as what appeared to be an electric saber swung wildly near the entrance of the bar. Patrons jumped aside in horror as a deep, raspy voice hollered people out of its way, threatening to shock the living shit out of any swine that dared linger in its path. In an instant, it was clear that our rendezvous had commenced.

Tall and lanky, wearing a woolen Native American–looking knit hat that trailed down past his shoulders, the ubiquitous aviators tight to the face, he shot a massive hand toward me. I placed my hand in his firm hold and gave back what I got — the beginning, I sensed, of a long and deep-rooted friendship.

He plopped himself into a chair, laid his armaments — a giant cattle prod and a hefty Taser — on the table. In that very second, the proverbial good times began to roll. We had a few rounds, talked about this and that, and connected on more than a few levels, not the least being the discovery that we both hailed from the dark and bloody ground of the great state of Kentucky. That fact alone sent Hunter into eloquent tirades ranging from southern chivalry to hillbilly moonshine-running to our fellow Kentuckian Cassius Clay. Within no time, the group was invited back to Owl Farm, Hunter's fortified compound just up the road from the tavern, where we babbled ourselves silly and, at about two-thirty a.m., blew up propane bombs with a nickel-plated shotgun.

This, I was to learn later, was my first test before being initiated into the "Too Much Fun Club."

Sometime later, I was working on *Donnie Brasco* in New York City when my phone rang one morning at about five-thirty a.m. "Johnny . . . Hunter . . . Listen, if they were going to do a film of the Vegas book . . . would you be interested? Would you want to play me?" I was stunned and tried to gather myself. "Well . . . What about it? Are you in?" Of course I was. Who wouldn't have been? I was beyond interested. It had actually been a dream of mine that I'd always thought an impossibility. We spoke a bit more about the hows, the whos, the whens, et cetera. It was then that I learned that there really weren't any. There was nothing — no script, no director, no production at all. It simply didn't exist. Not yet, anyway. He'd inquired for his own edification. He did that sort of thing a lot. Rhyme, reason, and rationale might have been totally invisible to the majority, but Hunter was always way ahead of the curve. Even amid what appeared to be absolute chaos, he was all too aware of exactly where the chips would fall.

We both acknowledged that there would be a great need for me to spend ungodly and potentially unhealthy amounts of time with him. We'd already established a pretty strong friendship from various other adventures together, such as a three-hour stint onstage at the Viper Room in L.A. I'd come to see Hunter and was then wrangled into doing the entire gig with him. He had insisted over dinner, minutes before he was due to be introduced at the club: Either I went onstage with him or he would cancel the whole thing right then and there. John Cusack had come 'round and was also shanghaied into participating. The three of us drove to the entrance of the club in some rented (I think) convertible. We inched our way down Sunset Boulevard with a life-size blow-up doll in tow and the ever-bespectacled Dr. Thompson spilling whiskey everywhere out of his large highball glass. Oh yeah, were we ever subtle. As we began to park, Dr. Thompson decided that the right thing to do was to heave the poor, defenseless sex maiden into the Sunset Strip traffic. One nasty screeching of tires and one horrified, ultra-high-pitched scream from Hunter, and all hell broke loose — more screeching, more screams, all eyes in our direction. A trail of madness in — literally — seconds.

Reunited with the sex toy, we calmly made our way inside and took the stage. The night got weirder and weirder, but my God, was it fun. Too much fun.

Meanwhile, the *Vegas* film finally got set up properly, and the time came for some serious soul stealing. I flew into Aspen and was greeted at the airport by Hunter in his '71 Chevy convertible, aka the Red Shark. We serpentined our way through the mountains and arrived at Owl Farm, where I was swiftly invited to put my things in the basement, where I lived for much longer than was planned and grew to be kind of comfortable with the brown recluse spiders that shared the room.

For days and nights on end we would sit in that Command Center and talk about anything and everything, from politics to weapons, our home state, lipstick, music, Hitler's paintings, literature, sports, always sports. We were talking one night about which sports he preferred and didn't. We were watching plenty of basketball and loads of football, so I asked him he if he had ever been a baseball fan, to which he replied flatly, "No . . . Baseball is like watching a bunch of angry Jews arguing on the porch." Once, a year later, we made a bet on the World Cup soccer tournament, France versus Brazil. He was absolutely, vehemently positive that Brazil was just going to cream France. I took that bet, one thousand dollars. We teased and prodded each other for weeks leading up to the match. The outcome bent in my favor; he promptly wrote me a check and sent it with this letter:

WELL, COLONEL, I TOLD YOU THE FUCKING GAME WAS FIXED. I just didn't think those prissy quadroon boys

*would go totally into the tank. They acted like stupid animals. They shit
all over themselves and disgraced a whole nation of gutless whores in the eyes
of the world. And it taught me another good lesson in WHY amateurs
shouldn't fuck around with gambling on games they know nothing about.*

Anyway, here's a check for $1,000.

Thank you very much for yr. business. I'll be back.

Okay,

Doc

His generosity was astounding. Never once did he try to wriggle away from my unending barrage of questions. He was always exceptionally patient and very giving. He was totally open regarding the details of his exploits, personal experiences, and memories, even the more private and intimate particulars from his past. He did not have to be. The more time together, the more intense the bond. For the most part, we were inseparable. And it felt good. The connection was profound and becoming more so.

I used to tease him that we were becoming a perversely dark and twisted version of Edgar Bergen and Charlie McCarthy, which really made him uncomfortable. I had by this point purloined an impressive amount of his clothing from the Vegas period and adopted his mode of dress: the aviator shades, a bush hat, short pants, athletic socks, Converse sneakers, cigarette holder clenched tightly between the teeth. If I took my hat off and aired out the chrome dome, he'd always beg me to cover up again. We'd saunter out of the house like freakish twins. For good or ill, there we were — a pair of deviant bookends on the prowl. Truly, the man should be sainted for putting up with my continual scratching away at the layers of his life. He stuck it out like a champion and couldn't have been a better friend.

There are countless other moments and experiences that I was fortunate enough to have gone through with Hunter, far too many to write about here. I was well aware that it was all going to happen only once in a lifetime. These were fantastic experiences. Some of the best moments of my life were happening to me, and luckily, I knew it.

Speaking as a fan: You owe it to yourselves to not be cheated, or shortchanged, by believing merely the myth. Understand that his road and his methods were his and only his, and that he lived and breathed his writing twenty-four hours a day. There are those of you who, based on Hunter's journeys and the mad stories that surround his life and memory, the excess and wild rantings of his lifestyle, might think that he was simply some hedonistic lunatic or, as he always put it, "an elderly dope fiend." I promise you, he was not. He was a southern gentleman, all chivalry and charm. He was a hilarious and rascally little boy. A truth seeker. He was a hypersensitive medium who miraculously channeled the underlying current of truth buried in lies that we have become accustomed to believing.

Hunter was a genius who revolutionized writing in the same way that Marlon Brando did with acting, as significant, essential, and valuable as Dylan, Kerouac, and the Stones. He was without question the most loyal and present friend I have ever had the honor of knowing. I am privileged to have belonged to the small fraternity of people in his life who were allowed to see more than most. He was elegance personified. I miss him. I missed him when he was alive. But, dear Doctor, I will see you again.

Colonel Depp
Los Angeles

GONZO

CHAPTER ONE

Coming of Age in Louisville

We had guns in our cars. We shot houses, mailboxes, garbage cans. We shoplifted. We broke into liquor stores. We'd jimmy a lock or break a window. I never paid a hotel bill when I was with Hunter. We'd just go out the window or the fire escape.

SANDY THOMPSON (now Sondi Wright) *met Hunter in 1958 and was married to him for seventeen years.*

Hunter was born different — very different. His mother, Virginia, and I talked a lot many, many years ago about Hunter as a little boy. He was angry. He was charming. He was a lot of trouble. And what I always used to say — which is interesting, in light of the end of his life — was that he shot out of the womb angry. And then he left that same way.

NEVILLE BLAKEMORE *grew up with Hunter in the Highlands neighborhood of Louisville, Kentucky.*

My grandmother owned a house a block away from Hunter's. I couldn't tell you the first time I met him; I just knew about him.

It was a neighborhood in which people would sit on the porch and talk to the people walking by. Washing was hung in the backyard to dry, and ironing was done with flatirons heated on stoves. Everybody knew everybody — the generations knew everybody, everybody knew the help, and so on. In the afternoon we'd listen to radio programs like *Superman* and *Sky King*. Television did not exist.

Hunter's dad, Jack, was born in Horse Cave, Kentucky, in 1893 and came to Louisville with his three brothers when his widowed mother moved here. His first wife, who was from eastern Kentucky, died in 1923 — two years after their first and only child, Jack Jr., was born. Jack Jr. was raised by his maternal grandmother in Greenup, Kentucky, so he wasn't around much. And he was a lot older; he served in World War II and Korea.

Mr. Thompson was a tallish man with glasses and gray hair combed straight back. He had served in World War I, and he was stern. Hunter's mother was Virginia Ray, who Jack married in 1935, and her mother was named — well, we called her Memo. Hunter was Jack and Virginia's first child — born on July 18, 1937. Mr. Thompson was an insurance agent, and Memo helped with raising the children and was always around the house. She'd read to us.

DEBORAH FULLER *was Hunter's personal assistant from 1982 to 2003.*

Hunter's mother told me that he was born a night owl. She cursed him for that — "Oh God, he never slept at the same time as his brothers." But Virginia loved him and was very proud of him. She told me he was very charismatic as a young man, even as a boy. Kids — boys and girls — would come around to the house and sit on the front steps to wait to walk to school with Hunter. But she also said that he was a feisty one — that he got in trouble quite a bit.

NEVILLE BLAKEMORE

My parents didn't like my hanging around with him — even when we were pretty young. They thought he was a bully. I think they may have been right. But we always wanted to go over to his house. Hunter was a magnet. There was always something going on. We had toy soldiers and we'd play these huge war games. World War II was a big influence. We'd play Germans and Japanese, and have battles all over the neighborhood. People would have cardboard guns and cap pistols and backpacks and helmet liners. Some guys had BB guns.

Hunter got his interest in guns from another neighbor, Joe Bell. Joe understood firearms when he came out of the womb. He loved them, and he always had the latest thing.

Hunter would go over to another friend's house, and behind the street where this friend lived was Bear Grass Creek and a culvert. A lot of African Americans lived on the other side of the creek. Hunter and his group would shoot these guys with BB guns and hurl racial insults, and the black guys would finally have enough and swarm down into the culvert and up the wall, and Hunter and the others would retreat into their friend's house and hide. They'd start these little mini–race wars.

Everybody had bicycles. Hunter used to ride his bike around the neighborhood, shooting matches with a clothespin shooter. You could make a shooter out of just a clothespin and a rubber band and a "strike anywhere" match, and all you have to do is squeeze the thing and out shoots a lit match. People used to burn their leaves in the fall, and they'd rake them into the gutters first. But Hunter would ride around the neighborhood and shoot these things into the leaves and start fires all over the Highlands.

Another time, when I was twelve or thirteen, I had all the neighbor kids over for lunch, and we played soldiers in the backyard. Hunter stole a bunch of my soldiers. I figured it out that night, and it really hurt me. My father said, "Well, I'm very sorry, but it shouldn't be that much of a surprise, because that's the kind of guy he is." That for me meant, "Okay, he's fun to be around, but be careful."

GERALD TYRRELL *also grew up a block away from Hunter.*

Our group would go to Cherokee Park to play football, or go to the basketball courts, or grab a dime and go downtown to the movies — we would go all over the place — but going to the library and reading books was always given equal billing. Hunter would say, "Let's go to the library," and seven or eight of us would grab our bikes and ride down. It'd be all grab-ass and being rowdy and loud marching up the steps of the library, and then we'd be quiet as church mice inside and each pick out a book and sit down and read for a couple of hours, and then put the books back and leave and be rowdy and grab-ass and ride our bikes home. And it wasn't just on rainy days. It was year-round.

PORTER BIBB *grew up with Hunter in Louisville.*

I first met him when we were eleven or twelve. Louisville then was a very elitist town, and very small. Geographically it's midwestern, but we all thought of it as very southern.

He lived in a slightly decaying middle-class neighborhood. It had been a prominent upper-middle-class part of the city, but it was within walking distance of downtown, and the city had gone out to the country by the time we were growing up. His mother, Virginia, was a wonderful, very intelligent, very hospitable lady who worked as a librarian. She looked like Betty Crocker. Hunter also had two younger brothers, Davison and Jim.

SANDY THOMPSON

He was very good-looking, tall, slender. He had this wonderful gait — and just a tremendous power of seduction. And he knew this very early on: how he could seduce not just women but men, children — anybody he really wanted to.

LOU ANN ILER *was Hunter's high school sweetheart.*

I was a new student at Highland Junior High when I met Hunter in ninth grade, in 1951. He was at my locker between classes, and before I knew it he rode home on the bus with me, and then he carried my books; he put his arm around me. It was a very innocent time. We'd go to the movies, which was only twenty-five cents a person — even with popcorn and a Coke you could have a very nice date for a dollar — and we would go to high school football games or walk from my house to the ice-cream shops. Sometimes we got around on the bus, or he had older friends who drove and we double-dated with them. Afterward he would drop me off at my house and say good-night, but once I arrived at my door, my mother knew I was home and she set a time limit: five minutes, and that was it. So after we said good-bye, Hunter would throw pebbles at my bedroom window, and he would stand outside my window and we would talk for another forty-five minutes or an hour.

He was very charming and handsome, and had wonderful manners, and treated me very well. I wouldn't take any guff from him, and I think he liked that. And I could out-stare him, which used to annoy him greatly. He had a lot of energy — I wouldn't call it sexual energy at that point, because it was ninth grade, in the fifties — but he was different from the other young men I dated. There was just a presence about him. And, yes, he would draw attention to himself.

In our sophomore year we were double-dating at a neighborhood theater called the Bard. Afterward he told me that he was going to go with the other couple, and he'd be back. In a few minutes, up drove a car with this little old lady in the back, all dressed up, screaming, "Help me! Help me! I'm being kidnapped!" Well, it was Hunter. He had dressed in his mother's clothes — he had a hat and a veil, and he had on her stockings rolled down to his knee, and he was screeching in this high voice. Well, I got so mad, because it called so much attention to himself. I started walking home, with Hunter following me in the car, hanging out the back window, shouting, "Please get in the car. . . . I promise I'll never do this to you again." I walked all the way home.

We dated through that summer, and then we both went to Atherton

[High School] in our sophomore year. Hunter was there for about six weeks, and then something happened — I don't know what — and he immediately went to another school. One day he was there and the next day he was at Male High School. I didn't see him for a while, and I started dating other people, but he kept coming in and out of my life. He would show up unexpectedly at my house.

PORTER BIBB

There were basically four schools. There was Male for the white males who were going to college. There was Manual for the guys who were not going to college and were going to be manual laborers or blue-collar workers. There was St. Xavier for the Catholics and Central High for the blacks. Male, though, was really an extraordinary place, even though it was a public high school. We had people teaching there who had turned down tenure at Yale and Princeton.

GERALD TYRRELL

Hunter went to Highland Junior High School and then Atherton High School for a semester, and then down to Male. It wasn't long before he joined the Castlewood Athletic Club and later the Athenaeum Literary Association. Those were the two organizations that shaped all our young lives — particularly Hunter's.

To get into both Castlewood and, later, the Athenaeum, you had to rush. Hunter loved to pledge people. One of the things he liked best was to have pledges throw "fits." We'd go into a restaurant, and all of a sudden on his command you'd throw an epileptic fit and scream and roll on the floor and carry on. Sooner or later they'd have to call either the police or the ambulance, and you'd have to run off. Hunter would be outside just doubled over laughing.

We were all very keen on athletics. We hired coaches and we played football against other teams in other parts of the city, and we generally won. Hunter played end, and I played tackle. In basketball we played in the city fifteen-and-under league. Three out of four years we won the league championship.

One of Hunter's big disappointments was that he didn't grow in the ninth and tenth grades, when he was fifteen and sixteen. He was short. It wasn't until his junior year that he grew — maybe three or four inches. But by that time it was all over — he was a smoker and a drinker, and he wasn't the athlete that he really wanted to be.

His best friend from his early days was probably Duke Rice. He was a skinny kid and not all that tall, and suddenly he shot up to be six-six or six-seven and got a basketball scholarship to the Citadel, where he was the only player of the time who was able to shut down Jerry West. Duke was the athlete that Hunter always wanted to be. And Hunter's little brother Davison was an All-American high school football player and went to Vanderbilt on a football scholarship. Hunter was surrounded by guys who had the sports dream, and he was really the best of all of us growing up in any of these sports — and then he stayed a little kid at the critical time, and then two years later it was too late to catch up.

Since Hunter couldn't be an athlete, he had to turn his energies to something else — and he turned it to social activities based around various shapes of bottles. Now when we took the bus downtown to the orange bars for hot dogs and orange drinks, we'd put gin in our drinks and go to the movies.

DOUG BRINKLEY *is the literary executor of the Hunter S. Thompson estate and the editor of three volumes of his letters.*

He learned that he could essentially become a leader or a bully by verbal extravagance and by doing the most outrageous pranks — that he could become cooler than the football quarterback or the head of some glib Kentucky high school club by being a wild-ass maverick ready to find the weaknesses in somebody and rip them to shreds. It gave him the upper hand.

GERALD TYRRELL

Hunter was the most charismatic natural leader I've ever been subjected to. I could walk into a room with him, and everybody would gravitate to Hunter. He just had a way about him. He was very appealing to all the girls, and he was a cutie. It was probably his mother's training: He was very nice to girls, almost chivalrous, really.

DOUG BRINKLEY

It's not easy for a working-class woman to raise three boys full of testosterone when you don't have a support system for it. So she turned to gin. Add to that the fact that Hunter at a young age had a bit of a deformity with his legs — the bowlegged walk that people would imitate later was there when he was young — and it kept him from being the sports star he wanted to be. It wasn't just that one leg was longer than the other — he had a bit of a pain problem with his back and spine, a birth defect in a sense. He didn't cultivate that distinctive walk that he had. He couldn't help it. He turned it into an asset, but he always thought of it as a deficit. And Hunter quickly learned that you can be made fun of when you have a deformity, and the way to not be made fun of is to take the Nietzschean offensive and lash out before you can even be hit, and get people afraid of you. He was railing after bullies or the people that he thought were screwing the little guy.

LOU ANN ILER

Hunter's father died in July between our freshman and sophomore years. Hunter showed up on my doorstep — I had a large porch — and sat for hours, not saying too much. One of the loneliest things I've ever seen was Hunter walking away from my porch to catch the bus on the night his father died. It was dark, and the streetlight was on. He wasn't openly emotional, but I held his hand. He had decided that he needed to be here.

SANDY THOMPSON

Hunter's father had been, from what I heard from Hunter's friends, quite a strict disciplinarian. So I'm guessing that he held Hunter in check. And then he was gone. Virginia became an alcoholic. And even though Hunter was drinking then, he hated Virginia's drinking.

DOUG BRINKLEY

Hunter never really liked Jack Kerouac's *On the Road* — he thought the writing was kind of sloppy and romantic and oversentimental — but he told me he thought Kerouac was a genius for two things: discovering Neal Cassady, whom Hunter thought was flat-out amazing, and using the literary construct of "looking for the lost dad I never had." Neal was never properly raised by a father. He didn't even know whether his dad was alive or dead, and the notion of a young son who never had a dad, looking for his biological father, appealed to Hunter a great deal. Hunter didn't get to know his father, and at times this loss would burst out as oedipal anger, but underneath it all was just a deep longing for the dad he never had and an unanswerable question of how knowing him could have made his life richer and different. He had to figure it all out on his own.

His mother stayed on top of Hunter and his brothers the best that she could, and it was her bringing books home from the library like *Huck Finn* and *White Fang* and making her boys read that turned Hunter into a writer. Hunter had a criminal cast to his mind, and he would have become a criminal if not for the literature that his mother infused into their household.

PORTER BIBB

Louisville had what we called literary societies, but they were basically social clubs. The one that Hunter and I were in, the Athenaeum

Literary Association, was 125 years old and very prestigious. We would meet every Saturday night for several hours, wear suits and ties, and different members would stand in front of the rest of the group and read something they'd written and be critiqued. After the meeting was over, you took off your tie and your jacket and went out and raised a lot of hell and got drunk.

NEVILLE BLAKEMORE

We published *The Spectator,* a literary magazine, and we'd put on a spring dance and a Christmas dance in the Crystal Ballroom at the Brown Hotel to raise money. Our dances were followed by breakfast — it was an excuse to stay up all night. And we'd have hill parties — there was a hill in Cherokee Park where you could go up on top and build a fire and sit around and sing, with dates.

PAUL SEMONIN *was an Athenaeum member.*

The Athenaeum was something that some of our fathers had been in, or even our grandfathers. It was the oldest literary society, and it was a social group — mostly upper-middle-class, people with family ties and things like that — and also a drinking group.

PORTER BIBB

Hunter and I and Paul Semonin hung out every day. We all believed we were Fitzgerald incarnate. Hunter was as passionate as the rest of us about this. This is when he started typing out Fitzgerald and Hemingway books word by word. I used to kid Hunter a lot and say, "You're not Fitzgerald. What the fuck are you typing *The Great Gatsby* for? That's the stupidest thing I've ever seen."

"You know," he said, "I just like to get the feel of how it is to write those words."

I just took that as pure pretension.

PAUL SEMONIN

Athenaeum was tied into the Louisville elite, and it had this atmosphere of tradition, which I think is important in understanding where Hunter came from. He has this element buried in his personality, and the older and wilder he got, the less it became obvious, but there was this sort of tie to the old American dream that seemed almost nineteenth century. It got mixed up with a lot of other things along the way — the counterculture, of course — but Athenaeum was a place where I could see that element in his personality blending with other elements which were quite contradictory and rebellious.

There was a lot of talk about *The Fountainhead* and Ayn Rand and the loss of individuality. It was one of the things that gave impulse to our rebellion. We wanted to become more individualistic — which seemed as much a part of the American dream as anything else — and we wanted to fight for that, to demonstrate it in varied, somewhat extreme ways.

PORTER BIBB

I was always amazed at Hunter's networking ability. He was solidly middle-class, yet he was hanging with some multi-multi-millionaire families. Paul Semonin's family owned half of Louisville. They were the biggest real-estate people around. My family was what we called "name rich and land poor." We lost tremendous amounts of land in the Civil War, but we still acted like we had it. Most of the people that Hunter was close to and who brought him into their circle were very, very wealthy people, and Hunter didn't have a sou. Here he was with a single mom — who had to *work?*

We were traveling in the circle of people who virtually ran the city, and we lived very luxurious teenage lives. There were debutante parties every other night in the summer, and huge banquets and teas and brunches. If you couldn't figure out a way to steal a case of beer from somewhere, you'd just go over to one of the girls' houses — they all had unbelievable bars, and the parents were very liberal.

But Hunter had friends in both high and low society. He took me to places in Louisville that I never would have known existed. We hung out in black nightclubs when it was still very segregated, got drunk, and did pretty much everything bad together. You'd see Hunter sometimes with four or five guys you'd never see in the social circles that he spent most of his time in — they were basically juvenile delinquents, and you knew they were going to end up as convicts for the rest of their lives. But they were doing something different and something interesting, so we would go along with them. They never seemed to get in trouble, and I didn't worry about it because in Louisville, if you have connections you're untouchable. I mean, I never bothered with taking a driving test to get my license. I just went down and told them my name, and they gave me my license.

We all had fake IDs and fake licenses. They just seemed to appear when you needed them, and we were drinking from fourteen on. But you really didn't even need them, because there was so much free alcohol everywhere. Every party at the country clubs, at the hotel ballrooms — it was all open to us. Not to 90 percent of the rest of the city, but it was totally open to us.

PAUL SEMONIN

We did some street theater things. We didn't think of them as street theater at the time, of course. We just thought of them as hijinks — like the fake kidnapping in front of the Bard Theater over on Bardstown Road, on the edge of the Highlands. Basically, we just got the idea of kidnapping a pal of ours from the ticket line and creating a scene. The guy — the kidnapee — was in on the joke. But we just grabbed him out of the line and stuffed him into a car and then drove off. He was screaming and resisting, of course. But we didn't anticipate that a local judge would be sitting in a restaurant across the street. He saw what happened and came running out of the restaurant after us as we were pulling away. We didn't know he was a judge until we read it in the *Courier-Journal* the next morning: "SUSPECTED KIDNAPPING AT BARD THEATER." But nobody got our license plate number, and nothing ever came of it

I later became a performance artist, and I constructed these sorts of confrontations in more of a professional way, but Hunter carried it on as part of his persona. It had nothing to do with gonzo or with journalism or even writing back then. It was more a finger in your eye to the establishment, or to society — but with a certain humor and a certain kind of bravado. I mean, this was '53, '54. We felt constricted or repressed in some way, and we were trying to explode out of that.

PORTER BIBB

He obviously intuited that he was different from the rest of us very early on. He had it in his head that he was going to do something else, but I don't think he knew yet what it was. Among other things, he saved every single thing that he wrote. This was way before Xeroxing, so he had to use carbon paper, which was real messy and time-consuming.

NEVILLE BLAKEMORE

Hunter wrote a third-prize essay for the Athenaeum *Spectator* called "Open Letter to the Youth of Our Nation," which began: "Young people of America, awake from your slumber of indolence and harken to the call of the future! Do you realize that you are rapidly becoming a doomed generation? . . . O ignorant youth, the world is not a joyous place. The time has come for you to dispense with the frivolous pleasures of childhood and get down to honest toil until you are sixty-five. Then and only then can you relax and collect your Social Security and live happily until the time of your death." He signed it, "Fearfully and disgustedly yours, John J. Righteous-Hypocrite." There was another essay, "Security": "Is security a utopian goal or is it another word for rut? . . . Where would the world be if all men sought security and had not taken risks or gambled with their lives on the chance that, if they won, life would be different and richer?" He ends by writing, "We shall let the reader answer this question for himself: Who is the happier man, he who has braved the storm of life and lived, or he who has stayed securely on shore and merely existed?"

There was another feature of the *Spectator* called "The Line-Up," which was just a jokey questionnaire laid out in columns. Here's what they had to say about Hunter in '53:

Alias: Marlon Brando
Usually Found: Innocent
Favorite Saying: "Why was I fined?"
Reminds Us Of: Dennis the Menace
Ambition: Be serious
Future Occupation: Undertaker

And in '54, his junior year:

Reminds Us Of: Al Capone
Usually Found: Cutting classes
Favorite saying: "Norvin did it." (That was Norvin Green, who was
    the guy Hunter used to get to do stuff, like "Norvin, I bet you
    can't steal her purse." "Norvin, I bet you can't throw a fit."
Ambition: Peace officer

PORTER BIBB

There were two basic industries in the '50s in Louisville: tobacco and bourbon. And we knew the people who ran the Brown-Forman distillery. They were part of our circle — Lee Brown, Martin Brown. Martin is now the president of Jack Daniel's, but he grew up with Hunter and me, and we'd hang out in their houses. If you needed a case of Jack Daniel's or Early Times, it was always there, because somebody's father worked at the distillery and got it.

NEVILLE BLAKEMORE

As Hunter got older, the stuff he did seemed to get more and more serious. You might say it switched from pranks to vandalism. There was a group that called themselves the Wreckers — I've always suspected Hunter was one of them, but it was never proven — that was behind two serious vandalism incidents in the east end of town. One of them was at Louisville Collegiate School, where they got in and tore the place up as much as they could. And then they vandalized the Highland Presbyterian church — they broke in and cut off the left sleeves of all the choir robes, among other things, and they left a note: "We're the Wreckers, and we're here to cause trouble." Hunter was suspected, and this detective on the Louisville police force, Dodson, was assigned to the case. Someone even put a fake ad in the Athenaeum *Spectator* that read, "Dodson Is Watching."

PORTER BIBB

People gave him, when he was growing up, a huge amount of latitude. I mean, he was a real bad boy. I was a real bad boy. Ralston Steenrod, who went to Princeton, was a real bad boy. We had guns in our cars. We shot houses, mailboxes, garbage cans. We shoplifted. I got arrested once. I had something like fourteen car trays in my trunk from the drive-in place that we all used to go for hamburgers. I don't know why I kept them, but they said, "This is grand larceny. What are you stealing that stuff for?"

We broke into liquor stores. We'd jimmy a lock or break a window. I never paid a hotel bill when I was with Hunter, and it wasn't his initiative as much as mine. We'd just go out the window or the fire escape. That was just normal.

PAUL SEMONIN

Hunter was a black sheep with the Athenaeum by 1955, his senior year. The Athenaeum was split between his partisans and the people who thought he was a disgrace, and they managed to vote him out.

GERALD TYRRELL

There was a period when I was probably his best friend. And then that stopped. He got in trouble, and my father put him off-limits.

NEVILLE BLAKEMORE

Ralston Steenrod, who was in the Athenaeum with Hunter and me, was driving, and Hunter and another friend Hunter knew from Castlewood were in the car. As they were driving through Cherokee Park, the guy said, "Stop. I want to bum a cigarette from that car." People used to go park and neck at this spot. And he got out and apparently went back and mugged them.

I don't know if he beat the guy up, and I don't know what he said or did, but he came back with the guy's billfold. I don't think Hunter and Steenrod had any idea what the guy was going to do. I don't even know if they knew what he had done when he got back in the car, because if they had, they could have tried to undo it. But the guy who was mugged got their license number and traced the car, and within a very short time they were all three arrested. The police may have come down to Male to take Hunter away in handcuffs. That happened at least one time, though that might have been the gas station robbery.

There were three events in the spring of his senior year. This was the last. Just before this he had been blamed for a nighttime gas station robbery, and before that he and some friends got arrested for buying booze underage at Abe's Liquor Store on Frankfort Avenue by the tracks.

So Hunter had a record, and he was already on probation for the other two things. He was given an alternative. There was a Judge Logan whose son, George, was in the Athenaeum with us, and Judge Logan went to Hunter's judge and said, "I know you've got to do something, because you've already given him an ultimatum of 'One more time and you're going to jail.' But please give him the ultimatum of jail or the military." And Hunter took the air force. He didn't graduate with his class.

PORTER BIBB

Nobody expected that Hunter would have this sort of problem. I mean, I got caught by the cops many times for doing horrible things, but I'd just tell them who I was, and they'd say, "Well, you better shape up. You keep doing this and you're gonna get in trouble, and I'm going to tell your dad." But nothing ever happened. Our best friend was the son of the mayor. The two other guys arrested with Hunter — well, one's father was the ex-DA of the city, and the other one's father was a very prominent lawyer. If I wanted to put a red light and a siren on my car, I would just tell the mayor's son, "Charlie, I want one of those things." It was that kind of a world, and Hunter was a part of that — until that moment right at graduation when the other two guys got sprung by their fathers, and Hunter's father wasn't there. Nobody sprung Hunter. He was hung out to dry.

We all dismissed that, but it stayed with Hunter for a long time.

DOUG BRINKLEY

Hunter wrote his mother these very philosophical letters from behind bars. They exude the desperation of a young man in jail looking for his freedom as well as contemplating how the rich get away with dastardly things and the poor don't — that the buddies that he was with in the Cherokee Park event were waltzing because they knew the judge, and that he was the poor kid on the other side of the railroad tracks with no dad. The game was fixed.

She was an extraordinarily loving, giving mom. They were very, very close. Hunter was running amok, and she didn't know what to do. She kept two of her sons fairly grounded. Hunter was the loose cannon. There was always a maternal disappointment that she perhaps had failed.

PORTER BIBB

He was such an outgoing, self-initiating guy that as one of his close friends, I never even thought to help. I didn't even go see him. He was there for a couple of days in a sort of temporary holding cell. It wasn't even a real jail. He's made up a lot of stuff about how terrifying it was and that he was worried about being attacked and everything. I think they called it Louisville Children's Detention Center. Then he had a choice given to him — go to juvenile prison or go into the military — and off he went.

He hadn't even applied to college, and it was unique that he didn't. Everybody went to college in the circle he was in, most of them to Ivy League schools. Hunter would probably have been in the top 25 students out of about 250. He didn't come to class a lot, but we all skipped around.

I remember asking him even before all this happened, "What the fuck are you going to do?" I mean, he could have gone to the University of Louisville or the University of Kentucky almost for free. And he said, "I don't know. Something. I'll figure something out."

LOU ANN ILER

Hunter was sent to jail for ninety days right before graduation, and at that point I really lost touch with him. As I was getting ready to go down to the jail to see him, my mother actually forbade me to do so. Then his probation officer got him released early with the understanding that he would go into the service. So Hunter got out of jail and literally went to the bus station, got on the bus, and went into the air force.

CHAPTER TWO

An Itinerant Professional

Hunter used to tell us that he was going to be a great writer but that he figured he'd have to do some sort of journalism to make a living in the meantime. He wasn't too happy about this, but he figured that if Hemingway did it, he could too.

DOUG BRINKLEY

The air force was his college. He learned a lot from various military types, and used this knowledge in his writing a lot — how the hillbilly grunt has to deal in a world of hard-nosed authority. Imagine such a rebellious spirit being forced into boot camp and mess hall drills and having to keep his boots polished perfectly and observe lights-out. Hunter would brag about his deviation from the rules, but that was one percent of the time. Ninety-nine percent of the time it was "Yes, sir!" But he was constantly studying the military culture. He really respected most of the officers; he became friends with a lot of them.

PORTER BIBB

We sent a lot of letters back and forth when I got to college. He'd gone off with the air force, so I started writing him as if he were my gay lover — thinking that the air force would read his mail — and he never responded. He didn't take the bait. But right after college I went into the Marine Corps, and he started writing letters to me as *my* gay lover (I was in Parris Island), and they definitely opened our mail and read it. They read it to the whole platoon.

JERRY HAWKE *served in the air force from June 1955 to May 1957, assigned to the Public Information Office at Eglin Field in Florida.*

Part of the function of my department was putting out the *Command Courier,* the base newspaper. Not long after I got there, Hunter came aboard as sports editor. He had been assigned to a radar unit, which was clearly not his bag. He managed to get transferred to the base newspaper. He loved sports, so it was a natural for him. He also had a moonlighting job with the local civilian newspaper, the *Fort Walton Playground News.* Hunter was a very good-looking kid, a boyish-looking guy, and even then he was something of a cutup. He had a very provocative sense of humor.

We had a common friend, a lieutenant colonel named Frank Campbell, who was the deputy head of the information services office. Frank was a delightful fellow, a former newspaper man, I think, a very literary guy. I had been an English major at Yale and had pretensions of being a writer. I had spent a summer at Oxford and was planning to go back there to read English. The four of us — Frank and his wife and Hunter and I — became very good friends. I would play duplicate bridge with Pauline and Frank, and Hunter would sit around and drink beer.

I remember very clearly talking about the great writers from the twenties and thirties — Hemingway, Fitzgerald. Frank was a big influence on Hunter — he really provided kind of a home away from home, and he encouraged Hunter's literary interests. Hunter was trying to do creative writing at the time. I remember his remorse for not having gone to college and his hope that when he got out he would go to Vanderbilt.

LOU ANN ILER

He came to see me in December of '56, just showed up at my door. He was still in the service, but he really wanted to start a relationship again, and I did not. He was not too happy, but . . . there's alcoholism in my family, and the pain that it caused me was something that I saw could happen with Hunter, and I wasn't going there. It was really a survival decision. It wasn't that I didn't care for him. We parted as friends.

Hunter probably got in more trouble than other people, but he wasn't that different in terms of his actual drinking. There was just always that energy, that tension. I don't know that he had the ability to stop himself once that energy took over. Hunter was exciting and had that edge that a lot of men didn't have. You'd be drawn to him like a moth to the flame. And when he wanted to, he could fit right in. It just seemed like every so often he had some energy that could not stand that type of constraint.

DOUG BRINKLEY

All in all, Hunter had a great billet. He was in Fort Walton Beach when it was still pristine, before it got developed. The most beautiful emerald waters in America are on that Florida Panhandle, and Hunter and his friends would go out swimming and surfing, and they drank. He would overdrink, but you didn't often find a twenty-year-old in the military who wasn't drinking a lot; they didn't hold that against him. It was just another part of being in the military — that wild male culture of strip clubs, boozy nights, a really raucous kind of comedy, and a kind of verbal hazing of each other. Hunter was a ringleader in all of those macho coming-of-age rituals.

He was pushing envelopes a lot with his sports coverage for the *Command Courier*, the base newspaper, and he wrote some extra stuff for the *Playground News* under the pseudonym Thorne Stockton. The officers eventually had to censor him and shut him down, but it wasn't out of disdain for Hunter. That's why he got the honorable discharge — he charmed those officers a lot too.

I think there is a misimpression that Hunter's air force years were one of him just flipping off authorities. In truth, he was an integral part of what was going on on the base and was respected by superior offi cers and the enlisted men. He just got into a tangle with some of the rules as a journalist. Quarterback Bart Starr was apparently finagling special treatment from the air force top brass so he could sign with Green Bay. Hunter found this appalling — or at the very least worth noting — so he snuck into base headquarters and found Starr's sui generis discharge and snuck it onto the front page of the *Command Courier* at the last minute. He had also made fun of radio and TV personality Arthur Godfrey when he had come to the base. Hunter was just pushing it too far; they had to call him on it.

GENE MCGARR *lived and worked with Hunter in New York City after Hunter was discharged from the air force.*

The last thing he did, in November of 1957, was to write up a press release describing a riot that took place at Eglin when the enlisted men attacked the women's quarters and the officer's mess — stole all the booze, got drunk as shit, attacked the women, beat up the officers. It was a very funny and colorful story — completely fictional, of course — and he sent a copy of it to the AP and to UPI, left a copy on his captain's desk, then drove like a son of a bitch for the gate.

He headed north; he'd read in *Editor & Publisher* about a small-town newspaper that wanted a sports editor. He wrote them a letter, and they said to come up. This was a place called Jersey Shore, Pennsylvania.

Now, it turns out that Jersey Shore, Pennsylvania, was just a bleak, hideous place with coal dust in the air. Dreadful, and no women in town that were worth looking at. Hunter got a room over a bar and started working for the paper, describing horse pulls and wrestling matches with "Popo the Killer Jap" and all kinds of things with this peculiar Dadaist approach. He wrote everything deadly serious. These things — like pro wrestling matches — were supposed to be laughed at to a certain extent. Everybody knows how it's phony as baloney, but he played it straight. Well, not exactly straight; he was writing things like "People were carried out of the ring with broken backs," "his neck was broken in three places" — stuff like that. Apparently nobody really cared whether it was true or not.

He's working there for a couple of months when the editor's daughter comes home for Christmas. She's a nice-looking girl, so Hunter immediately hits on her. They get together. One night, he takes her on a drive into the countryside in the editor's car. They pull into this side lane and start making out. They're having a fine time, but when Hunter tries to back out to take her home, he's mired up to the hubcaps in mud.

It's two o'clock in the morning. There's a farmhouse with a tractor sitting outside. Hunter goes up to the house, and he's loathe to wake up a farmer at that hour. The tractor's got the key in it, so he climbs up on the tractor, starts the goddamn thing, figures out how to put it in gear, turns it around, and runs it back down to the car. There's a chain at the end of the tractor to pull all kinds of farm equipment, so Hunter attaches the chain around the car's back bumper, puts the tractor in gear and eases out the clutch — and immediately rips the bumper half-off.

By this time, the farmer's running down the hill with a shotgun. Hunter explains everything to him, and the farmer calms down and actually decides to help him. He shows him, basically, how you don't put the chain on the bumper, you asshole, you put it on the axle. So he puts it on the axle and tows them out. Hunter's in the driver's seat and he's got the door open and he's looking backward to see where to steer, but he doesn't notice this tree. The tree catches the door and bends it completely forward. So now he's got a door and a bumper both hanging half-off.

They drive home. Hunter leaves the car in front of the editor's house, goes back to his apartment, and packs all his bags. He goes to the office and is waiting for the editor when he hears this horrible scraping noise coming down the street. It's the editor driving to work with the door and the bumper scraping the ground. Hunter gets up, walks out the door, gets into his car, and drives immediately to New York. That was the end of his Jersey Shore, Pennsylvania, experience.

JERRY HAWKE

I got out of the air force in May of '57. The Oxford plans had been scrapped, and I went up to Columbia Law School and was living in a shared apartment in New York City with my brother, who was a year ahead of me at school, and a fellow named John Clancy, who was a classmate of my brother. Clancy was a great character, a very bright, florid-faced Irishman. We all lived together in this old railroad flat at 110 Morningside Drive near Columbia.

Hunter called me and said he was leaving Jersey Shore and needed a place to stay. He wanted to come to New York. The way he put it, they sort of ran him out of town. He had to leave town so quickly that he left his watch in a pawnshop.

He enrolled in the School of General Studies at Columbia and took some courses. We had a deal where he wouldn't have to pay any rent but he had to do dishes and stuff like that.

One of the things Hunter did was sign up for book clubs. They'd offer you four free books up front if you agreed to buy so many books over the course of the year. Hunter would sign up, get the free books up front, and never order any other books — or if he did, he wouldn't pay for them. So he would get notices from these book clubs and would stiff them, or he'd send back some minuscule payment, which would only force them to trigger their whole process all over again.

ROGER HAWKE *is Jerry Hawke's brother.*

They'd send him letters, one after another. Finally when it got to a certain point, Hunter wrote them back, starting off very rationally but gradually getting crazier and crazier, to the point where he'd end up claiming that they owed *him* money — but that he didn't want their money and they could keep it. After that he'd never hear from them again. He used to read them to us. They were real gems.

JOHN CLANCY *was one of the roommates.*

Hunter used to tell us that he was going to be a great writer — he'd mention Hemingway and Fitzgerald in the same sentence — but that he figured he'd have to do some sort of journalism to make a living in the meantime. He wasn't too happy about this, but he figured that if Hemingway did it, he could too.

GERALD TYRRELL

I went down from Yale to Hunter's place in New York on spring vacation of my sophomore year to see him. He was living in this barren flat up by Columbia. I had to sleep in my overcoat on the floor. The only thing he had to eat in the refrigerator was a jar of peanut butter. I'm not even sure he had bread. There was a Chinese girl who lived next door, and Hunter said she fed him a lot.

GENE MCGARR

Around this time, Hunter and I started working together at *Time* magazine as copyboys. We worked the same daytime shift, starting at about seven-thirty or eight a.m. It was a miserably paid job, but a simple one. You deliver newspapers in the morning and then run copy from the editor back to the writer and from the writer to the editor and so on. Flunky work.

You couldn't get the job if you wanted to be a writer. They didn't want aspiring writers working as copyboys because all of a sudden, they would be rewriting the articles themselves and bugging editors with their own stuff. They wanted premed students or poor goofy anybodies, but no writers.

JERRY HAWKE

Hunter would get absolutely smashed and go around mouthing off and insulting all of his superiors at *Time*. He could drink a lot, and that got him into trouble. He eventually got fired because of that. He probably didn't last more than three or four weeks.

JOHN CLANCY

We lived uptown until the summer, and then Hunter and I shared a place in the Village. There was one bed, and a cot in an alcove that was very hard to sleep on. There was no mattress or anything, so we kind of shared the one bed. I worked as a teamster down on the docks. I'd go to work at seven at night and come home at eight in the morning. He'd be off to work at dawn, so we never saw each other during the week. But I'd come home around noon on Saturday after drinking with my coworkers — our "Friday night" started at eight a.m. Saturday morning — and Hunter and I would crank up what he called "the Fun Machine," with me on no sleep. We'd drive somewhere, or we'd just run all over the Village and drink and smoke and talk and argue and chase girls. And then on the weekends, if one of us didn't sleep in some girl's bed, we had to fight over who the fuck was going to actually use the bed instead of the horrible cot.

GENE MCGARR

Hunter almost never talked about his sex life, or about sex in general. You could never pin him down. He would never admit to having had sexual relations with anybody, or give you any details, except a couple of times. He told me once that if a girl wouldn't blow him, he wouldn't see her again. As far as he was concerned, a girl who wouldn't suck cock wasn't worth hanging out with, no matter how good-looking she was.

And I recall another time, we had met a stripper, a very pretty, nicely built girl, at Dirty Julius's or the Riviera, and he had a little affair with her. And there was something about the "standing tree" position — the girl was light and strong and athletic enough to perform in the standing tree position. Exactly what the hell the "standing tree" position was, I never found out, but it blew his mind.

JOHN CLANCY

I was going out with a girl that lived in an apartment down the street, and she had a roommate from Smith College who had a separate room. This girl and I were hot and heavy, and one night, about six months later, she told me that Hunter had been sleeping with her roommate. He'd been coming over the roof and down the fire escape and going in through the roommate's window. But the thing that impressed me was that Hunter had never said one word about any of this to me. I said to myself, "There's a man of principle."

GENE MCGARR

I was living on the Lower East Side, between the Bowery and Second Avenue, on the fifth floor. It was so bad that you could have cardiac arrest by the time you got up the stairs. I never locked my apartment door because I had nothing to steal — and if anybody actually wanted to climb those five flights, he deserved whatever he would steal. Hunter comes up one night, with a few other people, to visit me, and I'm not there, I'm out driving a cab. And I don't get any sense of what happened until the next day.

He's in there sitting with his friends and waiting for me, and drinking beer. And at one point, he gets up and takes his belt off. It's a hot summer night and all the windows are open all over the block, including mine. And Hunter starts whipping the wall, and he'd whip and then

scream, "AAIIIIIGH!!!" Whip, "AIIIIIGH!!! Whip, "AAAAAHH!!!"
It was loud. Everybody on the block could hear this. And every now
and then he'd stop and he'd go, "Do it again, do it again!" Whip,
"AAAAAHH!!!" "You can't do that, you son of a bitch!!"

Of course, to the neighbors, it's an outrage, a fucking outrage. Somebody calls the police, and two beefy cops come bounding up five flights
of stairs — they probably had apoplexy by the time they got to my
apartment — and pound on the door.

The cops come in and bark, "What the hell is going on?" They
check everybody for marks, but nobody has any marks on them —
they're sitting quietly drinking beer at the kitchen table. So there was
nothing to be done about it, no law being broken, nothing violated.
They just split.

I came home that night at about three o'clock in the morning. And I
don't know what's happened. There's a note, "We waited for you but
you weren't home" from Hunter.

The next day, as I'm coming up the stairs with a bag of groceries,
I meet this Chinese guy from just below me. We'd always gotten
along fairly well — "good morning," "good evening," smiles, pleasant-
ries. I think I borrowed some salt from him once. But he's coming down as I'm going up, and as I approach him, he flattens against
the wall, shoots me this horrible look, and starts mumbling in Chinese. And I'm wondering, "What the fuck is wrong with him?" I climb
up another flight of stairs and finally get to my floor, and there's a
little girl who lives down the other end of the hallway playing in the
stairwell. Her mother is working in the kitchen, and their apartment
door opens, the mother sees me — and runs out grabs the little girl,
runs back in the apartment, and slams the door. Then she peeks out
through the door to see if I'm still there. I'm thinking, "What's wrong
with these people?" Then I hear the story from Hunter about what
happened the night before. From then on, I was treated like King
Beast.

PAUL SEMONIN

I had a small room over on Charles Street right off West Fourth, which was only a block away from Hunter. We were practically roommates from April of '59 right on through the summer and into the early fall, until the winter of '60, when Hunter took off for Puerto Rico. We were getting more and more into the beatnik culture, reading Kerouac and Ginsberg. And of course Norman Mailer's early stuff was really important. That was teething for us until we were starting to live those kinds of personas in a way. That whole period forms this kind of continuum when you might say there was a kind of brotherhood of dare, a brotherhood of rebellion. Hunter was starting to work on *Prince Jellyfish,* which is the first novel or manuscript that I remember him actually sitting down to try and write.

As I recall, the essential character, the protagonist, is someone called Welburn Kemp. And those two names were a conjoined name of two different people from Louisville, one of whom had been killed in a car wreck — Welburn Brown — and another one, Penny Kemp, who was severely brain damaged in an auto wreck. They were heroes for young Louisvillians, in a certain way. And they both had tragic ends.

But Hunter hadn't found a voice. He didn't like what he was writing, but he never confessed to being inadequate. He just felt limited in a way that he didn't like.

GENE MCGARR

Hunter's place on Perry Street was two blocks up from the Riviera Bar and a fairly nice apartment house for Greenwich Village. It was a step above a tenement. But he was in the boiler room in the basement. Just an outrageous cave. I mean, the first time you brought a girl down there it was, "Holy shit." Because you went down the back rickety stairs and into the backyard, and you had to be very careful, particularly at night, to not strangle yourself on the clotheslines, which were all at about throat level if you were tall. You ducked under those and you got to this door and when you opened the door the first thing you'd see were the flames coming out of the boiler — the furnace — because the door was slightly broken and it wouldn't shut completely. The flames were dancing on the walls all around you, and the first door, right next to the furnace, was Hunter's apartment.

Hunter painted the entire interior black. Ceiling, walls — everything totally black, just to add to the atmosphere, presumably. The only way you could tell whether it was night or day, when you woke up, was one whole wall was barred windows that opened up on an air shaft, and you had to get on your back and press your head against the bars to look up. And there was a little triangle of the sky that you could see at the top of the air shaft. If it was blue, it was day.

I had been smoking marijuana since I was twelve or so, but marijuana was the first thing that Hunter and I did together. He didn't do it that much, and we weren't out looking for it, but if somebody turned up with some marijuana, we'd smoke it. The first time Hunter ever smoked, he got as sick as a dog. Later on, we did a lot of cocaine, a lot of acid. We kind of discovered a lot of it together. Something would come along, and we would try it. I think I was the one to introduce him to mescaline. He tried to get me into Adrenalin — shots of Adrenalin. I don't know where he got the stuff from. He once stuck a hypodermic full of Adrenalin into his ankle, and by accident he hit an artery and a needlelike thickness of blood just hit the wall of the room. He was a gorilla for a while once it kicked in, but at the same time scared shitless because this stream of blood was an awesome thing to see. He had to go to the hospital because it wouldn't stop.

One night, hot as shit, July, one hundred degrees and ninety-nine percent humidity, and it's midnight. We're with our girlfriends, and we can't stand Hunter's apartment anymore so we decide to go down to the Leroy Street pool a few blocks away. We climb over the fence, boosting the girls. And we strip down to our Skivvies and jump into the water and swim around. And, God, it's cool. But all of a sudden, over the fence come these five guys — local guineas — who decide that this is their turf. They start throwing our clothes in the water, and I start to get out of the water, but my future wife, Eleanor, gets there first and starts yelling like shit about throwing the clothes in the water, and these guys immediately turn to me, get around me, and start pegging me. So I start moving fast and pegging back at them, and then along comes Hunter. He jumps on one of the guy's backs and beats the shit out of him, and then he grabs another one. Between the two of us, we drive them back over the fence. We gather all our clothes up and figure we'd better get the hell of there, but before we're finished, over the fence come ten guys right at us. Well, it's another melee, but now there are too many of them. I'm getting hit, Hunter's getting hit. But somehow or another, we drive them off.

We finally put our clothes together and turn around to leave, and behind the fence we just came over must be fifty of them. I told my wife, "You and Connie" — I think it was Connie — "you get over the fence, and don't look back. I don't think they're going to bother you. They want us. Run for Seventh Avenue and do whatever you can to find a cop. Run like hell." So they go over the fence, and then Hunter and I gathered ourselves. Hunter was as brave as a lion. He waded right in. There was no fucking around. They started wailing and we started wailing. They started hitting me with bottles, and in the meantime, I can't see what's going on with Hunter. Thank God it only lasted about a minute. Somebody had called the cops, and the cops were right there. If the fight had lasted two minutes, both Hunter and I would have been dead.

PAUL SEMONIN

I arrived on a motor scooter just afterward. Both Hunter and Gene had a flair for the dramatic, and they could make it into almost an operatic event, but it was nasty — really nasty.

GENE MCGARR

The cops get an ambulance to take us to St. Vincent's Hospital. There's so much broken glass on both of us, they have to put us in this big room and hose little pieces of glass off of us. They have to sew up a cut over my eye and a cut above my right elbow. We get dressed and, as instructed, we go down to the precinct station house. They ask us what are we were doing at the pool. And I say, "Oh, shit — it was a hot night. We climbed over the fence to go swimming." They say, "Look, if you press charges against them" — and they've rounded up about ten of the guys by now, and they're in the station house — "they're going to press charges against you, and then we're going to have to keep you all in jail." I said, "I'll tell you what. Just give us a head start, and we'll leave." And sure enough, they did.

Hunter was a wreck the next day. Fortunately, he had this lovely girl to take care of him. But he started carrying a knife after that, a big bowie knife or something like that. I suggested brass knuckles, but he liked the idea of showing a big blade.

PAUL SEMONIN

Hunter talked about it being a bunch of vandals or delinquents who had stolen clothes from them or something, but I'm sure there was a provocation as well from Hunter and McGarr's side. They were always bristling and ready for fisticuffs if the chance arose, but this time it was a gang, and they were outnumbered.

GENE MCGARR

And of course there was the night of the cement in the Riviera. That was the day before he packed up and moved to Middletown, New York. He'd gotten some job as the sports editor of the *Middletown Record*. Eleanor and I went down to see Hunter, and he had a girlfriend with him in his apartment. He was excited. It was the last night in the dungeon, and he decided to celebrate by jumping up and grabbing a sack of flour and doing a dance all around his black-painted apartment until it looked like fallen snow everywhere. Then we walk out the door. He says, "Come on, I've got to go get stamps." And where he buys stamps is down at the Riviera. So we step out onto the catwalk into the furnace room. And there's this bag of cement, torn at the top, just sitting there outside his door, which really just looks like a bigger bag of flour. It was as though God wanted him to dance some more. Hunter grabs it, throws it onto his shoulder, and heads down the street to the bar. I say, "Hunter, what do you plan on doing with that cement?" He just says, "Stamps. I've got to have stamps."

We get to the Riviera, and I say, "Hunter, you going to go into that place with that bag of cement?" Again: "I've got to have stamps." I turn to my future wife and I give her my watch and my rings.

We open the door at the small end of the Riviera and march in. It's a Saturday night, so it's crowded. And as we walk through to the bar — silence. The whole goddamn place is quiet. Hunter gets to the middle of the bar, takes the bag off his shoulder, slams it on the bar, and this kind of mushroom cloud of cement rises from the top of the bag.

There are three bartenders on duty. There's a kind of middle-aged guy in the center, and the other two appear to be twenty-five-year-old middleweights, one at either end. The guy in the center looks at Hunter in silence and finally says, "You can't do this." Hunter says, "I want some stamps. What do you mean?" And the guy just says, "You can't do this." He's like a zombie, staring at the bag. Hunter says, "Come on, now." I see one of the middleweights coming around one end of the bar and the other middleweight climbing over the other end. I say, "Hunter, they're coming for us. Let's get the fuck out of here." He grabs the bag, it tilts backward, and some guy yells, "My suit! My fucking suit, you son of a bitch!" Then some lady screams, and a general melee begins. Everybody heads for the door, only the door is at the narrow end of the bar, and it's like a mob trying to get out of a fire. Hunter and I get swept along with them, and the bag keeps getting jostled more and more until finally it rips in half. And now everything's white. You can't see anything anymore. The stomping feet are sending the cement up into the air, the bag is in shreds, and we're lost in the fog. Everybody is still pushing for the door. It's a mob.

Outside, Hunter's girlfriend and my future wife are standing in the doorway of the haberdashery across the street. They can't see anything, and then all of a sudden — they later said it was like something coming out of a cannon — this incredible explosion of white powder comes bursting through the door, with arms and legs sticking out of it. Everybody empties out onto the sidewalk, and the stuff begins to settle on the two fucking middleweights. One of them chooses off Hunter. The other chooses off me. And the other people want to get in there and hit us, but one enormous guy takes control and decides to become the referee. And he insists on a fair fight.

About three punches are landed, and then we hear sirens in the distance. We run like hell up Tenth Street and down toward Hudson, and then sneak back over to Christopher to peer around the corner by the Riviera to see what's going on. The cops are there. People are brushing themselves off, and everybody's yelling and screaming. We all head to a bar about a block or two away, Hunter brushing himself off.

Later that night, we were sitting in a place called the Kettle of Fish, and this black guy came over and said, "I saw you! I saw you! That was the greatest thing I ever seen in my life!" Hunter had been wearing a trench coat that night, and this guy hands Hunter one of the shoulder epaulets that had gotten ripped off in the melee. The guy had saved it for him.

Hunter and I had to stay out of the Riviera for quite a while.

BOB BONE *had just come back from Europe and resumed his job in Middletown, New York, at the* Daily Record *in the summer of 1958.*

Hunter showed up at the paper soon after I returned. They hired him as a general assignment reporter. I think he may have covered some sports (because he was always interested in sports), but that wasn't his job there. I'm not sure how he happened to leave *Time.* I had the feeling that he quit in a huff or they fired him, but everything was always an emergency of some sort with Hunter.

Hunter and I began running around with the same girls. He had this place over in Cuddebackville where he tried to do some serious writing, and for a long time, a lot of us used to hang out at a house in Otisville, which is also in Orange County. There was an older couple there who liked to have young people around, and we'd go out there and drink Ballantine Ale until we all fell asleep.

GENE MCGARR

The only major industry in Middletown was the state mental institution. It's an interesting place. On Saturday night, when you party with these psychiatrists and psychiatric social workers, you begin to wonder how crazy the inmates might be, because these people were bananas.

BOB BONE

He was fired after just a few months for kicking in a candy machine. He was always skating on thin ice there anyway because he was too much of a character for the likes of the bosses. He didn't like to wear shoes in the newsroom, for one thing. The city council came through one day, and the publisher was rather upset because there was a reporter running around barefoot.

But the candy machine incident was the last straw. Hunter couldn't get anything out of the machine, so he just beat it — "savagely," to use his word — until it dislodged his candy bar. The interesting thing about it was that Hunter only took what he had paid for, but the whole rest of the newspaper room, including all the guys in the back shop, were eating free candy bars from the broken machine when the wrong person walked in. Hunter was deemed responsible, and that was the end of the candy man.

GENE MCGARR

My wife Eleanor's roommate at Goucher College in Maryland was named Sandy Conklin, and Sandy came down and hung out with us and met a guy who was a bond trader and hung out with him for a bit.

SANDY THOMPSON

I was going out with a guy who was a little older than me and who was in a stock brokerage firm in New York City. One night, Eleanor and I and Gene were at this bar called Christopher's in Greenwich Village, and I was with this guy who actually knew Hunter somehow. Hunter walked in, and I didn't really take much notice. Then Eleanor and I went back to college, and maybe a week later Eleanor said, "Oh, Sandy, I got this letter from Hunter. Do you remember Hunter? The big, tall, lanky guy?" I said, "Sort of." "Well, he has a cabin in upstate New York, and he said, 'When you and Gene come up to visit me, you need to bring whiskey, you need to bring blankets, and how about that girl — Sandy, I think her name was?' "

I graduated from college and got an apartment by myself on Thompson Street in Greenwich Village, and one Sunday I went to Washington Square Park, and there was some kind of a classical concert. And I was lying out there on the lawn, and there was this nice-looking young man lying on the lawn as well, and we started talking. I felt a little attraction for him and he felt a little attraction for me, and so we started seeing each other. That was Paul Semonin.

PAUL SEMONIN

Sandy and I went out in the summer of '59 for a little while. I took her out a couple of times, but once she connected with Hunter, that was it. It was never like someone stealing my girlfriend or anything.

SANDY THOMPSON

Paul and I were dating over that summer, and I remember times in August of '59 when it would be the three of us — Hunter, Paul, and myself. Sometimes we'd go for long walks along the East River. And now when I saw Hunter, I thought, "Oh my, you know, this is really something." There were two times when I was really, really taken in.

We were at Paul's apartment, a tiny place in the Village. It was very, very hot, and there was no air-conditioning. The windows were open, and he had a standing fan. Paul was on the windowsill, and I had made dinner for them. Hunter just lay down on the floor, lifted his shirt off of his back, and he gave me this talcum powder and said, "Oh Sandy, you know it's so hot. Do you think you could rub my back with this talcum powder?" So there I am, massaging this man's back and shoulders, and Paul is looking at us.

Another afternoon we all went into the Village apartment of some friend from Louisville. It was Paul and myself, and Eleanor and Mc-Garr. I remember lying on this sort of couch-bed and Paul was next to me, and everything's fine, we're all talking. And Hunter walks in down the stairs — this tall, lanky guy with Bermuda shorts and a big manuscript underneath his arm, which was *Prince Jellyfish*. And the only way to say it is that I was just gone. Absolutely gone.

The summer went on, and in September I started working for United Airlines. Paul and I stopped seeing each other. Paul was wonderful, but it just wasn't working for both of us. Then on Christmas Eve I was outside getting coffee, and when I came back there was a message from Hunter Thompson. He was at Viking Books, and would I call him back? I kind of seized up and got really, really excited, really tense, and

I called. Hunter said, "Oh, hi, well — yeah, ummm, I don't really know why I called. Well, I guess — ummm, would you like to have a drink somewhere tonight?"

I was supposed to go out to my father's house on Long Island that night to celebrate Christmas Eve and decorate the tree. It was my father's new house, his new bride, my brother was coming home from college — everyone was going to be there. I called Daddy and I said, "I can't quite make it at the time we talked about, but I'll get there." I walked over to the bar. No Hunter. Time passed. Still no Hunter. The bartender got a phone call from Hunter, and — this is a first and a last — Hunter actually called and said, "I'm going to be late. Buy her a drink, okay, and I'll be there." Maybe an hour later he walked in and immediately there was that chemistry, that seduction. We both sat there and talked, and about every hour I would go to the pay phone and call out to Long Island and tell them I was just going to be a little bit later. We were together for maybe three hours. The last train out to Port Washington was something like one o'clock in the morning. We were totally sensually connected, just wild chemistry. Hunter asked me whether I would come up to his cabin, and I told him I couldn't, which was a good idea, actually. And so I left and caught the last train out.

This was probably the highest I had ever been in my life. I was just so charged with this magic, this charisma — all these feelings. I was on top of the world. The next morning, I remember telling my father, "I've met a wonderful, wonderful man."

At the bar, Hunter had asked me if I'd like to go out when he was back in town the next week, and when I got back to the city, I actually called people I had been dating and made a date for every single night that week. I was certain that Hunter wasn't going to call, and I just didn't want to be sitting and waiting for the telephone to ring.

On Tuesday or Wednesday the phone rang — of course, at three o'clock in the morning. I really should have known right then. "Hi. Well, I'll be in town later today. How about we get together tonight?"

I called whoever I had to call, and I didn't say that my grandmother was ill, and I didn't say that I was ill. I said, "I have just met the most extraordinary man, and I'm really sorry, but I can't go out with you tonight." Hunter came over. I had a friend from college visiting me, and then she left, and Hunter and I spent the next seven days in my little railroad apartment. I had a tiny, tiny bedroom — just big enough for a single bed and a chest of drawers. The bathtub was in the kitchen. It was a sweet little place, and it was fifty-nine dollars a month. I think we actually went out once or twice to get more to drink. I had a little food in the refrigerator. But it was more about making love, talking, talking, drinking Christian Brothers brandy — really awful stuff, but when you're that young, you can drink anything.

After our seven days, Hunter went down to Puerto Rico.

BOB BONE

After my work in Middletown, I got this job in Puerto Rico, and then Hunter followed me and we began having some adventures down there too. The *Record* had sent me to Puerto Rico on assignment earlier for a story on migrant workers because we used to have a lot of them in Orange County. While I was down there, I met this fellow who had just started the *San Juan Star,* Puerto Rico's first English-language daily paper, and he hired me. That's where Bill Kennedy also worked.

WILLIAM KENNEDY *was the managing editor of the* San Juan Star *in 1959.*

In 1956, I heard about a new newspaper starting up in Puerto Rico and I applied for the job and got it. I was sick of Albany's journalism and politics and social life, a dreary dead end. I heard good things about Puerto Rico, and it was an expatriate life — Hemingway and

Fitzgerald go to Paris, go to Spain, go someplace. Puerto Rico was as far away as I could get at the time. I figured I'd rise in the world and become some kind of foreign correspondent. But the paper, a broadsheet called the Puerto Rico *World Journal,* lasted only nine months.

I met Dana in December and married her in January, the week after the paper folded. We went to Miami and I got a job at the *Herald.* But we loved San Juan and I quit journalism for the first time and went back to live there and write a novel. I became the Time-Life stringer and freelanced for magazines to stay alive while I wrote the novel. In 1959 the *World Journal's* editor started the *San Juan Star* and hired me as managing editor. I put the novel aside and took the job. Before publication we advertised for a sports editor, and Hunter answered the ad.

Hunter was twenty-two. He said he was twenty-four in his letter. In his application to be sports editor he said that the job interested him because it was in Puerto Rico, outside of the "great Rotarian democracy." Our publisher was a Rotarian, so that was the first misstep. He said he had kicked in the candy machine at the *Middletown Record* because it ate his nickel, and had gotten fired for it. He wrote, "I have given up on American journalism. The decline of the American press has long been obvious, and my time is too valuable to waste in an effort to supply the 'man in the street' with his daily quota of clichés. . . . There is another concept of journalism. . . . It's engraved on a bronze plaque on the southeast corner of the Times Tower in New York City." Then he added that he had to get back to his novel, which was with the Viking Press in New York."

In my introduction to Hunter's first volume of letters, I wrote about this time:

> As managing editor of the fledgling *Star,* I wrote him explaining that our editor was a member of Rotary, that we had a staff of offbeat reporters (and editors) who, like him, were writing fiction, and suggested he return to his novel, or perhaps start another, building

his plot around the bronze plaque on the Times Tower. "You should always write about something you know intimately," I wrote, and added that if we ever got a candy machine and needed someone to kick it in, we'd be in touch.

He received my letter at his home in Louisville in the same mail that brought Viking's rejection of his novel, and he sat down and wrote me: "Your letter was cute, my friend, and your interpretation of my letter was beautifully typical of the cretin-intellect responsible for the dry-rot of the american press. But don't think that lack of an invitation from you will keep me from getting down that way, and when I do remind me to first kick your teeth in and then jam a bronze plaque far into your small intestine."

I wrote back, saying that since he was the bushy-tailed expert on journalism's dry rot, we would pay him space rates to summarize its failings in three double-spaced pages that we would run in our first edition, along with our exchange of correspondence. I said I didn't know another publication that would give him the time of day, and signed it "Intestinally yours."

There was a fellow named Bob Bone who had worked with Hunter in Middletown, and we hired him as a reporter-photographer for the *Star.* Hunter had corresponded with him and then applied for a job at a new bowling magazine in San Juan and got it. Hunter showed up in the *Star*'s city room one day — presumably to kick in my teeth, but he proved to be very friendly. We went back to my house for dinner, and that was the beginning of our friendship.

Hunter stayed on in San Juan for a couple of months, but the owner of the bowling magazine proved to be insolvent, and Hunter never got paid for the stuff that he wrote, or paid very little. So he was just floating free. If I could have hired him at that point I would have, but there was never an opening.

I remember talking about an essay by James Baldwin about the writer's quest for wisdom. Baldwin viewed the generation of American literary giants — Hemingway, Fitzgerald, Dos Passos, and Faulkner — as looking at the world as "a place to be corrected, and in which innocence is inexplicably lost." Baldwin thought this was a simplistic vision, that the world was a much deadlier place now. This was 1962. The key phrase for Hunter was Baldwin's view that "innocence must die, if we are ever to begin that journey toward the greater innocence called wisdom." Baldwin was certain that "the curtain has come down forever on Gatsby's career: there will be no more Gatsbys." Hunter didn't buy this. He thought of *himself* as Gatsby, and he reveled in that kind of fate — that green light always receding, boats against the current, borne back into the past, and so on. This was a romantic notion that prevailed in him until he died. It first surfaced in our conversation and letters as a result of that Baldwin essay.

Salinger was one of his heroes at that time. He identified with Holden Caulfield, the rebel in the society, and he was talking about confrontation all the time. I think that the rebelliousness in Holden — swinging a chain mace at society verbally — was something Hunter was very good at very early on. But we'd talk about everybody. I remember he liked Styron a lot — *Lie Down in Darkness*. He didn't like Bellow very much. He tried *Augie March* and said it didn't get to him. He liked Algren, and so did I. *The Man with the Golden Arm* was one of my major books when I was a kid writer. We both liked Baldwin's essays, and I remember telling him to read Ellison.

He was reading voluminously — *Ulysses,* James Agee's *A Death in the Family, The Ginger Man* by J. P. Donleavy, Dylan Thomas, Mailer's *Advertisements for Myself,* Dos Passos's *U.S.A., The Plague* by Camus, *Don Quixote,* Proust, *Huck Finn,* D. H. Lawrence, *The Sound and the Fury, The Decameron, The Inferno.* It was the Western canon. He didn't think there were any serious women writers. He didn't know much about Flannery O'Connor, or if he did he didn't value it. He did like Isak Dinesen's *Gothic Tales.*

We often looked back on those days and those all-night conversations. Finally the sun would come up and we'd have some breakfast and call it a night. I remember how freewheeling it was. Also, we were drinking a lot of rum, one of the great liberating forces. "Drink is oil for unauthorized movement" is a line that came out of those conversations somewhere.

SANDY THOMPSON

I went down to Puerto Rico in March and spent a week with Hunter in Vieques, and again, it was total romance. Both of us were really smitten. I think Hunter really loved the fact that I had a college degree and that I had majored in international relations and then economics, and that I had traveled, and that I was a free spirit. And I had a great body. I really did. And Hunter — he was just gorgeous.

WILLIAM KENNEDY

Sandy was a beautiful girl, really gorgeous. They seemed to have a good relationship. We'd hang out and drink beer on the beach, or have dinner and the talk would be political or literary or about what was in the newspapers. I remember Hunter told her to bring money because he wasn't solvent. "If you're going to hang out," he said, "you've got to be able to support yourself."

SANDY THOMPSON

After a week with Hunter, I went back to New York. We decided that I would come back down in June, so I saved money and then went back. Hunter had this little concrete cabin right on the ocean about sixteen miles outside of San Juan. It was all jungle, and it was just the two of us at first. We had a single bed, with a net over it because they had mimis there, which are teeny, teeny mosquitoes that come out about four in the afternoon and cover everything. There were screens everywhere. This is where Hunter began *The Rum Diary*.

WILLIAM KENNEDY

He thought of *The Rum Diary* as *The Sun Also Rises* in Puerto Rico.

BOB BONE

After they lived in the cinder-block house, Hunter and Sandy lived for quite a while out at a place that had what he called a "voodoo center," a place called Loiza Aldea. You could only get there by a ferryboat across the river. It was all very spooky.

SANDY THOMPSON

Paul Semonin came down toward the end of our time there. McGarr was the wild guy, but Paul was a wild thinker, very creative, very soulful. He was an artist — he wrote, he painted. He and Hunter would talk late into the night about all kinds of things.

PAUL SEMONIN

I followed Hunter down to Puerto Rico. We ended up living there for about nine months, and Hunter wrote a little piece about me for the *Louisville Courier-Journal.* The headline was something like "Louisvillian in Voodoo Country." We were living out in a little place outside San Juan, which was a black community. It was pretty primitive — there were goats wandering around — and we had a little beachfront house there. But the myth surrounding it was that this was some sort of voodoo village.

Hunter did some interviews with me, but then when he showed me the draft of the article, every single quote from me was totally fabricated. I said, "Hunter, that's not what I said." But he sent it off and it was published. "Voodoo Country" is something that will grab the eye of any reader and pull him into the story, and Hunter was a master at that. That's what purpose his exaggerations and his buffoonery served — fantastic, eye-grabbing stuff for the reader.

WILLIAM KENNEDY

He had no income, he was drinking rainwater and getting eaten by sand fleas and he lived in a concrete, corrugated-tin-roofed blockhouse on the beach. After a while he upgraded to a better blockhouse.

SANDY THOMPSON

I wasn't really sure what I was supposed to be doing, except taking care of Hunter. I hadn't really thought much about a career. I had wanted to do something in international relations, maybe work at the UN. I also thought about being a photographer — I thought that would go well with Hunter's writing — but my father wouldn't put me through photography school after he put me through college. So I sunbathed a lot. I swam. I washed clothes. I fed him. I gave him feedback on *The Rum Diary*. I took care of him and made love.

WILLIAM KENNEDY

Hunter stayed in San Juan for a couple of months and then he got in a fight and was arrested. He wrote about this in *The Rum Diary*. Hunter and some friends walked out on a bar bill in this beachfront place near Vacia Talega, where he lived. I never knew what exactly happened, but some sort of fight erupted and the owner called the cops and Hunter and others went to jail. Somehow I helped him get out — I must have found someone who helped him post bail, but I'm very hazy on this. I told him he was nuts to get himself into that kind of a pickle, and then all of a sudden he was gone.

Hunter had written about tourism for a government PR agency and had gotten to know someone with a sailboat. I think they signed on as crew and went as far as Bermuda, where they were dropped off. I don't know the circumstances, but it was a dead end and the wrong place to be stranded and broke.

SANDY THOMPSON

The three of us left Puerto Rico for St. Thomas and then crewed on a boat to get to Bermuda. The whole crew, I think, was eight guys. The captain was a slightly older Australian guy, and something like the chairman of IBM's son was on the boat. We had these huge five-gallon containers of rum, and we drank a lot. Hunter would bark orders to me, and I was so used to it at that point — Sandy get me this, Sandy do this, Sandy do that — that I had no perspective. It was normal. I was young, and I was being told to do this or asked to do this, but by this extraordinary human being. I remember the IBM guy asking me, "What are you doing with this man?" I said, "Well, can't you see how extraordinary — " And he said, "Extraordinary? He's not being good to you." And I said, "Oh, that's just how it is."

We arrived in Bermuda in a storm, and we didn't go through customs. We didn't know anything about immigration and customs or anything, and we had no money.

GENE MCGARR

Hunter just wanted to get out of the United States. My wife and I were living in Spain in a little town outside of Málaga at the time, and what we were doing intrigued him. We wrote a lot of letters back and forth, and my letters were jolly as far as living in Europe was concerned. Our money went outrageously far.

SANDY THOMPSON

My mother, who was a travel agent in Florida, had a friend in Bermuda who owned a motel, so we ended up there. He was this Dutch guy, a raging alcoholic, and he let Hunter and me sleep in a . . . I don't know what you'd call it. It wasn't a regular room. Kind of, sort of a room. And it had a kind of, sort of a bed in it. Paul slept in the park, and then he would go to the yacht club and get showered and dressed because Paul could pull that off.

WILLIAM KENNEDY

I got cards from Hunter and also Paul, who said that Bermuda was one of the ten bottom places of the Earth.

GENE MCGARR

They seemed to think that since Bermuda is out in the Atlantic Ocean, from there they could catch a trap steamer or something and just hop over to Europe. Well, there's no traffic between Bermuda and Europe. There's traffic between Bermuda and New York, which is where they had started. But they didn't want to go back there.

SANDY THOMPSON

Hunter wrote an article for the *Bermuda Gazette,* and it was published with a picture of the three of us. Then we got a call from Immigration saying, "Wait a minute — who are you?" I was in the process of getting a job at a bookstore, and it was just about to happen, but you couldn't get a job until you had gotten your papers in.

We went to the consul, all three of us. Hunter did his absolute best. He had this story: "We were on this boat, and we're artists, and we're this, and we're that, and we're planning to work, and then we're leaving for Málaga . . ." And at the end of the story, the consul said, "Right. So what you can do is call your parents and have them send you a ticket."

We got hold of friends and got tickets back to New York. Hunter and I went up to see the editor of the *Middletown Record* and her husband, who lived in the Catskills.

The four of us were downstairs in the living room, and later in the evening the husband and I ended up in the kitchen getting drinks. The conversation was all about Hunter and how madly in love with him I was, and when we came back out Hunter and the woman were gone. I went upstairs to our room, and Hunter was sleeping on a mattress on the floor. The room was dark. As soon as I walked into the room and knelt down on the mattress, Hunter lashed out at me — literally. It was something that would happen a handful of times later throughout our relationship, and there was a great deal of emotional abuse as well, but this was the first time it was physical.

It was about me being alone in the kitchen with her husband. What had I been doing in the kitchen with her husband? That should have been a wake-up call for me, but the only wake-up part of it was "Be careful. Be careful. Don't make this man angry. Because maybe he'll leave you — and you don't want him to leave you, because this is exciting." We were newly in love, newly whatever — seduced by one another — and all I wanted to do was just make it right. And somehow I did.

It never, ever occurred to me to get my coat, slam the door, and walk out in the middle of the night. It never, ever crossed my mind.

GENE MCGARR

Hunter wrote me this really awful letter from Bermuda about how he and Sandy were stealing cabbages out of gardens and living in a cave. They had no money at all. Hunter was always very, very good at getting what he needed from people — all his life — but when he pled for any help that he could possibly get from me, I took him at his word that he needed help.

I sent him what was half our passage money home (and this was four months before we were going to leave), and I told him, very explicitly, in the letter, that I had to have this money back by this date at the very latest because this is our passage money. We've got tickets; we have arrangements on a Yugoslavian freighter out of Tangiers for New York City. Something like a week before the deadline, I still hadn't heard from him, so I wrote him a letter, saying, "Where the hell is the money?" The day after I send that letter off from Málaga, I get a letter from him saying he's off for San Francisco, and since I'm flush he's going to delay a little bit as far as the money he owes me. So I write a letter back to him saying, "You stupid son of a fucking bitch. You promised." Now he knows fucking well I'm depending on that money. For several days I was going nuts. Then I get a telegram from Sandy saying, basically, "He's gone."

Sandy had to go to my mother to get the money for my wife and I to get home.

✠ 🐃 ✠ 🐃

JOHN CLANCY

I moved to San Francisco in '59, and Hunter came out west shortly after that, and then Sandy joined him a little later. Dennis Murphy had written a book called *The Sergeant* that was later made into a movie with Rod Steiger. It said on the book jacket that Dennis Murphy lived in Big Sur, and there was a picture of the Big Sur compound where he lived. Hunter and I both liked the book, and Hunter wanted to meet Murphy, which is why he went to Big Sur in the first place: to look him up. The two of them met, and we'd play touch football with Murphy and his Hollywood friends, which was great fun as long as you weren't running hard toward the western part of the field because you might fall three hundred feet toward the ocean and die.

Hunter ended up living in the servants' cottage near the Big House, which had originally belonged to Murphy's grandmother. It was on the edge of a cliff. Dennis Murphy's brother Mike was one of the two guys who would soon start the Esalen Institute on the property. We would sit for hours in these amazing hot baths, screaming at each other about political issues. We lay around and drank beer. It was paradise, really. I never wanted to leave, but you couldn't make a living in the place.

One night Hunter and I were driving and a deer came off the side of the hill and crashed into the car, and it had a little baby with it. The deer itself was killed, and we threw it in the back and took it back with us and hung it up and gutted it and chopped it up into meat, but the little baby deer had a broken leg, so we put a splint on it. We got it hobbling around a little bit and drinking milk from a bottle, and we were feeling pretty good about ourselves. A couple days later Alan Watts, the great Zen Buddhist guru who was very popular and had a lot of followers at the time, came by and looked at the deer. He said, "Oh, I think I can help the deer. This deer needs some of nature's herbs." He started collecting these pieces of plants and cut them up and fed them to the deer while he pronounced these weird mumbo-jumbo phrases and touched the deer. The deer lay down and went to sleep, and Watts said, "The deer's going to be fine now." Well, about an hour later the little deer stood up, cried out, went into these quick spasms, and died. Hunter was outraged. "That fucker, that quack, that fraud, that charlatan! I don't believe in anything that he speaks. He killed a deer. He murdered it, that rotten prick!"

GENE MCGARR

The Murphys made him the caretaker for the place when they weren't around or old lady Murphy was on her own. How he talked his way into that I don't know. He was writing and living with Sandy in a nice little house that was very close to these fantastic hot spring baths. Two enormous square cement tubs with little ledges all the way around and the hottest fucking water in the world being fed right into it. Right in front of you was the Pacific Ocean, the rocks down below, sea lions barking — right there. And the sunsets were incredible.

My wife and I spent a few days with them. That first night I got so fucking drunk on red wine. One of the things that I recall, when I fell down into the weeds trying to get back to the house, was hearing my wife, Eleanor, say, "Leave him there. Don't bother, leave him there."

The next day, I really lit into Hunter about the money thing and his nonchalant "since you're flush" comment. Jesus. And he just sat there with his head down while I ranted. He had fucked me, and he knew it. I was confronting him with his basic selfishness, and there was nothing he could say. He never apologized for anything. I've never heard

Hunter say "I'm sorry" — ever. Hunter was shameless — borrowing money, asking people for help, making these weird deals — and he got away with it.

JOHN CLANCY

When my girlfriend Judith Spector and I got married, we had our reception at the Big House, and Judith had asked Hunter if he would please wear a tie for the occasion. As we drove in from the wedding to the reception, we saw a goat tied to a post out on the lawn. The goat was wearing a tie. Hunter never showed up.

SANDY THOMPSON

I was in heaven in Big Sur. Hunter was working hard. Jo Hudson, who became a friend of ours, was a sculptor who could do anything with carpentry and stone. He knocked out a whole side of our little two-story, one-room place and on the second floor he put in a giant plate-glass window facing the ocean. I found a job as a maid in a motel, and Hunter would write and get fifty dollars for something, or twenty-five dollars, or maybe even a hundred dollars. Our rent was only fifteen dollars a month, and once a week the postman would deliver food with his old station wagon because there were no stores anywhere nearby, and he gave everyone credit. We bought very little, but we'd get a gallon of cheap red wine, and Hunter always wanted these crescent pastry things — bear claws — and milk, eggs, maybe one box of groceries.

Joan Baez lived on the Esalen property too, on the other side of the canyon. She was living with a guy named Michael, and Michael's sister Jenny was living with Jo Hudson, so Joanie and Jenny and I became friends. Joanie had just cut her first album. She and Hunter had a not very great relationship because Hunter would hunt, and Joanie was against anything like that. They didn't connect.

I had two abortions when we lived in Big Sur. There was absolutely no way that we were ready, and we didn't discuss it. I just told him that

I was pregnant and that I would take care of it. I knew that if I had a baby, Hunter would leave me. There was no question. We weren't married. We had no money. He would have had to have left me, for himself. I mean, as a child he was a narcissist, and later he became a very well developed narcissist — a polished narcissist, actually.

I asked an ex-boyfriend for the money for one and my mother for the other one. They were very dramatic, especially the second. Hunter came with me to Tijuana both times, and the second time was all messy and ugly.

We were really poor for a long time. Every once in a while I would ask my mother for a hundred dollars, and she would always send it. Every once in a while she would send a little food. Being poor was actually kind of great, because once there was money, which was a lot of years later, then there was money to go out and drink.

We had to leave Big Sur after a year because Hunter had written an article for a men's magazine called *Rogue* about Big Sur and the baths. There was sometimes a gay scene at the baths, and Hunter mentioned this in the article. Well, when someone showed the article to Vinnie Murphy — the matriarch, the grandmother of the whole property — she flipped out. Her husband had this dream of the property becoming this incredible health spa and healing place, and she didn't know about the gay scene, and she didn't want anybody else to know about it. She came striding out with her assistant and said very majestically, "You're out of here!" Our fifteen-dollars-a-month place.

So we wound up back in New York. I got a job at a travel agency, and I would get dressed and put my hair up and put on high heels and go and make money, and when I came back, Hunter was writing. I had a steady income, and Hunter knew he could write; he just didn't think he could make a living at it yet.

I remember a couple of nights when he didn't come home until really, really late. That was my first inkling that he was more than a one-woman guy. I was worried and jealous. I'd call apartments at three in the morning to try to find him. Then Hunter left for Aruba. Right before he left, I came across a letter he wrote inviting another woman down there with him.

He was writing for the *National Observer* and some other papers, and he would send me articles and I would type them up. At first there was no such thing as a copy machine, so I had to type maybe ten copies of each article and send them out to New Orleans, Cleveland, wherever. The articles in those days had to be published some distance apart, like a hundred or two hundred miles apart. Hunter was a stickler for perfect copy: no mistakes, perfect margins. And then he made his way down to Colombia and then Rio.

BOB BONE

Hunter wanted to go to South America. He figured that was where the interesting stuff was. He had begun to make contact with the *National Observer,* which was becoming interested in South America, and he decided he was going to go down on a smuggler's boat. He'd heard that in Aruba people smuggled liquor and cigarettes into Nicaragua or somewhere like that, so he took a flight to Aruba and did indeed go on a smuggling boat into South America — to hear him tell it, anyway.

I had taken a job editing this small English magazine in Rio and got to Brazil ahead of Hunter. He was still up in Peru or Bolivia or somewhere, but he knew I was in Rio, and we eventually met up. I was there for slightly under a year in '62 and '63.

SANDY THOMPSON

During the time when Hunter was in Rio, I met this guy who was a law student at Harvard — nice-looking guy, wealthy. And he and I went out walking one night in New York, and we crashed a Leonard Bernstein party, which was interesting. I ended up getting to babysit Leonard Bernstein's children out on Fire Island. But this fellow invited me out to the end of the island on this big motorcycle, a BSA. The next day we went to the beach, and I had a bikini on while I rode on the back. He'd given me his helmet, and he made a sharp turn, flipped the bike, and I landed on my head unconscious. The next thing I know I'm in the hospital for a week — which meant that I couldn't type any of Hunter's things. So Bob Bone, who was living with me in New York (not romantically, though I always thought he was a little jealous that I wasn't involved with him), wrote Hunter a letter saying, basically, "Sandy can't do this. She can't write for you because she was in a motorcycle accident and she's in the hospital right now."

I got a letter from Hunter when I got back to the city that said, "It's over. You're on a motorcycle with some guy. That's it."

BOB BONE

Hunter could be absolutely, shockingly jealous. His letter to Sandy was brutal. Sandy was claiming it was all a very innocent thing, but Hunter was really upset about that and extremely intolerant. It shocked me because I had never seen him get that angry before.

SANDY THOMPSON

At the time, I was working in Queens as a receptionist for a company called Nuclear Research Associates. There were these young fellows there who were chemists, and they were making speed on the side. One day one of them came up to me and said, "You don't look so happy." I said, "Well, I'm in love with this man and he's somewhere in South America." The guy said, "We could make you a little happier."

They had four different levels of speed. I started out with the lowest amount. It definitely did make me feel better. I felt together, and sort of "up" — and then it got to be more and more, and of course I couldn't sleep.

When I came back and I read Hunter's letter, it felt like the end of the world. I don't remember how much speed I took, but it was a lot, and I took a bunch of writing paper and went to the top of the Empire State Building. Higher than a kite, but with a clear head, I wrote him this long letter about why we needed to be together. And it worked.

Then Hunter sent me a letter. He was writing me constantly — I went to the main post office in Manhattan every day — but this letter said, "I'm in Rio now, and Rio looks like a good place. It looks like finally I should settle here for a little bit, and this is where you should come." That's all I needed to hear. I quit my job and got a one-way ticket and wrote Hunter a letter saying I was coming. He sent me a telegram: "Don't come down yet — but when you do, I want you to bring my .44 Magnum." Which was in Louisville, Kentucky.

Well, I didn't want to wait, and I also didn't want to go to Louisville on the bus and break that gun down and then fly in a week, two weeks. I was ready. So I wrote him and said, "I'm coming," and I left. I had the speed with me. When I got off the plane, I called Bob Bone. Bob said, "Uh, hi, Sandy . . . well . . . Hunter, um, Hunter was not wanting you to come down right now, you know. He wanted you to wait until . . . he's not . . . he's not happy." Bob told me to get a room at the such-and-such hotel, which was right on the beach, and that maybe, maybe Hunter would come by. I said, "Okay, Bob. Okay."

BOB BONE

He was very upset when Sandy came down to Brazil when she wasn't expected to. I supported a lot of people in those days, including Hunter. None of us had much money, and Hunter thought it was quite an imposition for Sandy to suddenly become a responsibility or a liability in Brazil.

SANDY THOMPSON

I get over to the little hotel on the beach, get myself a room, take a little more speed, and I'm waiting and I'm fine. I'm fine because I'm high. There's a knock on the door, and Hunter comes in, and both of us just dissolve. We went out for dinner, he introduced me to friends. Everything was very, very "up," and then the next day he said, "I have to leave. You stay here, but I'm going to take an assignment" — I don't remember what country he went to, I think it was Uruguay — "because I'm so angry with you. At the same time, I'm madly in love with you, but I'm also so angry with you for disobeying me that I have to leave." And so he did, for about two weeks. And I was just fine. I got a cheaper room in the hotel, down in the basement. I started taking guitar lessons and learning the bossa nova. I worked on my tan. I wandered around the streets. I started learning Portuguese. And then Hunter came back, and he was okay. We moved into an apartment on the seventeenth floor, one block from Copacabana Beach.

BOB BONE

I was driving an old MG convertible with a friend of mine along Copacabana Beach, and I suddenly saw Hunter loping along. We picked him up, so now it was three of us piled in this tiny MG convertible. Hunter was a little bit drunk, but he said, "That's nothing. The thing that's drunk is in my pocket." He had a drunk monkey in his pocket. The way he explained it was that he got off the plane in Rio with the monkey and went to a bar, and somebody said they would buy him a drink as long as they could buy the monkey a drink at the same time. It probably was a bit of an exaggeration, but back in the MG the monkey had thrown up in his pocket for real, and he was kind of smelly.

That monkey eventually committed suicide. We figured it had the DT's. The maid saw it jump off the tenth-story balcony of the apartment.

Hunter had another animal back in his room. He was staying in some crazy little hotel, and we went back, and there was an animal there called a coatimundi. The Brazilians call them coatis. They're sort of a cross between a rat and a honey bear. Hunter's coati had no hair on his tail. Hunter claimed that he'd rescued it in Bolivia, that he'd bought it from some people who were mistreating it. Hunter had named it Ace, and Ace became famous for two reasons: One, he liked to play with soap; and two, he learned to use the toilet.

SANDY THOMPSON

One night just before carnival I was out on the street right in front of the building, and there was a samba group playing. And there was this guy, and he came behind me, and he was beginning to put his arms around my waist or something or other. I loved to dance, and Hunter loved to see me dancing. So I moved. The next thing I know, Hunter's got this Brazilian by the scruff of his neck, or maybe by his shirt. He's picked him up. And he says, *"Tienes problemas!"* Hunter would not let me out on the street after that. He locked me in the apartment for the rest of carnival.

BOB BONE

Another time Hunter and somebody else (I can't remember who it was) were shooting rats in a dump somewhere in Rio, and somebody called the cops, who came around and pulled them in. Hunter, of course, claimed that it wasn't them doing the shooting, that it must have been somebody else. As usual, he made friends with the cops, and they were all getting along great. And then at some point, Hunter put his feet up on the cop's desk, and bullets rolled out of his pocket. They threw him back in jail, but things turned out all right eventually. They called the consulate, and by that time Hunter had a little bit of cachet with the *National Observer.* It all blew over somehow.

SANDY THOMPSON

I was afraid to ask Hunter about marriage. I was afraid to bring it up, because I was afraid he'd say no, but I remember asking him once there.

I don't remember his response exactly, but it was along the lines of "That's up to me."

Hunter decided that it was time to leave Rio and that he was going to continue on in South America and write more articles for the *National Observer* and that I would go back to the States.

CLIFFORD RIDLEY *was Hunter's editor at the* National Observer.

There wasn't anything in his background that said that he was going to be good — his only credentials that I remember were from the Middletown paper — but we knew that he was good when we got his first piece. We were a national newsweekly, a broadsheet owned by Dow Jones that had just started up. Hunter probably wrote a piece a month when he was in Latin America, and a lot of them ended up running on the front page. We were fairly flexible about length — if something was good and it was long, we had the space — but he probably averaged in the neighborhood of fifteen hundred words, for which we paid him a hundred fifty, or two hundred dollars if it was a helluva job. With rare exceptions, he didn't mind the editing, though in fairness to him, he was three thousand miles away and wasn't seeing his stories for six weeks or so after they came out.

We didn't have a problem with him injecting himself into his stories. We were going in the direction of personal journalism at that point, experimenting with allowing more personality in our pieces. Given today's journalistic climate, though, we might be a lot more skeptical about some of his details; the rich British man hitting golf balls from his penthouse terrace over the downtown slums of Cali, Colombia, in-between sips of his gin and tonic is a little *too* perfect. He *may* have embellished just a *tad* . . . but there was no arguing over the quality of his writing. He was extraordinary for us, and for journalism at that time.

I found him quite easy to deal with, aside from his letters and cables perpetually bitching about money, and subsequently about being sick.

The needing-money part we basically accepted as true. We didn't pay a lot, and as far as we knew he wasn't writing for anybody else. The other stuff about his health — well, obviously hyperbole was Hunter's stock-in-trade, and we understood that. Did we literally believe every account of his health, when he's saying that he's so hobbled that he was using a leg of his camera tripod as a cane to help him walk at the rate of a hundred yards an hour? No. I would read excerpts from Hunter's letters to me to the other editors nearby, and eventually one of us said, "Maybe we oughta run some of this stuff." So I pulled a piece together out of the best parts.

His ambition, from the moment that he and I started dealing with each other, was to be a novelist. He'd refer to *The Rum Diary*, which he carried around with him, and his idols were the literary heavyweights. It was clear to me that his aspiration was to one day have his name among them.

WILLIAM KENNEDY

For Hunter it was a career and lifestyle breakthrough. His life was professionally itinerant after he went to South America for the *National Observer*. He went anyplace and wrote whatever moved him in his own way — up to a point. It was heavily edited, and there were limitations on what he could say. But it established his name, modestly, and he managed to distinguish himself through subject matter and attitude. He had an editor he respected. But after a few years and a couple of rejections he soured on the paper — which *was* rather straitlaced, with a centrist Republican attitude. He called it a "dead man's train." And eventually he moved on.

He was having no success with *The Rum Diary*, which he thought was his best work up to that point. He was finding success with everything journalistically, but he still wanted to become a novelist.

After I got a couple of rejections of my novel as being too downbeat, I advised him to write an upbeat novel. But he didn't, and neither did I.

We exchanged stories of grief and rejection and he sent word if he got some money. Once he won sixty dollars on a quiz show.

What we didn't know was how you got published. After Hunter left San Juan, there was a lot of correspondence back and forth about agents and publishing. I got an agent who had an A-list of writers, and I sent Hunter over to him, but he said he didn't want to represent anything like what I Iunter was doing. Hunter eventually found someone to represent *Prince Jellyfish* and later another agent to represent *The Rum Diary* before it was finished.

We were very honest about one another's work. He wrote me after I published *The Ink Truck* in '68 and said, "I haven't read *The Ink Truck*. Sandy read it, and she didn't like it through the first half and then the second half she sort of liked it. But if I do read it, I'm not going to admit it." I presume this was in retaliation for my negative input on *The Rum Diary*. I was rooting for him to publish, but not that work as it was; and I was hardly alone in this view. The book was full of digressions and wisdom — his essays on the state of the world, the nation, journalism, Puerto Rico.

SANDY THOMPSON

I worked for my mother's travel agency for a couple of months, and then one weekend I decided to go up to Louisville to see Hunter's mom. While I was up there, we got a phone call or a letter or a telegram saying that Hunter was on his way home. In fact, I think he was in Florida, and he was going to take the train, or the bus.

I remember Virginia saying to me that whenever she knew that Hunter was coming home to Louisville she was scared She knew there would be tension.

That same day, some friends of Hunter's came over. They were being very gracious and asked if I'd like to come out and ride with them. I loved to ride horses, so we went out. I did not realize that this was a polo pony — not only a polo pony, but a *green* polo pony. I wasn't on this horse five minutes when he threw me and I landed on my shoulder. I just went back to Virginia's, and that night I couldn't sleep, so we went to the ER. It was a dislocated shoulder.

The next day Hunter was home, and there I was in the hospital. I knew that wasn't going to go over well. The hospital told me that I was free to leave, but I was in this wheelchair with my arm in a sling when Hunter came in. We hadn't seen each other in months. Hunter said, "Well, that's the end of that." And I'm thinking, "The end of what?"

I found out later he had had great plans to come home and sweep me off my feet and get married. We went home to his mother's — she was at work in the library — and with my arm in a sling we broke her bed making love. She was under the illusion that we were each sleeping in separate rooms, even though we had been living together for three years, and she came back, and she was just wild from this terrible, terrible thing having happened in her home.

The next afternoon I was upstairs, and Hunter and his two brothers, Jim and Davison, were downstairs, and Hunter called up and said, "Sandy, come on down." I came downstairs, and we got into the car with the two brothers. Hunter and I were in the back, Davison was driving, and I said, "Where are we going?" Hunter said, "Indiana." I said, "What for?" Hunter replied, "To get married." That was my proposal. I said, "Oh."

GERALD TYRRELL

Hunter's mother persuaded Hunter to get married, so he got married across the river from Louisville in Jeffersonville, Indiana, in a marriage parlor.

SANDY THOMPSON

So we went to this town in Indiana. The first thing we had to do was get our blood test, and then we had to wait overnight for the results. We went to this cabin on a property that was owned by one of Hunter's wealthy friends, and it was all lovey-dovey, and we were lying — once again — on a mattress on the floor, naked and half-asleep, and all of a sudden there was this banging on the screen door. Hunter got up, pulled on his drawers, and went to the door. It was the owner of the property, the father of his friend, this Scotsman wearing a kilt, and he yelled, "Who is cohabitating in my house? You will get out of here. You will be out of here within an hour, or I am calling the law." Hunter had already been in jail, and this wouldn't help. So we got out of there (I don't remember where we stayed) and made it to the justice of the peace the next day.

I've got my arm in a sling and I'm wearing Hunter's big sweater, and the justice of the peace starts reading this thing — you know, sacred stuff — and he looked over at me and said, "What happened to your arm?" I said, "I fell off a horse." He said, "You fell off a house?" I said, "No, a horse." "Oh. Okay, you're married." That was May 20, 1963.

GERALD TYRRELL

Jimmy Noonan had an impromptu party afterward, and that's the only time I met Sandy. Hunter had been down in South America doing some kind of drugs, and he was strung out. He was having trouble talking; his whole manner of speech had changed. He was speaking in this guttural, staccato way, where he'd spit things out quickly and you'd have trouble understanding him. He seemed to be having a hard time finishing sentences.

SANDY THOMPSON

From Indiana, we went down to my mother's in Florida and spent a little time there. My mother adored Hunter. But my father thought otherwise. Anything he had ever heard about him was terrible.

My father was a serious Republican, and straight — really straight — and my mother was soulful, passionate, and an alcoholic. Virginia told her, when we got married, "I'm worried for Sandy. You know Hunter.

He's a lot to handle. Trust me: He can be really . . ." She probably wouldn't have said "violent." She might have. And my mother said, which I've never forgotten, "Don't worry about Sandy. She'll take care of herself."

SANDY THOMPSON

My whole life was completely wrapped around Hunter. I would send my father articles, but my father wouldn't respond. My mother kept in touch with me because she wanted to make sure that I was okay. But when people in my family died, or when there was a wedding in my family, I was not there.

We headed back to New York, and then Hunter and Paul got a job delivering a somebody's things cross-country.

LOREN JENKINS *met Hunter in the fall of 1963 in Aspen.*

I'd been in Africa teaching school for the Peace Corps and was about to go up to graduate school. Hunter and I had a mutual friend, a lady from Louisville, Peggy Clifford, who had a bookstore in Aspen. She said, "You two should meet. You have a lot in common." And Hunter breezed in. He had a job driving someone's stuff out to California and had a full truckload.

So we met, we talked, had a drink, and then he went west and I went east, and after my first year in graduate school, by process of elimination, I decided that the only hope for me was journalism, and the only person I knew at the time who'd been a journalist was Hunter. So I wrote to him and asked him, basically, "How do you break into this racket?" He wrote me back a very funny letter, a typical Hunter screed about how fucked the profession is, but then he wrote, "There are two things you should know if you're going to get in to do this. First, all editors suck. Second, if you correct something on a manuscript when you're typing, don't use x's. It doesn't look neat. Use alternate m's and n's — it makes it neater." These were his two pieces of advice.

SANDY THOMPSON

By the time I flew out to meet Hunter, Paul was living in a cabin in the Aspen mountains, and Hunter and I visited him before renting a small house on the Woody Creek Road. I remember being at Paul's and pouring them wine. Paul had an outhouse, and I went out to the outhouse and I got sick. And I thought, "What's this?"

I saw the doctor that week, who confirmed that I was pregnant. I don't remember Hunter's reaction exactly, but it definitely wasn't bad. I was incredibly happy.

Hunter shot elk so I could eat elk liver, which is what I ate the whole time I was pregnant with Juan — after which of course I never wanted to see another piece of elk or venison ever. I had that and salad and powdered milk. Hunter was kind and thoughtful all through the pregnancy, and then we were getting ready to leave for California. We were going to stay in some fantastic cabin that Denne Petitclerc, who was a fairly successful screenwriter, had outside of Santa Rosa, outside of Glen Ellen on the top of a mountain. I was eight months pregnant, and in February it was thirty below in Colorado.

It was not exactly Hunter's idea of the American dream — going across the country in an old Nash Rambler with almost no money and his wife eight months along. But we got there, and Hunter went to meet Denne, and I could see them talking, and Hunter looking really, really agitated, and then Hunter came back to the car and said, "He's already rented it."

He said that there was a place on the property, but that it wasn't a whole lot. It was actually a shack — not a bad shack, you know, but a tin shack with a little kitchen and a big room, and then a little room off that which became Juan's bedroom. It was great. It had electricity and running water.

At nine months, at about six o'clock in the morning, my water broke. Hunter drove me to Santa Rosa Hospital. Juan was very easy. The doctor said that I could have had this baby in a field. I was just elated, and I was very glad that it was a boy. I thought that Hunter really wanted a boy. That was March 23, 1964.

WILLIAM KENNEDY

Hunter loved Fitzgerald, and he named his son Juan Fitzgerald Thompson after Scott and also after the other Fitz — John Fitzgerald Kennedy.

SANDY THOMPSON

When we brought Juan home, he slept with us. We had a Doberman at the time, Agar, and the dog slept with us too. Agar was the first, but later we had other Dobermans: Darwin, who was the all-star, and Benjie, who had two litters of puppies. We kept one of them and called him Weird. His actual name was Speed Wizard, and he was very weird.

The mattress was on a box spring, not on the floor, so we were getting up in the world, you know? I nursed Juan, and I was in absolute heaven. Here's Hunter and here's my son. It was an extraordinary feeling of power, of love, of everything good.

I got pregnant again a year or two later. Hunter didn't want another child, but I definitely did. I wanted another Hunter, of all things. But I'm Rh-negative and Hunter is Rh-positive, and in those days, if that was the case, only your first child lived.

None of my other children lived after Juan. There were five. The first one was probably at two or four months, and it was a true miscarriage. And then I had a full-term baby. Well, she was born with the cord tied around her neck, and she was blue. She was Rh-positive, and Aspen Valley Hospital didn't have blood. When the baby was born I didn't look at her because I sensed that something was wrong.

I dealt with it initially by just going crazy, by going out into the field, in my head, next to the hospital bed, and nothing was real. There were all these flowers out there. And in my mind, I thought, "You know, if nothing is real, the baby's not dead." I went into this place, and Hunter looked at me, and he said, "Sandy, if you want to leave, if you need to leave and go out there for a while, then you do that. But you have to know that Juan and I need you." It was one of the most beautiful things he ever did, and of course I came back.

Hunter and a friend buried the baby — Hunter had named her Sara — by the Roaring Fork River.

MICHAEL SOLHEIM *was a bartender in Sun Valley, Idaho, in 1963.*

Hunter came up to Sun Valley to talk to some people who knew Ernest Hemingway for an article he was doing for the *National Observer.* He and a local guy walked into the little bar I had, called the Leadville Espresso House, which used to be a church and still had a steeple and a bell. It was a bar disguised as an espresso house. I had had conversations with Hemingway there.

Hunter was asking this guy questions about Hemingway and taking notes, and then he and I talked for a little, and I said to myself, "I'm going to like this guy." It was that quick. I ended up closing down early, and we went back to my cabin and talked more, and at some point late in the night, Hunter wanted to know if we could go up to Hemingway's house in Ketchum, so up we went. The door was open, and we could hear the caretaker snoring in the background. For Hunter it was all about going into the vestibule, the enclosed space where Hemingway had shot himself. I hit the light switch and the sconces came on and we stood there.

Hunter would come back to Sun Valley or Ketchum now and again and see my wife and me. He'd write us a lot and he'd let us know when he'd be coming through. Our time together was as simple as listening to comedy LPs and smoking weed. I'd put on these albums from *Beyond the Fringe* and Peter Sellers; at one point I put on General Douglas

MacArthur's farewell speech, his address to the joint House session. "Old soldiers never die, they just fade away."

Another time he was writing an article for *Pageant* about Robert Mc-Namara, the secretary of defense, and I had some stuff I'd got in the mail from some kind of a sex club lying around my place, and with it came this postcard. You could write on the back of it and check off boxes to express your interest in some of the damndest things you ever heard of in your life, and this club would promise to put you in touch with somebody in your neighborhood with similar views. It was called Club Wow. So Hunter, in his article, accused McNamara of wearing a Club Wow button on his lapel.

DR. BOB GEIGER *met Hunter in Sonoma, California, in 1964.*

I had just started my practice in orthopedic surgery and my then wife and my daughter, who's Juan's age, maybe a year old at that time, were out in the town square. My wife came home and said, "I met this gal, and she had a baby, and we started talking." Turns out her husband's a freelance writer, and my wife said, "I told her that, 'Gee, my husband's a doctor, but he writes.' So I invited them over for dinner."

Hunter and I hit it off, and from then on they were both around. He was about twenty-seven, and I was thirty-three. There was a series of misadventures that ended up getting Hunter and Sandy and Juan thrown out of the little house they were living in just above Sonoma. Hunter and I were doing a little target practice at four in the morning, and the landlady — it was this little cottage on some property out in the country — lived next door. There were some gophers in the lawn out in front of this place, and the obvious way to kill gophers is to shoot them. It makes sense, doesn't it? It made sense to us. But it didn't make sense to the landlady. So the next day, Hunter and Sandy moved in with us in Sonoma. We were house-sitting at a condo complex with a pool, and there was no one else in this complex. We had a three-bedroom place, so there was room for Hunter and Sandy. Sandy could hang around the pool with Juan, and so it worked out real well.

I had published a novel, and Hunter had this horse's-ass idea that it was supposed to be important to be a fiction writer. I would try to point out to him, "Hunter, you are writing fiction. All writing is fiction. Experiences you experience, and words are words, so everything is fiction. This is just its own kind of fiction." We'd argue about that.

PAUL SEMONIN

A couple of years after we were in Puerto Rico together, when Hunter was down in Latin America and South America writing stuff for the *National Observer,* I was becoming much more politicized. I went to Africa and ended up at the University of Ghana getting a master's degree in African studies. There was a colony of African American exiles in Ghana, including people like Maya Angelou and Julian Mayfield; Malcolm X came to visit, and I met him and became very interested in the political direction he was taking just before he was assassinated, and of course I was writing to Hunter about some of this stuff. But as I was writing and identifying in some ways with the black struggle, the civil rights struggle — but even more with black radicals — Hunter addressed one of his letters to me as "Niggerboy."

I mean, that's it in a nutshell. He pulled a deep race card out of his pack and used it as an insult. Although if you look at many of the letters he wrote, he would often use these ridiculous "Dear so and so" addresses. Part of it was insulting and part of it was humor and part of it was just provoking you. But there was always this race element buried in his character which popped out every now and then, and it was nasty.

Hunter was always pushing you, always testing you, seeing how far you'll go before your loyalty breaks, or before you've had enough. And it created a kind of inner circle of people who stood the test. It's like hazing, but there could be that feeling, if you're on the other end of it, that he was mocking you in some way. It was a part of his character from a very early stage. And it was partly what later led to us parting ways. It grew kind of tiresome and unproductive.

DR. BOB GEIGER

I know that different people have accused Hunter over the years of having kind of a Neanderthal attitude towards blacks or minorities. Sometimes he would use the word "nigger" when he was writing, and he was very quick with racial jokes and things like that. But in terms of where his real sentiment was, it was the opposite. When we were getting together, we would get all fired up about this shit. At one time, Hunter and I were planning to — thank God we didn't do it — we were going to get a truck and run guns down to Mississippi to help out with all this crap that was going on in Mississippi in '64 and '65. We figured that maybe we ought to level the playing field, and a truckload of guns would do that.

Hunter and I each tended to have our own ideas. Hunter was a great guy to argue with because he would listen to what you said. Very few people do that. He would change his mind on the basis of what you said. And if someone's going to actually pay attention to what you're saying, you argue a little differently than if you're just saying things to hear yourself say it, though when when you got Hunter and Clancy and McGarr and I together, you couldn't hear anything.

JERRY HAWKE

Hunter and John Clancy were kind of kindred souls. Clancy had a really wild streak to him, and that appealed to Hunter.

I used to get telephone calls from Clancy and Hunter in the middle of the night. They would generally be drunk. It started when they were together in San Francisco; later, they would put in conference calls. I remember listening to operators come on at two o'clock in the morning: "Will you accept a collect conference call from John Clancy and

Hunter Thompson?" "No!" So a few minutes later, they'd ring back with a paid call and Hunter would say something like, "I've got a very important question. Do you still feel the same way about *The Great Gatsby?*"

JACK THIBEAU *is a poet and actor who met Hunter in 1961.*

Clancy was a vicious attack lawyer. You wound him up and it never stopped. He would come after you with guns, knives. Because he was crazy, and he had no mercy. And he was brilliant; he was at the top of his class at Columbia.

ROGER HAWKE

Clancy was insane.

DR. BOB GEIGER

McGarr was not eminently sane, either. He was a very handsome big guy who would come on to all the chicks. Hunter and I and Clancy would usually just insult them. Even if Hunter tried to not be insulting, he would insult the girls. So you always had this dynamic: If McGarr would come on too strong, Hunter would get upset at that. It didn't bother me that much. If McGarr was coming on to my wife, I'd just say, "Well, that's McGarr." Hunter, though, would get very defensive, and say that McGarr was abusing me. He was very loyal and protective that way, surprisingly.

Hunter went after McGarr with a tire iron one time for coming on to my wife. McGarr and I were out in the front yard boxing at my place in Sonoma. Bare-knuckled boxing, which was a mistake. McGarr was a good boxer, but we weren't hitting each other hard. We were playing, really, but McGarr had been coming on to my wife, and Hunter walked out and thought we were serious. He went to his car and got this tire iron and started chasing McGarr around, and then suddenly he got in his car and disappeared for two days. He was embarrassed that he overreacted. Sandy was looking frantically for him. I said, "I think he drove off like a dog that's bit somebody and doesn't want to get caught." But you have to realize that this was booze too. This wasn't high-powered drugs or anything. Maybe there was a little grass around.

Hunter decided he wanted to be closer to the action, so they moved down to a place right across from the University of California Medical Center in San Francisco. He and I rented a trailer and I moved them down, which was another adventure because the mattress flew out of the trailer, as it usually does.

It was there where he mostly wrote *Hell's Angels*.

CHAPTER THREE

San Francisco, Hells Angels, and Merry Pranksters

I saw him two days after they beat him up. Both of his eyes were filled with blood. His ribs were taped. He could hardly stand up.

SANDY THOMPSON

We moved to San Francisco and got a place at the top of Golden Gate Park, right at the edge of the Haight. The Haight-Ashbury scene was just beginning — this was in '65.

We had very little money. Every once in a while there would be an article and a little more money, and one of these was the piece for *The Nation* on the Hells Angels. So that's where it all began. Ian Ballantine, who would become Hunter's book editor, came out from New York and offered Hunter a contract.

DR. BOB GEIGER

I'd drive down to San Francisco to see Hunter when he was writing *Hell's Angels*. The bedroom had been converted to a studio for him, and Sandy and Juan were sleeping in the living room. It was kind of a typical old San Francisco apartment, long and narrow. He had drilled holes through the ceiling and tapped into the phone line of the empty apartment upstairs, so for a little while he was able to use the phone as much as he wanted.

SANDY THOMPSON

I was working for a Realtor and I made ninety dollars a week, so there was two dollars or something that he could spend on beer. He heard the Jefferson Airplane and got friendly with them, and he took acid for the first time. They all came back to the apartment and then the band left and Hunter was there with me and Juan, who was in a crib. I didn't know anything about acid, except that it seemed awfully dangerous. Hunter said, "Get me my gun." I had hidden the gun. I said, "Absolutely not." He started to get really angry. And he said, "If you don't get me the gun . . ."

There was no way I was going to get him the gun while he's on acid. I had no idea if he was going to kill me, if he was going to kill my son . . .

He said, "If you don't get me that gun, I'm going to throw this boot through the window." These were plate-glass windows, big windows. And he did. He threw this boot — *wham!* — through the window, and I was shaking. I reached up — this was a mom protecting her son — and scratched his face. There was blood. And it was weird, but he stopped. I guess that jolted him.

Hunter had a motorcycle, and he went out and got on it and rode up to Bob and Terri Geiger's in Sonoma. I called up there an hour or so later and said, "Is Hunter there?" I had no idea if he could possibly make it on acid or not, not knowing anything about acid. And Terri said, "Oh yeah, he's here. And you know, I've never seen him like this. He's out there coloring with the two little girls." They were maybe two and three years old.

DR. BOB GEIGER

We got into it a little bit when he showed up because I started bawling him out about it, telling him that it was inappropriate behavior to attack Sandy or to be negative to Sandy.

SANDY THOMPSON

When Juan was an infant, Hunter was very sweet with him — in the first year or so. By the time he was two, he just wasn't there for him. Hunter told me, "Juan's *your* novel." He could come out and be there when he needed to be there, for someone or something. He could rise to the occasion, and then when he didn't have to, he could sink back into the uncharming self.

Hunter wanted to keep his really dark self away from Juan, but he wasn't making any changes in his behavior so that he could be a father to Juan. He stayed out of the picture. I mean he was physically there some of the time, but mostly he was asleep, or he was at the bar, or he was out of town. Juan's time with Hunter began about ten or twelve years before Hunter died.

Hunter did not like Christmas, and he didn't believe in Christmas trees. But when Juan was two years old we had a tree, and we continued to have a tree for Juan so that when he got older he would know Christmas. Hunter would get up for a couple hours while Juan opened presents, and then he'd go back to bed. He didn't behave badly, and he would get me a present. But we never celebrated my birthday, ever, until the year that I left him.

JACK THIBEAU

We first met at a bar before a football game with John Clancy and then took a cab across Golden Gate Park to Kezar Stadium.

He was writing *Hell's Angels,* and he told me I looked like an Oakland undercover cop covering the Angels. I just sort of shrugged that one off, and he goes, "Reach into my pocket and grab some of those brownies." There was a whole mess of brownies that he said one of the Angels had given him. I nibbled on some. By the time we got to Kezar, we were unredeemable. He started screaming epithets during the game — "RIP HIS THROAT OUT!" — stuff like that.

He had a sheepskin jacket on and one of those slouchy golf hats. He was like a weird-looking collegiate type and passed for a sort of odd aristocrat. He spoke very well, and he was very literate. He seemed to think he was some sort of rich guy.

The quarterback for the Forty Niners was named John Brodie. At one point there was a lull in the game. There was a big play about to happen, and Brodie goes up to get behind the center, and everybody's quiet. And Thompson screams, "JOHN BRODIE WEARS HIGH HEELS!" Everybody turned around, including some old lady, who said, "Young man, will you please stop using that nasty language?" And Hunter says, "Madam, we come here to vent our spleens and get rid of the daily drudgery of our lives. If you and your husband don't like it, why don't you go to the opera?" They got up and left.

After the game, Thompson paid some hippies with a pickup truck to drive us around all night. He just kept the guys stoned and drunk, and we're driving through alleyways in San Francisco's residential districts. All of a sudden Thompson bangs on the hood of the truck and asks the driver to stop and jumps out of the truck and runs up to this house and disappears inside. He comes out about five minutes later, jumps in the truck, bangs on the hood, and we take off again. And I said, "What did you do?" He said, "I had to make some phone calls." I said, "Did you know those people?" He said, "No, but they shouldn't leave their door open in the middle of the night. I mean, luckily all I wanted to do is make a few phone calls. I had to call my agent in New York."

We ended up spending a lot of time in these nasty-ass bars around Kezar. Once I took him to a North Beach bar down on the waterfront, and some guy started bothering him — you know, some fucking drunk just harassing people — and Thompson punched him right in the fucking mouth. Boom-boom-boom and "We'd better get out of here." He just fucking knocked the shit out of him very quickly. So we hurried out the door and we got about half a block down the street, and he said, "Let's go back. That was fun."

JOHN CLANCY

One day after a Forty Niners game, we were drinking with David Pierce, the mayor of Richmond, California, at Hunter's place. Out of nowhere, Hunter leapt up and fished a shotgun out from underneath the couch, threw open the back door, screamed really loudly, and fired both barrels out the door. After all this, he ran back to us, carefully placed the shotgun under the couch, sat down, and grabbed his beer. Hunter seemed completely amazed and surprised when a few minutes later there was a knock on his door — a cop. Hunter invited him in and told him to look around, and Pierce started talking about how he's the mayor of Richmond, and Hunter's this famous writer on the way up. I just kept my mouth shut. Eventually the cop just sort of warned us to keep our noses clean. He scoffed at "Mr. Mayor" — I don't think he actually believed this for a second — and said to Hunter, "Good luck with your writing. I tried to do that once, and it's a lot harder than it looks."

PAUL SEMONIN

Hunter spoke about the Hells Angels in a strange kind of way. There was an identification with the Angels as outcasts — downtrodden outcasts, and victims, if you will. He saw them as a kind of emblem of honor and rebellion. It wasn't only Hunter, but people like Ken Kesey as well who somehow thought that an alliance between the Hells Angels and the peace movement was going to make or break the whole struggle. They invested a lot of their energy into that.

I think Hunter's perspective on this goes back to his kind of survivalist character, the way that he identified with some of these extreme elements that were actually quite right-wing. If you look at his writings about the Hells Angels, there's not a more unsavory kind of bunch of characters, and yet he somehow idolizes them. He does it in a very subtle way, but he makes their struggles something that reflects both a failure and a rebellion against certain things in American culture and society. His own descriptions of it, and the parties that Kesey threw, are just horrifying. He saw some things which I thought were worthy of some kind of a critique, or some kind of intellectual space that he needed to have and didn't seem to have. We talked some about this, because I was there while he was writing the manuscript. But this sort of thinking just was not on Hunter's radar then.

SONNY BARGER *was the president of the Oakland chapter of the Hells Angels.*

There was a guy named Birney Jarvis, who was an ex-Frisco member and a writer for the *Chronicle*. Somehow or another he and Hunter hooked up, and Hunter was introduced in a San Francisco club and then they brought him to us. We're a very democratic club and the whole Hells Angels had to vote on letting him visit — Oakland, San Francisco, San Jose, Richmond — whatever charters were around in '66. We voted on doing the book and then we worked with him to do it. Hunter was the first person that ever approached us about a book, and he got the story. He had the cooperation of the club — not *my* cooperation.

He was definitely different. He didn't fit in. We hung out at his house, and wherever we went, he went. And I don't think Hunter ever tried to act like one of us. He always knew that he was apart from us. Some people get into thinking they're one of us, and they really run into problems. I don't think he ever tried to put that front on. Which is a very good thing for him — and for us too.

SANDY THOMPSON

They brought their mamas over too, and they were all very sweet to Juan. One of them said once, "We've got to keep it down. The baby's sleeping." I had no idea that they had killed and raped and done horrible things because when they were at our apartment, they just talked.

Hunter would go to a bar in Oakland, the El Adobe, to see them, but he was very diligent. They would take Seconal with beer, and when all that kicked in, they would be *monsters*. He'd stay until he knew they'd taken the Seconal, and then he couldn't leave soon enough.

Sonny would come over, and Tiny. I remember going to a couple Hells Angels parties, but we didn't stay late. And of course there was the party at Ken Kesey's.

Hunter had met Kesey at a radio show, and Kesey said, "I'm kind of interested in the Hells Angels. Do you think they might want to come and meet my friends?" Hunter told him that he could arrange that, and then one Sunday he said to me, "Let's go for a drive." Which was really bizarre: Hunter, on a Sunday afternoon, like a normal human being, saying, "Let's take the little family for a drive." Juan was with us, and he was still an infant.

We drove up through these big evergreens, and we knew that Kesey and the Merry Pranksters were under surveillance at the time. There were narcotics agents and police in the hills looking to catch anybody doing anything wrong. And then we saw this huge banner stretched across the road and across the river that read, "The Merry Pranksters Welcome the Hells Angels." I can't imagine what the law must have thought when they saw that sign.

Neal Cassady was there, and Ginsberg, and Cassady's ex-wife. Kesey played this four-hour documentary of the Magic Bus and the Merry Pranksters doing their thing. After a while you couldn't watch anymore. It was just endless people smoking and being high and being silly; smoking, being high and silly; smoking, being high and silly.

Kesey's children, who were maybe five or seven, were there too, and people were high, and drunk, and dancing; they were taking acid, though Hunter didn't. The kids had taken acid too. At some point we jumped in a car with Ginsberg to go get some booze. We got stopped by the police, and they asked us who we were. All Ginsberg would say was "I'm a poet . . . I'm a poet," which Hunter and I thought was funny.

When we got back, I noticed some of the Angels going outside of Kesey's house, where we were all hanging out, from time to time passing through a side door. When we got back in the car to leave, Hunter was very, very agitated. He said, "Do you know what just happened? There was a gang bang in the cabin next door to the main house." Hunter just happened to open the door. She wasn't screaming or yelling or resisting, he said. She might have been passed out part of the time. It was not violent, but it was continual; lots of different Angels got involved.

This was the scene he wrote about toward the end of *Hell's Angels*. It was very disturbing to him. He felt partially at fault for bringing them all together, and he felt sick.

DR. BOB GEIGER

People think that *Fear and Loathing in Las Vegas* is dedicated to me because they think I was supplying Hunter with drugs, but the main reason is that I would drive down to San Francisco almost every night, and Hunter and I would read through the *Hell's Angels* manuscript page by page, word by word. I had a different idea of the way he should be writing it than he did, and I was absolutely wrong.

I would say, "Hunter, why are you writing about these losers? These guys are crazies, and you're glorifying them. They're nothing. You wouldn't stop to piss on them if they were on fire, so why the hell are you writing a book about them? In essence, you're kind of glorifying them in this book. Even though you're not saying positive things, you're giving them all kinds of publicity." And he would listen to me. Remember, some of those articles in the *National Observer* were stories I wrote. But he said, "No, these guys are really showing us where society is going." And I totally missed it, because he was absolutely right.

SONNY BARGER

He would fire a gun out the window of his apartment in San Francisco trying to impress people — to me, that is the stupidest thing anybody can do — and he would talk himself up that he was a tough guy, when he wasn't. When anything happened, he would run and hide, like what he did at Bass Lake.

Bass Lake was the big run of the year, the Labor Day run. We had a place up there, and one year Hunter drove up in his car and met us. We'd be there, two, three, four days. Tiny Baxter might have been the sheriff; Sergeant Ring was the guy that ran the show up there. Sergeant Ring and I had a very good understanding. But Hunter jumped in his car for a beer run and a couple of us went with him. The first store we went to was a bust, so we went to another store. "These fucking punks ain't going to run us off. We came here to get beer, and they aren't going to tell us, 'You can't buy beer.' " But we get to the other store, and there was a group of mostly sheriffs waiting for us — there might have been three or four locals with them — and we got in a little verbal argument with the sheriffs there and we were going to fight, and Hunter jumped in the trunk of his car. When he's got citizens around him, he'll shoot his gun off and talk loud, but when the shit comes down, he's out of there. When it was settled, he came out. He didn't write about that part in the book.

JOHN CLANCY

I went over to Hunter's place one Sunday to have a few beers and head to the football game — the Niners were playing the Packers that day, and we were all pretty excited — and nobody was home. I was furious. The big game was about to start and he was really late, and suddenly he comes screeching up and says, "I'm sorry I'm late, but the Hells Angels beat me up last night when they found out they weren't going to get any royalties out of me. I probably wouldn't have even made it, but I knew you guys were waiting for me." He was bruised, and he had these welts on his face, and his nose was definitely broken and pushed in. This had happened the night before or maybe around midnight. He was pretty battered but certainly coherent. We walked to the game. He didn't seem to be *really* badly injured.

SONNY BARGER

We hadn't seen Hunter in months, maybe a year, and he said that his editor told him, "Finish the book or you're not getting paid." He said himself that he got a bottle of whiskey and an ounce of coke and wrote the second half of the book overnight. When the book was done, he came back around to us and said, "I'd like to go on this run with you." We went up to Squaw Rock. It's a big rock, 5,200 feet high. Supposedly in ancient folklore, the squaw's boyfriend was fucking another squaw down at the bottom. She climbed up on the rock, jumped off, and landed on them both and killed them. But anyway, it's up in northern California.

So we were up there. Hunter says it was an argument over whether his Triumph or BSA or whatever he had was faster than Junkie George's Harley, which is total bullshit. Junkie George was the name of the guy that beat him up, but it had nothing to do with that. We were there and George got in an argument with his old lady — George's old lady, not Hunter's. They got in an argument, and George slapped her. You know, guys do that. Well, when he did that, his dog bit him. But when his dog bit him, George kicked the dog. And Hunter jumps right in. Now, Hunter's run with us for a year. He knows policy and procedure, and he says, "Only punks slap their old ladies and kick their dogs." And George says, "Well, I guess you want some too" and started beating him up. We let George beat him up for a couple of seconds, and then we stopped him. To hear Hunter talk, he was beaten half to death.

We stopped it. We put him in a car and told him, "You better get the fuck out of here. You're outgunned." He went to the sheriff's department, and they told him, "Get the fuck out of here. You're bleeding in our jail." Well, he left. And then his book was a myth I had to live with.

JACK THIBEAU

I saw him two days after they beat him up. He looked like death warmed over. He was staying at some crash pad getting ready to leave for Aspen, and both of his eyes were filled with blood. His ribs were taped, and he was sleeping in a sleeping bag on the floor of this empty house. He and Sandy had moved out of their place and put all their stuff in a trailer, which was parked outside this house.

Juan and Sandy were already in the car. And as Hunter got out of the sleeping bag, he could hardly stand up. I tried to help him, but he said, "Oh no, no, don't help me." So he crawled up the wall from the sleeping bag and managed to get into his clothes and hobble out to the car. He got out up to the car, and then he sent me back into the house to the refrigerator for a six-pack of beer.

He made a mistake. He trusted them a little too much, and they got him. Sonny Barger's great statement was: "You treat me good, I treat you better. You treat me bad, I treat you worse." That's the way they do it. If one Angel fights you, they all fight you. He just made that one last run he shouldn't have.

SONNY BARGER

Of course he doesn't want to admit he set it up. The best part of it was we wanted a keg of beer when the book was sold. That's what our payment was, and he didn't give it to us. That's why I've never spoken to him. When I got out of prison the last time, in '92, Hunter called my wife and wanted to talk to me. I didn't want to talk to that mother-fucker. And then he wanted to know what the problem was, and she told him, "You never gave him a keg of beer." "Oh, if that's all it is, I'll buy him one now." Well, mate, fuck you, you're twenty-five years too late. We didn't want money. We wanted a keg of beer.

It's a funny thing. Hunter's probably one of the best writers that we'll ever get, but I didn't care about that. The Rolling Stones are prob-ably the best rock & roll singers left, but they're total fucking jerks in my world. I met them at Altamont. I didn't like them before they came out, I didn't like what they did when they came out, and I didn't like what they said about us afterwards. I don't think that people realize that just because you're really good at something, it doesn't make you a good person.

JAMES SILBERMAN *was the editor in chief of Random House in 1965.*

I got onto Hunter because he had written this very good piece in *The Nation* about the Angels, and the subject seemed great. He didn't need any help writing the book, but he needed help organizing the narrative. He hadn't yet discovered his full voice, but he was already beyond stan-dard journalism. He was his own subject. He was putting himself into situations and not only letting them develop, but making them develop. He was interested in results. I said to him, "Hunter, I know how you do your research. You tie yourself to a set of railroad tracks and wait for the train." That's what happened at the end of *Hell's Angels*. He was on the tracks the whole time he was working on that book.

From Hell's Angels: The Strange and Terrible Saga of the Out-law Motorcycle Gangs *(1967)*

By the middle of summer I had become so involved in the outlaw scene that I was no longer sure whether I was doing research on the Hell's Angels or being slowly absorbed by them. I found myself spend-ing two or three days each week in Angel bars, in their homes, and on runs and parties. In the beginning I kept them out of my own world, but after several months my friends grew accustomed to finding Hell's Angels in my apartment at any hour of the day or night. Their arrivals and departures caused periodic alarums in the neighborhood and sometimes drew crowds on the sidewalk. When word of this reached my Chinese landlord he sent emissaries to find out the nature of my work. One morning I had Terry the Tramp answer the doorbell to fend off a rent collection, but his act was cut short by the arrival of a prowl car summoned by the woman next door. She was very polite while the Angels moved their bikes out of her driveway, but the next day she asked me whether "those boys" were my friends. I said yes, and four days later I received an eviction notice.

. . . Actually, their visits were marked by nothing more sinister than loud music, a few bikes on the sidewalk, and an occasional shot out the back window. Most of the bad action came on nights when there were no Angels around: one of my most respectable visitors, an advertising executive from New York, became hungry after a long night of drink and stole a ham from the refrigerator in a nearby apartment; another guest set my mattress afire with a flare and we had to throw it out the back window; another ran wild on the street with a high-powered Falcon air horn normally carried on boats for use as a distress signal; people cursed him from at least twenty windows and he narrowly escaped injury when a man in pajamas rushed out of a doorway and swung at him with a long white club.

One of the worst incidents of that era caused no complaints at all: this was a sort of good-natured firepower demonstration, which occurred one Sunday morning about three-thirty. For reasons that were never made clear, I blew out my back windows with five blasts of a 12-gauge shotgun, followed moments later by six rounds from a .44 Magnum. It was a prolonged outburst of heavy firing, drunken laughter and crashing glass. Yet the neighbors reacted with total silence. For a while I assumed that some freakish wind pocket had absorbed all the noise and carried it out to sea, but after my eviction I learned otherwise.

. . . [Terry the Tramp] had been up all night and was groggy from pills and wine. It was a cold wet day, and on the way to my place he had stopped at a Salvation Army store and bought the shaggy remains of a fur coat for thirty-nine cents. It looked like something Marlene Dietrich might have worn in the twenties. The ragged hem flapped around his knees, and the sleeves were like trunks of matted hair growing out of the armholes of his Hell's Angels vest. With the coat wrapped around him, he appeared to weigh about three hundred pounds . . . something primitive and demented, wearing boots, a beard, and round black glasses like a blind man.

Letting him answer the doorbell seemed like a final solution to the rent problem.

TOM WOLFE *is the author of numerous bestselling books.*

Hell's Angels is a beautiful mixture of very brassy reporting — I mean, to be with those guys as much as he was is like *inviting* that last scene — and very real thinking. He hadn't been trying to interpret the Angels all through the book, and then at the end he comes up with the meaning of the Angels — "Exterminate all the brutes!" — which is from Conrad in *Heart of Darkness*. It was an awfully good combination of real reporting, real thinking, and the comic style.

SONNY BARGER

He didn't belittle us. If there's any falseness to the book, it's more on the glamorous side than on the detractive side. He made us even more of a myth than we were at the time.

JAMES SILBERMAN

He'd come up to the offices on Madison Avenue when we were still in this mansion, and he'd sneak down the halls with this yachting foghorn attached to an air canister, which he'd blast, and we'd send out for the whiskey, and he'd hang around and talk. He soon became one of those authors who are a celebrity in the building. When Hunter was around, people showed up to take a look at him. It was life as performance art.

During one of these visits, Hunter had brought a snake, four or five feet long. He couldn't carry it around with him everywhere, so he wanted to leave it in the Random House building. So he put the snake in a cardboard carton, which for a snake is nothing to get out of, and taped it up. Sometime during the weekend the snake got out, and the weekend guard looked up from his post and saw this gigantic snake slithering across the marble entryway. The guard got some sort of blunt instrument and quite brashly killed the snake.

When Hunter came in on Monday morning and found that his pet snake had been beaten to death, he was in a total rage. That snake story came up once a year for all the rest of the time that I knew Hunter. It had nothing to do with him being at all at fault for leaving a giant snake in a cardboard box in a midtown office building. It was this insane, crazed night watchman who had lost his head.

While I was having lunch with Hunter, I saw an agent I knew, Lynn Nesbit, and brought her together with Hunter. I thought it would be a very good match, and Lynn made a deal with Hunter.

LYNN NESBIT *was Hunter's literary agent for thirty years.*

He had already written *Hell's Angels,* so he was already very much on the map of celebrity. He was an incredibly good-looking and very strong man, and he was obsessed with getting enough money for his work. He had to depend on his writing, and he also spent money like it was going out of style. The arguments we had about money went on and on.

He'd come blundering into our offices, and there were always some secretaries there who were rather smitten with him. Some people were terrified of him. He'd be talking at the top of his voice with some strange baseball cap on and a bag full of his funny things. Even when it was quite cold out, he'd be in shorts.

WILLIAM KENNEDY

I noted the transformation of Hunter into a public personality for the first time when he was doing publicity for *Hell's Angels* in 1968. He was in New York and he turned up with a cowboy hat and very bizarre sunglasses, bright red or green, glow in the dark. It was a costume for Halloween, and that persona was what he was after, that look. I asked him, "What are you made up for? What are you trying to prove?" He had always shown up at my house wearing sweaters, slacks — clothes, not costumes. But now the image was foremost. I believe Hunter was captured by that persona, and that his writing was transformed. More and more it was about that persona, not about what it used to be about. And it seemed he was reveling in it.

JACK THIBEAU

David Pierce, the mayor of Richmond, was having a birthday party across the bay, and I told him I'd come over and celebrate. Hunter was there, and he was whacked on something. I asked him what it was. He kind of hiked up his pants and said, "These drugs could knock down an elephant." I said, "What do you mean?" He said, "I'm either high or I'm low, I can't tell which where . . . which when . . . how I feel, you know?"

It got late, and Hunter said he had to go home and write, and I didn't have a ride home. Hunter said that he'd drive me but that he had to stop off at the Angels bar in East Oakland. We got on his BSA and rode down the hill. Hunter stopped the bike and pulled off his helmet and gave it to me. I said, "No, it's your helmet. Wear it." He just said, "Do as I told you. Put that helmet on." So I did and we went around the corner, and there was a long run to a stoplight, about two hundred yards, and the light was green. By the time we went through the stop-light we were going about sixty miles an hour. He hit third gear, and the streets were very, very, very slick. We must have gotten up to about eighty, and then Hunter hit a turn, and all of a sudden I was being catapulted end over end. I felt like I could have rolled through it, but my knee hit a railroad track at eighty-five miles an hour

I don't know how long I was unconscious, but I woke up and saw that my pants were ripped, and there was some blood. I picked my leg up and it began to flop around like a fish. I saw a bone protruding. I hollered over to Hunter, who was maybe twenty yards away. He was unconscious, and the BSA looked like a mutilated machine. Then I saw some lights coming from the highway, and I realized they were police lights. All of a sudden Hunter was on his feet holding a bowie knife, standing and facing the police. And he said, "All right, you've been tracking me for months now, you cocksuckers." Like they were a rival gang. "It's about time we got it on. I'm sick and tired of it."

The police pulled their guns and said, "Put down that weapon, or we're going to use force." And Hunter said, "I've had it with you moth-erfuckers." The police got the knife away from him, and I saw that Hunter had a huge gash on his forehead, which turned out to be a con-cussion. As it turns out, he had a broken hand too.

They splinted my leg and put me and Hunter in an ambulance and took us to a hospital. While they were checking my insurance, Hunter came up with an expired Blue Cross card and said he was paying for everything. Then he disappeared. The hospital got a call about ten minutes later from a bowling alley — there's a guy there bleeding all over the place, pounding his fist on the counter demanding beer. I woke up in intensive care with my knee raised above my head with two pins through it, and I had to stay that way for three months.

Hunter came to see me maybe once a week. He brought me a hot television set, some books. He'd come at two, three o'clock in the morning up the back stairs, drinking beer, smoking grass. The night nurse would give me a shot of morphine, and Hunter would say, "You know, you're going to turn into a junkie taking that shit, man." I said, "Well, it's getting me through the day and night." He said, "Yeah, you're going to end up in fucking prison taking that shit. But don't worry, they'll cut you off. They'll cut you off eventually, man, and then you'll be fucked."

CHAPTER FOUR

Freak Power in the Rockies

Every afternoon our whole staff would end up in the Jerome Bar with Tom Benton and Hunter and a whole bunch of people. We all did mescaline, LSD, cocaine, opium if you could find it, but — this sounds funny — in moderation.

LOREN JENKINS

I don't remember thinking anything bizarre about Owl Farm at all in those early days. I mean, hey, it was the sixties . . . what was strange? Everything was there, you sort of accepted it, and . . . we were all strange, right?

JOHN CLANCY

After Hunter moved to Woody Creek, I'd get a legal case in Denver, go skiing in Aspen, and then swing by Hunter's place on my way home. One evening when I pulled up, Hunter had the stereo cranking good and loud. He came out of the house and put this big bag of pot up on the roof. One thing led to another, and Hunter dragged the couch out of the living room into the snow in the yard, poured gasoline onto it, and set it on fire. Then he walked back to the house with this huge ball of fire going up in the air. He looked me right in the eye and said, "I am a master of tools." A friend of his was ducking up from behind the burning couch firing tracer bullets out of a machine gun over the couch, and then Hunter said, "Holy shit!" In the glare of the flames, it looked like there was a thousand pounds of pot up on the roof. We expected the police would be on us any minute. "Jesus," Hunter said. "We'll go to prison for life."

GEORGE STRANAHAN *was Hunter's Woody Creek neighbor.*

Before Hunter moved out to Owl Farm in '68, he was in a little apartment in Aspen. My friend Bob Craig, who was the executive director of the Aspen Institute, and I were buying real estate in Woody Creek for protective purposes. Craig was making friends with Hunter and called me one day and said, "I think I have a good tenant for this place that we just bought together, namely Hunter Thompson. Maybe you've heard of him. Nice folk, a writer." I now was Hunter's landlord. He was renting the place, with about 140 acres behind it, for $375 a month.

If I did get a check from Hunter, which was irregularly, I usually got a little letter along with it. I think it was his way of apologizing, though he'd never actually apologize or write "I'm sorry." Never.

I was still in my academic career — I was a theoretical physicist at Michigan State — so I didn't meet Hunter until I came out the next summer. Sandy called my wife and said, "Hi, neighbor, we live down the road. We rent this house from you. Why don't you come on down for dinner?" I drove up in an old jeep, and Hunter came out the door and said, "Oh, good, you've got your jeep. We have to go down and pull my motorcycle out of the creek" — those were his first words — which we then did. I admired his motorcycle, particularly the fact that it was a Bultaco Matador. Soon thereafter I ordered my own Bultaco, and I would get riding lessons from Hunter, which basically meant getting your wire cutters and maybe a pistol and going trespassing. We'd go across hayfields, and if there was a fence we cut it.

But then we went in for dinner, and Hunter said, "Eat these." It was my first experience with pure, very high grade mescaline. Sandy had put the turkey in at about one in the afternoon — she told us that — and at about eleven she opened the oven to take it out. The mescaline was . . . I was hungry. The turkey, of course, just collapsed.

TOM BENTON *was an Aspen-based graphic artist.*

In 1965, I had a little gallery in Aspen, and I rented out part of the gallery to a girl that ran a frame shop. One day she came to me and said, "Tom, you gotta see these damn pictures from this crazy guy who came in and wants me to frame them." And so I looked at them. They were pictures of Hells Angels, and some of them were kissing and touching tongues. When the guy came in to pick up the stuff, she introduced me to him. Right then, Hunter and I became friends. He seemed crazy enough.

JUAN THOMPSON *is Hunter and Sandy's son.*

We moved into Owl Farm when I was around four. Before that, we rented a house on George Stranahan's property. In some ways the experience was like that of any of the kids around Woody Creek whose parents were ranchers or farmers or whatever. Things like guns were a part of life. They were just lying around. Much later on, I moved them all to the gun safe, but for a long time they were propped up in corners by the doors. Very early on, there was a very clear understanding that you don't mess with the guns. It never occurred to me to actually pick one up until much later. I got a BB gun first, and then a .22 rifle when I was eleven.

The hours my dad and I kept were quite different. He didn't get up at a certain time every day. It would be three, or six, or seven p.m. Sandy would make dinner for me and then breakfast for Hunter. He'd be eating bacon and eggs and reading the paper, and I'd be finishing my dinner or doing my homework before bed. My friends at school thought that was funny, and at the time I thought it was funny too: My dad wakes up at five p.m., just in time for the evening news.

My mom provided a basic framework of functional childhood — meals and toys and reading and all that. Reading was very important. I read a lot.

SANDY THOMPSON

It was one of my jobs to get Hunter up. When he came to bed, I'd be asleep, and he'd wake me up and say, "Wake me up at one." So I would, though he usually didn't get up for a couple hours after that. I'd be busy making the right breakfast, because he had some very specific ideas about what breakfast should be, and there were maybe four different ones that he liked. One was a Spanish omelet with bacon. One was mayonnaise and peanut butter on top of toast with bacon on the top. There was some sort of a spinach thing. There was huevos rancheros. And then maybe six cups of coffee. With the last cup of coffee, he'd start in on the beer, and maybe four beers, five beers later he started on the whiskey. It was pretty orderly, pretty structured.

As I was busy making the coffee and the breakfast, he'd come out into the kitchen yelling about something or another. Sometimes it was directed toward me, and sometimes it wasn't. Maybe even most times it wasn't. But it was scary. Somebody comes in yelling, who's big, and angry. It's scary. It makes for that angst in your heart. You shake a little bit. And then later on in the day, when you've had a drink, it's a lot easier.

Hunter didn't drink fast. It was more like a drink an hour. Problem was, when you stay up for twenty-four or thirty-six hours, it accumulates. But Hunter could really hold his alcohol for a long time. And he could hold the drugs. I mean, I saw him with some powerful political figures when he was on acid, and no one knew the difference. The one thing that really brought him down was opium. I only saw him do that twice. Otherwise, he could function. I mean, was it completely changing the way he was, and what he was saying, what he was doing? Of course. But he could function, just like a functional alcoholic, or a functional coke addict.

JACK THIBEAU

I think Hunter preferred drugs to women, actually. And he liked women who understood that.

SANDY THOMPSON

At Owl Farm, you did a lot of cocaine, and at times you did too much. That's not a problem. You just take something else. If you're really bad, you take quaaludes. If you were not so bad, then you just smoked a good strong joint. But you could always go up. And you could always come down. There were so many options.

GENE MCGARR

Sandy and Hunter had some rough times because he just never stopped. I mean, he would fuck a fire hydrant. There were instances later, in front of the Jerome hotel in Aspen, when she would be howling up at him, "I know you're there, you son of a bitch. I know you're in there fucking somebody." But it got to the point where you couldn't get in touch with Hunter.

SANDY THOMPSON

One night Hunter and I went to a party in Aspen at the house of a woman who was a good friend of Jack Nicholson's and had been close to Timothy Leary. Hunter was the big deal because he had written *Hell's Angels*, and it was my first excursion into the world of him being adored. There were drugs around, and some very pretty women, and all of a sudden I was just this little wife in Woody Creek, and all these women were hanging all over Hunter. I went into one room and everybody's drinking and high, and this woman was sitting on Hunter's lap with her arms around him kind of cooing, and I went ballistic and ran outside, sobbing hysterically. Hunter came after me. It was a new stage of a never-ending drama, the beginning of all the attention. That was the beginning of "Oh, Hunter . . ."

Fortunately, during the time when we were married, I only knew about one woman, and I had thought that he ended that. But it turns out there were women the whole time. I just came across a letter in a box of my stuff from a woman to Hunter — about wanting to see him again, wanting him to know how she felt, da, da, da. As it turned out, my friends — or our friends — knew that I really, really couldn't have handled the truth. I could not have handled Hunter going out with all the Jerome cocktail waitresses and everybody else. So I didn't know about all of this until much later, which is very good, because I would have cracked up. I almost cracked up when I found out about the one.

GENE MCGARR

Sandy always answered the phone. And Hunter was always "not available." She was shielding him from all the calls from friends of his that she didn't approve of. And I was high on that list.

JACK THIBEAU

Sometimes I couldn't tell his paranoia from his reality. He seemed to enjoy both. Sandy just got worn out, I think. He would take her out to dance, take her out every month to a party, and she would dance like a fucking Frank Zappa character out of one of the songs, and then he would wrap her up, throw her in a car, and take her back home for the night.

SANDY THOMPSON

I did cocaine for maybe two years. It's a terrible drug. Marijuana — and some other drugs too — make you feel loving, make you feel connected, make you feel good, make you feel warm. With cocaine, it was all about the ego. You felt really sharp and really, really smart, and strong, and more powerful than the person next to you. But there was no sense of connection. It's not a drug to make love with. Not a drug to be in a community with. It is a completely self-centered, egoistic drug.

But when I took LSD with him, I was clean. I didn't have that angst anymore. I was absolutely at the same level as he was. He was still the king, but I was a very, very important queen. It was a great escape. And it was also great fun, mostly. I've had friends who used LSD to really explore things spiritually, but for me, and for Hunter too, it was really more of an escape.

✝ 🐃 ✝ 🐃

PAUL SEMONIN

He called me in '68, when I was living in New York, and wanted to meet in Chicago and go to the demonstration at the Democratic convention together. I was disillusioned with the way the whole country was going and just told Hunter that I wasn't interested in that. But I always mark that time as when his political consciousness really kicked in. He wasn't a part of the movement in that he wasn't any kind of radical character. I don't think he identified with any group per se, but he could see that some of the protest movement and the antiwar stuff was important. And of course he always had this thing about the Kennedys. When Bobby Kennedy was assassinated, that probably drove a stake into his heart.

JAMES SILBERMAN

All his writing was about the loss of some mythic world that he may once have inhabited. It was no accident that *Gatsby* was his favorite book. I said to him at one point, "You're really writing one lifelong book called *The Death of the American Dream*." And that stuck.

PAUL SEMONIN

I don't think he ever felt identity with the political ideas. He felt identity with the rebellion; he could see how it tarnished the ideals of an American identity. He was never very ideological about his thinking. He didn't join any groups and was kind of a maverick character all along.

SANDY THOMPSON

I saw Hunter cry exactly twice in my life. One had to do with our dog, and the other was the night he got back from Chicago. He broke down telling me what had happened. The police had fired tear gas into the crowd of people demonstrating at the convention, and he was right in there. He talked about people being hit, and brutally hurt, and the violence, the horror of it all.

GAYLORD GUENIN *was the editor of the* Aspen Illustrated News *in 1969.*

Our offices were in the basement of the Jerome hotel, and one day in comes this madman with a letter to the editor, screaming and yelling. I couldn't understand what he was saying; I didn't have a clue who he was. His letters to the editor were all signed "Martin Bormann" — Hitler's deputy after Rudolf Hess was captured. I asked an editor at the paper, "Who the hell is this guy?" I thought he was a wacko. He'd come into the office on almost a daily basis just to see what was going on, or he'd have some grievance about one of the politicians in town. His letters to the editor were essentially political, attacking or complaining about the local sheriff, or police, or whatever. And at that time, Aspen was really going through a transition. The old guard was still pretty much in political power, and the young people, like Hunter and a lot of others, were coming to town, and we were a hundred times more liberal than what was here.

JOE EDWARDS *was living in Aspen in the spring of 1968.*

I had just graduated from law school and was sitting in my office when some guys from the physics institute in town walked in and said, "Are you aware of what's going on in municipal court?" I wasn't, really, but they said, "Well, it's really appalling. The city police are harassing these hippies. . . ."

Haight-Ashbury was breaking out, and hippies were drifting across the country. They were coming to Aspen and hanging out. There had been a petition from the businesspeople to the city council to get rid of undesirable transients, and there were six kids that had been thrown in jail for hitchhiking — and everyone got sentenced to three months. One of them was fourteen. He'd been in town ten minutes and now he was in jail with no shirt and no shoes. Guido Meyer, the police magistrate, a Swiss who came over after World War II, looked over his reading glasses and said, "You dirty hippies are messing up our town. We've got to clean you up. Ninety days." That was the whole trial.

I filed the first civil rights suit in Colorado under the federal laws that were being used to help the blacks get registered to vote — against the city police, the city magistrate, and the city council. We had our preliminary hearing in Denver, and the chief judge lambasted the city and said that this was the most outrageous situation he'd ever seen. The city promised they weren't going to do this anymore.

Suddenly I'm the hippie lawyer. Anybody that gets busted for smoking dope, they come to see me. And that's how Hunter had heard of me. He called me one night about two or three in the morning, woke me up, and introduced himself and started saying that we needed to straighten out this town, that things were out of control. And they were, a little bit. Carrol Whitmire was the sheriff, and he and his staff were of the same mind-set as Guido Meyer. His staff would beat up handcuffed prisoners, spit on them, and kick them with their cowboy boots.

PAUL PASCARELLA *is an artist who moved to Aspen in the fall of 1969.*

There were a lot of us coming here who had more or less dropped out and come to Aspen in the span of a year or two. It seemed like the mountains around the town were some kind of huge two-dimensional protective barrier with a superstructure behind them holding everything back. At the time, Aspen wasn't a hip place. When you left New York and said you were going to Aspen, people said, "Where? Colorado?" They didn't know where Colorado was. You either went to California or Chicago or something, maybe New Orleans — but Colorado was definitely not on the map.

JOE EDWARDS

When we all came here in the sixties, or sometimes even earlier, Aspen was a fixed-up old mining town. The main street through town was paved, and nothing else. There were no stoplights. There were no condominiums, and no big hotels or lodges other than the Jerome, which had been there for a hundred years. Everybody was living in these old miner cabins or Victorian houses that had been fixed up, and suddenly in the summer of '68, while this was all going on with the hippie trial, a developer from Chicago came in and built what's called the North of Nell condominium, and across the street they built these Aspen Square condominiums. Most of them were a block long and three stories high. Before that, you could walk around downtown and see the skiers coming right down into town a block away from you, and in the summer you'd see the wildflowers, and people would just carry their lunch bag up on the ski hill and sit down or go for a hike. When I first came to town, we'd ski off the mountain and down the streets to the bar and leave our skis outside. All of a sudden, you couldn't even see the ski hill anymore.

Hunter started saying that we've got to get politically active, that we've got to take over and foster a recognition amongst the younger kids that they've been disenfranchised. He had me meet him at the

Wheeler Opera House, which was showing this movie called *The Battle of Algiers*. After the movie, we went over to the Jerome hotel and sat in the bar for a couple hours and talked politics, and he went over his point again: that we needed to organize all the young people, all the bartenders and ski bums, the kids working the ski lifts and in the restaurants and bars; that we had the numbers; that if we could just get them registered and get them interested and get them to participate, we'd have the political power to change the town.

At this same time, the dozen or so lawyers in Aspen got together and put a petition to the city council to remove Guido Meyer from the magistrate's office. Guido ran a restaurant in town and had no legal experience at all, and he had this almost Nazi attitude. The DA brought to the attention of the district judge the prisoner abuse that was going on, primarily by the undersheriff. So the undersheriff was removed from office by order of the district court, which was highly unusual, and Guido Meyer was replaced by the city council as a result of this embarrassment. Things were changing, and Hunter wanted to push it even further.

PAUL PASCARELLA

We weren't even really hippies. Some of us had long hair, but we were ex–Special Forces and marines, so that didn't go so well either. We were all peace and love, and we were stoners, but we didn't take any shit from anybody. Hunter became this sort of figurehead, the leader of the underground, and we all sort of rearranged Aspen.

JOE EDWARDS

One thing led to another, and a group of people coalesced around Hunter and I, and he brought in people that he knew that I didn't. He brought in Bob Craig, who was the president of the Aspen Institute for Humanistic Studies and who lived right next door to him in Woody Creek, who gave us his office in the redbrick building catty-corner from the Hotel Jerome to use as our campaign headquarters, and all of a sudden I was running for mayor.

TOM BENTON

Hunter, myself, and Joe Edwards had formed something called the Meat Possum Press, really just to expose the "greedheads," as we called them. There was a board of directors — friends of Hunter, like Oscar Acosta, John Clancy, Bill Kennedy, Loren Jenkins — and Hunter and I were editors. The first thing that the Meat Possum Press did was purchase a fifty-millimeter flare gun, and we would go out at night in the middle of town and fire off these beautiful flares just for the hell of it. If you fired them up in the air, this red or green parachute would pop open and float down to the ground, but if you fired it down an alley it would bounce off buildings for a whole block and then shoot across the block. It was wonderful. I still have the gun.

That's when Hunter and I started calling ourselves doctors. At some point somebody had bought me a subscription to the *Los Angeles Free Press,* and every week I'd get it, and the back page always had this ad — "Get your doctorate of divinity degree for $10" — so I went to Hunter and said, "Look, man. Wouldn't it be nice if we called ourselves "Dr. Thompson" and "Dr. Benton?" And Hunter said, "Yeah, that'd be good." So I said, "Well, give me ten bucks."

It was through a thing called the Missionaries of the New Truth, and it was run by Alan Baskin in Evanston, Illinois. They had some guy in a basement there cranking these certificates out. We got them, and Hunter said, "This is great, because you get cut rates on hotels. And you know, it always sounds good in an airport when you hear 'Paging Dr. Thompson.' "

Since Hunter was now a doctor of divinity, he could marry people legally, which he tried once. When I saw him afterward, he said, "It didn't come off very well." He had this electrotherapeutic machine with him — when you turned it on, this blue flame would go shooting up the tube, and if you got it close to your skin it would arc across — but apparently he was waving it at the couple and he got the thing too close to her nose, and the current leapt across and hit her nose and scared the hell out of her. He said, "I'll make a deal with you. You do all the weddings and I'll do all the funerals."

JOE EDWARDS

We'd be up in our law offices in the second story of the Wheeler Opera House, and Hunter would climb up the fire escape at ten o'clock at night and come in the window with his six-pack and a bottle of whiskey and cigarettes, and we'd sit and talk until the wee hours planning our campaign strategy and designing the advertisements.

I wound up being six votes short of winning, but the probusiness candidate, who was endorsed by the city council, lost by a landslide, and all the other people we were supporting won office. The police chief was fired, and the whole mood of the city shifted. We still had this issue of Carrol Whitmire over in the sheriff's office, though, which is a separately elected position. Whitmire had jurisdiction over the whole county. That's how Hunter decided to run for sheriff. When I lost, there was criticism that my candidacy was just too far out there. Hunter thought he would widen the "out there" span quite a bit and be the farthest-out candidate you could possibly imagine. He originally did it, I think, as a lark, not really having any serious thought that he might win.

ED BASTIAN *met Hunter in the summer of 1969 at a Sunday afternoon volleyball game at Owl Farm.*

I had just helped manage Governor Rockefeller's campaign when he ran for president in '68 and then Governor Romney in New Hampshire and then a congressional campaign in Iowa. I really learned about organization, but after Rockefeller I became more radicalized. I was working in New York on underground films, and before that I had been in Vietnam as a photographer. Before that I had been in college in Iowa, where I was playing basketball and being a jock. Hunter sort of combined all these attributes — the jock thing, the political thing, the social-activist and human-rights philosophy thing — and there were just so many parts of our respective personalities that meshed.

Michael Solheim was the official campaign manager, and I ended up being a sort of manager of logistics. When I got involved in Hunter's campaign, things were pretty chaotic. It was really running on his charisma, and there'd been some interesting work done with Tom Benton's posters.

TOM BENTON

Hunter walked into my studio one day and said, "We should do an Aspen wall poster." I said, "What the hell is that?" He said, "It's gonna be one single-sheet thing, and it'll have your graphics on one side and my writing on the other." He would write about local politics and other things. We would get together at night at my studio and I'd work on the graphics while he would write the whole damn back page in one night. Of course, that night might take a day and a half. Hunter was always nocturnal. That's one thing that kept our friendship going.

ED BASTIAN

Hunter shaved his head to look like a cop. There were a lot of elements in the campaign that were a kind of parody of what a real-world cop would be like or look like or act like. On one hand you had a very radical rhetoric and platform of tearing out the streets and sodding them over, and all bad drug pushers would be put in stocks in front of the courthouse and rode out of town on a rail, and there'd be no profiteering on drugs. But on the other hand, Hunter dressed himself up to look like an L.A. cop, with these serious sunglasses and a shiny bald head. He was quite an imposing figure already, and the shaved head also allowed him to refer to Whitmire as "my long-haired opponent."

We conned the sheriff into a debate at the Wheeler Opera House. We filled the place with hippies, and there was poor Whitmire onstage looking very straight and trying to be a pleasant, amiable guy because he realized he had walked into a difficult situation. Hunter was up there next to him with his bald head and his sunglasses and cigarette holder and a can of beer, and he destroyed the guy. Hunter was really acerbic and was really playing to the audience. They were asked if they were going to enforce marijuana laws in Aspen, and Whitmire would say, "Yes, it's my duty as a law enforcement officer to do that." Hunter would say something about the unjust drug laws in America and how they lead to profiteering on drugs, which leads to the criminialization of drugs and so forth. He gave answers that were both very intelligent and very political. Whitmire was ridiculed, which precipitated some really tough stuff later in the campaign.

TOM BENTON

Whitmire knew how to handle drunks, car wrecks, cowboys, and that stuff, but had no idea how to handle the new wave of young people, or drug people — people with a different agenda. The business community was afraid. They thought that the new crowd on their way here was going to eat the local babies and cats, and all they did was make flutes. Some guy jumped up and asked Hunter, "What are you going to do about drugs? Everybody knows you take drugs." He said, "Well, I'll tell you what I'm going to do. This is the only time I'll talk about it. I do not like needle-injected drugs. I'm dead against them, and I won't chew jimsonweed on the job. Other than that, I don't want to hear anything about it."

Afterwards people were coming out of the auditorium, and one guy said to me, "You know, he didn't sound like a moron. He didn't sound like a freak to me. He makes a lot of sense." And another guy said, "Well, hell yes. He's got a degree from Columbia" — which was nonsense, of course.

ED BASTIAN

A guy who appeared to be a Hells Angel arrived at Hunter's house on a chopper and said he was sent from California by Sonny Barger to tell Hunter to get out of the campaign or they were going to burn his house down and kill him. Then he rode off.

JOE EDWARDS

In the middle of the campaign, the existing sheriff retained this undercover agent, a guy who had worked for the Alcohol, Tobacco and Firearms division of the Treasury Department as an informant. Whitmire paid him money to come to Aspen to infiltrate Hunter's campaign and set Hunter up to be arrested for having illegal weapons. This ATF guy came to town dressed up like a biker, with a big leather vest and his Harley, and started hanging out at the Jerome hotel.

MICHAEL SOLHEIM

There was a lot of activity going on at the Jerome. We had our headquarters upstairs in Parlor B, and one day a guy named Chuck Bromley came up there to cause trouble. He thought it would be a good idea if some of the guys on the other side got the shit beat out of them, and he said he would do it, but he'd need a little help from our people. Then we got a call from somebody in Denver saying, "Watch this guy. He's trouble, and he's not what he seems to be." So we kept an eye on him. He just kept wanting to start trouble. When we had issues with our opponents, he'd say, "You don't have to put up with any of that stuff. That can all be handled."

He accused us of a couple of other things, and then he left, and then he called Joe on the phone. He had just been over talking to the opposition, and he told Joe, "I will deny saying this, but if I were you guys, I would get Sandy and Juan out of that house up there. I would bring them into town. I would close down my election campaign headquarters" — which were here in the hotel — "and I would arm myself. These guys are furious." We all went out to Hunter's and armed ourselves to the teeth. Bill Kennedy was there, really stunned, I think, that he was on the floor of Hunter's kitchen waiting for bullets to come zipping through the window.

ED BASTIAN

Oscar Acosta, the Chicano lawyer who had run for sheriff of L.A. County — who later became the "Samoan attorney" from *Fear and Loathing* — came in to advise on the campaign and to help Hunter and to be a buddy. Actually, a whole weird assortment of people showed up in town, some bringing guns. There was one lawyer who was carrying around a .357 Magnum pistol, and a couple of us had to take his gun away because we were scared that any violence that might take place would destroy our campaign. We were really minding our p's and q's, but we had to ride herd on this cast of characters that showed up.

Hunter and Oscar and I were sitting in the bar at the Jerome one night after closing, talking about the campaign and tactics and philosophy, and when we walked out at about two in the morning onto Main Street, a police deputy who was sympathetic to us stopped us on the street and said, "Hey, you guys should know — that guy that's been hanging out in your office? Well, we found a car on Main Street parked in a place it shouldn't have been and we towed it in and opened up the trunk and found a trunkload of automatic weapons. We found out where the guy is staying and we went to his motel and brought him in for questioning, at which point he showed us his identification as an ATF agent and says, 'You can't arrest me. I'm here on federal business.'"

The sheriff, we found out the next day, called in some people from the Colorado Bureau of Investigation, who said they had done some kind of a survey of the town and then had a meeting with Hunter and Joe Edwards and said, "We advise you to get out of the campaign; we found out that there are five or six direct threats on your life." Suddenly we saw the other side of things. What began as a lot of fun with this wonderful way of doing politics with strong language, sometimes offensive language, sometimes poetic language, and pranks and parties to get out the vote, and all of that had become something different. Six months earlier, I had been studying Buddhism and making a film with the Dalai Lama in Dharamsala, India, and now I found myself involved in a political campaign with death threats — and I'm toting a gun? At that point, Hunter could have easily said, "Hey, that's enough of this." But we carried on.

JANN WENNER *is the founder and editor of* Rolling Stone.

Hunter sent me a letter out of the blue in January 1970. He must have been an early *Rolling Stone* reader, and he wrote, "Your Altamont coverage comes close to being the best journalism I can remember reading — by anybody." Having been a fan of *Hell's Angels* before I started *Rolling Stone,* I sent back an open-ended offer for him to write for us. He wrote that he was too busy to write, since he was running for sheriff of Aspen. Around this time, he was writing the Kentucky Derby piece. I suggested he write about his sheriff's campaign, and in part it could be seen as a prelude to our push in 1972 to get our readers to register to vote. That was just after eighteen-year-olds were given the right to vote.

One day he called — I'm not sure if he had an appointment or not — and came in to the office to see me. At that time *Rolling Stone* was in a redbrick building south of Market, which was then an undeveloped warehouse and industrial area. In retrospect, what I saw was already classic, fully formed Hunter. Here's this big guy, kind of awkward and clumsy — not knocking anything down exactly, but kind of lumbering in. He had his Converse sneakers and wore a pair of shorts and a polyester multicolored shirt, I think the famous one with red circles on it. He was also outfitted with a gray bubble-top ladies' wig and had those small-lens dark glasses on and was carrying his leather satchel. And he had his cigarette holder.

I'd seen a lot of stuff, and I really didn't know anything about the local Aspen legend, but this guy was strange. He sat down and put his satchel on my desk and started to slowly unpack things. I sat there watching all this — and at this point I was a pretty busy young budding entrepreneur trying to get things done — and he was very slowly unpacking his satchel, pulled out a couple six-packs of beer, a bottle of scotch or something or other, can openers, knives, cigarettes, smoking paraphernalia, notebooks. An air horn. He put everything out on the table, and then he slowly sat down after circling the room and started to mumble as he took more things out. Everything with Hunter was protracted. One thing that was always true of him was that any movement took fucking forever — and this was *mild* Hunter, the beginning of the gonzo Hunter. We sat and talked — or I should say he talked — for an hour and a half or two hours. He was charming, fascinating, and weird, but he was taking forever.

He accepted the assignment to write about the sheriff's race. It brought national attention on Hunter and the political machinations in Aspen. Right from that point, I felt that we were on a crusade with Hunter. It was crazy but very serious.

From "The Battle of Aspen," by Dr. Hunter S. Thompson (Candidate for Sheriff) **Rolling Stone** *67; October 1, 1970*

Tentative Platform
Thompson for Sheriff
Aspen, Colorado, 1970

1) Sod the streets at once. Rip up all city streets with jackhammers and use the junk asphalt (after melting) to create a huge parking and auto-storage lot on the outskirts of town — preferably somewhere out of sight. . . . The only automobiles allowed into town would be limited to

a network of "delivery-alleys." . . . All public movement would be by foot and a fleet of bicycles, maintained by the city police force.

2) Change the name "Aspen," by public referendum, to "Fat City." This would prevent greedheads, land-rapers and other human jackals from capitalizing on the name "Aspen." . . . The main advantage here is that changing the name of the town would have no major effect on the town itself, or on those people who came here because it's a good place to *live*. What effect the name-change might have on those who came here to buy low, sell high and then move on is fairly obvious . . . and eminently desirable. These swine should be fucked, broken and driven across the land.

3) Drug Sales must be controlled. My first act as Sheriff will be to install, on the courthouse lawn, a bastinado platform and a set of stocks — in order to punish dishonest dope dealers in a proper public fashion. Each year these dealers cheat millions of people out of millions of dollars. As a breed, they rank with sub-dividers and used car salesmen and the Sheriff's Dept. will gladly hear complaints against dealers at any hour of the day or night, with immunity from prosecution guaranteed to the complaining party — provided the complaint is valid. . . . it will be the general philosophy of the Sheriff's office that *no* drug worth taking should be sold for money. . . . This approach, we feel, will establish a unique and very human *ambiance* in the Aspen (or Fat City) drug culture — which is already so much a part of our local reality that only a Falangist lunatic would talk about trying to "eliminate it."

JOE EDWARDS

"The Battle of Aspen" was almost 100 percent accurate. Everything he said in there actually happened. Some of his writings can be wild exaggerations, but in this case, with very little exception, everything that he said in there was done.

ED BASTIAN

Hunter took all of this very seriously. Yes, he was a writer whose career was just taking off, but he was also a ringleader, and he became very good at getting involved with or creating events that he could write about.

The campaign was attracting a lot of attention, and Hunter was very charismatic, and the media were coming in from around the country and from England, but what I realized was that nobody involved at that point knew how to run a campaign. It took a while to get some serious strategy instituted, but we did, and I think that's why we got as close as we did.

JOE EDWARDS

The polls started looking like he might have a chance of winning. The impetus and the steamrollers started going, and suddenly everything got more and more serious and more fine-tuned as that became apparent. We started getting even more energized.

ED BASTIAN

But then everybody was wondering, "What happens if we win?" Hunter never really saw himself as a working sheriff. He saw himself as carrying the vision, carrying the mission, making a big statement, and changing the culture of this town.

TOM BENTON

Hunter said, "I've got it all figured out. If I win, I'll take my salary and the undersheriff's salary and combine them and give them to one guy who knows how to run a nuts-and-bolts sheriff's department. I will be the figurehead who will sit up and listen to the people and make decisions."

The guy who was really going to run the office if Hunter had been elected was Dick Kienast, who was going to be his undersheriff. Dick had been a city police officer, but he quit because he disagreed with the heavy-handed attitude of the police. Dick had been a divinity student earlier, and he was soft-spoken and very smart, and a very good administrator.

JOE EDWARDS

On election night, Hunter wound up losing by, I think, 274 votes out of 2,000 or 3,000. It was pretty damn close. The night of the election was wild. The Jerome was packed body to body in all the halls and all the way up the stairs; you could hardly get in. Hunter was walking around with his cigarette holder and his shaved head and an American flag wrapped around his neck, and people were cheering.

JANN WENNER

Had he taken it a little more seriously at the start, or had it been his second try, he would've been elected sheriff.

TOM BENTON

If we'd had another two weeks, he'd have been sheriff.

PAUL PASCARELLA

I think what lost him the few hundred votes he needed was his idea of changing the name of Aspen to "Fat City." These old people got all upset. But it was a very exciting time. It showed me that voting worked. We changed this little valley by registering to vote and coming out with some posters and doing the work and getting all the freaks involved.

ED BASTIAN

It was a big downer that night, but in the next few days we got over it. Hunter was a realist. I don't think he was depressed about it. It was an experience, and he began moving on.

JOE EDWARDS

In between that election and the next one, the district court ordered the undersheriff removed from office, so Whitmire had further embarrassment. And the next time there was an election for sheriff, Dick Kienast ran and won and became sheriff for eight years. And of course the city police changed too, so now instead of wearing these militaristic uniforms, the police and sheriff's departments started wearing blue jeans and blue-jean jackets. For a while, Dick Kienast had them not even carrying sidearms.

The attitude of the police became laissez-faire. They refused to co-operate with any of the federal undercover agents regarding marijuana, primarily because in those days everybody — at least everybody under thirty or thirty-five — was smoking dope. None of our officers would participate in their raids or their busts, and they didn't have enough manpower to do it on their own.

The whole tension of harassing the younger people disappeared, and the whole attitude of policing in the community shifted from beating up people to helping them and seeing what their problem is and getting them to social services or rehabilitation. If they found you drunk, they'd help you home. And to a great extent it's remained that way for thirty years.

Bob Braudis was Dick's undersheriff, and Dick hired everybody who had the same attitude — let's just keep things low-key, let's be a service to the community and not a harassment. When Kienast decided he didn't want to do the job anymore, Braudis stepped into his shoes and has been sheriff ever since. He's continued that same program that Hunter originally had in mind, and it's been just wonderful. Hunter changed the culture of this whole area. He was the catalyst that got the whole thing going.

GEORGE STRANAHAN

Our social club at that time was the Jerome Bar. It was Hunter's court salon. Michael Solheim was manager of the bar and Hunter's buddy.

MICHAEL SOLHEIM

The bar was being run totally wrong. The people who were running it thought it'd make a great African-themed bar, and the interior was filled with swords and spears and shit. The clientele was mainly winos and a low-end crowd. I told the owner when I started, "The group of people you saw here for the sheriff's campaign will be back." He loved that, because his hotel rooms were packed then, and there were people in the bar all the time. I changed the place back to a Victorian theme and made a whole different thing out of it, and it became popular fairly quickly; we were the only bar in town that was busy all the time, day and night, all year round. There's no doubt that Hunter hanging out there was a draw, and there were a lot of girls coming through as well. Most of the colorful people in town seemed to hang out there.

Hunter and James Salter and I were watching the NBA play-offs there one day, and then another couple guys walked in and came over to us. One of them knew us, and I looked at the other guy that he'd come in with and said, "You know, you've got a familiar look about you. Aren't you a friend of [ski racer] Billy Kidd's?" As it turns out, he was a friend of Billy Kidd's, but he was also Robert Redford. We all sat around and talked for a while. Redford wanted to talk to Hunter about *Hell's Angels*. He really liked that book.

Another time Hunter and I were sitting there watching some football and who shows up but Allen Ginsberg. I said, "Hunter, here comes Allen." And he said to me, "Don't say a word." Hunter owed him some time together. Well, here the fucker was, but Hunter didn't want to pay him back that time. So we just stayed quiet and Ginsberg walked right by us.

PAUL PASCARELLA

One time, when we were watching football at Owl Farm, Hunter was threatening Juan with a cattle prod, but he was always great to Juan. He always really loved Juan. It's kind of like that thing with dogs — if you rough them up a little, they like to play like that. In a sense it was never really anything harmful. He never pinned him down and drilled him with electric jolts or anything; it was just a threat and a lot of running around.

But Juan was always different; he was always so quiet. I don't remember him being around all that much. I think he was off in some other part of the house or off with Sandy.

SANDY THOMPSON

I helped start the Aspen Community School, which is right next to Owl Farm. I think that really, really helped Juan. I had no idea how bad things were for Juan until we left. I really didn't know.

JUAN THOMPSON

I've often wondered how much so-called childhood trauma is the result of an adult's comparison and questioning of what they experienced with what they thought they should have experienced. At the time I didn't question any of this. It's only later, when you learn more and grow up a bit, that you can say, "Hey, this guy was always high."

Given the time period, looking back now, the values look extreme, but at the time they weren't. My mom and dad and their friends came out of the sixties and shared a system of beliefs and some similar assumptions about life's problems. For the most part, drug use was taken for granted. In the environment in Aspen in the late seventies there was a lot of drugs, so it was pretty natural for kids to try them. There were two or three years where I tried them out on weekends — nothing that serious to where it became a problem.

Politics were very liberal. Some families were a lot more open, some were more structured. I do remember going over to a friend's house when I was young and sitting down with his family for dinner and them saying grace. That was odd. But I just took it all in.

GAYLORD GUENIN

Every afternoon our whole staff at the [Aspen] *Illustrated News* would end up in the Jerome Bar with Tom Benton and Hunter and a whole bunch of people. We all did mescaline, LSD, cocaine, opium if you could find it, but — this sounds funny — in moderation. I mean, there was a period in Aspen, in the late sixties and the early seventies, where everyone was doing copious amounts of drugs. In the Jerome, not only would they sell drugs, but they had the mescaline flavor of the week. One week it'd be raspberry, the next week strawberry, the next week grape. Hunter's real intake is one of those things that you cannot be certain of, because Hunter made such a show of his drinking. I'd wonder — was he really doing that much cocaine all the time? Or was it a lot for show? But if we're talking an over/under situation, I'd take "over."

PAUL PASCARELLA

The Jerome Bar was our base. Hunter always took up the far end of the bar where it turned, by the back door. Because there was a television, we used to watch sports there. There were some pretty big people floating around in those days — Bob Rafelson, Jack Nicholson, and Don Henley — but I remember at one point thinking that out of all my famous friends, Hunter was the only genius.

Back in those days, Aspen was really cool. It was adventurers, mountain climbers, exceedingly wealthy people that chose their own path. You'd be sitting in the bar and you could be sitting next to Hunter, or some bikers from Massachusetts, or some heir to some huge money thing — but you all looked the same. If you were just some rich person from out of town, that didn't cut it. And if you didn't know these people, you were out.

CHAPTER FIVE

The Golden Age of Gonzo

✦

What were we doing out here? Did I actually have a big red convertible out there on the street? Was I just roaming around these Mint hotel escalators in a drug frenzy of some kind, or had I really come to Las Vegas to work on a story?

RALPH STEADMAN, *the British artist, met Hunter at the Kentucky Derby.*

I got a call one day from a magazine called *Scanlan's,* and I thought *Scanlan?* What type of magazine is that? It's the name of a little-known pig farmer from Nottingham. It was a very anti-establishment thing. They got on Nixon's blacklist. J. C. Suarez was the art editor, and Don Goddard, who had been the foreign editor of the *New York Times,* was an editor. He'd found my book, *Still Life with Raspberry,* and he'd brought it back to America.

Hunter had asked Pat Oliphant, the famous political cartoonist, to do the illustrations first, but Oliphant was on his way to England for a cartoonist convention.

J. C. Suarez said to me, "How would you like to go to Kentucky and meet an ex–Hells Angel? He's looking for someone specific. He wants someone who becomes part of the story. He's a tall guy and he's shaven-headed, you know, and he wears hunting jackets." For two days I walked around Churchill Downs asking for "Hunter Johnson." I looked at people, did a few drawings here and there. I actually tried to be a journalist, a visual journalist, doing what Hunter eventually called my "filthy habit" - drawing people.

I was in the press room one day and I had a beer. Suddenly I turned around and this tall man said, "Hello, I'm Hunter S. Thompson. I was told to look for a matted-haired geek with string warts. They said you were weird — but not this weird." I said, "I'm sorry, I'm from England, I don't . . . ," and Hunter said, "I'm pulling your leg; don't worry. I see you drink. Would you like to have another beer and sit for a minute and talk about things? It's a strange assignment, because I've come back home and I'm feeling a bit weird being here."

Through that whole week, we consumed enormous amounts of alcohol. I don't think we ever stopped, actually. We liked beers, and we both had this funny thing about chasing beers with whiskeys, and we just got more and more plastered. But what I didn't know at the time was that Hunter stayed up most of the night. I would knock on his door at eight o'clock in the morning with a bit of a hangover, and he'd shout, "Who's there?"

"It's me, Hunter. I thought we should get to the track and try and start looking at things."

"What the fuck is this?! I haven't had any sleep. I've been up all night. Give me two hours."

It was just bizarre, frankly. When he walked into a room, everybody noticed him. He'd have a drink in one hand, a cigarette in the other, and his foot wouldn't go on the floor. He'd be sort of perched and looking 'round, with a funny hat on. I thought the one-foot-off-the-floor thing was his way of making an impression, but later he told me he'd had some football injury when he was younger, which gave him this peculiar limping gait.

At one point early on, he said, "I wish you would stop doing that." "What's that?" I asked. "That filthy habit you have of making little scribbles of people," he said. "They take it personally, you know. Those things could get us into trouble, because they're rather ugly. I don't mind them myself, you know, but they really are ugly things. You've got to stop it." I said, "Oh . . . well, that's what I *do*. This is my first American assignment." And he said, "Maybe it is, but you can't keep drawing people like that. It's something with Kentuckians particularly. That's not a drawing to them — it's an insult. It's like telling people, 'You're the ugliest piece of shit I ever saw' or something. You'll get in a fight."

The next night we met his brother Davison in a restaurant, and I drew him, and it was a horrible picture. Hunter said, "You've upset my brother, you know that? And not only that, but people are looking. I really don't think we should stay around much longer. As it happens, I have mace in my pocket, so we can get out of here. People don't like what you're doing. It's a nasty, unpleasant thing."

"But it's what I came to do, Hunter."

"Well, do it later. We've got to get out of here." And he maced the restaurant. *He maced the restaurant!*

It was a terrible thing to do. I mean, we got maced too. The whole damn place got maced. People were coughing and sputtering, "Get me outside!" It was the first time I realized: "Oh God — this is not an ordinary person. This is somebody that does things with a paranoiac fever."

At some point during that week, though, Hunter began to like my filthy habit of drawing and would say, "Draw that one, Ralph. Draw that, over there." He liked the idea because he thought it was a way of saying something about a person that he couldn't say in words. But after our first week doing this sort of thing at the Derby, Hunter hadn't got a fucking thing down except notes in red ink in one of those spiral notebooks.

SANDY THOMPSON

When he wrote the Kentucky Derby article for *Scanlan's*, the drugs and the booze and all that stuff was getting involved in his life. This was no longer the Hunter who would sit down and rewrite a piece three times. He could get out a page, maybe, or a paragraph, a really neat, wild paragraph — and then some gibberish He couldn't come out with a full piece.

RALPH STEADMAN

He was always going to be against the people who belong and for those who don't, and this particular story was about the people that he really despised in Louisville — the establishment that had rejected him many years ago. He was back to settle a score. They had made him know he was not going to be anything, certainly not a writer.

Over breakfast on the last morning, he said, "I have to go see my mother; she's having a bit of a problem." I think she was being institutionalized for a while because she drank a lot. I met her and she said, "*Hell* no! I'm more worried about *his* drinking than I am about mine!" They were both at it, I guess. I'm not trying to malign her, because she was wonderful, a terrific lady. But that was on Hunter's mind.

DOUG BRINKLEY

A lot of his correspondence with his mom was about filling her in on his financial situation. She was broke a lot, and he was always trying to get money for her. If Hunter got two hundred dollars for an article, fifty bucks would probably go to Virginia for what he considered a loan from some other time. They shared in each other's financial difficulties a lot. Once her boys left, she had to make it in Louisville by herself, and Hunter had to make it in a world of freelancing where dollars were hard-earned.

WILLIAM KENNEDY

"The Kentucky Derby Is Decadent and Depraved" is a wonderful story, really a departure piece, and I think that that was a moment where he used all his fictional talent to describe and anatomize those characters and just make it all up. I'm sure some of it was real.

RALPH STEADMAN

The second story we did was in September. Hunter called me and said, "Ralph, I don't know if you're interested, but I've been asked by *Scanlan's* to go to the America's Cup in Rhode Island. I'd like you to be there. Maybe you could do something to help pilot a three-masted sloop or something." I felt I had to go. In a strange way I felt chosen, whatever that means — maybe by accident. It was journalism of outrage. There was no market for journalism of outrage at that time.

We got there, and Hunter found this captain who took us out to this huge boat, and he had an idea that he'd do a story by trying to get onboard both these racing boats, the *Gretel* and the *Intrepid*. He said, "We really could kick some ass! These people are horrible, with their filthy two-million-dollar yachts with gin lounges on the front of them, and everybody sitting there drinking their mint juleps and their gin and tonics and whatever else they have — it's filthy, Ralph. It's an expression of decadence I'd like you to see."

For some peculiar reason I got seasick. I was in a terrible state standing up on the deck and trying to remain, well, not sick. He didn't demand that I take the psilocybin. He said, "Maybe it will make you feel better. Try one." That was all. And I tried one, and that's when the screaming red-eyed dogs started. It was a full moon, but all the reflections I saw were red. The next thing I knew I was saying, "I feel like Hitler." It was a really awful panicked feeling.

Hunter kept barking, "We have a mission." I didn't quite know what the mission was. He said: "You're the artist from England, Ralph. What do *you* want to say about the America's Cup?" I couldn't really come up with something on the spot, and he said, "Well, Ralph, I have this idea. If you find something you want to write on the side of the boats, I have these spray cans here, a black and a red. We should write something." I said, "How about 'Fuck the Pope?'" He said, "Are you a Catholic, Ralph?" I told him no, that this was just what I was going to write. I shook the spray cans, and that alerted the guard on one side of the jetty. By this time it was hopeless. The drugs scoured my brain. I was seriously put into such a catatonic state by psilocybin that I would write "Fuck the Pope" on the side of a boat. I was going to do it.

Then I had to go down to New York because I needed a doctor. I was palpitating, and I had to take Librium to bring me down. They put me out for twenty-four hours. Awful. I flew back to England, and I insisted on standing up on the plane. Every time I closed my eyes I saw purple things moving, and wings. I believe I was harboring devils of a kind. Hunter said I was up for ninety-six hours.

SANDY THOMPSON

When "gonzo" first happened, Hunter's first reaction to it was terrible guilt — just terrible. They didn't get it. But he could also see that here was an avenue; people seemed to really like this, and they were going to pay him for it. He thought it was gibberish.

It was past deadline, and the editors of *Scanlan's* were trying to get the Kentucky Derby piece from him, and he said, "I can't send it to you; it's gibberish." They said, "Send it anyway." It wasn't up to his standard, but finally he sent it. And what do you know — they called and they said it was great. Hunter knew it wasn't; it was outbursts of greatness and wildness. But it wasn't a final draft by a long, long shot. He did not feel good about that.

DOUG BRINKLEY

The Internet is full of bogus falsehoods propagated by uninformed English professors and pot-smoking fans about the etymological origins of "gonzo." Here's how it happened: The legendary New Orleans R&B piano player James Booker recorded an instrumental song called "Gonzo" in 1960. The term "gonzo" was Cajun slang that had floated around the French Quarter jazz scene for decades and meant, roughly, "to play unhinged." The actual studio recording of "Gonzo" took place in Houston, and when Hunter first heard the song he went bonkers — especially for this wild flute part. From 1960 to 1969 — until Herbie Mann recorded another flute triumph, "Battle Hymn of the Republic" — Booker's "Gonzo" was Hunter's favorite song.

When Nixon ran for president in 1968, Hunter had an assignment to cover him for *Pageant* and found himself holed up in a New Hampshire motel with a columnist from the *Boston Globe Magazine* named Bill Cardoso. Hunter had brought a cassette of Booker's music and played "Gonzo" over, and over, and over — it drove Cardoso crazy, and that night, Cardoso jokingly derided Hunter as "the 'Gonzo' man." Later, when Hunter sent Cardoso his Kentucky Derby piece, he got a note back saying something like, "Hunter, that was pure Gonzo journalism!" Cardoso claimed that the term was also used in Boston bars to mean "the last man standing," but Hunter told me that he never really believed Cardoso on this. Just another example of "Cardoso bullshit," he said.

PAT BUCHANAN *was a Nixon adviser and speechwriter.*

I met Hunter in New Hampshire when he came to interview the old man. We used to go up to New Hampshire to campaign for two or three days, then take the former vice president down to Florida, where he could relax and get a tan and let our advertising do the talking for us. We won the primary on March 14 after a six-week campaign, and Hunter and I were holed up in some hotel in Nashua on a snowy night and discovered that we were in possession of, I forget, either a gallon or a half-gallon of Wild Turkey. Now, I had a lot of stamina in those days, and the two of us stayed up all night arguing fiercely about communism. It got pretty vicious and brutal by dawn.

We got Hunter to interview Nixon in the car driving from Nashua to the airport where we were going to catch our Learjet. Hunter got out of the car right by the plane as they were gassing up and snapped his Zippo to light his cigarette. My friend Nicholas Ruwe, a great advance man, knocked it out of his hand. We thought we were going to be blown to kingdom come.

Hunter and Nixon had talked about sports all the way out to the airport. Later, Hunter said it was laid out as a rule that sports was all he could talk about with the old man, but I don't recall limiting him like that; that's all they happened to talk about, I guess.

WILLIAM KENNEDY

In time he found a way to turn himself into this singular first-person itinerant journalist who was interesting no matter what he wrote about. He put himself into the picture and he became the story.

JANN WENNER

It felt natural. We had the same goals; he had the talent, and I knew how to handle it and had a place to put it. We had many all-night talks about our goals, our ideals, what we could do together. We liked each other enormously. We recognized in each other the belief that work and play should be as close as possible. And I was a great foil for him.

I was starting to ski again, and I had friends in Aspen, so I'd go stay with them, or I'd stay at the Jerome, or I'd stay with Hunter. But soon it became clear that I wasn't going to both visit Hunter and ski. His hours didn't really allow that. So if I wanted to ski, I started staying elsewhere and then going out to Owl Farm at night to visit him, or meeting him in town . . . but that invariably meant five other people were involved.

I was staying at a condo as the guest of this incredibly wealthy man — the original financier of Intel. I invited Hunter to have dinner with us at the fanciest restaurant in Aspen at that time, the Paragon, and Hunter arrived with the usual amount of commotion and ambled over and said to this man, "It's wonderful to have the honor to meet you." I had told Hunter beforehand to be cool, that this guy was worth a billion dollars, et cetera, et cetera.

Hunter sat down and said, "I don't want to bother anybody, so I brought my own food." He put a package wrapped in butcher paper on the table and opened it. It was a huge piece of liver covered with maggots. The guy nearly puked on the table, then got up and left; you had to fall on the floor laughing.

"Strange Rumblings in Aztlan" was Hunter's next assignment after "Freak Power in the Rockies." It was a serious piece of pretty standard reporting, not really the kind of thing that Hunter would become known for, but he wanted to do it because he had a very close friend, Oscar Acosta, who was right in the middle of the La Raza movement in L.A., and we all thought this could be a good heavy-duty piece. Hunter was fascinated with Oscar. And it was in the middle of writing and reporting this piece that Hunter took the assignment to go to Vegas for *Sports Illustrated* to do a quickie on the Mint 500 motorcycle race.

DOUG BRINKLEY

Hunter used to claim that the phrase "Fear and Loathing" was a derivation of Kierkegaard's *Fear and Trembling.* In actuality he lifted it from Thomas Wolfe's *The Web and the Rock.* He had read the novel when he lived in New York. He used to mark up pages of favorite books, underlining phrases that impressed him. On page sixty-two of *The Web and the Rock* he found "fear and loathing" and made it his. I asked him why he didn't give Wolfe credit. Essentially he said it was too much of a hassle, that people would think he meant Tom Wolfe, his New Journalism contemporary. Not many of his friends knew this. His Aspen buddy Dan Dibble did. Maybe a couple of others.

JOE EDWARDS

After Hunter's run for sheriff, he joined some law enforcement organizations and started getting all sorts of literature sent to him. One was this thing about a district attorneys' convention about drug enforcement that was going to be held in Las Vegas. Hunter thought, "What a great, outrageous thing to do — to get stoned as hell and go to that convention," and that's what he did. He and Oscar, who is another whole story. Oscar was crazy. I think he ultimately got killed, or shot, or something. He used to carry a .357 around, and he had these wild eyes. I was very careful around him.

JANN WENNER

In the middle of doing "Strange Rumblings in Aztlan," Hunter was staying at my house in San Francisco. That's where he started to write "Vegas" on a red IBM Selectric that I had had set up on a rolltop desk in the basement. I remember him showing me the first ten pages, asking me if it was worth it to keep going. It was pretty brilliant stuff, way off on a tangent — just that amazing list of what was in the Cadillac's trunk. I had no idea where he was going, but I said, "Yeah, we'll go with that, but let's finish this other thing first." To his credit, he did finish the Aztlan piece.

CHARLES PERRY *was the first copy chief of* Rolling Stone.

He was going to finish the Aztlan story in the office, so they made him a little area in the record library where he could work. I did not tolerate deadline-itis. Hunter was just a guy with a book about the Hells Angels, and I was trying to impose deadlines on everybody. One day I stuck my head into his office and said, "Hi, Hunter! I'm Charlie Perry. How are you doing?" and he said, "Oh, it's going great, it's going great!

I really got the momentum. It's like a train on greased wheels. If I can just keep this momentum up." I didn't know exactly what to make of that, but then two days later, I asked him how he was doing again, and he said, "I lost my momentum. I've been up for two days on speed. I haven't changed my clothes. I think my feet are rotting."

DAVID FELTON *was an associate editor at* Rolling Stone *in 1971.*

You had to give up a lot, as a traditional editor, if you were working with Hunter. I remember calling him once after our fact-checkers had gone over a piece of his, and telling him, "They called the hotel from your story — there *is* no room 303." And he said, "Don't worry about that. Let's move on."

He had a lot going on that I didn't know anything about. We'd work together all afternoon, and all of a sudden he'd make a phone call and two beautiful twins would show up. Where did they come from? I had no idea. He was always looking for a new thrill. One time at *Rolling Stone* he got hold of some kind of weird makeup that was a horrible, ghoulish white, and he put it all over his face. It looked like he had OD'd or something, and he walked all around with it. He thought it was hilarious. Another day he put a recording of screaming rabbits in the speaker system in the office.

But the thing about working with Hunter was that it got worse. From the very start, he was doing battle with Jann over expenses. When he was in Las Vegas covering the DAs' convention, I remember getting a phone call from him — I think it was a total setup — but he had Oscar screaming in the background, and it was all about how Hunter couldn't control Oscar, and it was all because Jann had refused to pay their expense money, and Oscar had used all their money to buy a flute. It was just a big act, and it was very funny, but it was kind of terrifying. They were basically living out that story while he was on the story.

Sometime around then I went out in San Francisco with Hunter and

Oscar, and Hunter had me pull up to Jann's house, where I think Hunter was staying. Jann wasn't there. Hunter said, "This'll just take me a minute." He went into the house and came out with Jann's stereo amplifier under his arm. He was kind of grinning as he got in the car, and he said, "Now we're even."

JOE ESZTERHAS *was a reporter at the* Cleveland Plain Dealer *in the fall of 1970.*

I went out one Sunday to report on a shooting in a bar on the east side of Cleveland. A Hells Angels type of motorcycle gang had shot up a bar and killed three or four people. Two or three weeks later I got a call from Paul Scanlon, the managing editor at *Rolling Stone.* I wrote five thousand words about it for *Rolling Stone,* and a couple weeks after it came out, I got a note from Hunter Thompson that said, "I don't know you, but I read your piece and now there are two of us that know enough about motorcycle gangs to write about them. And the fact that there's two of us really pisses me off, but nice going." I can't tell you what that meant to me, because *Rolling Stone* at that point was *the* hot publication. I had read *Hell's Angels,* and I really admired Hunter's work. The fact that he had sent me this note really, really moved me. I wound up doing a couple of other freelance pieces for *Rolling Stone,* and eventually they hired me full-time.

I was a real heavy drinker and knew how to enjoy drugs, but I was nothing compared to this guy. We would have breakfast at eleven in the morning, and it would consist of five or six Bloody Marys and twelve or fourteen lines of coke. By the middle of the day I was nearly passed out sitting at my desk, but he could do that all day. But with all the drinking, all the drugs, I never saw Hunter not in control of himself. His constitution was really amazing, but that was also a macho thing between him and me. I think it had to do with violence. I learned how to fight at a young age — well, either fight or negotiate. Hunter, I think, got a big charge out of that. I prided myself, as did he, on being in control. No matter how much you drank, or how many drugs you did, the manly thing was not to give up your control, not to pass out on the ground, not to be out of your skull. To still maintain your cool and your sense of manhood, your sense of macho.

TIM FERRIS *joined* Rolling Stone *as chief of its New York bureau in 1971.*

I came out to San Francisco to meet everybody and get to work. My first day there, we were having a meeting — talking about the budget, actually — and Hunter appeared, looking much as we remember him now, in shorts, with that weird bowlegged gait of his. He had an open beer in one hand and part of a six-pack in the other, and a cigarette, and he was wearing a lady's wig — and lipstick. Jann asked Hunter if he wanted to take me out on the town and show me the sights, and on that first time out, Hunter managed to misplace two rental cars in the same evening. We remained friendly ever after.

PAUL SCANLON *was managing editor of* Rolling Stone *for most of the 1970s.*

There was a round oak table in the editorial bullpen, and Hunter would make this big production out of opening up his satchel and unpacking it. We all kind of wandered over to see what was going to come out — fresh grapefruits, notepads, a can of mace, a tape recorder, a carton of Dunhills, spare cigarette holders, a bottle of Wild Turkey, a large police flashlight, lighter fluid, a bowie knife — the usual stuff.

One day Hunter came in, and I'm standing there with Charlie Perry and another editor, Grover Lewis, and he pulls out a sheaf of manuscript, legal sized and all neatly stapled together, and he handed one section to me and one to Charlie and one to Grover, and then stomped out. It was the first chapter of "Fear and Loathing in Las Vegas." I went into my office to read it, and I started howling when the bats started coming out of the sky, and by the time I finished reading it, I was pounding on my desk and I couldn't stop laughing. I wandered into Grover's office, and he was hunched over his desk wheezing. I thought "Shit, he's having a seizure!" And he turned around, and there were tears in his eyes and he couldn't stop laughing.

We spent the next hour just reading lines back and forth to each other. Everybody was really flat knocked out. I know Jann was. Nobody expected it.

CHARLES PERRY

We passed around the manuscript to the editors, and it took us a day to read it and observe it. I remember someone saying that the day after you read it, life just seemed incredibly dramatic, like you never knew when a pack of pythons might come attack you from the corner.

PAUL SCANLON

Later that afternoon at Jerry's, which was the staff watering hole across the street, the editors toasted Raoul Duke and our good fortune while we recited our favorite lines — "One toke? You poor fool! Wait till you see those goddamn bats!" We were like goofy schoolkids.

CHARLES PERRY

Even at *Rolling Stone,* which had been journalistic in its approach to things, the accepted way of talking about psychedelics was the Timothy Leary way, which was essentially as a spiritual experience. Hunter was writing about the fact that sometimes when you're on acid, you're just totally fucked up. It was a breath of fresh air.

JANN WENNER

Working with Hunter was already a major hand-holding job. It meant a minimum of two, maybe three people assigned to the task, including me. It was too much for any one person to handle, even that early on, because of the hours and the time Hunter took. He liked having a team of people working on his stuff. He liked the company, and he liked the crisis atmosphere. I could never change that pattern.

But "Vegas" was completely different. He did that on his own. It took him several months to write it. He'd send me pages. I'd change a word here or suggest a little thing there, but it was already completely formed. I'd ask him to write transitions to make the narrative more complete, but he politely and firmly refused. It was his pure fantasy, coming directly out of his own mind. There was no real reporting involved, except when he wanted to go back and do the district attorneys' conference, which was hysterical and had pure gonzo potential.

Memo from Hunter to Jann Wenner, written as he was finishing Part II of "Vegas"

Jann . . .

The central problem here is that you're working overtime to treat this thing as Straight or at least Responsible journalism . . . whereas in truth we are dealing with a classic of irresponsible gibberish. You'd be better off trying to make objective, chronological sense of "Highway 61," The Ginger Man, *"Mister Tambourine Man," or even* Naked Lunch.

Despite these onerous comparisons, I suspect the point still stands. And the real nut of the problem is that I seem to resent any attempts to tell me how I should write my gonzo journalism. I realize that this stance is rude & irrational, but I guess I tend to operate that way now and then.

This gibberish is no more "journalism" than Steadman's art is "illustration." Charlie [Charles Perry, RS associate editor] was lamenting the fact — and I agreed — that one of Ralph's drawings would have been nicer if he'd included a herd of bats. But he didn't — so I offered to draw them in myself, with an ink pencil. Charlie was horrified. Which was

*exactly the right reaction. I wouldn't touch one of Ralph's drawings —
and for the same reason, I can't work up much enthusiasm for treating
"Fear & Loathing" like a news story. No doubt the holes and kinks
should be filled, but for some reason I just can't work up much zeal for the
job. Maybe after 12 or 20 hours of sleep I might think differently, but I
wouldn't count on it. Let's keep in mind that this was never a commissioned
work of journalism; it was a strange neo-fictional outburst that was deemed
so rotten and wasteful, journalistically, that neither RS nor Spts.
Illustrated would even reimburse me for my expenses. So I'm not in much
of a mood, right now, to act grateful for any editorial direction. (No doubt
I'm wrong and bullheaded on this score, but the way this thing developed
has made me feel sort of personal about it; irrationally possessive, as it
were — and at this stage of the action I'm not real hungry for advice about
how the thing should be handled. It's been an instinct trip from the start,
and I suspect it's going to stay that way — for good or ill.*

*Anyway, I've worked myself into such a stupor of crazed fatigue
that I can't even sleep — and when I went into the office today Hank
[Torgrimson, RS accountant] was ready to have me arrested for Stealing this
typewriter. Things seem to be breaking down — after a long run of Good
Work. So I think it's time to go home. I'll call you on Monday or Tuesday
and see how things look then. But my general feeling is that you have a hell
of a lot more important things to concern yourself with than perfecting the
chronology of Vegas/Fear & Loathing. I have the feeling that it's a pretty
fair piece of writing, as it stands, and I've developed a certain affection
for it. . . .*

*I like the bastard. So why not get on to more important things? (I'm not
seriously opposed to any cutting or editing, but don't expect me to get wired
on the idea of adding big sections that I didn't feel like including in the
first place.)*

*OK for now. I'm in a massively rotten mood, trying to stay awake until
plane time — seeing double, feeling bugs under my kneecaps, etc.*

Fuck this — maybe I'll send another chunk(s) of Vegas II when I get back home — but let's not worry or count on it. We have enough, and 90% of it is absolutely right — on its own terms.

And that, after all, is the whole point.

Ciao,

H

JANN WENNER

We agreed from the get-go, after he'd written 5,000 or 10,000 words, that we would publish it in two parts for our fourth-anniversary issue. We knew it was quite special, and we put it on two consecutive covers.

From "Fear and Loathing in Las Vegas: A Savage Journey to the Heart of the American Dream," by Raoul Duke
Rolling Stone 95; November 11, 1971

I drove around to the Circus-Circus Casino and parked near the back door. "This is the place," I said. "They'll never fuck with us here."

"Where's the ether?" said my attorney. "This mescaline isn't working."

I gave him the key to the trunk while I lit up the hash pipe. He came back with the ether-bottle, un-capped it, then poured some into a Kleenex and mashed it under his nose, breathing heavily. I soaked another Kleenex and fouled my own nose. The smell was overwhelming, even with the top down. Soon we were staggering up the stairs towards the entrance, laughing stupidly and dragging each other along, like drunks.

This is the main advantage of ether: it makes you behave like the village drunkard in some early Irish novel . . . total loss of all basic motor skills: blurred vision, no balance, numb tongue — severence of all connection between the body and the brain. Which is interesting, because the brain continues to function more or less normally . . . you can actually *watch* yourself behaving in this terrible way, but you can't control it.

You approach the turnstiles leading into the Circus-Circus and you know that when you get there, you have to give the man two dollars or he won't let you inside . . . but when you get there, everything goes wrong: you misjudge the distance to the turnstile and slam against it, bounce off and grab hold of an old woman to keep from falling, some angry Rotarian shoves you and you think: What's happening here? What's going on? Then you hear yourself mumbling: "Dogs fucked the Pope, no fault of mine. Watch out! . . . Why money? My name is Brinks; I was born . . . born? Get sheep over side . . . women and children to armored car . . . orders from Captain Zeep."

Ah, devil ether — a total body drug. The mind recoils in horror, unable to communicate with the spinal column. The hands flap crazily, unable to get money out of the pocket . . . garbled laughter and hissing from the mouth . . . always smiling.

Ether is the perfect drug for Las Vegas. In this town they love a drunk. Fresh meat. So they put us through the turnstiles and turned us loose inside.

JANN WENNER

Hunter would infuse everything with drama; whatever he was doing was always full of energy and craziness — things were always at stake, and there would be crises. Going to the district attorneys' conference was going to be this dangerous undercover mission. He was going to go right to the edge of this or that.

Then we were haggling over expenses. The magazine was on a shoestring at the time, and I had to say, "No, you can't rent a Cadillac." *Rolling Stone* was small; we were still in our third year. If people were making $125 a week, that was a lot. The idea that he wanted to rent a Cadillac was out of the question. What was his famous line? "You can't cover the American dream in a fucking Volkswagen."

His first book of letters is consumed with correspondence about money and expenses. It's embarrassing. That, and then how he was going to slice either "Vegas" or something else up into several books.

He was really trying to maximize the money coming in. I guess as a young and struggling writer with a wife and kid, he had to do it. But it was also a little over the top. Hunter loved to live well, so he was constantly spending money. He was always in debt to four or five or six people. He was always in debt to me.

GEORGE STRANAHAN

He always had this kind of Robin Hood thing, that it's okay to take things — if somebody's got plenty, it's okay, you don't have to pay them. In fact, they owe you. He always felt entitled to more than he got — that there was a certain societal abuse of his talent, that society was not giving him enough. Lord knows he knew very well how to spend it! He was financially imprudent. I was his landlord, so I talked to him about it. At a certain point in the early seventies, I said, basically, "You guys are irregular with the rent payments, and I understand a writer's life might be irregular, so let's just recut the deal to make it into a lease-purchase instead of just a rent." That made him much happier, because he wasn't just writing a check. He was struggling, and I was not, and it really irked him that he was taking his meagerness and sending it to me.

He attracted "financial advisers" like leeches, and eventually he'd get around to wondering, "Where's the money?" Well, these other people got it; they sold him a bill of goods because he didn't really have a good feeling for how you handle money. It wasn't his strength. He spent plenty. He spent everything he got, ever.

JANN WENNER

He knew he had his hands on a great piece of writing. After we published "Vegas," he became dominant in our world. In that four-year period from the start of "Vegas" to the campaign trail and Watergate in 1974, working with Hunter probably consumed a quarter of my life. I had other people working with him on the road or in the office, but I had to basically keep the same schedule he did until the story was done. He would never let me turn a piece over to another editor; in the end, I had to do every word of it. And, of course, I loved it.

TIM CAHILL *was an associate editor at Rolling Stone in 1971.*

I didn't have to work directly with Hunter. I'd spend one night out with him and then spend two days recuperating — but when I'd run into him two days later, he'd still be going from the last time I saw him. He looked like he could take care of himself — there was some physical power there. This confused me as time went on, because had I abused myself the way Hunter continually did, I suspect that I would have deteriorated physically quite rapidly.

He was always yelling at himself, like "AAHHHH!!! CAZART!!!" and then there would be these long silences, which meant that he was probably writing. He would sometimes leave notes in the office when he wasn't there that said, "Don't even try to look for me." He'd run to a nearby indoor pool and swim, which no one would ever know about.

JANN WENNER

Everyone loved to be around him — even Charlie Perry, who would grumble about Hunter's complete disregard of a practical and helpful deadline schedule. He'd come to San Francisco relatively often and stay at my house. Of course, those were the early days. We all had stamina on our side. By the time of the campaign trail in '72, the idea of Hunter staying at my house really wore itself out. So we moved him out to the Seal Rock Inn overlooking the Pacific Ocean at the absolute western edge of the city. It was also good to get Hunter away from people just so he could have the space to work. People wanted to hang out with him, both legitimate — all his fellow workers and bon vivants — and illegitimate people — the crazies, whom he was quite tolerant of.

CHARLES PERRY

After "Fear and Loathing," people in Colorado were giving him stuff they'd written, thinking he could get them in *Rolling Stone*. I was the poetry editor, and he sent me a package of poems from other people once with a note that said, "I don't know about this stuff. If you feel the same way, send it back to them with this." He included a prepackaged rejection letter that read:

> *You worthless, acid-sucking piece of illiterate shit! Don't ever send this kind of brain-damaged swill in here again. If I had the time, I'd come out there and drive a fucking wooden stake into your forehead. Why don't you get a job, germ? Maybe delivering advertising handouts door to door, or taking tickets for a wax museum. You drab South Bend cocksuckers are all the same; like those dope-addled dingbats at the* Rolling Stone *office. I'd like to kill those bastards for sending me your piece . . . and I'd just as soon kill you, too. Jam this morbid drivel up your ass where your readership will better appreciate it.*
>
> Sincerely,
Yail Bloor III, Minister of Belles-Lettre.
>
> *P.S. Keep up the good work. Have a nice day.*

We actually sent it out to a couple of people, thinking they would appreciate it. One person took it to a lawyer and asked whether he could sue us, and the lawyer said, "No, you don't have a leg to stand on . . . but could I Xerox it?"

TIM CAHILL

Hunter imitators were all over the place. All these writers were writing this gibberish, but they lost sight of one of Hunter's saving graces, which was that he was hilarious. He couldn't have been effective without his humor. But there were dozens and dozens of Hunter imitators who all thought that they should be published.

RALPH STEADMAN

A lot of people around Hunter have tried to be like him, but I found the best way to get on with him was always to be myself. I was gentler, but my drawings were wilder. As he said to me, "You're a liar, Ralph. You're worse than me, and weirder."

Actually, what I thought was pathetic later on was not so much watching people try to be like Hunter as try to write like Hunter. It doesn't work. He was writing something that came out of the way he talked. And it's an extraordinary thing, because he was such a bad speaker, but if you could catch it, it was a bloody good sentence.

JANN WENNER

You just couldn't help, when you were around Hunter, picking up some of his mannerisms and his expressions. No one was immune to it. To this day, if I hear a loud noise, I overreact in a sudden, startled way, jumping out of my seat, shouting, "What the fuck?!" like he did. I can't shake it.

WILLIAM KENNEDY

When he started working for *Rolling Stone* he could write anything he pleased. Look what he did with that assignment to cover a Las Vegas sheriffs' convention. That's hardly journalism. Yes, it's grounded in historical fact, he was there, there was the convention, he did have an assignment, and so on; and he claimed it was all true and that he could prove it with his notes, but that only makes his notes a transcript of his performance and his wild and fanciful imagination, the first phase of the novel. What he then wrote was a singular work that was a mutation of the fictional form, which is why his place is secure, because nobody can ever do that again. You can't duplicate him; it's just so obvious when anyone tries. There's no way you can follow that mind or that career.

JANN WENNER

Rolling Stone at that time was a collection of journalistic misfits, all of them extremely talented. They all recognized the talent and eccentricity in one another and shared a common purpose. The leader of the pack in the office came to be Joe Eszterhas, but the star was always Hunter. It created a bit of a rivalry. Joe was jealous, but Hunter never seemed to feel that at all. He never did anything but treat Joe in the most magnanimous and generous fashion, as he treated everybody. Likewise, Joe was deeply respectful of Hunter's talent and charm.

Tom Wolfe had a great deal of respect for Hunter and wrote wonderful things about him in his New Journalism anthology. I introduced them to each other for the first time when they were both writing for *Rolling Stone*. In fact, the first installment of the *Rolling Stone* version of "The Right Stuff" opens with a lede passage that's an homage to Hunter's style.

TOM WOLFE

Hunter had been very kind to me when I was writing *The Electric Kool-Aid Acid Test*. I had gathered from *Hell's Angels* that he had been present when Ken Kesey and his Merry Pranksters gave a party for the Hells Angels, which had happened before I had even known about Kesey and the Pranksters. I called Hunter up from out of the blue, and he sent me some tapes he had recorded at that crazy party, which was really generous of him.

JANN WENNER

Hunter appreciated New Journalism and read its practitioners. He felt part of that fraternity of Wolfe, Talese, and Halberstam, whom he was very fond of, and Eszterhas as well. He knew he was different from them, but he also knew that he was one of the writers of that era who formed the fraternity. Of them all, he was the most unique: He was the wild man, and he was the genius.

WILLIAM KENNEDY

He liked the idea of being part of the New Journalism — and Tom Wolfe did include him in his book that codified that genre — but Hunter wanted more; he wanted to transcend it, and he did. He wanted to be singular, and he was.

PAUL SCANLON

One night, Jann summoned me and two other staffers over to his house. Hunter was there wearing this reddish-purplish tie-dyed shirt with what looked like a bull's-eye over his stomach, and he proceeded to pull that ruse of shooting 151-proof rum into his navel with this huge horse syringe. It was really, really big. He didn't actually do it, but he had us believing that he was doing it. He'd make this elaborate presentation of filling the syringe, and you saw the rum bottle and everything, and then he'd turn around and crash over and make these noises — "Ugghhh!!! Aggghhh!!!"

JANN WENNER

He'd come in the office, and there'd be a batch of mail from his fans. Every tenth letter had a joint in it or some pills or something. Hunter would open them up and usually take the stuff.

It was during that period he first brought the plunger in — what appeared to be a horse-sized hypodermic needle. Hunter would take this monstrous gadget, plunge it into a grapefruit, extract the juice, and then shove the needle in his stomach in front of everybody. Of course, it was a needle that retracted and went back up into the plunger, but it looked very real. Hunter loved to see people recoil in fear and revulsion.

PAUL SCANLON

I went out drinking with Oscar a couple of times, which could be a bit frightening. Oscar was scary. He was a real sweetheart, but he was big — big and scary. Very intense, way more so than Hunter. Hunter could be very gentlemanly and almost shy sometimes, and Oscar was anything but.

There was a falling-out at some point. Oscar felt like he was being ripped off by Hunter — that he had been somehow used, by Hunter and by Jann. On one of his last visits to *Rolling Stone* — I believe he was banished — he carved his middle name, Zeta, on a wooden shelf in the men's room.

JANN WENNER

Oscar had a capacity to go crazy. He had no restraint. He was really bright and had a lot to say, but he was so full of anger and frustration because he felt his sheer size — he was imposing — and being Chicano distracted people from what he was trying to get across. He wasn't a bad writer, but I think he was also jealous of Hunter's talent. But he had this wonderful sense of humor and a great talent for having fun. I never felt threatened when I was with him. Oscar and I used to take acid and go out to topless bars. This was kind of second nature with the Brown Buffalo; I mean, why not?

Oscar usually had a knife or a gun, but my impression was that he wouldn't use them. In reality, he was more temperate than that, but he could fly off the handle. We all think he died in Mexico in some kind of drug deal gone bad. He had possibly done some ridiculous thing that offended people, and he didn't have Hunter's gift of pulling back and charming everybody. He'd go too far.

From "The Banshee Screams for Buffalo Meat"
Rolling Stone 254; December 15, 1977

When the great scorer comes to write against Oscar's name, one of the first few lines in the Ledger will note that he usually lacked the courage of his consistently monstrous convictions. There was more mercy, madness, dignity and generosity in that overweight, overworked and always overindulged brown cannonball of a body than most of us will meet in any human package even three times Oscar's size for the rest of our lives — which are all running noticeably leaner on the high side, since that rotten fat spic disappeared.

He was a drug-addled brute and a genuinely fiendish adversary in court or on the street — but it was none of *these* things that finally pressured him into death or a disappearance so finely plotted that it amounts to the same thing.

What finally cracked the Brown Buffalo was the bridge he refused to build between the self-serving elegance of his instincts and the self-destructive carnival of his reality. He was a Baptist missionary at a leper colony in Panama before he was a lawyer in Oakland and East L.A., or a radical-chic author in San Francisco and Beverly Hills. . . . But whenever things got tense or when he had to work close to the bone, he was always a missionary. And that was the governing instinct that ruined him for anything else. He was a preacher in the courtroom, a preacher at the typewriter and a flat-out awesome preacher when he cranked his head full of acid.

The Brown Buffalo ate LSD-25 with a relish that bordered on worship. When his brain felt bogged down in the mundane nuts and bolts horrors of the Law or some dead-end manuscript, he would simply take off in his hotrod Mustang for a week on the road and a few days of what he called "walking with the King."

Oscar was not into serious street-fighting, but he was hell on wheels in a bar brawl. Any combination of a 250-pound Mexican and LSD-25 is a potentially terminal menace for anything it can reach — but when the alleged Mexican is in fact a profoundly angry Chicano lawyer with no fear at all of anything that walks on less than three legs and a de facto suicidal conviction that he *will* die at thirty-three — just like Jesus Christ — you have a serious piece of work on your hands. Specially if the bastard is *already* thirty-three and a half years old with a head full of Sandoz acid, a loaded .357 Magnum in his belt, a hatchet-wielding Chicano bodyguard on his elbow at all times, and a disconcerting habit of projectile-vomiting geysers of pure red blood off the front porch every thirty or forty minutes, or whenever his malignant ulcer can't handle any more raw tequila.

JANN WENNER

Ralph [Steadman] was always crazier than Hunter. I knew it and Hunter knew it. Ralph really was a mad genius, and he really did act on what he believed in, whereas Hunter knew how to modulate. Hunter and I could be businesslike and think about what was realistic to do and what was better not to do. Ralph, once he got on a crusade — well, that was the end of it. He wouldn't compromise. He was pure, and Hunter saw that.

RALPH STEADMAN

One thing he was fond of saying was "We are not like the others, Ralph."

JAMES SILBERMAN

The Vegas book didn't sell fabulously well in hardcover, at least not with the first printing. It became a big bestseller in paperback. Jann would agree that it was a big success in *Rolling Stone*.

I thought it was really going to take off, and printed a lot of copies of the book. There were 20,000 copies — out of a printing of 60,000 or 80,000 — left over in our warehouse, and when Hunter was notified about this, he said, "How much are they?" He made an offer to buy all 20,000. His plan was to keep them — "Let them age," as he put it — and then little by little let out some autographed copies as he needed money.

JANN WENNER

Hunter did in fact tell me that we should get all the remainders and buy them for a dime a copy or something like that — I think there were 7,000 available. We tried. Hunter was always looking for a scheme or a business adventure for us to get involved in, and it was always fun to do anything with him — despite the fact that most of these ideas were overwhelmingly complicated, with little reward, but lots of fun in the scheming. I wrote to his publisher and said we'd like to buy them. But for whatever reason it never came to pass.

Later on, though, he decided somehow that I *had* bought them. I don't think he really believed it, but it sounded good and it was getting traction as a story: that I had buried them and was going to sell them after his death and make a fortune off him. It really was too funny to deny, and a lot of people believed it.

JAMES SILBERMAN

Somehow the books got lost. The last time I was with Hunter and Jann together, Hunter was still complaining to Jann that he thought that the books had been put in the *Rolling Stone* warehouse and that Jann had lost them, that Jann owed him whatever these books were worth. Some first editions of *Vegas* turned up in the antiquarian catalogs for a hundred dollars, a hundred and a quarter — so he would have had a good return on his investment.

JANN WENNER

The summer after *Vegas* was published, my wife, Jane, and I drove from San Francisco to Woody Creek and spent a week in the cabin next door to Hunter. It was sunny, green, the Rockies at their best, with Hunter, Sandy, and Juan in a golden moment. Hunter had two exceptional books under his belt and a stable gig at *Rolling Stone*. We were all enjoying the moment immensely. I was trying to figure out what Hunter would do next. What was the best and biggest story? We agreed that he was going to go to Vietnam.

Maybe a month after that, I had hesitations and thought it would be better if Hunter covered the 1972 presidential election. I was fearful he would be angry that I pulled the Vietnam assignment, but he loved the idea of the campaign trail and agreed to it immediately.

He saw it better than I had in terms of how much he could devote himself to it. We would have full-time coverage of a presidential election in our rock & roll–and–drug magazine. What we thought of right from the beginning — we were trying to make some kind of splash — was that he'd move to Washington. Well, that may or may not have been the smartest idea, but it got him there. We put him on payroll with a salary of $17,000 a year, which was big for us then.

TIM FERRIS

There was the great *Rolling Stone* editors' confab at Big Sur — a weekend at a motel and in the Big Sur hot springs. It was 1971. There was a kind of tension between the lifestyle that most of us were living individually and the requirements of actually sitting through long meetings in a corporate setting. On the very first full day of the conference, there were people there that could barely hold their eyes open because they'd been up all night with Hunter or with one another.

I mainly remember testy declamations involving stylebook matters and Charlie Perry being irritated that someone would put a comma inside a parenthesis or something, which I mention just because although many of us would seem today to be taking advantage of the fact that we were living in the sixties, there was a unanimous, universal dedication to quality of craft among a very fine group of writers and editors. There was a certain amount of playing around going on, but everyone, Hunter included, was very serious about trying to do their best work and to expand what they could do.

That first night at Big Sur, Hunter drove his car up onto the sidewalk in front of his room at the motel and then climbed over the hood of the car to get into his room and lock the door — the idea was to discourage anyone from hanging on the door to try to wake him for the morning session.

JANN WENNER

By the time of the Big Sur editorial conference, Hunter and I had already made the agreements and written the contracts for his book on the campaign. The Big Sur confab was a weekend-long gathering of all the editors from San Francisco, New York, Los Angeles, and London at a motel near Esalen. At night everyone would hit the hot springs, pretty loaded. That great series of pictures of Hunter taking a highway patrol sobriety test came from that weekend.

It seemed like a good idea at the time to discuss where the magazine was going and gather some story ideas. But Hunter had a fantasy that everybody else on the staff should come to an agreement that he should go to Washington. He wanted to take the temperature of the room and have some kind of consensus. He didn't want to do it if he was going to be considered some foreign organism to the editorial body, if everybody else thought that *Rolling Stone* really shouldn't cover politics — of course, knowing all the time that we were going to do it anyway. But it was a useful conceit that both gave him spirit and energized the staff for the year ahead.

Hunter didn't actually make some of those meetings. They'd go on for four or five hours. When he did show up, he'd bring noisemakers and toys and prank gadgets; other times he sat quietly. The Big Sur conference turned out to be a one-of-a-kind event in our little universe.

CHARLES PERRY

We'd be trying to tackle all these serious issues, and Hunter would pull out all this weird stuff that he bought by mail order from *Police Chief* magazine. I remember there was a stick-on flashing red light like the ones you see on cop cars. Hunter would slap it on top of a table in the middle of a meeting.

JANN WENNER

He had a flashing red police light that you could mount by suction cup, and there was an air-raid siren, and later on a toy hammer that made a shattering-glass sound. He loved to get people going, and knowing how much pleasure he got out of this, part of our routine became that he would pull some prank and then I'd overreact to make it more fun for him. Later he gave one of the hammers to my kids as a Christmas present so they could use it on me.

JANE WENNER *is Jann Wenner's wife.*

Max Palevsky had a computer company with some other people that he sold to Xerox for a billion dollars, which, in the sixties, was an enormous amount. Max was also a very active Democrat and either had invested or was going to invest in *Rolling Stone*. So he had invited us all down for a weekend at his home — Jann and me, his secretary, a few editors, a couple of the business people, and Hunter.

Max had an ultramodern, very large ranch-style house in Palm Springs with a wonderful staff and a butler dressed in a white jacket with a black bow tie. The staff had been cooking all day and was getting ready for dinner — it was getting near cocktail time — and Hunter came over to me and said, "Jane, I want to tell you something." And I said, "What?" And he said, "Listen, you can't tell anybody, but I just have this one tab of acid left." He said he'd already taken one, and now I went through that little "Shall I? Shall I not? Shall I?" I took it.

Everybody was called to dinner, and we all sat around the table, and this butler came out carrying this huge silver platter with a thirty-pound slab of roast beef, blood dripping down, and the roast beef was *moving*. I looked around the table, and this seemed to be happening to everybody. Hunter had said the same thing to each person in the room separately and dosed everyone — and then we all started laughing. Nobody ate anything.

It was classic Hunter — with the twinkle in his eye and the devilish grin. Somehow he always made everybody feel special, that it was going to be your moment. He'd make you want to be naughty because he made everything sound so good. He had a way of getting you to go along with him on any ride.

JANN WENNER

When we realized that Hunter had dosed everybody, it turned into this wonderful all-night party in hot tubs and Jacuzzis. That was Hunter in action.

Everybody there was drug-friendly. Hunter really didn't fuck them over — he just had fun with them. There was a confrontational Hunter who could be very abusive, especially to people that worked for him, but he was never out to hurt anybody. He would never give anybody drugs they couldn't handle.

So he moved to Washington and got a house there with Sandy and Juan. Sandy was pregnant at the time. They'd had a miscarriage and an infant death already, so they were full of hope about this. And then she miscarried again.

SANDY THOMPSON

The last baby that I had, at Johns Hopkins in Washington, D.C., in '72 — he was taken at seven and a half months. We thought he was going to be fine. And he developed hyaline membrane disease, which is what John Kennedy's baby died of — which is also now curable.

JANN WENNER

It was a very sad moment. It had been a time of such big hope and change: They were moving from Woody Creek to Washington, and Hunter had his first full-time job in years as the national affairs correspondent of *Rolling Stone*. He'd put his son in school, and they had a nice suburban home. But it didn't slow Hunter down. He wanted to get on the road.

CHAPTER SIX

A New Voice on the Campaign Trail

Hunter worked his ass off. He knew he didn't know about politics, so he insisted that you explain every detail. That's why he was so much better informed than most of the political reporters traveling on the campaign, because they were covering it by the book — and Hunter didn't have the book. He was making one up.

SANDY THOMPSON

We lived in D.C., right on the edge of Maryland, in Rock Creek Park. It was just sort of a regular brick house that *Rolling Stone* paid for, but across the street was a park, and it was at the end of a cul-de-sac, and we had the Dobermans there, and Juan went to this weird so-called school. It was really alternative. He'd started off in a regular public school because I couldn't find anything else for him in D.C., and he was completely bored. He was so much further ahead than everybody else. I had taught him to read when he was four. There were maybe eight kids. They tore up telephone books, and I don't know what else they did.

JUAN THOMPSON

I'm not sure if it was even really a school by most standards. Our "class" would be things like driving to New York City and back stuffed behind the backseat of VW bus. The "classroom" was this old, really run-down second-floor apartment in a pretty bad part of Washington. Some days in between field trips we'd just do something weird like kick a big hole in the wall. Academically it was a wasted year. But it was fun. We were six years old and running around Washington, D.C., without supervision. We'd all walk a few blocks by ourselves just to get lunch.

JANN WENNER

Sandy was not only his wife but also his full-time assistant. She was the one typing the manuscripts, filing, and doing all the administrative work, and she was also the recipient of Hunter's abusive behavior and unrelenting late-night irritability. When Hunter was in a rage, Sandy would just take it, though in retrospect everything was milder then. At that time we all kind of laughed at it — the stakes weren't so high, and he wasn't so crazy.

JUAN THOMPSON

I knew my dad worked at a newspaper, and I knew Nixon was bad. Very bad. That's all I knew. Hunter didn't sit down and talk to us — this was more from overhearing conversations.

JANN WENNER

Max Palevsky was also one of the principal funders of the McGovern campaign, and through Max, I was able to meet Frank Mankiewicz, McGovern's campaign manager; he'd been Bobby Kennedy's press secretary. One Sunday morning Hunter and I went to see Frank at his home — a large colonial house in Chevy Chase, Maryland. Hunter and I had smoked this rather serious joint before heading over there. In the car we developed an extreme case of the giggles. We were cackling hysterically while we were walking up to his door and wondering if we were going to make it through. We tried not to look at each other, but we'd sneak a look and start giggling all over again. This was our first major move in big-time politics.

The door opened, and we suddenly went very serious. Frank laid out his whole theory of the campaign — how and what they would do, state by state, what candidacies would fall apart — and lo and behold it all came true as Frank predicted. He had a clear and accurate vision of it, and he told it to Hunter, which was a big part of why Hunter was able to call the campaign so accurately and understand it so well.

It took Hunter a while to find the right voice on the campaign trail, for him to feel the whole story out. He started developing the style and seeing how far he could push it, to see how gonzo he could really go while in the middle of this heavy-duty mainstream story. Hunter was on the road all the time. The press corps noticed almost immediately that he was doing something new, and we both soon discovered that his stuff was being read by everybody in the McGovern campaign and practically every member of the national press corps. This put both Hunter and *Rolling Stone* on the map in a way we hadn't been.

GEORGE MCGOVERN, *the South Dakota senator, ran for president in 1972.*

The first time I met him, in '71, he was in a phone booth in Madison, Wisconsin. Somebody said to me, "That guy with his back to you in the next booth is Hunter Thompson," so I turned around and said, "How ya doing, Sheriff?" He sort of glowered at me and said, "What do you mean by that?" So I repeated it. "Things going okay, Sheriff?" I knew that he'd run for sheriff, but he couldn't seem to believe that I knew that. He didn't seem to mind being greeted that way by somebody running for president.

I announced for president in 1971, almost two years ahead of the '72 election. That had never been done before in American history. Most people thought it was crazy, but not Hunter. He said to me, "If a guy wants to run for president, let him say so, for Chrissakes." He then attached himself to my campaign and followed me night and day. Sometimes it would just be the two of us on a little putt-putt airplane going somewhere. But he was filing stories with *Rolling Stone* regularly during that period, along with Tim Crouse.

TIM CROUSE *was a writer for* Rolling Stone *in 1972.*

At the time Jann called a gathering of the tribe — virtually the whole masthead — at a motel in Big Sur, I was aware of Hunter from "Fear and Loathing in Las Vegas," but I'd never met him. He showed up in the middle of a big meeting one morning wearing a hospital robe and a blond wig, holding a drink. I never did find out why he had been in the hospital or why he had on the wig.

I was fairly new to the magazine and had no experience at all as a political reporter. But I had gotten up my gumption and insisted that I be sent to cover the New Hampshire primary. Jann finally said okay, on the condition that I work as Hunter's assistant. I was a little grumpy about this at first, but it didn't take me long to figure out what a good deal I'd stumbled into.

There was a sprawling lodgelike hotel called the Wayfarer in the woods outside Manchester, New Hampshire, where all the politicians and reporters stayed during the primary. We had rooms close by each other. My first job was to get Hunter up in the morning. I knocked on his door, and there was a long, loud eruption of curses. I realized within about three seconds that this wasn't directed at me. It was just the life force announcing itself through Hunter's early-morning self.

JACK GERMOND *was covering national politics for the Gannett papers in 1972.*

Hunter always had so much foreign matter in his body, he would sometimes go crazy. I remember him walking into the entrance of the

Wayfarer Inn. Outside they had a little covered place where cars pulled up, and the roof was propped up by two-by-fours. Hunter got out of the car with Tim and walked into one of these pillars, and he thought someone had come out and hit him with a two-by-four. He went bananas until Tim calmed him down and convinced him that nobody could have hit him, that it was just an accident.

TIM CROUSE

From the beginning, Hunter treated me as part of a team. At the end of the day, we would get together, order room service, and sit on the floor, eat our club sandwiches, and process the events of the day. Hunter was what you could call a creative listener — responsive, shrewd about the subtexts of any conversation, constantly putting you on your mettle. He was quick to seize on anything that you might know that could be of use to him and to offer anything he might know that would be of use to you.

He also had a funny kind of vulnerability. He was convinced the other reporters were dissing him — that they weren't treating him with the respect that his experience as an established journalist and author entitled him to. "Listen," he told me, "we're going to get these bastards — or you are. Here's what you do: Keep a notebook and watch them, and any time they screw up, any time some guy forgets to wipe his nose or anything — write it down." Within a week, Hunter's rancor had evaporated, and I'd become fascinated by the people I was observing.

After New Hampshire, I went to Washington, D.C., where Hunter and Sandy were living in a modest suburban house with their son, Juan, a well mannered Doberman named Benjie, and a mynah bird named Edgar who was trained to say, "Fuck Humphrey." For me, that house was a kind of Neverland. Sandy was sweet and endlessly patient, devoted to fostering what she saw as Hunter's genius.

The first day I was there, Hunter came down to a sunporch off the living room, and Sandy took me aside and whispered, "Now, at this point he isn't to be disturbed." Then she came out from the kitchen with a breakfast tray — grapefruit, scrambled eggs, toast, coffee, juice, and his newspapers and mail carefully laid out. It was rather like Phineas Fogg being served by Passepartout. That was his quiet time, when he marshaled his resources.

After that, he got down to work. He was very open with me about his process as a writer. I was with him in the room upstairs where he had his IBM Selectric set up on a card table. He would sit with his elbows out to the sides, his back very straight, and he would get this sort of electric jolt and blast out a sentence. Then he'd wait again with his arms out, and he'd get another jolt and type another sentence.

Watching him, I began to realize that he was trying to bypass learned attitudes, received ideas, clichés of every kind, and tap into something that had more to do with his unconscious, his intuitive take on things. He wanted to get the sentence out before any preconception could corrupt it.

One of Hunter's methods of composition was to write a bunch of ledes and then somehow fit them together. By lede, I mean the opening portion of a story, which is ordinarily designed to pack more of a virtuosic wallop than the sections that follow. Early on, I remember, Hunter showed me a stack of ledes he'd accumulated, as if he were fanning a whole deck of aces. On a tight deadline, my job would sometimes be to stitch together the lede-like chunks that Hunter had generated. Ideally, the story would function like an internal-combustion engine, with a constant flow of explosions of more or less equal intensity all the way through.

When we got to Milwaukee, the Wisconsin primary, Hunter's assignment was to cover Humphrey and Muskie, who were the frontrunners. My assignment was to cover the poor underdog, George McGovern. Lo and behold, McGovern pulled off this upset and won.

So the little story I had became the big story. Hunter immediately fell into the role that I'd played for him. I was sitting at the typewriter, having been up for two days straight, and he was pouring coffee into me and rubbing my shoulders and giving me pep talks and feeding my copy to the mojo wire and dealing with Jann. Just to keep things from getting too sweet, he kept saying, "Jann's going to fire you for this for sure. This is the end of you and *Rolling Stone*."

GEORGE MCGOVERN

I thought it was interesting that the two people who covered me the closest during that period worked for *Rolling Stone,* but I got to know Hunter quite well. I was intrigued with him, as I think he was with me. We had entirely different personalities, but we hit it off right after I started the campaign. He used to tell me I was an honest man — and I don't think he delivered that judgment on very many people. He also said, "You're the best of the lousy lot," but I always took that as a compliment.

He used to take my wife and me out to dinner when he'd come to Washington. We went into a nice restaurant, and this young woman said, "Can I take your drink order?" Hunter said, "Bring me four margaritas and four bottles of beer." And this young woman said, "Well, sir, there are only three of you." He said, "I don't care if there are thirty-three. Bring me four margaritas and four bottles of beer." I think she assumed that Eleanor and I would get part of that, but I knew better, so I said, "Get us a couple of vodkas on the rocks." You felt a little self-conscious sitting in an upscale restaurant with a guy with four margaritas and four bottles of beer, all just freshly opened, sitting in front of him.

TIM CROUSE

I was with Hunter for the better part of a year. Sometimes he was ragged with fatigue, but his natural tact and generosity never quit. It was a wonderful time, and there was never a cross word between us, except once. I was busy interviewing people at one of the conventions, and Hunter asked me to get him a certain statistic. I'd seen him invent stuff in his stories — including things about me — and I thought, "What the hell," and just made a number up. He said fine, and I went about my business and forgot about the whole thing. All of a sudden, I got this phone call from him, and he was livid. He'd somehow found out that the statistic wasn't right. "How could you do this?! How could you do this?!" It wasn't a performance, as so much of his indignation was, but real shock — one way I could tell was that when Hunter was truly stung, the bad language tended to drop out of his vocabulary. From then on, I was quite scrupulous about facts.

Hunter set a high standard for himself at the beginning, and he felt he needed to rise to that standard or surpass it with every piece that followed. That put a considerable strain even on someone with his exceptional stamina and skill. But he was fearless. With Hunter there was this constant demonstration that if you wanted to make something happen, you just had to plow ahead and do it on your own terms, and not let anything stop you.

AL EISELE *was a Washington correspondent for the Knight Ridder papers.*

The first time I met him was at a bar on Capitol Hill. He pulled out of his pocket a handful of red and blue pills and said, "You want some?"

He was viewed with a combination of love and fear by the other reporters. I think they were all mystified by him at first — he was such a different animal than you usually see in the press corps — but most of them quickly came to appreciate the fact that he was a pretty good writer. He wasn't just there for show. Even the big mainstream writers from the *New York Times* and the *Washington Post* — R. W. Apple and that crowd — grudgingly learned to appreciate and respect him. The younger reporters, of course, loved him.

JACK GERMOND

There were some stiff-necks who resented Thompson's presence on the campaign, who thought you had to have certain credentials to be covering it, but most of us liked him.

He was odd, obviously. Before the California primary, we were all staying at the Hyatt House on Wilshire Boulevard. Hunter would arrive at the pool at about noon every day with a tray of room service following him on which he'd have his usual six Heinekens — he loved Heineken — several grapefruit, and a bottle of gin. That was breakfast, and he'd do it day in and day out. How in the world he managed to function we never knew.

JANN WENNER

The Washington wizards and the gentlemen journalists never saw anything like Hunter. He could hold his own with them, and what he was publishing was funny and original and more right than they ever were . . . and on their own turf. He had access to everything, and it was fun for me to tag along. Somebody from McGovern's campaign said, "There's only two things we read to find out what's going on: the *New York Times* and *Rolling Stone.*" A few years later, William Safire called *Rolling Stone* "the house organ of the Democratic party."

From "Fear & Loathing in the Eye of the Hurricane"
Rolling Stone 113; July 20, 1972

Sick dialogue comes easy after five months on the campaign trail. A sense of humor is not considered mandatory for those who want to get heavy into presidential politics. Junkies don't laugh much; their gig is too serious — and the political junkie is not much different on that score than a smack junkie.

The high is very real in both worlds, for those who are into it — but anybody who has ever tried to live with a smack junkie will tell you it can't be done without coming to grips with the spike and shooting up, yourself.

Politics is no different. There is a fantastic adrenalin high that comes with total involvement in almost any kind of fast-moving political campaign — especially when you're running against big odds and starting to feel like a winner.

As far as I know, I am the only journalist covering the '72 presidential campaign who has done any time on the other side of that gap — both as a candidate and a backroom pol, on the local level — and despite all the obvious differences between running on the Freak Power ticket for Sheriff of Aspen and running as a well-behaved Democrat for President of the United States, the roots are surprisingly similar . . . and whatever real differences exist are hardly worth talking about, compared to the massive, unbridgeable gap between the cranked-up reality of living day after day in the vortex of a rolling campaign — and the fiendish ratbastard tedium of covering that same campaign as a journalist, from the outside looking in.

For the same reason that nobody who has never come to grips with the spike can ever understand how far away it really is across that gap to the place where the smack junkie lives . . . there is no way for even the best and most talented journalist to know what is really going on inside a political campaign unless he has been there himself.

Very few of the press people assigned to the McGovern campaign, for instance, have anything more than a surface understanding of what is really going on, in the vortex . . . or if they do, they don't mention it, in print or on the air: And after spending half a year following this goddamn zoo around the country and watching the machinery at work I'd be willing to bet pretty heavily that not even the most privileged ranking insiders among the campaign press corps are telling much less than they know.

FRANK MANKIEWICZ *was George McGovern's campaign director.*

What impressed me — and indeed continued to impress me — was how opposite he was from the general public's notion. I always thought he was much cleaner than what people thought. He was carefully groomed — clean shirt, clean shaven, short hair, coherent. This was this wild druggie? Not on your life. I'm still not sure. . . . I mean, I've seen enough testimony for the contrary, but I've never quite believed that he was as off the rails as everyone says. I only got that from his writings. He came across as straight, very straight. Sometimes nasty straight, but never wild, never rude.

He had better access to our campaign than any other reporter. He was around, and he was friendly. It was partly a case of no one else treating us seriously at the beginning. But in addition to that, I thought he was the smartest. Someone like Johnny Apple could fill the *New York Times* with good stuff. Johnny understood the mathematics of what was happening, but I thought Hunter better understood what was really happening. There wasn't anything that was going to hurt us, because we were outside the pale — and if anything did come up, I would say to Hunter, "Hey, listen — lay off that for a couple of weeks at least."

PAT CADDELL *was the pollster for the McGovern campaign.*

Hunter was very hands-on; he was doing great stuff. But he was also covering the whole campaign, so he would be down in Florida with Muskie — where the famous incident with the Boohoo happened.

Hunter had met this guy who borrowed his press pass. The next morning, Hunter was supposed to be on the Muskie train in Florida, but he overslept — he blamed the Muskie people for not waking him up — and this guy, who Hunter referred to as "the Boohoo," got on the train with Hunter's credentials and started attacking everyone on the train and taunting Muskie at every stop. Hunter was still asleep back in Palm Beach.

JANN WENNER

Monte Chitti, who was a friend of Hunter's, was the Boohoo. Hunter was not about to run amok on the train himself. He was too much part of the press corps and knew that he had to maintain that access. He was dead serious about his mission.

It was also totally up Hunter's alley to let some live mice out or give his press pass to some drug crazy and see what would happen and then later say, "Gee, I don't know how he got my pass. It was lying around, and he must have stolen it." Of course, people would always believe Hunter, but you knew. Why would you believe Hunter? Of course he gave Chitti that credential.

PAT CADDELL

For the first couple of primaries he was all over the place because nobody thought that we were going to win; even though *Rolling Stone* was basically for McGovern, we were seen as a somewhat hopeless cause. But when we emerged, Hunter really became full-time, and that's when he became really immersed, when he wasn't making the famous California trips to Humphrey's campaign.

Hunter didn't act like a maniac, unless you hung out with him off the record. Maybe it showed up in his writing, but in terms of politics, Hunter worked his ass off to understand what was going on. He saw things that nobody else was seeing. He came to it with an eye and an understanding that this was a historical moment, that something was happening, and there was a war, and this was somehow the crucible of what was going on. He knew he didn't know about politics, so he insisted that you explain every detail, and he would pick it up like that. That's why he was so much better informed than most of the political reporters traveling on the campaign, because they were covering it by the book — and Hunter didn't have the book. He was making one up.

✛ 🐃 ✛ 🐃

JANN WENNER

Hunter quickly became a guiding spirit of the magazine during the course of the '72 campaign trail, but that came with a price. In virtually every issue where something of his would appear, the deadline would be totally butchered. Everything and everybody was focused on these biweekly three- or four-day sieges. I was galvanized. My God, that smell, that acrid odor of the stylus on that treated paper coming out of the mojo wire just outside my office door . . .

All of this was punishing on the staff. I didn't give it a lot of attention, really, until the production department put together a nasty memo insisting that I try to get Hunter's copy in on time. I forwarded it, and his reply was basically "Sorry, but fuck you people if you can't tough it out." Some of them were working twenty-four to thirty-six hours straight on the final closing, so their humor was stretched a little thin.

Hunter loved having a place that was devoted to him from the top to the bottom. The whole operation that we had at *Rolling Stone* was in great part crafted toward receiving his material, getting it in shape, and publishing it on his schedule. He had his own private newsletter with a readership of a million.

SARAH LAZIN *was an editorial assistant at Rolling Stone in 1971.*

I was trying to fact-check Hunter's stories from the campaign. They'd usually start coming in on Saturday night around seven, and I'd be there until early in the morning standing over the mojo machine. We all decided that in order for this to be taken seriously as real journalism — and to get the humor, and the irony, and the exaggeration of it — it had to be fact-checked thoroughly. If you got someone's age wrong and someone else's quote all wrong, the whole thing could be perceived as fiction, which it wasn't. It was as honest and as true as anything anybody had ever said about Nixon or any of the candidates.

Problem was, his copy came in so late that it was really, really, really hard to check it. I had discussions again and again with the editors and with Jann about "How do we fact-check Hunter Thompson?" He had one piece where he wrote that Ed Muskie was addicted to Ibogaine. How do we check that?

Fear & Loathing: *CORRECTIONS, RETRACTIONS, APOLOGIES, COP-OUTS, ETC.*
Unpublished memo from Hunter to Jann; 1972

For various reasons that probably don't mean shit to anybody but me, I want to get straight — for the record, as it were — with regard to some of the most serious of the typographical errors that have marred the general style, tone & wisdom of "Fear & Loathing."

I have tried to blame various individuals in the San Francisco office for these things, but each time we trace one of the goddamn things back to its root, it turns out to have been my fault. This is mainly because I never seem to get my gibberish in to El Ropo [Charlie Perry, aka "Smokestack El Ropo"], who has to cope with it, until the crack of dawn on deadline day — at which time I have to get him out of bed and keep him awake by means of ruses, shocks and warnings while I feed my freshly typed pages into the Mojo Wire, which zaps them across the nation to El Ropo at the rate of one page every four minutes.

This is a fantastic machine, and I carry it with me at all times. All I need is the Mojo wire and a working telephone to send perfect Xerox copies of anything I've written to anybody else with a Mojo Wire receiver . . . and anybody with $50 a month can lease one of these things. Incredible. What will they think of next?

The only real problem with the Mojo wire is that it tends to miss or skip a line every once in a while, especially when we get one of those spotty phone connections. If you're playing New Speedway Boogie in the same room, for instance, the Mojo machine will pick up the noise and garble a name like "Jackson" so badly that El Ropo will get it as "Johnson" . . . or "Jackalong" . . . or maybe just a fuzzy grey blank.

Which would not be a problem if we had time to check back & forth on a different phone line — but by the time El Ropo can assemble my gibberish & read it I am usually checked out and driving like a bastard for the nearest airport.

So he has to read the whole thing several times, try to get a grip on the context, and then decide *what I really meant to say* in that line that came across garbled.

This is not always easy. My screeds tend to wander, without benefit of such traditional journalistic landmarks as "prior references" and "pyramid reverse-build foundations."

— 000 —

I still insist "objective journalism" is a contradiction in terms. But I want to draw a very hard line between the inevitable reality of "subjective journalism" and the idea that any honestly subjective journalist might feel free to estimate a crowd at a rally for some candidate the journalist happens to like personally at 2000 instead of 612 . . . or to imply that a candidate the journalist views with gross contempt, personally, is a less effective campaigner than he actually is.

Hubert Humphrey, for instance: I don't mind admitting that I think sheep-dip is the only cure for everything Humphrey stands for. I consider him not only a living, babbling insult to the presumed intelligence of the electorate, but also a personally painful mockery of the idea that Americans can learn from history.

But if Hubert meets a crowd in Tampa and 77 ranking business leaders offer him $1000 each for his campaign, I will write that scene exactly as it happened — regardless of the immense depression it would plunge me into.

No doubt I would look around for any valid word or odd touches that might match the scene to my bias. If any of those 77 contributors were wearing spats or monocles I would take care to mention it. I would probably follow some of them outside to see if they had "America — Love it or Leave it" bumper stickers on their cars. If one of them grabbed a hummingbird out of the air and bit its head off, I think it's safe to say I would probably use that. . . .

. . . but even if I did all that ugly stuff, and if the compilation of my selected evidence might pursuade a reader here and there to think that Humphrey was drawing his Florida support from a cabal of senile fascists . . . well . . . I probably wouldn't get much argument from any of the "objective" journalists on the tour, because even the ones who would flatly disagree with my interpretation of what happened would be extremely reluctant to argue that theirs or anyone else's was the flat objective truth.

On the other hand, it's also true that *I* will blow a fact here and there. A month ago I wrote that a registered independent in Colorado could vote in either the GOP or Democratic primary — which was true last year, but the law was recently changed. Somebody wrote to curse me for that one, and all I can do is apologize. In 1970 I knew every clause, twist, sub-section & constitutional precedent that had anything to do with voter-eligibility laws in Colorado. (When you run for office on the Freak Power ticket, the first thing you do is learn *all* the laws.) But when I moved to Washington and got into the Presidential Campaign I stopped keeping track of things like that.

The only other serious error that I feel any need to explain or deal with at this time has to do with a statement about Nixon. What I wrote was: "There is still no doubt in my mind that he could never pass for human. . . ."

But somebody cut the word "never." El Ropo denies it, but our relationship has never been the same. He says the printer did it. Which is understandable, I guess; it's a fairly heavy statement either way.

Is Nixon "human?" Probably so, in the technical sense. He is not a fish or a fowl. There is no real argument about that. Most juries would accept, prima facie, the idea that the President of the United States is a *mammal*.

He is surely not an Insect; and not of the lizard family. But "human"

Hunter S. Thompson, age eight, in his hometown of Louisville, Kentucky. *(Courtesy of the Hunter S. Thompson Estate)*

Hunter with brothers James (center) and Davison (right).
(Courtesy of the Hunter S. Thompson Estate)

Airman Second Class Thompson, sports editor and columnist for the Eglin Air Force Base paper, Valparaiso, Florida, 1957. *(Courtesy of the Hunter S. Thompson Estate)*

The young writer at ease in 1959, near his cabin in Cuddebackville, upstate New York. *(© Robert W. Bone)*

Hunter enjoys the scenery from his cabin. He was fired from a nearby small-town daily newspaper after he kicked in a candy machine. *(© Robert W. Bone)*

Hunter with his future wife Sandy Conklin at a Caribbean airstrip. *(© Robert W. Bone)*

Puerto Rico, 1960, the beginning of *The Rum Diary* period. Left to right: Hunter, Peter Flanders, Bob Bone. *(© Robert W. Bone)*

Hunter, Sandy, and their son, Juan, at home in Woody Creek, Colorado. *(Courtesy of the Hunter S. Thompson Estate)*

Hunter reading the paper in a rare quiet moment during his campaign for sheriff of Pitkin County, Colorado. *(David Hiser)*

Hunter awaiting election returns at his campaign headquarters in the Hotel Jerome, Aspen. *(David Hiser)*

He shaved his head so he could call the incumbent sheriff "my long-haired opponent." *(David Hiser)*

Artist Ralph Steadman's
rendering of Raoul Duke
sneaking out of his hotel in
Fear and Loathing in Las Vegas.
(Ralph Steadman)

Hunter and Oscar
Zeta Acosta at
Caesar's Palace in
Las Vegas, 1971.
Oscar was the model
for Dr. Gonzo, the
"300-pound Samoan
attorney," in *Fear and
Loathing in Las Vegas.*
(Cashman Photo)

Rolling Stone editor
in chief Jann Wenner
and Hunter plot
presidential
campaign coverage
during a
Big Sur editorial
conference in 1971.
Nobody got around
to asking Thompson
why he wore a
hospital gown. *(©
Annie Leibovitz / Contact
Press Images)*

On the campaign trail with Senator George McGovern. The two men became lifelong friends. *(© Annie Leibovitz / Contact Press Images)*

Relaxing at Owl Farm with one of his Dobermans, 1972. *(Courtesy of Jann S. Wenner Archives)*

Stalwart collaborator and coconspirator Ralph Steadman, at Jann Wenner's home in San Francisco, 1973. (© *Annie Leibovitz / Contact Press Images*)

Hunter exhaling a mouthful of lighter fluid as Jann attempts to make a point in his New York home, 1976. (© *Annie Leibovitz / Contact Press Images*)

The political wizards of *Rolling Stone* visit Doe's Eat Place in Little Rock, Arkansas, to grill a presidential candidate. Left to right: William Greider, P. J. O'Rourke, Jann Wenner, Hunter Thompson, and Governor Bill Clinton. *(© Mark Seliger)*

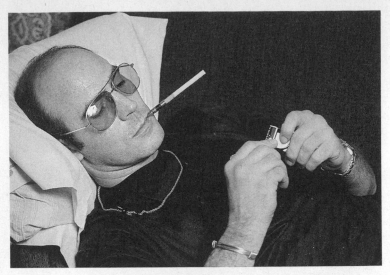

Relaxing at Owl Farm in the 1980s. *(© Lynn Goldsmith)*

Totally in his element, Woody Creek, Colorado, 1987.
(© Annie Leibovitz / Contact Press Images)

Settling a score with his old adversary, an IBM Selectric typewriter, Woody Creek, 1989. *(© Paul Chesley)*

Hunter's kitchen at Owl Farm was his command center, where he worked, entertained friends, and generally held forth. *(© Paul Harris / Pacific Coast News)*

Outside his home in Woody Creek, where he lived for more than three decades, 1990. *(© Paul Harris / Pacific Coast News)*

Hunter at the Woody Creek Tavern in 1990. He was a regular at the bar. *(Dean Krakel / Rocky Mountain News / Polaris)*

Hunter and his bullet-riddled portrait of Jann Wenner, replete with fake blood. *(Deborah Fuller)*

Deborah Fuller was Hunter's steadfast assistant and good right arm for more than twenty years. Hunter is on his way to *Rolling Stone's* twenty-fifth anniversary party. *(Courtesy of Deborah Fuller)*

At home in 1993. The skull pin in the hat was a gift from Keith Richards. *(William J. Dibble Jr.)*

Hunter and Laila Nabulsi at ease, early nineties. She would eventually produce the movie version of *Fear and Loathing in Las Vegas*. *(Ralph Steadman / Courtesy of Laila Nabulsi)*

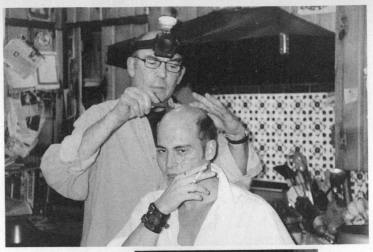

Making sure
Johnny Depp
looks authentic
as he prepares
to portray
Raoul Duke on
the big screen.
(Deborah Fuller)

Johnny Depp, clutching calla
lilies, and Hunter at the
New York premiere of the
film *Fear and Loathing in
Las Vegas,* June 19, 1998.
(Albert Ferreira / Globe Photos)

Taking a spin with
son Juan and one-
year-old grandson
William in Woody
Creek, 1999.
(Deborah Fuller)

Hunter and good friend Pitkin County sheriff Bob Braudis at the Jazz Aspen Snowmass Labor Day Festival 2000. *(Steve Mundinger)*

Hunter and Anita Thompson on their wedding day, April 23, 2003. *(Louisa Davidson)*

Hunter shows Will the tools of his trade. He doted on his grandson but was shy about admitting it. *(Deborah Fuller)*

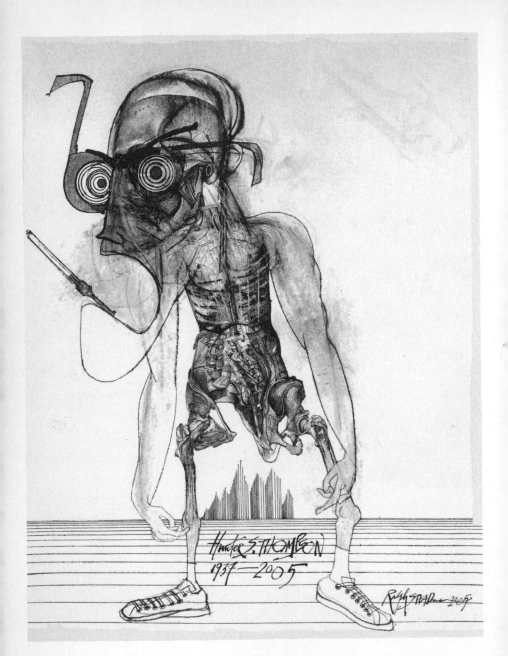

Ralph Steadman's final tribute. *(Ralph Steadman)*

is something else. A mammal is not necessarily human. Rodents are mammals. An extremely intelligent Bayou Rat called "Honeyrunner" was once elected to the city council in DeFuniak Springs, Florida. Nobody called him "human," but they say he did okay on the job.

It would take a really sick and traitorous mind to compare the President of the United States to a Bayou Rat, regardless of intelligence. So maybe El Ropo was right. By almost any standard of responsible journalism the President must be referred to as "human." It is one of those ugly realities — like the Amnesty Question — that we will all have to face & accept.

— 000 —

The only other thing I had in mind was to say — to all the people who keep writing me those vicious goddamn letters — is that I get a really fine high boot out of reading them. I read them all, screening the best ones for good lines to steal. About a week ago I got one from somebody in Chicago, calling me a "Crypto-faggot Bulldog-nazi Honky-fascist Pig."

I can really get behind a letter like that. But most of the stuff is lame. I'm not running a goddamn "Dear Abby" service here. Anybody with problems should write to David Felton, Bleeding Heart Editor, at the San Francisco office. He's *paid* to get down in the ditch with lunatics. And he *likes* it.

But I have more important things to do.

Politics.

Human Problems are secondary.

— 30 —

JANN WENNER

People used to ask me how much of Hunter's stuff was true. Really, 90 percent of those things that he said or things he did were true. And if you believed the other 10 percent, God bless you. I'm not about to change your mind about it.

PAT CADDELL

In November — the issue where *Rolling Stone* used Tom Benton's poster of "re-elect the president" with swastikas in the eye sockets of the skull — what Hunter wrote below that skull was some of the most brilliant stuff ever written about politics. At the top he started, "On Tuesday, November 7th, I will get out of bed long enough to go down to the polling place and vote for George McGovern. Afterwards, I will drive back to the house, lock the front door, get back in bed, and watch television as long as necessary." It goes directly to the sadness of it.

From "Ask Not for Whom the Bell Tolls . . ."
Rolling Stone *121; November 9, 1972*

Nixon represents that dark, venal and incurably violent side of the American character that almost every other country in the world has learned to fear and despise. Our Barbie doll president, with his Barbie doll wife and his box-full of Barbie doll children is also America's answer to the monstrous Mr. Hyde. He speaks for the Werewolf in us; the bully, the predatory shyster who turns into something unspeakable, full of claws and bleeding string-warts, on nights when the moon comes too close. . . .

At the stroke of midnight in Washington, a drooling red-eyed beast with the legs of a man and a head of a giant hyena crawls out of its bedroom window in the South Wing of the White House and leaps 50 feet down to the lawn . . . pauses briefly to strangle the Chow watchdog, then races off into the darkness . . . towards the Watergate, snarling with lust, loping through the alleys behind Pennsylvania Avenue and trying desperately to remember which one of those 400 iron balconies is the one outside Martha Mitchell's apartment. . . .

Ah . . . nightmares, nightmares. But I was only kidding. The President of the United States would never act that weird. At least not during football season. But how would the voters react if they knew the President of the United States was presiding over "a complex, far-reaching and sinister operation on the part of White House aides and the Nixon campaign organization . . . involving sabotage, forgery, theft of confidential files, surveillance of Democratic candidates and their families and persistent efforts to lay the basis for possible blackmail and intimidation."

"Ominous" is not quite the right word for a situation where one of the most consistently unpopular politicians in American history suddenly skyrockets to Folk Hero status while his closest advisors are being caught almost daily in nazi-style gigs that would have embarrassed Adolph Eichmann.

SANDY BERGER *was a speechwriter for McGovern.*

My most vivid memory of him is the day after the campaign. We had spent election night in Sioux Falls, South Dakota . . . or Sioux City, South Dakota . . . or Rapid City, South Dakota. In any case, it was South Dakota. It was a devastating loss, obviously — forty-nine states — and we all flew back to Washington on the charter the next day. My wife came to meet the plane, and right as we arrived back in town, Hunter said, "Yeah — I need a ride," and so did a couple other people. So we all packed into the car with my wife, and I started driving out of National Airport when somebody said, "Oh, my God! I left my suitcase on the tarmac." I made a U-turn in the road going out from the airport — up over a curb and over a concrete island — and started driving back to the airport. If you read *Fear and Loathing on the Campaign Trail,* Hunter took that little snapshot and used it as a metaphor to show the nihilism and despair of the McGovern campaign staffers after the campaign. Here I was basically prepared to kill myself to go back and get a suitcase. I think it's a good example of Hunter's technique, which was to take some event and then explode it into a story line that was compatible with the story already in his own mind. We were defeated, despairing and dispirited. Well, actually we were just exhausted. It was the quickest way to get back to the airport, right? But for Hunter, what I did was a kind of existential act at that point.

GEORGE MCGOVERN

He flew into Washington the week after the campaign ended. His book was almost done the day we voted, but he had a couple more questions he wanted to put to me, so I had one final interview with him in my office. He teared up more than once. He took it very hard. There was no question in my mind that he grieved over it, and that he was serious. He alternated between a sort of sweet fury and genuine grief. He couldn't even stand to look at me.

PAT CADDELL

A year later, we all had a party at the McGovern house in Washington. It was a big one. Afterward, Hunter and I and Warren Beatty were in this car, and Hunter was racing down the street with a bottle of Wild Turkey between his legs. He literally drove a police car off the road. "Hunter, that was a cop!" I said. He went, "Holy shit!" And out the window goes the bottle.

We finally pulled up to this bar and started to get out to go inside — except Hunter forgot to put the car in park, and the car rolled straight into a row of motorcycles owned by these tough-looking Puerto Ricans. Hunter started jabbering something apologetic to these guys, and we all jumped back in the car and raced deep into the Maryland suburbs and ducked into a driveway to hide from the cops. They were still constructing I-95, and somehow Hunter managed to get into the construction — he said it was some kind of shortcut — and almost drove off a half-finished bridge into the Potomac. He was jumping medians and scaring the shit out of everybody. I remember looking at Warren, who was whiter than a sheet.

That evening — or morning — ended with Hunter driving to Bethesda Naval Hospital, where Nixon was being treated for viral pneumonia, and walking up to the front desk with his fairly official-looking kit bag with him and saying to the receptionist, "I'm Dr. Hunter S. Thompson, here to treat the president."

TIM FERRIS

I spent a lot of time with Hunter at his home and in various hotels and all that, and certainly he was a theatrical guy, but I don't think he was playing up his alcohol or drug use. It was constant. I mean, I've never been with him in any setting in which he wasn't drinking or taking drugs — well, very rarely. The exception is when we used to work out down at the Watergate Hotel gym. We did some weight-lifting, but Hunter always liked swimming more than anything else, so we did that. And then we'd go up to that little Watergate bar and get ripped.

Around that time, I was leaving New York to go on tour with David Bowie. Jann was in New York, and we had had a meeting. I had my bag with me because I was on my way to the airport, and Jann fired me — which happened periodically in downturns. When I called Owl Farm, Sandy answered and said that she had just spoken to Hunter, who was in his room at the Watergate. I asked her how things were going, and she said, "Pretty well, but we're worried about money. That's what we were just talking about. We only have four hundred dollars left in the bank and we don't know where any more money is going to come from." We talked a bit more, and then I hung up and immediately called Hunter. He said, "How's it going?" I said, "I just got fired by Jann." And Hunter said, "Do you need any money? I can lend you four hundred dollars."

GEORGE MCGOVERN

I thought *Fear and Loathing on the Campaign Trail* was remarkable. You may have heard Frank Mankiewicz's famous quote from when that book came out — "It's the most accurate and least factual book about the campaign" — and there was some truth in that. He had a lot of insights that I think were on target. There are some that weren't, but that's true of everything.

After the campaign, every now and then I'd get a big scrawled fax from him. He might write six words on an entire sheet of paper — just goofy stuff that I couldn't make sense of sometimes. The scrawl would cover the top of the page and then run to the bottom, usually at a forty-five-degree angle. I saved them. He'd call me once in a while, and I called him. Sometimes I'd get up in the morning and there'd be a message that he had called, and the message box would indicate that it came in at four o'clock in the morning.

PAUL SCANLON

I was Tim Crouse's editor on "The Boys on the Bus" article. And a year or so after both of their stories had come out, Hunter was the toast of everything in sight. There'd be these journalism conventions in New York and Washington that a bunch of us would fly out to. I'd meet all these guys from the Washington press corps, and they would go on about, "Oh, my best friend Hunter . . ." — Hunter this, Hunter that. I finally ran into Hunter, and I said, "Jesus Christ! Everybody in the Washington press corps is your best friend!" He just gave me that kind of half-cocked smile.

SANDY THOMPSON

A long time ago, he really didn't want to become the gonzo person. He wanted to be read and thought of as a serious human being, a serious writer. And what happened was different. I mean, *Fear and Loathing in Las Vegas, Hell's Angels* — he rewrote and rewrote and rewrote and rewrote those. He had a lot of pride in those. With *Fear and Loathing on the Campaign Trail,* things were beginning to get harder for him.

There were editors who would piece things together for him, which he had never had to do. He didn't want editors to even touch his stuff, never mind fit the pieces together and then string transitions to hold those things together. That's not what he had meant for himself.

JANN WENNER

You had to get him started writing his pieces on location from wherever he was on assignment. He had to get the feel and the groove going there — and it usually began with the weather. He had to describe what the town looked like, what the motel looked like, if the rain was beating down, what the waves were doing. If he didn't get the geography and the weather established and get at least some chunk of the narrative going, you were in trouble. You had to keep him there until that was done, so that meant sending him the Selectric typewriter and the mojo wire. Even if the deadline wasn't for two months, you had to keep an ongoing writing schedule with him. You couldn't go away and then come back and say, "Give me your pages in a week."

He could always sniff out the fucking deadline. Over all the years, every single time I'd try to give him a slightly fake deadline — and sometimes a double-fake deadline, knowing he'd sniff out the first one — he would always find out.

He needed his audience and his editor there on the spot, and it was too much for any one person to handle. There was always going to be me and some combination of people on every piece. No matter how hard I tried to delegate the work — even knowing full well I'd come back and do the final edit — he wouldn't let me off the hook for more than a day or two before people were running to me and I would have to step in and start orchestrating everything.

A few days into a piece, I'd say, "Well, we have a lead. We're cool with the lead." I'd start writing headlines and subheds for various sections, and Hunter would start labeling the inserts by letter combinations. Sometimes he'd name the inserts if the letters weren't working. Early on, it would just be "Insert A" or "Insert B." Later we'd start getting to "Insert ZZ" or "Insert X-Ray." You always had to save time for him to write transitions. He needed someone to organize that for him because he was always so up against the deadline he didn't have time to do it himself.

You needed to know his rhythm, and you needed to know your pharmacology — what he was taking, what you shouldn't be feeding him or allowing him to eat. In addition to me managing the whole show, there would be an assistant here, and at his end he had his assistant, so there were at least four people in this drama.

Hunter understood what I was trying to do, which was give him somebody to talk to at two in the morning because I didn't want to do it, but until I entered the picture, he really wasn't going to hit fourth gear. He'd do the basics, but he wasn't really going to do the big stuff unless it was going to inconvenience me. Just knowing that I was at the other end, pacing around and being kept up and troubled, was meaningful and necessary in his mind. His attitude was that if I was going to get the fine stuff, I had to pay for it, or show how much I loved it, and we were in this together, no matter the hour; buy the ticket, take the ride.

You'd start laying the whip on a week or two weeks before the final deadline. You had to have a feel for just how much physical stamina everybody had left. You had precious natural resources here — limited natural resources — and you wanted to use them wisely. You knew that on deadline there were still going to be pieces of the story missing that you weren't going to be able to publish because he still hadn't written them. He'd *planned* to write them, but you had to say, "In the three days we have left — in the seventy-two hours of writing skill, drug stamina, and sheer physical strength on his part — we will have to do triage here."

You had to know when to say, "Okay, look, Hunter. It's time for 'the Wisdom,' " which was essentially the wrap-up where he reached his conclusions and imparted his vision. Sometimes he'd write this very early. In the early days, the end of the piece might be the first thing he had written. Usually he would start off in the middle somewhere with a scene that he liked and that he was comfortable with, that he knew he could get flowing right. He'd write that and then see where it went. It all depended on how much time he had.

You also had to know how late you could keep him up. About three days was the limit. Things would get going at a certain point, and you just had to have a feel for where he was. Had he produced eight pages? Was he on a good streak? Okay, let's keep him up, keep him writing. At some point when the productivity started to fall and things were slowing down, you'd let him rest. But all the time you knew that in the end, like a racehorse, you were still saving strength to pull out a final twelve-hour stretch, straight through to the last word.

SANDY THOMPSON

What happened, of course, was more about the image. And the way it turned out was absolutely not the life he dreamed.

JANN WENNER

There was a divide, I thought, with people who entered his life later on. There was always this phenomenon of people who wanted to be closer to Hunter than anybody else. People would tell me how to work with Hunter, how to get him to write, the right way of handling him. I did not pay attention, but Hunter loved all that. That came with the fame and the groupies. Hunter wanted it, and everybody was getting something from the transaction, so I just smiled quietly.

There are people, and he was one of them, who when they smile at you — Hunter had that smile — it's as if the sun has come out, and you feel the warmth of it. A lot of charismatic people have that. Hunter invited you inside his conspiracy to have fun. Everybody felt very special, like they had some kind of moment or special understanding with him. I never begrudged anybody their time with Hunter.

JANN WENNER

The first time he pulled the fire extinguisher trick on me was one night in 1973 in my house in San Francisco, when we were sitting around taking acid. It was two or three in the morning; the fire was going; Joni Mitchell was on the stereo. Hunter was fussing around doing something, and I was listening to the music and quietly drifting. Hunter took this fire extinguisher sitting in the corner, aimed, and opened up on me. It's like an explosion of chalky dust, and it's quite unpleasant, especially if you have a head full of acid. It's the only time I really got angry at him and told him to get the fuck out of the house. I think he was truly shocked by my reaction, but of course he loved that too, and he reveled in the story for years.

Later that year I was at Owl Farm, and it was Sunday afternoon, and what do we do on a Sunday afternoon? Take acid and watch the football game, of course. I was never a football fan, but now I've got a head full of acid once again, and I'm looking at the game very intensely and listening to Hunter carrying on, and I start thinking, "Wow — these guys are like gladiators! They're like modern-day gladiators! Like the Roman games." I had what seemed like this wonderful, original insight, and it was "Eureka, Hunter, I've got the next story," and I laid out this whole theory of the Roman empire. Well, obviously it was no new insight of any kind. But Hunter was stringing me along, knowing exactly where it was going — he being a football freak. He was on the verge of a dream assignment: writing about the NFL. He was just reeling me in.

MARGOT KIDDER, *the actress, and her then-husband Tom McGuane met Hunter in early 1974.*

Tom and I went over to meet Hunter at his hotel in Miami, where he was supposed to be writing a piece about the Super Bowl. He'd set up his mojo machine on a table, but of course he hadn't written his article. So he said, "You — get under the table." So we got under the table and pulled the plug in and out of this thing while Hunter fed pages that he'd just typed a bunch a random letters on, and then he got on the phone to Jann saying, "I don't know what's the matter with the god-damn machine you sent me — it's not working. I'm trying to get the pages through." And I remember thinking, "Holy mackerel — here's a live one."

PAUL SCANLON

We had a moment, which I regretted, after Hunter had finished the campaign trail book, around the time he was working on "Fear and Loathing at the Super Bowl." We were sitting at Jerry's bar, and I had the temerity to lecture Hunter, saying it was time to maybe take some time off, drop the Raoul Duke persona, lay off the drugs and the booze a little bit, and get back to being the guy who wrote *Hell's Angels*. And he stared at me while he reached into his safari jacket and pulled out a tab of blotter acid. He looked me in the eye, put it in his mouth, and started chewing.

JANN WENNER

The continuum of Hunter's writing was practically seamless, except perhaps for the Super Bowl. Watergate extended and continued this ongoing assignment he had covering politics, and Hunter could extend his anti-Nixon obsession that dated back at least to 1968 in an even darker and deeper way.

Hunter expressed many times that there were similarities in our re-lationship and that of the cofounders of *Time:* I was Henry Luce, who got wealth and empire, and he was Briton Hadden, the genius who died young. He and I wanted to use *Rolling Stone* to get the youth vote out and to put our people in charge of the country — an extension of the sheriff's race, in a sense. We had this common political agenda that we were working on together, and Hunter felt he was also, to some degree, advising me on how to run *Rolling Stone*.

Hunter could have run the place himself. He was smarter than everybody. He had a good grasp of strategy and where people were going. He had an ability to think two or three steps ahead, or to look at the other person and their interests and their needs and what they'd want out of the situation so he could anticipate that, much like a lawyer.

I looked to him for advice. He gave me quite a few simple but profound insights about being a leader, what the nature of that was. But I also learned never to hire a friend of Hunter's. I tried several times. I knew all of them and I became friendly with a lot of them, but I should never have done any business with those that I did.

CHAPTER SEVEN

Failed Deadlines and a Failed Marriage

A lot of us who knew him well were concerned about the excess and the self-destructive behavior. So I'd say a few words like, "Hunter, I'm worried about you." But you usually only did it once, because Hunter always had an answer: "It's my life, my decision . . . it's how I make my living."

JACK NICHOLSON, *the actor, is a part-time Aspen resident.*

One of the first times I met him, he pulled out a gun in the middle of a house. And me, I'm not that relaxed in that kind of situation. It was out at Monte Chitti's house, and he was quizzing me: "Anybody who can say what *this* is . . . ?" He was holding a round disk that looked like a cross between a hockey puck and an alarm clock, and he was curious if anybody could guess its use. It was a pacemaker. That was when he pulled out this gun. Me and a friend of mine jumped out the window, because guns can go off — I never look at them any other way than that.

ANJELICA HUSTON *is an actress.*

Jack and I used to stay with Bob Rafelson in those first couple of years, '73 and '74, but by the next year or two, Jack had bought a place and we were living there. Aspen then was a place that didn't have a lot of prejudgment. It was a kind of free-for-all — and a great free-for-all.

The first time I met Hunter was at a New Year's Eve party at Abatone restaurant in Aspen. There were a lot of drugs going around. I was sitting in a booth with Jack and a bunch of other people, and this guy came over and punched out the lightbulb from this hanging lamp above our table. The light and the bulb just kind of exploded and rained shards of glass down over these naked Cornish game hens on our plates. Nobody was eating them anyway. I've never been one to enjoy overt displays of violent behavior, but he would do these things with a smirk on his face. I don't think he was interested in my reaction per se, but in a general reaction.

I don't remember a lot of discussion that night. It was pretty much him going around and punching out the lightbulbs all over the restaurant, which was not really the way for him to endear himself to somebody — or to a group at large — but everybody was very tolerant and said, "Oh, that's Hunter." So my first impression of him was that he was a bit of a loose cannon, a little dangerous . . . and I must say that my opinion didn't change or alter over the years.

Jack's known as a wild man, but actually he's quite firmly planted, and a Taurus. He stands pretty steady on the Earth. Being around Hunter would have completely debunked that wild-man idea about Jack, because I think by comparison he was mild and very stable.

I don't know if I ever "wanted" to be at Owl Farm. Hunter always had a lot of work going on — the television was on; there were papers everywhere — he always had a lot of notes, data coming in. He was like someone at the controls of a master ship — you always had the idea that this had to be done, and this was urgent. There was a strategic, almost militaristic atmosphere, except that everything was very off-the-wall. It was a little bit like being down the rabbit hole with Alice.

Whether in snow or in summer, Hunter always wore shorts, always had his cigarette holder, always had some kind of fishing hat with one side up. There was that sort of bumbling thing about him. He was very large, and he would kind of lurch, so being around him always contained, for me, the promise of something monumentally scary happening. He mumbled a lot, so I understood maybe 30 percent of what he was saying for a good number of years, but as my ear became attuned, I understood quite a bit more.

BOB BRAUDIS *is the sheriff of Pitkin County, Colorado. He first met Hunter upon arriving in Aspen to ski in 1970.*

I had to learn how to interpret mumblese. When you were with him, it was a lot easier. Over a staticky phone line, at first it was impossible. He could speak the equivalent of a paragraph with no spacing between the words and no punctuation.

WILLIAM KENNEDY

God, those rambles. He would call at four in the morning and start right up, and you couldn't even find a point where you could say, "I have to hang up. I have to sleep." He presumed you were vitally interested in the nuances of his relationship with his agent, whom he had just had a fight with, and how much money was involved and what she did or didn't do, and on and on. Finally I'd have to say, "Shut up, Hunter — I've got to tell you something!"

Sometimes he'd call and you couldn't even understand what he was saying. I would listen to it two or three times on the answering machine and you'd know it was Hunter, but that's about it.

BILL DIXON *managed McGovern's campaign in Wisconsin, Oklahoma, Missouri, and Texas.*

I was the first employee of the U.S. House of Representatives assigned by Peter Rodino to work on the impeachment of Nixon, and

Hunter came out to set up his headquarters in the Washington Hilton for a few months in 1974. There wasn't much written about impeachment of the president, but I had the Library of Congress get me as many books on the subject as they could get their hands on. Hunter arrives, and I go over to meet him that night at the Hilton, and I'm real excited because I've read these four books on presidential impeachment. I walk into his room, and Hunter's got eight books on presidential impeachment. Somehow, between Aspen and his arrival in Washington, he had assembled a better library on presidential impeachment than the Judiciary Committee of the House of Representatives had been able to assemble.

PAT BUCHANAN

When I was working at the White House, Hunter wanted to talk to me. I was too busy during the week, so I told him to come over one Saturday to our Watergate apartment. My wife was a little worried after all the stuff she'd read and heard about Hunter and was asking me how wise I thought it would be to let this kind of, you know, stark raving wild man into our house, but I said, "Well, I'm a pretty fit man — I think I could handle him."

He came over, and we talked for a long time and then we went down to the pool. Hunter was swimming in this pool like a shark, and I was telling him about all the guys from Watergate and what they were like. He wrote it all up and described me as "a half-mad Davy Crockett storming around the ramparts of Nixon's Alamo." Then Chuck Colson, Nixon's special counsel, asked me, "What's his story?" Hunter had written that Colson should be tied by his testicles behind an Olds 88 and dragged down Pennsylvania Avenue. I told Colson that Hunter tended to exaggerate.

PAUL SCANLON

Hunter was trying to crash a cover piece on Nixon's resignation and only had three or four days to do it, and when I left Friday night he was sitting in Jann's office blasting the stereo and looking out the window with his IBM Selectric humming. When I came in the next morning, he was still sitting there — the page was blank, and his cocaine vial was empty. I felt badly for him because you could almost see the drops of blood coming off his forehead.

JOHN WALSH *was the managing editor of* Rolling Stone.

Hunter and I got through the Super Bowl piece and went into the spring of '74, but as the summer progressed and Nixon fell deeper and deeper, it was harder and harder to get articles out of Hunter. Somehow he couldn't bring himself to do it — here was the biggest story for him, the Nixon resignation, and we had all the pages he needed for coverage, and he was in Washington, D.C., and all he could say was "I can't find the drugs. I can't do this." This was almost the epilogue to *Fear and Loathing on the Campaign Trail,* and it was right in front of him — and he couldn't do it.

JANN WENNER

You could think of all of Hunter's political writing up to this point as one unified story — the Nixon story or the struggle over the American dream. He did a couple of pieces which were inspired, but after the campaign was over, Hunter thought, "Well, look — we've met all these people; we've made all these friends, and we can't just let this base of knowledge and *Rolling Stone*'s reputation and credibility and its involvement with this audience and my knowledge of the players go to waste." We wanted to keep the fight going, and he came up with the idea of the Elko conference — which then consumed him and me for another couple of months as we put it together. He nominated his list of people that we would bring to this small desert town of Elko, Nevada, at the

Commercial Hotel, with this giant fifteen-foot-high stuffed polar bear inside the entrance and a low-rent casino for locals. Hunter picked the location.

SANDY BERGER

Jann wanted to convene a meeting in Elko, Nevada, in February 1974 to help define the future of liberalism and the Democratic Party. Jann thought of himself as something like the William Randolph Hearst of his generation, and he was going to gather the best talent he could and stick them out in the middle of no-place, and from that would emerge a manifesto. Hunter was the maestro of the manifesto. So we all went to Elko, which really is the end of nowhere. You go to Reno, and then you just keep going.

JANN WENNER

We got Dave Burke, who was Teddy Kennedy's chief of staff; Adam Walinsky, Bobby Kennedy's speechwriter; a few people from the McGovern campaign: Pat Caddell, the pollster; Rick Stearns, one of the great field organizers; and Carl Wagner, a strategist. I had in the meantime met Dick Goodwin, who had written speeches for John F. Kennedy. I liked him a lot and appointed him Hunter's successor as a political correspondent. His girlfriend at the time, Doris Kearns, came as well. Sandy Berger, who later became Clinton's national security adviser, was also there.

I'm not sure exactly why Hunter picked Elko — maybe because he had driven through there a couple times, and it just appealed to his sense of the absurd: "Let's bring these people to the middle of fucking nowhere, where we will put together a conspiracy that will win the next election." We wanted to put everybody in a place where they could concentrate, negotiate the differences between the McGovern camp and the likely Kennedy campaign to come.

Hunter's symbolic object this time was the tire checker — a heavy two-foot-long wooden baton with a thick metal ring nailed to the end. It was used by truckers to knock the sides of the tires to check air pressure on their eighteen-wheelers, and he distributed one to everybody who attended the conference to use as a kind of personal gavel and totem. I'd conduct the meetings with it. We spent three days going back and forth in all-day sessions in a large suite. Hunter put American-flag decals up on everybody's doors and a huge flag in the conference room. I remember going to pick up Dave Burke at the airport on a *Rolling Stone* charter — a very distinguished, heavy-duty behind-the-scenes political operative, the guy who masterminded Teddy Kennedy's Chappaquiddick response. We'd flown him in from New York City to make some heavy deal with another wing of the party, under our supervision.

SANDY BERGER

Hunter gathered what seemed like a rather copacetic group of people — which turned out to be quite the opposite. Instead of thinking about how we could define the future, the conversation quickly descended into a brutal attack on the McGovern campaign by the Kennedy people. Carl and I were still raw from having gone through this experience, so we lashed back, and this descended into a first-class food fight. And the last thing Hunter was able to do was lead a discussion — you would not hire him as the mediator for a major securities case — so he sank into despair and sank deeper and deeper into his chair. He was trying to get us to talk more about the future, but it just was getting worse and worse.

He went off after the first day of this to a nearby truck stop and bought us each tire irons and then came back and said, "If you're gonna fight, you might as well do some damage."

PAT CADDELL

Elko was Hunter's last moment, when he gave up on everybody. He was so fucking mad — at me and everybody else — because we weren't taking this thing seriously enough about stopping Nixon and the war. He was expecting daily that we would somehow come up with the answer.

JANN WENNER

It was interesting stuff to talk about, but what it boiled down to was that if you want to win an election, you have to have a candidate. A platform, or a big theory, doesn't really count for much. Hunter and I flew back to my house in San Francisco together with a shoe box full of cassettes recorded at Elko and labeled "The Half-Moon Tapes." We listened to some of them, and we started to make plans. I was going to write something and he was going to write something, but in the end it was too much work.

It was a great moment nonetheless. It reflected our crusade to tap both Hunter's talent and *Rolling Stone* itself to set a sweeping agenda, and for the magazine to make a lot of things happen. Of course, the new political dynamic of Watergate soon made all that moot.

SANDY BERGER

I still have the tire iron.

PAT CADDELL

Elko put Hunter off politics for a long time. For almost two years he didn't get involved, and then when Teddy Kennedy was going to run, Hunter reappeared as a Carter fan and beat me into supporting Carter — then blamed me later for supporting Carter. That was a fucking scene you wouldn't believe.

He was also very serious about running for the Senate in '74, when Gary Hart was going to run. I was helping Gary at the time. He hadn't decided to run yet; he was still exploring it. And then Hunter called me one day and he said, "I'm going to run against this Gordon Allott asshole out here in Colorado. Don't you think we should organize a campaign?" This was in '73. And then Gary was going to get in the ring, so Hunter said, "Okay, that's fine. I'm going to run as an independent. I'll help Gary."

It was serious enough at one point that Gary told me that he knew Hunter really well too, and it was clear this wasn't going to work. My point to Gary was "Let's let Hunter figure this out himself." The thing was not to say to Hunter, "You can't do it." That would be, uh . . . a real bummer. So Hunter and I had these conversations about what the campaign would be like. We would talk about how he wanted to hunt Allott down and harass him. He was going to run his ass into the ground. It wasn't a joke. He wasn't the dilettante that people sometimes make him out to be. That would be his defense when it didn't go well, but I'm telling you, in his heart he really was serious, and that's what Hunter was not given credit for.

But once Hunter realized that Gary was serious and was nominated and might win, he dropped out. Hunter liked Gary. He also understood his complications and contradictions, and when Gary was being a horse's ass.

RICHARD GOODWIN *was a speechwriter and adviser to John F. Kennedy, Robert Kennedy, and Lyndon Johnson.*

I saw Hunter all the time in Washington, and then he came up to Ethel Kennedy's house, Hickory Hill, when I was staying there around '74. There's no doubt Hunter liked the Kennedys. Later I brought him up to Jackie's apartment on Fifth Avenue in New York because he'd said he wanted to meet her. He was very quiet and polite and courteous, but I figured one meeting with Hunter was probably enough for her, so that was it. But at Hickory Hill, I'd wake up and look out the window, and there would be Hunter in the swimming pool. I found out later that Ethel was a little worried about Hunter's presence around the kids — but mostly he just swam.

JANN WENNER

He was letting his energies and his talent dissipate. Take his assignment for the Ali-Foreman "Rumble in the Jungle." He should have just written an 8,000- or 10,000-word description of it and been done with it. There were all the characters, and the craziness that was going on in Zaire at that time. It was one of the best sports stories of a decade, and Muhammad Ali was one of his idols. He was from Louisville, and Hunter always said he was some sort of distant relative.

RALPH STEADMAN

Hunter and I were in Zaire for about two weeks. Bill Cardoso was there from the first, and at one point the fight was postponed and we were all given the option to go or to stay, and Cardoso decided to stay. He became an absolute wreck drinking and smoking and developed a vicious cough. I made a drawing of him and I called him Mr. Mandeliman. I've got all the drawings from the trip, and I never used them again because Hunter never filed a single word about the fight, or about Zaire, or about anything.

I couldn't even go to the fight — Hunter had sold our tickets on the day of the fight itself, maybe ten minutes before we were supposed to be there. I watched it on television.

NORMAN MAILER, *the novelist.*

Zaire was fascinating. There were a great many of us writers there who loved prizefights and were absolutely, completely attached to the idea of the fight. It was a very exciting fight, and we'd covered it for weeks. Then Hunter came in, and it was so typical of Hunter: Here was the convocation of experts, and his experience throughout most of his life was that convocations of experts were concentrations of bullshit.

He figured he was going to ace the whole goddamn thing. He had a basic knowledge that he wasn't going to learn more about prizefights in a week or two than the rest of us had already known for years, and so he had to make an end run around us. And what he decided to do was to see the fight with Mobutu, who was the dictator of Zaire. He made a real effort to get together with Mobutu — and failed.

RALPH STEADMAN

I said, "That's it, then, isn't it, Hunter? It's done." And that's when he said, "If you think I came here to watch a couple of niggers beat the shit out of each other, you've got another thing coming." That was Hunter — he was terrible. He said, "I'm not going now. I don't want to see the fucking fight. You can go somehow, Ralph. I don't know how, but watch it on television or something. We didn't come here for that. We're doing something else. I'm trying to find out where the money came from to put this fight on. Not the fight itself. That's not important." All Hunter was interested in was finding out where John Daly — this entrepreneur who was supposed to be the promoter of the fight — had got the money from to put the fight on.

On the night of the fight, Hunter had a big bag of marijuana, and he took a bottle of Glenfiddich I had bought him down to the pool with a bucket of ice and the bag, threw the marijuana into the pool — everyone else was off watching the fight, you know — and dived into the middle of the marijuana and then just hung by the side of the pool, smoking and drinking and loving the whole meaningless nature of it.

I did a drawing of the eighth round when Foreman went down after Ali hit him. I drew the punch. I made it up almost as though I had seen it. I had to.

NORMAN MAILER

The bet he'd made was that the fight would be a bummer, and that he could still ace us even though he'd spent his time swimming when the fight was on. Instead it was one of the great fights of all time, and he was shut out entirely from it.

I saw him on the plane home, and there he was, full of good spirit and knocking down a great many beers in a row. I remember that in terms of his immense adaptability — he'd take huge risks, and if they blew up on him, so what? There was always another risk to take, and he'd move on. But that was probably one of the least successful ventures he went on.

The first time I had met him, years earlier, I saw a totally different Hunter. He was just a young writer on the make and not very interesting — a rather conventional sort of guy. He was sort of doing some journalism and talked to me about his ambitions a little bit. Nothing out of line, nothing unpleasant, but I wasn't that impressed. Afterward, of course, I was most impressed with him, because of his daring, but when I first met him I never would have pictured him being the guy who would break that many shibboleths one after another and take that many chances. Damned interesting — it was like he left one part of his personality behind and got into another.

SANDY THOMPSON

When Hunter was in Kinshasa, I went to see a therapist for the first time. Hunter, of course, was very anti–anything like that. It was ridiculous. He thought there was absolutely no merit to therapy, to psychiatry — none whatsoever. I had tried to get better on my own, and the reason I wanted to get better was really so that I could be better for Hunter. I could maintain for Juan — I thought, anyway, that I could maintain for Juan.

I found a Gestalt therapist, and he saw me for three hours in one session every week for twenty-five dollars — at his place. After the very first time I saw him, I walked outside, and it was a beautiful day in September, and I thought, "Maybe, maybe I'm okay. Maybe I'm okay." I had no self-esteem, no self-worth. I mean zilch. And when I came out of that three hours, my eyes opened and I could feel the air and see the sky — and so I continued to go to him.

Then Hunter got back. I came into the house, and he was passed out on the couch in the kitchen. He had malaria, because of course he had taken too many malaria pills, and he didn't wake up for two days. Then he woke up and he gave us some ivory that he'd stolen and gotten through customs, and then he passed out again for a long time.

PAUL PASCARELLA

Sandy was his wife through thick and thin. One time Hunter and I had a fight about Sandy. I don't want to say what it was exactly, but he wasn't treating her very well. I was living out in Castle Creek and I said, "Sandy, listen — if it gets too intense, come and stay." Hunter went crazy when he found out that I told her that. He said, "I'm going to shoot your horses." I just said, "Fuck you, Hunter. You shoot my horses, I'll just come over and shoot your whole fucking place up." We got into this thing for about a day or two. It didn't go on for too long, and it never really went into action.

JIMMY BUFFETT, *the singer-songwriter, moved to Aspen in the early seventies.*

I lived down-valley, and through a mutual friend, I got invited over to Hunter's house — of course I was a huge fan — and then he came down and saw my show in Denver with a bunch of guys from Aspen, and we just immediately locked in. There was a little bit of a groupie thing for me in the beginning because Hunter was such an outrageous character.

When Hunter and Sandy were fighting like crazy, Hunter called me and said, "I gotta get Juan outta here." I said, "Well, have him come stay with me." He came out and was kind of our cabin boy. I took Juan sailing for a summer on the boat. Things were so crazed in the domestic scene, but there was always a soft side of Hunter that people didn't see. All that other stuff, to me, was a front that Hunter put up because he loved whipping people into shape, but under there was a pretty interesting guy.

MARGOT KIDDER

I got to know two Hunters — and I expect there were about twenty of them. But women got to know a side of Hunter that men didn't, because of that Ernest Hemingway nature of feeling very competitive with other men. They feel a great need to keep their macho up in the presence of other guys. But there was a side to Hunter that I think almost all women who got to know him saw — God knows I saw it — which was a very sad, sweet, lost little boy who was very eager to please.

Hunter and my husband would be strutting around trying to out-peacock and out-drug each other. I used to scream at him, "Don't kill my husband!" After spending these nights having tried to snort as many drugs with Tom as possible, Hunter would come over the following day and just talk to me, being very contrite and very concerned' about my baby, and talking a lot about his son, Juan, and how much he loved him. He'd bought Juan a blowgun, which seemed an odd gift for a five-year-old.

SANDY THOMPSON

When Hunter finally realized I was seeing a therapist, he was very angry. Obviously, for him, if I got well, I would leave him — which is exactly what happened. But on the nights before my appointments, Hunter would try to keep me awake. I'd go downstairs to the basement. He'd follow me. If I'd start to fall asleep, he'd poke me with his elbow to wake me up.

I saw the therapist for six months. Maybe the second or third time, I decided, "I'm not going to do any more acid. I'm not going to do any more coke. I'm not going to do any more . . ." And he said, "Now, calm down, calm down. Just take it easy. I don't want you to go off everything right away." But gradually, I got rid of everything. Alcohol was the last thing to go, and it was the hardest for me.

That was the beginning of my coming out. And after a period of time, I began to get very angry with Hunter. It was so hard for him, because this woman who had adored him, who would have given her life for him, was now looking at him with these eyes that were angry. Where had the love gone? Where had that little girl gone?

I said to him, "When you've held someone's head under water for eighteen years, do you think that when they come up out of the water the first thing they are going to say to you is 'Hi'?" I mean, he understood. At least on some level. It was always hard for me to know — really hard. What was at the core? The bad guy or the good guy?

MICHAEL SOLHEIM

I always liked Sandy. When Hunter and I were in Cozumel when he was working on a story called "The Great Shark Hunt," we got into talking about her. He went so far as to quiz me about whether I was having an affair with her. That really surprised me. Sandy and I were friends, and I'd hold her when she was in tears over stuff that was going on, but I would never do that.

JANN WENNER

I never fully understood how she could absorb all the abuse. We used to work very closely on deadlines — she was typing up clean pages, faxing them to me, keeping Hunter awake, putting him to sleep, everything. You'd always hear him in the background of phone calls, screaming violently — "Goddamn it, Sandy, you fucking dingbat, I am going to tear your fucking throat out . . . ," and so forth, and you'd chuckle a bit and just keep working. You got used to it. Juan stayed with us in the summers, and he was an adorable but submissive kid. Sandy was, bottom line, a very old-fashioned stand-by-your-man gal, despite the hippie-and-drug trappings. We'd have dinner often after they split, and she was still devoted to Hunter — but alive and happy.

SEMMES LUCKETT *managed a restaurant in Aspen in 1974.*

I'm from Mississippi, and I could see that underneath all of that bluster of Hunter's was really a southern man who appreciated manners. He was formal in a weird way. He stood up when women walked into the room.

My mama came to Owl Farm, and he was the perfect gentleman. He would send her copies of *Rolling Stone* whenever he had a piece in it. One day years later, Mother was in a car with my aunt, and I had to drive them to Oxford, Mississippi, to hear William Buckley speak, and my mama was reading Hunter's latest story — which was kind of weird. But then we were in a horrible wreck, a terrible wreck, and my mama was grievously hurt and just bled all over the issue. When she came home from the hospital a couple of weeks later, she had me tell Hunter that she had laid her life on his lines. Hunter sent her a letter, written with silver and gold felt pens. He wrote, "Dear Celeste, Don't worry — we will be in charge in heaven, and we will wallow in fun while settling many scores. Love, Hunter."

JAMES SILBERMAN

Hunter liked people. He wasn't a recluse; he wasn't a misanthrope or any of those things. I think he really liked people. And once he decided you were okay, you were okay from that point on. Unless you did something.

RALPH STEADMAN

When he made an insult, the words he used were perfect. It might have been a long sentence, but it wasn't too long. And it was deadly. It was worse than a double curse — it was a kind of contempt that no one had ever felt before or mentioned to this person to make them understand how awful they were. And the shame they would feel at hearing those words — that was something else that always came with him.

He berated most of his friends a lot, but somehow it was funny. His way of expressing love for people was to be both angry and insulting. I always thought that when he was the most rude to me was when he loved me the most. I guess if he insulted you, he really liked you. But the outrageous dressing-down that he'd give you undermined your whole sense of self-esteem. He would just tear it to bits.

SEMMES LUCKETT

Somebody once said, about my time with Hunter, that I was essentially pulling an oar in the water while Hunter was throwing matches at the wind. There were times I was furious at him. He never hollered at me, though. He was always real good about that.

Hunter had this huge satellite dish. We'd spend all afternoon calling whatever newspapers were in the town of the team we wanted to see to get somebody on the phone. I would say, "Well, look, I'm calling for Hunter S. Thompson" — and somebody there would always know about Hunter — "could you tell me what TV station is broadcasting the game today?" And they'd give me the phone number of the TV station, and then I'd call the TV station and use Hunter's name again, and somehow I'd be able to get to some engineer or somebody to tell me what satellite the game we wanted to watch was going to be on. But it would always be a wonderful time — fueled by massive amounts of everything.

JANN WENNER

You'd see him with drug dealers, politicians, NFL players, musicians, multi-millionaires. Hunter, like everybody else, liked the rich and famous. He liked movie stars. He charmed everybody, and people would cut him extraordinary leeway. He was so damn funny. But one of the things that hurt Hunter was that his legend started to overwhelm him; he started paying too much attention to it, and cultivating it, and brought too many people around him. He liked all the attention, and it got in his way. Fame got in his way.

I think the Uncle Duke thing in *Doonesbury* was bad for him. I told Hunter that he should have sued Garry Trudeau and stopped it. It was a clear appropriation of Hunter's literary property. He used to hate Garry for it, and he used to complain, but at the same time, Hunter allowed that to happen, and in doing so he crossed a bridge that was very hard for him to come back across. In part, that's why his political coverage fell apart: He was now too much a part of that world. His original theory was that he'd go to Washington with no concern about burning bridges. But after a while he became friends with these people, became enamored of his own reputation, and it became difficult for him to work. I don't think he handled it all that well.

JOHN CLANCY

Hunter was always pissed off at Garry Trudeau for the Uncle Duke character. He wanted me to sue him. I told him, "You should be grateful. This guy makes you out to be friendly and nice, basically. You're not."

SANDY BERGER

Around 1974 and '75, there were two convergent events. One was the emergence of Uncle Duke in *Doonesbury,* and the second was a long profile of Hunter done by Sally Quinn in the *Washington Post.* Hunter was outraged — absolutely indignant — about both Sally's piece and the appropriation of his persona by Garry Trudeau without any kind of remuneration. Sally had, in her piece, quoted Hunter as saying something to the effect of, "I don't know why people get so upset about my stuff — three-quarters of what I write I just make up." He said that was defamatory and just wrong, and that he never said any such thing, and that what he wrote was the truth. At this point I was practicing law, and he wanted me to sue Garry Trudeau and Sally Quinn and the *Washington Post.* I listened to him go on for quite a long time and then said, "Well, I don't think those suits would be successful, Hunter." And he said, "Why wouldn't they be successful? It's self-evident!" And I said, "Well, first of all, truth is an absolute defense in defamation" — and he got so angry that he hung up. I didn't hear from him for months.

SALLY QUINN, *a reporter for the* Washington Post, *first met Hunter during the 1972 election.*

He had this little coterie of people following him around, these worshippers. He was like the Pied Piper. He sort of liked that, and it was fun to watch. We had a number of friends in common — Jann and Pat Caddell were among them, and may have introduced us — and we became very friendly right away. I was working for the Style section of the *Post,* covering politics and writing features and profiles, and whenever he'd come to Washington, he'd give me a call. I'd heard about him, so I knew what to expect. And I've always been attracted to renegades. I was not intimidated by his bad-boy reputation. These kinds of guys are always really sweetie pies underneath, and that's what I adored about Hunter.

I dated Hunter for a while. We had a sort of relationship, but it was obviously long-distance, because he'd just blow into town now and again. It was not serious. For me it was just fun, but I adored him. He was the sweetest man I've ever known. He was absolutely adorable.

He was also the most shy person around women that I've ever met. Whenever we'd be together, he'd be absolutely tongue-tied and in a cold sweat he was so nervous. He was a real southern gentleman. He always would open the door for me, and whenever he'd meet me, he'd be standing there with a little bouquet of flowers. There was something so incredibly touching about him. I don't think I've ever been treated as well by anybody as I was by Hunter. On the sidewalk, he would walk on the outside, next to the curb — you know, so that if the horses came by, they wouldn't splash mud on me. "Courtly" is exactly the word I'd use. He used to kiss my hand all the time and pull the chair out when I sat down. I didn't know anybody who did that.

The contrast between the way he was with me and his public persona couldn't have been greater. He was extremely respectful but just really shy and very insecure about himself as a man in a male-female relationship. He didn't have a lot of confidence in himself that way, so all the bluster and the screaming and yelling and whatever — I just found it amusing. He was always much more comfortable talking about his work, and what he was doing, and other people, and politics. When things got personal, he'd just get sweaty and clammy.

He never talked about his wife. It was mostly about political gossip and who was doing what. It was a most exciting time — the war was going on, and Watergate. We had a lot to talk about. He was always pumping me for information. When he threatened to sue me and all that, it was just bluster. I never took any of it seriously — he was just doing a number. Hunter and I were never not friends.

✛ 🐃 ✛ 🐃

JANN WENNER

It just seemed like the natural thing for Hunter would be to move from the story of the impeachment to the next big story about America — the fall of Saigon. I could see it, he could see it, everybody could see it. It was preceded by this frantic attempt to get him over there. All the nuttiness of making arrangements for Hunter to travel or go anywhere was now exacerbated by the desperate endgame situation in Vietnam. Once he got there, I started getting all these somewhat frightening faxes from him asking what he should do. Should he go with the retreating army? Should he make contact with the Vietcong? I had no idea what the right move was. I kept saying, "Hunter, you have to make your own decisions. Talk to people there." And he seemed overwhelmed.

PAUL SCANLON

Hunter and I were supposed to work on "Fear and Loathing in Saigon," which didn't amount to much, just one truncated piece. It was mostly me waking him up at four in the morning, Saigon time.

LOREN JENKINS

"Fear and Loathing in Saigon" should have been his masterpiece. I was crushed, because the fall of Saigon was such a nutty time. The only person that could've written it was Hunter. I was writing for *Newsweek* then, dealing with the classic sort of duh-duh-duh-duh-duh *Newsweek* story, and I kept thinking, "God! I wish I was writing for *Rolling Stone*," because it was just that zany madness that would lend itself to a great *Rolling Stone* story.

It was the end of the war, '75. April 30 was the evacuation, but there was a period of about six weeks before that when it was clear the end was very near. It was just a matter of whether it happened today, or tomorrow, or next week. The South Vietnamese army started crumbling, and refugees started fleeing south, officers were abandoning troops . . . I mean, terrible chaos.

At some point during this time, Hunter called and said, "I'm coming in. What's it like there? What's it all going to be like? Dangerous?" And I said, "Well, shit, it's a *war*. It *is* dangerous, and it's mad." My then wife was in Hong Kong, and Hunter came through Hong Kong on his way over and went to visit her because he knew her, and also to get briefed on what was going on.

I needed money — big money — because we saw that the end was coming, and I had a whole staff, and I didn't know whether we were going to have to buy a plane or how the hell we were going to get out.

So I asked Hunter to go by my office in Hong Kong and pick up forty thousand dollars in crisp hundred-dollar bills. I said, "Be sure to tape it to your body — don't carry it in a bag, because it'll be searched." He landed at the airport, a little nervous, and looked up at this sign which said, "Please declare any foreign cash you bring in over a hundred dollars or you'll be subject to prosecution." But he got through and made it to the Continental Hotel, where I had my office, and asked for a room. I'd asked for them to get him a room, but now they didn't have one. Someone told Hunter to wait until I got back from the front and we'd try to figure it out. When I got back, the guy at the desk said, "Hey, there's some guy looking for you. I think he's from the CIA." The CIA in Vietnam always looked really American, and certainly, running around in a Hawaiian shirt with shorts on was not press or the military.

From the moment he arrived, he was going on about his life insurance. I mean, that's almost all he talked about. "What do you think about flying halfway across the world, going to war, and Jann cancels my life insurance?"

LYNN NESBIT

One day a forty-foot fax unrolled across my office floor — all about Jann and the expenses and "Where is my life insurance?" and "He's canceled it."

JANN WENNER

Hunter always needed a foil — a partner or companion or nemesis of some kind — throughout everything he did. Obviously it was Oscar in *Vegas* and Nixon for much of his political writing. And through all of the long years that we had together, I was the substitute foil whenever there was nobody else around to have a crisis with. I understood it, and I enjoyed it most of the time. There was the schtick about money. If he wanted to have a crisis and complain about something, that would be it — I'd sucked him dry of some amount of money or wouldn't pay his expenses. We understood that to be laughs and fun, and it mostly never concerned me.

The only thing that really did was when he went around saying I canceled his life insurance. Finally I said, "Hunter, if you say that one more time, I'm going to go out on a campus tour and explain how I was the one who came up with the idea that you should have life insurance, and I was the one who named your wife and child the beneficiaries. Let's just put that one to rest, because that's kind of an ugly lie." So we did.

LOREN JENKINS

Eventually he got installed in the Continental Hotel and went out on a trip. I was his patron. There was a lot of suspicion about Hunter S. Thompson. This was the old, boozy presixties generation of correspondents, and they thought he was a freak — a "druggie" and all that. But everybody — all the troops there, all the Americans — was stoned. The war was a druggie's war.

Hunter wanted to go to the front. Basically, you just got in a car, drove until you couldn't drive any further, saw what was happening, and drove back. So he went out with one of our cars — I had all sorts of vehicles and several correspondents and photographers. I think he was with Nick Profitt, one of our correspondents. They loaded up the jeep, and Hunter appeared in the morning with his cooler full of beer, and off they went.

He came back after just a couple of days. There was a curfew every night around seven, and you weren't supposed to be out, but the Continental Hotel — Graham Greene's hotel from *The Quiet American,* this classic French colonial hotel with slow-revolving fans and high ceilings — had an inner courtyard where at night we ate and drank. At this point it was really just the press corps left, and every night after curfew everyone sat around getting drunk and talked about what was happening and wondered what we were all going to do. All these sort of mad debates — "What happens when the North Vietnamese arrive in Saigon?" "Are we gonna stay here? Are they gonna kill us?"

But then after just a couple of days there, Hunter all of a sudden said, "I have to go to Hong Kong," and jumped on some plane. He bought a footlocker full of electronics on Jann's tab — walkie-talkies and all this other stuff — and then flew back [to Saigon]. He was trying to distribute all this stuff, to organize us, and of course everyone else in the press was just sort of, "Who gives a shit?" I don't think anyone took him seriously. I mean, here you've got all these really war-hardened foreign correspondents, and they've done this sort of thing before. We weren't going to carry walkie-talkies and talk to the mother ship.

All this fear-talking, and people at night getting drunk and stoned and ranting and raving about commies with horns on their heads and rumblings on the streets — I think Hunter took it all to heart and thought, "Shit, I don't want to be around for that." Because all of a sudden he said, "I'm gonna go. I've decided that the place to watch all this from is Laos." Well, the last place you wanted to watch it from was fuckin' Vientiane! Laos was the middle of nowhere, clearly out of the picture on anything. But he picked up and left. The last thing I think I said to him was "When this is over, the place to go is Bali." I gave him the address of a little hotel on Sanur Beach called the Tandjung Sari and said, "If I get out of here alive — if I'm not dead in the streets — you can reach me on Sanur Beach."

From "Interdicted Dispatch from the Global Affairs Desk"
Rolling Stone *187; May 22, 1975*

It is 3:55 on a hot, wet Sunday morning in Saigon, and I am out of ice again. It has been raining most of the night and the patio bar here in the Hotel Continental closed early. The paper in my notebook is limp and the blue and white tiles on my floor are so slick with humidity that not even these white-canvas, rubber-soled basketball shoes can provide enough real traction for me to pace back and forth in the classic, high-speed style of a man caving in to The Fear.

This empty silver ice bucket is the least of my problems tonight; all I have to do to get it filled is go out in the darkened hallway and wake up any of the three or four tiny, frail-looking old men in white pajamas who are sleeping uneasily out there on green bamboo mats behind the circular staircase leading down to the lobby. The slightest noise or touch will wake them instantly; and after sleeping outside my room for almost a week, they have learned to live with my nightly ice problem in the same spirit of tolerant fatalism that I have learned to live with the nightly thumping sound of artillery fire outside my window, five or six miles to the south. It is a sound I have never heard before — not even from a safe distance — so I can never be sure if the faraway, deep-rumbling explosions that rattle the ice in my bucket every night are "outgoing" or "incoming."

There has been a notable lack of distant artillery fire tonight — which is probably an ominous sign, because it means the Viet Cong and North Vietnamese troops that already surround this doomed volcano of a city on three sides are no doubt spending these peaceful, early-morning hours rolling their doomsday 130 MM siege cannons into place out there in the mud just north of Saigon's defense line around Bien Hoa and the remnants of what was once the biggest U.S. Air Force base outside the continental U.S. The ARVN 18th Division that was sup-posed to protect Bien Hoa — just fifteen miles north of Saigon, on a four-lane concrete highway — has apparently been ground into ham-burger in the weeklong battle for Xuan Loc. Latest reports from the front, as it were, say that two of the 18th's three regiments no longer exist, for one reason or another, and that the third is down to an effec-tive fighting strength of 500 men.

To: Paul Scanlon, Rolling Stone, San Francisco Telex RS 34 0337
From: Hunter Thompson, Global Affairs Desk, Hotel Continental,
Saigon, April 20, 1975

Everybody here is becoming very edgy and kind of bone-marrow nervous. Advance units of the NVA are now only five miles out of town and they could immobilize the airport at any moment with artillery fire and that would cut us off from all access to the outside world except by Marine helicopters. It's also possible that a rocket could hit at any moment near enough to send me running over to UPI with whatever I have, hoping to get it on the wire before they begin operating under emergency conditions and not using their Telex for anything but their own copy. So if you stop receiving from me and don't understand why, check with UPI and find out if the situation here has turned weird.

Loren Jenkins, the *Newsweek* bureau chief, just sent his local fixer out to the black market to buy us two flak jackets, two helmets and maybe a few bayonets, which are suddenly a hot item here.

I've been trying to buy a revolver, but again for obvious reasons they cannot be had for any price at this time. Some of the press vets are saying we should get some M-16s into this hotel, so the place can be defended — at least until Marine choppers arrive — from rampaging mobs who might figure the last Americans they'll ever have a chance to get even with, as it were, are the 500 or so correspondents trapped downtown in the Continental and the Caravelle. You might also advise Jann that the three-unit, triangulated walkie-talkie system I brought back from Hong Kong is now being used by other press here in the hotel and in the event of a sudden emergency it will definitely be pressed into service by the people in charge of evacuation. . . . We have only two hours left before curfew, and I can't get from here to UPI after nine tonight without risking being shot and the people at UPI have advised me not to take the risk because the ARVN troops and police out there in the street have orders to shoot anybody moving around and ask questions later.

There are a lot of people here who think the ARVN will make a gallant last stand and hold for at least a few days at Bien Hoa before fleeing back into the city. . . . But my own feeling is that the battle for Saigon is already over and once the elite 325th NVA Steel Division starts moving they will not even stop for a joint break until they get all the way into Saigon.

. . . Jesus I just got very repeat very reliable word that things have suddenly changed dramatically for the worse and we can expect the big move on Saigon to begin rolling tonight or tomorrow but I can't give any details via Telex for obvious reasons . . . But you can expect my copy flow to be interdicted, as they say, at any moment from now on and in fact you may have to use this stuff as either the ending for the piece or as some kind of intro/editor's note, explaining why my story sounds so jerky, garbled and unfinished. We are working under extreme tension here.

LOREN JENKINS

Well, the shit came down, the North Vietnamese came into town, and we all evacuated off the roof of the American embassy in helicopters. I spent four days on a carrier in the South China Sea sailing to Subic Bay in the Philippines and made my way through to Bali, Sanur Beach, the Tandjung Sari Hotel. I checked in to a nice little two-story bungalow with the rooms upstairs and a sort of salon downstairs, right on the beach, with a thatched roof, thinking, "War's over, all done."

But on the first night, at about three in the morning, there's this racket and gunfire and loud sounds and explosions. I jumped up — shit, I've been covering the Vietnam war for two and a half years; I'm jumpy! — and there's Hunter, standing down in the salon with his tape recorder blaring. He'd found the Tandjung Sari in the middle of the fucking night and decided to wake me up with these sounds of war.

We spent the next week or ten days on the beach, talking about our Vietnam War, talking about life. Sandy had arrived from Aspen with a jar full of a concoction that was basically organic mescaline. We sat on the beach for a good long time.

It was such a good story. It was a classic story. Hunter was always going to write it — he just never got down to it. It really was my great disappointment.

JANN WENNER

I think maybe he just got frightened in Vietnam. It was the first time that Hunter — coming off the campaign trail with his success and this image of himself as a guy who could handle guns and confront the real danger — had to deal with genuine life-and-death consequences that were far more extreme in every way than what he might have seen on the campaign trail or with the Hells Angels. Compare the Hells Angels to the Vietcong for a moment.

He wasn't a war correspondent, that's for sure. Maybe he didn't have time to recover from Watergate. I don't really know. He left Saigon. I think it was just too much for him. He left town before the story was over and before he could write it. Once he went on vacation — Hong Kong, I think — he just never disciplined himself to write the piece he did have. Like Zaire, he just threw it away.

He couldn't deliver less-difficult things later, like the Grenada invasion, which was a story handed to him on a plate, and the Ali fight. I had a lot invested in it. Why would he float around in the hotel pool in Kinshasa and not go to the fight? These were all serious failures, and it went on for a decade.

JANN WENNER

I guess if you look at any writer of his stature, with that kind of talent, they go through periods when their stuff is genius and periods when their stuff is weak. We tried to put him on another campaign in '76 — he had been down in Georgia a couple of years earlier with

Ted Kennedy and saw Carter give a speech that apparently blew his mind — but he didn't really engage with the Carter campaign.

JIMMY CARTER *is the thirty-ninth president of the United States.*

In 1975, Hunter spent a few days in our home because I was contemplating a presidential campaign. He interviewed me for many hours, tape recording extensive conversations about every conceivable subject, some of which were quite discomforting. Later I learned, with some relief, that he had lost all the tapes.

He tried for another session of interviews after I became a prominent candidate, and my staff tried to schedule certain times for him to fit in with other journalists, but Hunter felt that he should be given top priority in order to replace the lost tapes. He threatened my press secretary, Jody Powell, if he didn't gain immediate access — one night he even built a fire in front of Jody's hotel room door in an attempt to smoke him out.

BILL DIXON

Hunter's intuition and instincts were better than most of the hundreds of members of the national press corps that I've dealt with in the last thirty-four years. Somehow he managed to smell out the truth while others got bogged down in the facts. When no one had ever heard of Jimmy Carter, Hunter went down to cover Carter's Law Day speech in '74 and came back with the only recording of the speech in existence and said, "Listen to this. This guy is the real thing."

JIMMY CARTER

Much later, while my family was skiing at Aspen, Hunter would join us to talk about old times and other places, telling me that he still had my Law Day speech in his automobile and still made everyone listen to it.

JACK GERMOND

In '76, we were covering the Florida primary and staying at a hotel off lower Biscayne called the Four Ambassadors. Hunter was there and called me on the phone one day and said, "Can you come to my room? I've got a problem, and maybe you can help me." So I went to his room, and as it turns out he'd been having a sort of writer's block about Jimmy Carter. He'd heard Carter give this Law Day speech, and it impressed the hell out of him, but he couldn't get started on the piece. I walked into the living room of his suite, and he's sitting there in his underwear with a big iron tub full of ice and Heineken and a bottle of gin and a bunch of grapefruit and a typewriter set up on this table, and all around the room were thirty or forty wadded-up sheets of paper. He'd start a lede for his piece, decide it wasn't any good, and rip it out and ball it up and throw it away. He thought I could help because I knew Carter so well — I knew Carter earlier and better than most people at that time — so we tried to walk through it. I said, "What are you trying to say in this piece?" He said, "I'm trying to say essentially that Carter is a very different kind of cat." I said, "Why don't we start there? 'Jimmy Carter is a very different kind of cat.' What's wrong with that?" And all he could say was "Nah — that isn't quite what I mean!"

He told me that he didn't feel comfortable with the fact that he liked and admired Carter because of that speech. He said it made him feel odd.

DAVID FELTON

I don't think there was an editor at *Rolling Stone* that worked with Hunter after "Fear and Loathing in Las Vegas" that didn't at one point break down in tears. I did myself.

The problem was, when he was on cocaine, from my perspective, he really had a hard time concentrating on his writing. It would be very frustrating to him. He couldn't write more than one sentence that was about the same thing as the previous sentence. He'd be coked up, plus he'd be on uppers and all this other stuff, and he would mojo you, wire you three or four paragraphs, and then you would have to spend the next few hours trying to make the sentences deal with each other by adding some transition words or something like that. He'd be up for three or four straight days struggling with a piece, and you'd have to stay up for that length of time to take the morsels as they came in and work on it, so you didn't have any sleep either. Then he'd crash for a day or two, and you still had to stay up during that time and keep working on what he'd sent you. So basically, during a weeklong stretch you'd gotten no sleep, he'd gotten some, and you were just frayed. The copy department and the art department and the printer would all be waiting for the story, and they'd start getting disgruntled and angry. Right around this time, Hunter would pull some sort of bullshit — he'd make some sort of serious threat or something, and you couldn't take it — and boom: breakdown.

At some point I'd be scolding him, saying, "It's ridiculous. You're just fucking over everybody, even your friends." Then he would calm down, and everything would be okay. It was just a feeling that everybody was being victimized. It was like dealing with a child — and I've been a child myself as a writer, so I know it isn't easy — but you're treating him as delicately as you can because you don't want to get him on a tangent where he's raving instead of writing. At some point *you* end up raving because it's so difficult.

PAT CADDELL

Hunter later blamed Carter for being a disappointment, particularly since he had believed in Carter. But that's why it's so important to understand what it was he saw in Carter. That Law Day speech blew me away when he played a tape of it for me. Carter was speaking from notes. It was Carter talking about justice and about how rich people have justice and poor people don't, and how he had power, and all of them in the audience had power. It was a lot about class issues. That's what turned Hunter on about Carter.

ED BRADLEY *was a Washington correspondent for CBS when he met Hunter in January 1976 in New Hampshire.*

I remember it being cold and snowy, and in some big hall at a campaign event, I saw this guy in the back of the room wearing a silver jacket with "Porsche" spelled out down the sleeves, and I knew it was Hunter. He had the cigarette and, well, Hunter was Hunter. At some point, I think we ended up in the same bathroom, and we introduced ourselves to each other. He knew me from television, and I knew him from reading *Rolling Stone* when I was a radio stringer in Paris and then when I'd buy it at the PX in Vietnam.

There were a lot of late nights, and on a lot of those late nights I had very long phone conversations with Hunter, exchanging ideas and opinions about the campaign and what was going on. When he went back to Woody Creek, we talked a lot at night. It didn't make any difference where you were and how late it was — you knew that Hunter was up. The last conversation I had before I went to sleep was with Hunter.

BILL DIXON

At a certain point in his life, his notoriety, his presence, would change the room or change the story. I don't think that happened until after he was credited — probably quite properly — with having a lot to do with Jimmy Carter winning such a closely contested election.

✛ 🐃 ✛ 🐃

ED BRADLEY

That May I ended up in some place close to Denver. The campaign was on a western swing, and the Carter campaign was going home.

There was going to be a four-day period where there was nothing happening. Instead of going back to Washington, I went to Woody Creek, at Hunter's invitation, and stayed at Hunter's house. I slept downstairs in the War Room on a bed with satin sheets.

Of course, Aspen was very different then. I think there was a chicken wire fence around the airport. You had two airlines that flew in and out, and on Rocky Mountain Airways flights — which were not cabin pressurized — there was surgical tubing hanging down from the airplane's ceiling so you could suck oxygen on the way in and out. I stayed at Owl Farm for three days. Sandy was there; Juan was there. I have pictures of Juan walking around in the yard reading a book. He must have been eleven or twelve years old. The first night I was there, we had dinner and sat out and talked, and then Hunter crashed at something like a normal bedtime because he'd been up for two or three days, so we started off on an even keel.

MICHAEL CLEVERLY *is a writer and artist who lives in Aspen.*

My first memory of hanging out with Hunter was at the end of the bar at the Jerome. He and I were just sitting there having a drink, and these two hippies — a boy and a girl — came up to us. They'd been on a pilgrimage to find Father Gonzo, and there he was! They came up and genuflected and all that stuff. The girl was really buxom and wearing something that showed her cleavage very nicely. The guy was like a little dust ball, but he whipped out this vial of cocaine and said, "Do you want a bump?" or whatever we called it back then. Hunter said sure, and he took the vial, unscrewed it, poured it out on the broad's boobs, and shoved his face in there and started snorting. He held up the vial, and there was a tiny bit left — from a full vial — and he gave it to me. I dumped the rest of it in my hand, snorted it up, and gave the vial back to Hunter. He gave it back to the kid and then turned his back on them.

Aspen was not a shopping destination. It still had more of a flavor of a western town — on the Fourth of July, people would ride their horses into the Jerome Bar, and there would be horses tied up outside. There was a pub crawl called Ruggerfest, which was a three-legged race that anyone could enter. You'd have to do a shot and a beer at every one of more than a dozen bars around the core of the town. People would keep their womenfolk inside. It was the sort of wholesome antics that you would never, ever see now. And the Jerome had the most beautiful waitresses in the whole world.

KALLEN VON RENKL *started working as a cocktail waitress at the Hotel Jerome in 1975.*

We used to have to wear long dresses. We had to dress very elegantly at that time. You could wear short skirts if you were the day shift, but not the night shift.

JACK NICHOLSON

For a while there, I had one of those big TV screens up in the attic, so the Jerome contingent came to my house on Sundays. We were all a no-nonsense group. I would burger them up or whatever we did. It was a good way for all of us that knew one another to get together and harrumph for whatever hideous thing we'd done Saturday night. A lot of them, frankly, were dope dealers — some of them retired and some didn't; many of them went to jail — and a lot of them were skiers. Hunter was not one of them. Skiing takes a certain amount of effort. You've got to peel yourself out of bed at a certain point and get a bunch of gear on.

MICHAEL CLEVERLY

If you were talking about something that you really didn't know that much about, that was sure to get him. He did not suffer fools gladly. He did not suffer the uninformed. I don't care who you were — if you knew what you were talking about, he would sit down and listen. The busboy could teach him something if he had something to say. But God help you if you tried to bullshit your way through it — or get between him and a pretty girl. You'd better hope she didn't pay attention to you. He was a stallion. God, he was unscrupulous when it came to women.

WILLIAM KENNEDY

Any meeting was the occasion for an all-night party at some saloon, Elaine's or down in the Village, or when he became affluent, in his hotel suite, which was a circus. The food and booze from room service, the vast amount of shrimp and Chivas — nobody could eat or drink that much, not even Hunter. Eight or ten people couldn't.

He came to a party at our house in 1977 with a pocketful of LSD somebody had given him, and a lot of people around the house were suddenly doing LSD. He came in around midnight. E. L. Doctorow was here that night — he'd been reading in Albany at the university, and we gave him a party. Hunter was speaking in Saratoga, at Skidmore, I think, and one of my students went up and brought him to our place. Doctorow was leaving out the back way around midnight. Hunter walked in the front door. They missed each other by minutes. They never met.

The party went on until four o'clock the following afternoon, when I took Hunter to the train station. Some of us never went to bed. People drifted off, but some went to work and came back. Somebody came in with a hypodermic full of Adrenalin, and Hunter injected it

LOREN JENKINS

We shared a lot of political discussions, discussions about the state of society, a lot of interesting conversations about the world, concerns about Aspen. He was always good company. But his persona, his fame got in the way. There were really two Hunters: There was the personal Hunter that you knew as a friend, who you'd really want in a pinch. Then there was the public Hunter, which was all about show and living out his legend.

Obviously a lot of Hunter got clouded by the gonzo side, but a lot of people never understood what a great political analyst he was. In another world — without drugs — he would have been Karl Rove.

WILLIAM KENNEDY

Conversation with Hunter was no longer an exchange — it became mostly a conversation about Hunter, with all those unbelievable stories. He was always a nutcase in a way, but he kept surviving these outlandish events and ingestions and going on to produce terrific work. It was wonderful to witness this, but it wasn't conversation like the old days. It was a monologue. Nobody could match those stories, or the personality behind them.

LAILA NABULSI *was a production assistant on* Saturday Night Live *in 1976.*

John Belushi was my best friend. One night just before the show I went into John's dressing room — it was just a little room with a couch — and someone was lying there. I could see the shorts and the long legs and the sneakers. It could have been the pot dealer. You never knew who was going to be around.

John says, "Laila Nabulsi, Hunter Thompson. Hunter Thompson, Laila Nabulsi." John and Danny [Aykroyd] had gone on a road trip commissioned by *Rolling Stone* and had stopped by Hunter's along the way, and when they came back, John was talking about him a lot.

My fate was sealed in that second. Here was this tall, good-looking —

well, actually I couldn't even tell if he was good-looking. I couldn't really look at him; there was all this energy going on.

After the show we all ended up at a party. Every once in a while I'd feel this presence and look up, and Hunter would be staring at me with his cigarette holder in his mouth. At some point, John came running over to me and did this typical song and dance about "I have to go somewhere. But I'll be back. Could you take Hunter back to my apartment? I'll give you the limo — just make sure he gets in the house, okay? I'll be there." I could only imagine what he was up to, but he was doing the whole eyebrows-up thing and using his best charm. I looked at him and joked, "Okay, but I'm not gonna fuck him."

What I didn't know at the time was that John had already gone to Hunter and said, "I need to go somewhere. I'll give you the car. Go back to my apartment, and I'll meet you there in an hour. Is that okay? What do you need? Do you need anything?" And Hunter pointed at me and said, "Her."

He was staying at the Gramercy Park Hotel, and I ended up staying there with him for about two weeks. I hadn't quite got the hang of his humor, so it was tense — because I was scared sometimes. We were sitting in the bedroom talking, and every now and again he would go into the living room, and I'd hear these weird screams — lamenting, hideous, agony-filled screams. Then he'd come back into the bedroom and pick up right where we'd left off and act like nothing happened. I thought, "He's insane, and I have to get out of here." I would have to get out of the bedroom and over to the door, but I thought he would do something to me if I tried to get out. And then he went out to the living room and did it again, screaming, "Oh God! . . . Oh God!!"

The third time he went out and screamed, I flipped into anger as a defense — out of fear, I think — and I said, "Stop that! Why are you doing that?" Hunter started laughing, and he said, "I can't find my lighter." In that second, I got the whole thing — the humor, the drama. I saw that it was a show.

I didn't know he was married. I found that out toward the end of the two weeks. So that put me off. Plus I was only twenty-two. When he left, I was relieved; it just seemed too much. But we had this back-and-forth that went on for a couple of years. Sometimes he'd come to town, but it was always a little weird.

SANDY THOMPSON

Juan and I had left Owl Farm and Hunter in 1977, but we came back after Hunter literally swept me off my feet at a sidewalk café in New York City. Juan was returning from a trip to Ireland with my mother, and we met him at the airport and went out to John Belushi's for the weekend. I remember John getting the go-ahead for *Animal House* on the phone and turning to his cats and telling them they'd be wearing gold collars soon.

JUDY BELUSHI *was John Belushi's wife.*

The most sane time I ever spent with Hunter was the first year John and I rented a summer home on Long Island. Hunter came out there with Juan and Sandy, and it was just a lot of barbecuing and boating and maybe the Wild Turkey didn't start until eleven o'clock in the morning. It was much more of a quiet time; we had a lot of fun and we laughed a lot. I remember Sandy saying that it reminded her of her happiest memory, which she said was sitting on her couch with Hunter sleeping on one side and their baby sleeping in her lap and her dog sleeping on the other side. I could relate to that because when you have someone in your life who is so high-energy and so dangerous, there's a real peace when they're sleeping.

LAILA NABULSI

John Belushi had that aura of someone who doesn't have a lot of time — that's why he was a little frantic about everything. I think Oscar [Acosta] had that too. They were both holding on to the end of that tornado, and somehow I think they knew it was just not gonna last.

SANDY THOMPSON

Hunter and Juan and I flew back to Owl Farm to try again. Everyone was happy to see us together at Jimmy and Jane Buffett's wedding, and everything held together for a few months. I said, "Hunter, it's really simple: I have to stay strong, and you have to stay good."

By the end of a year, I knew Juan and I had to leave again. I had no idea how we would live, and so I decided to go to travel agency school in L.A for a week. I mentioned this to Hunter several weeks beforehand but then didn't mention it again. I'm sure at this point he knew it was really over. He was angry and, I think, absolutely terrified. On the day of my flight, several hours before I was to leave, Hunter realized what I was doing and, for the last time, became very physically violent with me in the kitchen. He totally lost control.

I took the flight anyway, and when I was in L.A., I was also seeing men. Hunter called one night at three a.m., and I wasn't there. I knew that he would be angrier than angry, and when I came home a week later, Hunter had had a very bad time. Juan was distraught. I just held him and held him, and then I started moving out. When Hunter came down, I called the police because I was afraid of what might happen. When I had left the year before, Hunter had thrown my clothes out onto the driveway and set fire to them.

JUAN THOMPSON

This was just the world I grew up in. I wasn't conscious of it. It was sometimes scary and a little unstable, but for the most part it was okay. But what would I have compared it to? It was only when I got to college that I started to examine my relationship with my dad, and it was only then that I realized it really was quite different from what most people experience.

BOB BRAUDIS

Sandy was moving out and taking what she thought was her property by agreement, and she was taking the stereo. Hunter threatened to kill her or something, and she called the cops. I didn't go, but all the deputies who responded put on flak jackets. This was before Kevlar body armor. We had a locker filled with World War II–surplus flak jackets — the kind of thing you'd wear while flying over Berlin. So all of a sudden the whole shift is heading down to the Owl Farm wearing flak jackets because they're afraid when they show up to protect the stereo that Hunter's going to open fire. He had an arsenal, and everyone knew it.

SANDY THOMPSON

With Hunter, there was never a hint of a mature relationship. It was two people who couldn't really be honest with each other, who couldn't really communicate with each other, who weren't working out differences, working out problems, making compromises — nothing like that. Hunter was the king, and I was the slave. I was the happy slave — until I was neither happy nor a slave.

I had no life. I lost contact with my aunts and uncles and cousins, and mostly my brother. My whole world revolved around Hunter. I didn't have friends because I couldn't just bring them into the house, with the chaos and violence and bad tempers — you couldn't subject your friends to that. I didn't have time to do that, even if I would have been able, because I was taking care of him and taking care of the house. I was feeding him. I was writing whatever needed to be written. I was his executive secretary. I was his bookkeeper. I was his accountant. I was everything. I was living for Hunter and his work — for this great person, this great writer, who was so disciplined — and then when he couldn't write anymore, what was I doing? It was sad to see. I was taking care of a drug addict — who loved me and who was also terrifying me.

I had asked Hunter once, when he was in a rare calm mood, "Do you know when you're about to change? Are you aware of it?" Hunter said, "Sandy, do you know what it's like? I'm just standing here, and I have a sense that something is about to happen. And then I start to turn my head, and it's here. The monster's here."

JUAN THOMPSON

When Sandy and Hunter separated, I sided with my mom. It just seemed like the thing to do as a child. Hunter and I had remained distant. I didn't think he was a very nice guy.

He didn't take jokes very well. He was better dishing it out than taking it. I had some serious confrontations with him a couple of times, and he was not receptive to that. It was always clear that there was no point in trying to alter his habits. "That would be foolishness," as Hunter would say. It wasn't like he was an alcoholic who would go on a binge and then be all remorseful and say, "I won't do it again." No — he was totally unapologetic and unrepentant. And he was consistent. So what are you going to do?

What I had growing up was really more a fear of discipline rather than any discipline itself. I think Hunter's anger is well known. His anger was something that as a child I had no desire to experience. He had quite a temper, so there were some scary, scary times, especially for a child. Different people have different ways of coping with that, but my way was to try to mediate and calmly, rationally resolve things. That didn't work well at all. It took me a long time to realize that was not what they were looking for.

MICHAEL SOLHEIM

Hunter and I had meeting after meeting after meeting up at my office at the Jerome about how to deal with the divorce. I'd been divorced once before, and I explained to him how it's done. We'd try to talk about Juan, and about money, and he'd say, "I'm not giving her anything, that miserable bitch!" But mainly what had to be done was to talk him down. His energy level was too high. He was violent, in a sense. He wasn't being violent, but he was on the verge of it, and it was something that had to be addressed. I had to tell him, "Don't go crazy and get the cops involved." He had a lot of anger.

SANDY THOMPSON

After Juan and I left, people knew that Hunter was in a lot of pain, that he was hurting. It was pretty obvious — he boarded up the front door of Owl Farm and didn't want to talk to anybody, didn't want to deal with anybody. He had a friend of his, who was a friend of Jimmy Buffett's, find the saddest love songs — songs of loss — that he could think of and put them all on tapes. The friend said, "Oh my God, Hunter — I can't do that to you. You can't handle that." Hunter said, "I have to. So make them." And he made them. There's a lot of Dolly Parton, and some just tragic, tragic love songs he listened to.

SEMMES LUCKETT

He wouldn't open the door — I mean, he nailed his door shut. There was a big brouhaha among all his friends, so I called him. This was before caller ID, so we had coded rings. At that time the code was one ring, hang up, and then call back — then he would know it was a friend — and I said, "Now, Hunter, are you okay? Because this is showbiz, you know what I mean?" And he would say, "I'm okay, yeah — it's still showbiz."

DEBORAH FULLER

I first moved to Aspen in the summer of '79, which is when I met Sandy. I was looking for an alternative school for my daughter, and somebody said, "Sandy Thompson and her husband send their son, Juan, to the Community School right up the hill from their house." We became friends, and while Sandy and Juan were looking for a house, they lived with my daughter, Kristine, and me. Loren Jenkins and his wife, Nancy, lived in the house next door, and when it was time to deal with the divorce and Hunter wanted to see his son and talk with Sandy, he would go visit Loren and Nancy and then walk across the alley to my house.

That's how I met Hunter. He liked good weed, and I always had some around in those days. During the divorce negotiations, their lawyer suggested that Hunter and Sandy each have one person with them when they met, so Tom Benton and I would accompany them, but then we would leave Sandy and Hunter to themselves.

GEORGE STRANAHAN

Hunter's only asset as far as the divorce was concerned was the land Owl Farm was on, which he hadn't really paid for, and Sandy said, "Well, I own half of the land, and I don't want it because I would have to be next to that asshole Hunter." She basically said, "Will you trade me a little piece of land here?" and I said "Okay," and I did the same deal with Sandy — if in the future you ever sell this land, I have right of first refusal. And you can't sell for twelve years. And sure enough, eighteen months later, she said, "George, I've got a new boyfriend from New Zealand, and I'm going to sail around the world and open a coffee shop in Turkey. Will you buy my land back?" I said, "But I gave you the land. Now I have to buy it back?" And I did.

JUAN THOMPSON

She spent about ten years just traveling. She bought a boat and sailed on that for fifteen years or so. She did a lot of things. She'd been completely devoted to Hunter and focused on his life and concerns for sixteen years or something, and then once they were divorced, she decided to go explore other stuff. She traveled for — God, I don't know. A long time.

CHAPTER EIGHT

Wreckage in the Fast Lane

Hunter was working on Songs of the Doomed *and got in a fight with his editor over some insanely minor point. He went ballistic in the middle of the night and destroyed a typewriter — just beat it to death with a phone. There was metal Selectric shrapnel flying all over the kitchen.*

LAILA NABULSI

Every year at *Saturday Night Live* they had a Seder. Being Palestinian, I never went. But one year Paul Schaffer made me go, and Bill Murray came running up to me and said, "Oh, my God — you're alive! I talked to Hunter last night, and he said he heard you were dead. He's staying at the Coconut Grove Hotel in Miami." I started laughing and said, "Well, thanks. Now I know where he is. I guess that's what he wanted me to know."

Billy realized he'd been totally set up. But of course I called Hunter — he was on his way to Jimmy Buffett's place in Key West — and then Judy Belushi and I went down to visit him. I bought a white bikini and a gold bracelet and didn't really think about it until we got down there, and then I realized, "Wait a minute — what have I done?"

Judy went back to New York the next day, and I stayed for two weeks. Hunter was working a lot with a writer named Tom Corcoran on this screenplay that Jann had commissioned them to do called "Cigarette Key." It was a story about dope smugglers in Key West, and Tom was ghostwriting it for Hunter. Hunter kind of enlisted him. That's when Hunter and I formally fell in love.

JANN WENNER

I got a development deal with Paramount Pictures at a time when the top three films in the country were *National Lampoon's Animal House, Cheech & Chong's Up in Smoke,* and *Midnight Express.* Drugs and magazines! That's the ticket! I had met and lined up both Michael Mann and Oliver Stone as potential directors for a script by Hunter. I was trying to get the sort of sunny Jimmy Buffett version of the marijuana-smuggling trade, but Hunter wanted to go darker. Ultimately, of course, I couldn't bring him to deliver a script — but he was having a great time living down there on Paramount's money. It got nowhere, but we had a great time hatching the plan for the screenplay, having dinners, and drinking.

JIMMY BUFFETT

I was probably responsible for his Key West years. I must have been high on something when I offered to let him use my apartment down there in those days. I was on the road, and he immediately turned my apartment into some kind of sex palace. He was trying to work on some kind of a movie for Jann, and of course he didn't have much written. He'd talk to Jann on the phone for a long time and bullshit him to the nth degree. I'll never forget him lying on the floor, pushing and pulling the plug in and out of the outlet for the fax machine, and then getting up and going, "Goddamn fuckin' Jann, this piece of shit you sent me!!" He'd do that routine for forty-five minutes — putting that cord in just so it would work a little bit, and then taking it out to create a totally fake problem to buy himself a few more days. That was a pretty good Hunter trick.

LAILA NABULSI

He could hang out and really just *be* in those days — listen to music, look at the sunset, and relax. He'd have breakfast with a notebook next to him. And he'd be writing and talking — there was always something going on, whether it was the movie [*Where the Buffalo Roam*] that was coming up, or this script. But at that time, he was a great romantic. He liked the peacefulness.

JIMMY BUFFETT

Hunter loved Key West because in those days there was such a crazy end-of-the-world mentality down there. There were still cockfights right down the road, and the navy was there, and there were tourists and a whole drug culture.

There were times when Hunter was way out of control, and I'd stay away from him, and I would tell him so. I always tried to position myself so that I could leave and never get put in charge of Hunter. I had enough crazy characters in my band.

I did have to have a conversation with him once. I said, "You know, I got to live in this apartment. You guys have got to kind of take it easy here. You can stay here, but you've got to watch the rules."

About two months later, I was on the road and got a call from my accountants in California about a $10,000 or $12,000 phone bill. I don't know how a phone bill like that was even possible, but Hunter made it happen. I can't remember whether I ever got that money back.

I introduced him to the Amazing Rhythm Aces, which was one of this favorite bands, and to Jim Harrison, and I know I introduced him to my brother-in-law, Thomas McGuane — and when those two were running together, when they were both fueled up, it was quite a thing to see.

ANJELICA HUSTON

I remember the first night I met Laila. Hunter had brought her over to Jack's house in Aspen at Maroon Creek, and Jack was having a Jacuzzi. She had just come back from a trip to Florida with him. Hunter went downstairs to talk with Jack, and I stayed to talk with Laila. I think they must have left around four o'clock in the morning. She and I had a lot to say to each other, and we became instant friends and have been best friends ever since.

LAILA NABULSI

Later that year, Hunter and I went to San Francisco, and then we visited Billy Murray in L.A. and stayed with him. He was starting to shoot *Where the Buffalo Roam.* Hunter loved Billy, and he was happy about Billy being in the movie, but I don't think he was too happy about the script, and he got less fond of the director, Art Linson, as time went on. We didn't go to the set that much.

Later we came back for the filming of the ending — they thought it didn't work very well, and they wanted Hunter to write a voiceover. We stayed at the L'Ermitage. Hunter wrote a beautiful voiceover about Oscar: "Gone but not forgotten. Forgotten but not gone. I won't believe it until I can gnaw on his skull with my very own teeth" — that kind of thing. In the end, Hunter and Linson did not get along very well at all. Hunter thought his choices were cheap and silly, and the movie didn't have the weight or the aesthetic that he would have wanted.

MITCH GLAZER *was a twenty-two-year-old writer for* Crawdaddy *when he met Hunter through John Belushi.*

Hunter's presence is so strong that it fucks actors up. When they do him, an interesting thing happens. I was around Billy a lot right after he did *Where the Buffalo Roam.* I'd see him do sketches on *Saturday Night Live* and not be able to shake Hunter. People were coming and talking to him about it. And then when we did *Scrooged,* years later, there were still scenes where I'd see Billy doing Hunter.

The difference between Murray and Belushi or Hunter is that Billy would take no for an answer. They wouldn't. Hunter and John both shared a sense of possibility, and they seemed to have no limits. There was no governor on the night. It was like being around Huck and Tom, going off on adventures. Everything was possible, and they had total access, and so you found yourself in really exciting, really strange places, from sitting with Louis Malle and Candace Bergen overlooking Central Park South to some weird drug dealer's place in a sweaty back room on Avenue A at five in the morning.

LAILA NABULSI

I went back to *Saturday Night Live* in the fall of 1979 and then back out to Aspen on Thanksgiving, and that's when Hunter sort of proposed. I moved in the day before New Year's Eve, which was my twenty-fifth birthday. Bill Murray and his girlfriend were staying with us.

A lot of the local wackos were used to coming over at any time of the day or night, but I decided that that couldn't go on all the time, and I had to kick a few people out. So things changed a little bit. I settled into getting up, reading the paper, making breakfast, opening the mail.

Hunter used to get up around four in the afternoon. There were usually calls to make and things going on and requests for this or that. There was the running of Owl Farm. I would pick up supplies and peacock food from the co-op. We built a cage on the porch so you could observe them at night from inside the house. They had a pecking order, and you'd get to know them. There was one named Hannibal; there was an Oscar. We had a cat that just showed up one day and stayed, Jones. Ralph Steadman did a book all about Jones. He was a great character. He tolerated us, basically. Later he had that other cat, Screwjack, which showed up in a snowstorm.

ANJELICA HUSTON

Laila always seemed to be easy and pragmatic and normal in terms of her day-to-day behavior, and very careful with Hunter. She provided him with a sort of social legitimacy. She cushioned him. It was almost as though she could explain him. She interpreted him and understood him in a nonjudgmental way, and enjoyed him, whereas I'm a bit more catlike. I don't like public disruption, wild trajectories — and that was always the atmosphere around Hunter: Anything Can Happen. Her acceptance of occasional — well, much more than occasional — lunacy was in fact a comforting thing. She was very brave.

LAILA NABULSI

I felt I could talk to him about anything. I mean, it wasn't just a romantic thing. Hunter understood me in ways nobody ever had. When it came to relationships, Hunter was very conventional. We were engaged, and there was a formality on some level which makes you feel very comfortable. I always knew I was loved, and he knew he was loved.

We did a lot of family stuff, actually. My mom came out and stayed with us, and we went and visited Hunter's mom, and we went to his brother Davison's for Christmas, and we invited them out. We also had Juan on and off. He was about fifteen at the time. Hunter was a really good dad in a lot of ways — he was very consistent and had a good moral sense of what was right and wrong. He didn't make Juan behave in a certain way; it was more just about manners in general. Juan might get away with being a little weird, but he would never get away with treating me badly.

I think Hunter always assumed he would have this stable home life, with a wife and kids and a family. In a very traditional way, he was the man leaving the homestead and bringing back the elk to feed the family. He'd come back to his stable environment, where things were nice and peaceful, and cook some food and hang out. I was right after Sandy, and in that sense, I think Hunter and I both thought we were going to create that thing again.

✛ 🐃 ✛ 🐃

JANN WENNER

He took some dumb writing assignments. The bar for him at *Rolling Stone* was set very high, and we both were equally aware of that and wanted it kept that way. I was unwilling to offer him or accept second-rate work, so if there was an easy-money gig or some goof-off, he'd do it elsewhere.

LAILA NABULSI

In 1980, Paul Perry, an editor at *Running* magazine, sent Hunter a letter asking if he'd like to do a story on the Honolulu Marathon. Hunter said he would if they gave him this, that, and the other thing and flew over Ralph. We rented these two little houses for Christmas, because the marathon was in late December. Christmas in Hawaii — that was the big lure.

The houses were right on the water, and there was a pool as well. We had this image of swimming in the ocean and everything just beautiful and peaceful. No one told us that the sea is really rough during the winter months. It was raining every day. The ocean was coming over into the pool. One night we had to evacuate because the water was coming up to the houses. We felt they had sold us this idea of Christmas in Hawaii, and it was a lie.

TOM BENTON

He wrote me a note from Hawaii that said, "Tom, I am Lono." I said, "Lono? What the hell does he mean, he's Lono?" So I looked it up. Lono was a kind of crazy Polynesian god that used to carry a little boy-child around. The people put him in a canoe and sent him away and never saw him again, and then Captain Cook arrived, and they thought Captain Cook was Lono returned. The people had a lot of guilt about it, and then they had to shoot Captain Cook. They had to kill him, so they'd done Lono in twice. So when Hunter wrote to me and said, "I am Lono. I feel at home here and I know I am Lono," I called him up and said, "For God's sake, don't tell anybody over there that you're Lono. This would be too much for them to take."

LAILA NABULSI

Fireworks were legal in Hawaii, so we bought red Chinese firecrackers that come in a long strip. You're supposed to uncoil them and hang them on a tree or something. They came wrapped up in a tightly wound cake, and we found that if we just lit the end of the fuse of the cake, the whole thing would blow up like a bomb.

The first person we bombed was Captain Steve, who was this old guy Hunter had found who had a little shack on the Big Island, and a big boat, a humdinger. Hunter's whole mission out there was to catch a fish — a marlin — and Captain Steve was an obvious fan and slightly in love with Hunter.

They would go out deep-sea fishing all day, and Hunter just couldn't catch a fish. Hunter would berate Captain Steve endlessly: "You don't know how to get marlins. . . . There's no fucking marlin. . . . You don't know what you're doing." Poor Captain Steve was practically having a breakdown by the end of it. I would say to Hunter, "He's a shell of a man. You've ruined him."

RALPH STEADMAN

Hawaii was a hell of a trip, though we didn't catch a fucking thing. Hunter went back later because he couldn't stand the shame of not catching a marlin. It was a hopeless task. If we went south, we should have gone north. And the engine stuck. I felt worse than ever because I hate fucking boats. I was doing it because I thought, "This is the story, and we have to do a story." Everything was urgent. Everything *had to be done.*

We'd show up at these places and start hanging out and see what turned up. Really. He didn't know what the story was either. He just had these odd sayings. "There are no fish. Why did they lie to us?" Or another: "Fuck you, I'm rich."

LAILA NABULSI

Captain Steve had this tiny little place that was about the size of a hotel bathroom with a little porch, and we went over there in the dead of night. We were giddy like teenagers. We took the cake of firecrackers and put it on the porch, and Hunter lit it.

RALPH STEADMAN

Hunter said it sounded "like God's own drumroll." Isn't that nice?

LAILA NABULSI

We turned around after we got far enough away and drove by to see what was happening. Hunter turned the headlights off as we got close, and there was Captain Steve, naked, with a hose. The house was on fire.

I know that Captain Steve knew it was Hunter — who else could it be? We drove home laughing hysterically, but we also felt like kids who'd gone too far. The terrible thing was that we didn't know that Captain Steve's eighty-year-old father had come to visit and was in the house when we bombed it.

RALPH STEADMAN

As an Englishman, a Welshman, I don't think I could ever feel wholly comfortable in that situation. I was there as an interloper. I was there because this was the story, and I was asked to go and do it.

LAILA NABULSI

Somehow, all of this turned into the idea of a book. We had so much fun material from all of it, and Ralph was doing all these drawings. The book was also really just a way to keep going back to Hawaii. Hunter would say, "I can't remember what it's like — what it smells like, We've got to go back." But every time we left Hawaii, I thought, "We can never come back again. We've burned every bridge."

ALAN RINZLER, *the former head of* Rolling Stone's *book division, edited* Fear and Loathing on the Campaign Trail '72.

Hunter wanted to do a whole book about their experiences in Hawaii, and that eventually became *The Curse of Lono.* There are some wonderful things in that book, but it was also the beginning of the end — at least of my tenure with Hunter.

When we got to work on *Lono,* things began to deteriorate. Hunter was having so much trouble writing. The effects of alcohol and drugs didn't paint a pretty picture. It was ugly, and it was debilitating, and it made it very hard for him to work. I was now a director of Bantam Books, and we gave Ralph and Hunter a lot of money, and we signed a contract — and nothing happened. Finally I flew out to Woody Creek and moved in at Owl Farm for several days, and we started to hammer out the book.

He began to evolve this concept of the original voyage of James Cook, the English explorer, who was mistaken for the Hawaiian god Lono and worshipped — and then killed — by the Hawaiian natives. Meanwhile, he wanted to write about how he had gone deepsea fishing and caught this huge marlin — which he actually, finally did, just like Hemingway. The fishing story got sort of grafted together with the Lono story until Hunter truly convinced himself that he was the reincarnation of Lono and that everybody was out to kill him.

LAILA NABULSI

It was a nightmare. I had a huge stack of pages that sort of ran in order, and Alan and I stood at the kitchen table every day and went through it. Hunter would get up at four or five, and he was supposed to write an outline or maybe some transitions, some things that would make it work. I'd have to go through all the pages and changes with him, because Alan would have left by now, so I'd have to tell Hunter about the whole day and then get him to write.

Hunter would say, "Okay. Okay. I'll write the transition." And then he'd write something completely different — which was fantastic but had nothing to do with what you actually needed. Sometimes he just wouldn't do it — he'd go off on something else. He'd be up all night, and then the next day Alan would be back. It was a nightmare, and it was endless.

ALAN RINZLER

The first time I visited Owl Farm we nailed the concept, and I went home to New York. And nothing happened again, so I had to go back. Hunter wasn't returning my calls, didn't even want me to come, and when I got out there, didn't want to let me in the house. He was really hostile, and he didn't have anything, and he didn't want to work, but I hung in there and stayed and stayed. He did anything to distract me, and himself, from the work that had to be done: We'd drive in his convertible at high speeds with the top down into Aspen for these expensive meals that we couldn't eat; he'd lock us in some concrete bunker and set off long strings of firecrackers that left us stinking of cordite and deaf for hours — anything to avoid actual work.

LAILA NABULSI

Hunter agonized over everything. Then Alan had to come out and torture both of us. Hunter hated the book. That was the other thing:

You'd be working so hard, and then Hunter would give up and say, "It's shit. It's horrible. It's terrible. It's not worth it. Fuck this."

ALAN RINZLER

One night Hunter fell asleep, or passed out, and I went all over the house and down to the basement and gathered up every single manuscript page or notebook I could find that was about this project, including — literally — brown shopping bags with notes scrawled all over them. I made a big pile of them, wrapped them up, and flew back to New York. I copied everything and sent the originals back to him with a note that said, "Thanks, Hunter. You're done." I put *The Curse of Lono* together in the basic form that it came out in, which is why it's a little incoherent. There are a lot of disparate elements. It was a patchwork, a cut-and-paste job. It doesn't quite make sense, but the language is really good. That was basically the end of our relationship.

JANN WENNER

To me, he was just spinning his wheels. I don't know where *Lono* fit into what he was supposed to be doing. I never read it. It just seemed like an indulgence, a chance to live the easy life and sport-fish in Hawaii for not too much work. But even easy work was hard for Hunter.

MIRIAM GOOD *and her husband, Lloyd, own Sugarloaf Lodge on Sugarloaf Key in Florida.*

Hunter stayed here quite often starting in 1980. He was in Key West, and then he came out here. I don't think he planned to stay that long, but the Mariel boatlift started. Castro let 130,000 Cubans leave the country, and Miami Cubans came down here with their boats to pick up their relatives. When you looked at the highway, it was a stream of boats being towed. There was no food left in Key West because they took everything with them on their way down here. Then Castro opened up the jails and the asylums and said, basically, that if these people wanted to take their relatives, they had to take the rest of these people. It was a wild time down here.

Hunter was staying at the lodge when all of this was going on, and he convinced *Esquire* magazine to fund him to write this story. I don't think he ever wrote it. He pretty much watched it all happen from the TV in the bar. Whether or not he was writing at the time, I don't know, but he was doing something all night long, and then he'd sleep for a couple hours and then so on.

LAILA NABULSI

Hunter said he wanted to write a book called *The Silk Road*. He wrote a long memo to his agent: "A story about people who got caught in the fast and violent undercurrents and, finally, the core of the action of the great Cuba–to–Key West Freedom Flotilla in the spring of 1980 — a bizarre and massively illegal 'sea lift' which involved literally thousands of small private boats that brought more than 100,000 very volatile Cuban refugees to this country in less than three months. . . ." He was going to do it next, but he never did.

MIRIAM GOOD

I have no idea how he found out about our lodge. There was a group of people having dinner in the bar one night, and somebody recognized Hunter, and he and Laila checked in the next day and stayed for a few months. They settled into his routine, and we all got used to that. Soon he had a relationship with everybody in the family. He and my husband, Lloyd, had some kind of sports bet going on every day. Hunter had breakfast in the bar, usually around noon, with his drinks lined up, and everybody got used to that. It was quiet, and people didn't harass him. It just seemed to suit him, and he went out and about doing what he did. There were times when he had his boat here and he went out, but whether or not he fished or what he did, I don't know.

We were only a party to the alcohol part, but the rest went on too, and of course in those days in the Keys that was not a problem. Bill Murray and several other friends came down, and they all had a wonderful time. He had just done the Hunter part in the *Where the Buffalo Roam* movie, and he had Hunter down. It was almost scary — he had the walk and all the rest of it.

We have two sons, and we had a dolphin in those days, and Hunter was very involved with all of that.

LAILA NABULSI

They had a one-eyed dolphin called Sugar. You had to go get the fish to feed the dolphin from the kitchen, and then you had certain tricks that you made Sugar perform, like jumping and singing, by doing the right hand movements. One night Hunter jumped in the pool with her, with his snorkel and everything. He just said, "I'm going to talk to Sugar," and Sugar came up and stood straight on her tail in front of him and yapped at him for fifteen minutes. And Hunter talked back to her. They had a whole relationship.

MIRIAM GOOD

He was very accessible and very friendly to everyone. Then one day they left early in the morning, and they left a copy of *The Great Shark Hunt,* and Hunter wrote in the front of it:

Dear Lloyd and Miriam,
 You have too many dependents for me to list all their names on this page.
 Fuck the doomed. Indeed — but you ran a decent hideout. It was a good

place to hide from the movie. I'll call you about my boat — we need to get it back to Boog's.

And thanks for running a good inn, which is better than a bad book.

Then I guess he decided he'd been too nice — on the next page it says:

Nevermind — I caught some weird disease in this place, and I will damn well see you in court.

LAILA NABULSI

John Belushi came up to stay with us at Owl Farm in September '81, and he was not in great shape. Hunter was trying to distance himself because Judy was there with John. John kept getting in these situations — he stole somebody's truck and went to town, or he'd hitchhike into Aspen, probably to buy drugs, and then come back hours later. Hunter didn't want to be perceived as the one who was making John fall off the wagon, so Hunter kept saying things like, "I'm going to the Holiday Inn to watch the football games," and try to get away from all of that. Hunter wasn't mad at him. He was basically in "It's not my fault" mode. He didn't want to be blamed.

After John died in March of '82, Hunter and I went to New York for the memorial, and then he went home and I stayed to look out for Judy. But then Hunter decided that he and I were going to go back to Hawaii, and there was no question — I was going back to Hawaii. I was going to be with Hunter. I *was* with Hunter. I just had a short break because of the John stuff.

But this time, a certain amount of the fun seemed to have gone out of our lives. I wanted to move into another phase, and I know that's what Hunter and I had planned, but I guess I had assumed that everything would go differently than the way things were going now. And when it didn't or it couldn't, it became harder to deal with all the other stuff.

After John died, things changed, because then I was more worried about Hunter. It got harder. I was tired. I wanted things to be more normal again, and they were starting to get less normal. More stuff was going on, and it was just getting a little crazy. John dying was really part of it.

BOB BRAUDIS

Hunter and I were friends way before I became sheriff. And over almost thirty years I don't believe I've lost any friends because I put on a badge and strapped on a six-shooter. The relationship with Hunter has been puzzling to a lot of people. I don't believe that drug use is a crime of moral turpitude. We had a simpatico philosophy regarding drug use, and I didn't see a lot of craziness in Hunter's drug use. The guy could drink twenty-four hours a day and never get stupid. With Hunter's peccadilloes, or some of Hunter's behavior that I didn't approve of, I treated it as a challenge to help him. So I accepted the fact that Hunter was a recreational user or an addicted user of several substances, most of them legal. My main relationship with Hunter in the criminal realm was that he did commit some crimes, and he wrote about them, and he was prosecuted and worked out plea bargains most of the time. Hunter was very discreet in protecting my reputation, and I accepted his lifestyle.

One thing that always defined our relationship was the fact that I think he was a little afraid of me — and I wanted to keep it that way. He would admit it. When I'd give him the stink-eye, I could tell he was listening. He was pretty fearless, but when I told him, "Hey, you don't do this shit," he'd listen.

GEORGE STRANAHAN

A lot of us who knew him well were concerned about the excess and the self-destructive behavior. As a friend, I felt that I at least had to talk to him about it — if not for his sake, at least for my sake, so that I could say I tried. So I'd say a few words like, "Hunter, I'm worried about you." Many people did that. But you usually only did it once, because Hunter always had an answer: "It's my life, my decision . . . It's how I make my living." That kind of thing. And it was so logical that you'd say, "Okay, I'm not going to revisit that conversation."

ED BRADLEY

It was Hunter's life. He had been doing it most of his life, and I didn't feel that I was going to be the one to change him, because I don't think he wanted to change. I think he enjoyed that life, and he would have been miserable living any other way. Hunter was an alcoholic, a serious alcoholic. Hunter got up and drank for breakfast, he drank all day, he drank all night. And he was a drug addict — he started with drugs in the morning, he used drugs all day, he used drugs all night, and sometimes he'd stay up for two or three days on drugs. He was a serious addict.

Once I said, "You know, man, I'm really worried about you. How can you continue like this? What kind of shape are you in?" And he said, "Well, you're right, Ed. . . . I could stand to lose ten pounds."

JANN WENNER

Hunter was a drug addict. He loved drugs. He took massive amounts of them. And if you were with him, you took them. I'm sure some people didn't — I suppose — but for most everyone, it was almost impossible not to. He enjoyed drugs, all kinds of them, day and night, really with no break for years on end. At a certain point I don't think he enjoyed it anymore, but by that time he was hopelessly addicted.

ANJELICA HUSTON

Laila's a sensible girl. She protected Hunter a lot and nursed him a lot and cared for him, and I think it became evident to her that she just could not go on doing that. I don't think I ever questioned Laila's decision, and I don't think it ever really merited an explanation. I got it. Being in a relationship like that, when you realize the person is outside your sphere of influence, you realize there really is no other thing you can do other than lick your wounds and find a quiet place.

LAILA NABULSI

John's death had more of an effect on me than on Hunter. He didn't act like John, but there were similar amounts of drugs around, so I started to freak out that he could die. It was a conversation I had with his doctor that set me straight about what addiction was, and what alcoholism was; that Hunter really was addicted and really was an alcoholic; that this was something that had been going on for a while, and that my life was going to be this unless he did something drastic about it. I didn't realize then that I couldn't make him do it.

I think he felt judged, which is not what I wanted to do. I just thought, "If you love me, you'll do this." There were only a couple of people who really understood what was going on: Jann and a few others. Basically, the rest of his friends had the attitude of, "He's Hunter Thompson — what are you worried about?" There was no support system.

JANN WENNER

Laila asked me to try to get Hunter to get into AA or some program. So at her urging — beyond urging, really; it was pleading and desperation — I sat down with Hunter one night at my apartment in New York and had a conversation about it. He admitted that he screwed up his career. "Well, why don't you do something about it? It would be great for you, and for all your friends." I explained the benefits in terms of his writing and his ability to be productive again.

Hunter was extremely gracious. "I know you're sincere. I know you mean well, and I appreciate you having the courage to say this to me, because most people won't; but this is just never going to happen." He didn't deny anything at all. He had said to me often throughout his life, beginning much earlier than this, "I'm a dope addict. A classic, old-fashioned, opium-smoking-type dope addict. I admit that freely. That's who I am." And he was also an alcoholic, and that slowly destroyed his talent and finally his life.

LAILA NABULSI

I threatened to leave if he didn't go to rehab. He finally said he'd do it, but making it happen and finding the right place was like pulling teeth. He insisted that it be someplace near the water, so we found a place near the water in Florida. The deal was he would stay there for thirty days and then I'd stay with him at Owl Farm.

He lasted a week. He had a drug dealer who lived in Florida bail him out of rehab and pick him up. That fucking guy called me and said he was going to pick Hunter up and take him to a plane, and I said, "Don't! Let him stay there." And he said, "Hey — it's *Hunter Thompson,* man . . ." That's when I realized that there would always be *that guy* who Hunter could get to go along with whatever he was doing. And there were more of them than there were of me. His counselor down there told me, "He's not ready. He did it for you, but he didn't do it for himself."

His fear was that he wouldn't be able to write — and that was the most important thing, ultimately. He had created such an edifice around him that it was hard for him to break out of it without thinking that he would be publicly humiliated. He didn't know how to back-track. He said he'd made a "career decision."

That was the beginning of the end. Around September, I told Hunter that I was going to go to New York for a couple of weeks to work on this book with Judy. It was just a way to get out of there and away from everything for a minute. I took a toothbrush with me, and I never really went back.

It got to a point where I just didn't want to be responsible. Life was getting bigger on his end, in all sorts of ways. I didn't want to be the secretary all the time and do all the work, but it was required because who else was going to do it? Money was tight then. It wasn't like we could have just easily hired somebody. But mostly it was because he didn't like it. He was so private about his life at home that to him, it was weird to have somebody coming in to do the books. But I was tired and I didn't want that job, which is what my life with Hunter was becoming.

TERRY MCDONELL *was the managing editor of* Rolling Stone *in 1982.*

When the Roxanne Pulitzer story broke, it occurred to me that this was just too perfect. Guy de la Valdene, who was a great friend of friends of mine in Montana — along with Buffett, Tom McGuane, Jim Harrison — was living in Palm Beach and was a friend of Roxanne's, so I knew a little bit more about the story than what was appearing in the tabloids, which was sensational enough.

I thought, "Perfect. Hunter should go there." He loved Florida. I told Jann I was going to do that, and he laughed and said, "Good luck. That'll never happen." And what I realized was that the two of them had determined that they were never going to do anything together again, because it was just too hard. They had pushed their particular theater too far. But I thought it would have been tragic not to go back and do it again sometime.

The relationship that Hunter had with *Rolling Stone* — even if it was not going to be with Jann in the same way — was important. So I proposed the story, and Hunter, of course, said no, he'd never work with that little fucker again because, of course, there were hundreds of thousands of copies of *Fear and Loathing* in some warehouse somewhere. I heard about it all the time, that and the canceling of the insurance in Saigon. I was immediately brought into that swamp.

But I started talking to Hunter on the phone, and I think what happened was we enjoyed it, or I filled a gap for him or something. He loved the idea that *Rolling Stone* wanted him to write again, because he told everyone that Jann had come crawling back on his knees. But in one of those conversations, I asked Hunter if he remembered how good it felt to really work. And that struck him, and over the next twenty years or so, he would bring that up. He had been not working much at that time. But he got that; he wanted to work, and he wanted his work to be great. I never felt adversarial with him like so many other editors have said. I felt conspiratorial.

I think that that was the little trigger that got him on the plane to Palm Beach. Of course, once he was there, the Cadillac convertibles and the wind whipping through the palm trees and the lesbians drinking champagne as they did four-wheel drifts around the corners took precedence.

ROXANNE PULITZER *and Hunter were friends for more than twenty years.*
Hunter and I first met in '82 at my divorce trial in Palm Beach, Florida. He was there every day for twenty-one days, in the front row. There was Tom Brokaw, the *New York Times* — and there was Hunter in his Hawaiian shirt and cutoff khaki shorts and TopSiders. On the first day of the trial, when Hunter walked in and sat down, the judge said, "I'm so honored to meet you, Mr. Thompson." He didn't want to meet anybody else in that front row except for Hunter. I had never met him. I'd heard of *Fear and Loathing,* but I have to admit that at the time I was not a reader of *Rolling Stone,* so I didn't know much.

The trial was a lambasting — and, I think, the first divorce trial that really stood out since the Gloria Vanderbilt custody case in terms of taking the press for that kind of ride. Maybe it was because of my husband's name, or because I was the younger woman from the wrong side of the tracks, and now there I was in Palm Beach with two beautiful children. And we had the drugs, the sex, everything — it was the seventies, for Chrissake. I lost custody of my own children, and the only way my ex-husband could strip them away from me was to say I was a voodoo witchcraft queen and a cokehead. He had to do that to win. All of a sudden he's saying, "She made me have a ménage à trois with her and her younger girlfriend. She introduced me to cocaine." I was twenty-eight before I even saw the drug.

I lost everything. It was a shock — an incredible thing, a bad thing. Of course Hunter had to come to Palm Beach to cover it for *Rolling Stone*.

PAT CADDELL

He really had this thing for underdogs, and he really had a thirst for justice. Even if the underdogs didn't vote with him or under- stand what he did, he thought they were much more genuine than the whores. Take his Roxanne Pulitzer story. Everyone was making fun of her — well, it turns out that most people are ass-backwards mother- fuckers. He exposed that community for what it was — that sort of wealthy, patrician corruption — and he put it in a social context. He was deeply passionate, and he cared, and it was not his persona to pre- tend to care. That story is the greatest attack on the Gatsby class since *Gatsby*.

From "A Dog Took My Place"
Rolling Stone 400/401; July 21–August 4, 1983

There is a lot of wreckage in the fast lane these days. Not even the rich feel safe from it, and people are looking for reasons. The smart say they can't understand it, and the dumb snort cocaine in rich discos and stomp to a feverish beat. Which is heard all over the country, or at least felt. The stomping of the rich is not a noise to be ignored in troubled times. It usually means they are feeling anxious or confused about something, and when the rich feel anxious and confused, they act like wild animals.

There are hideous scandals occasionally — savage lawsuits over money, bizarre orgies at the Bath and Tennis Club or some genuine outrage like a half-mad eighty-eight-year-old heiress trying to marry her teenage Cuban butler — but scandals pass like winter storms in Palm Beach, and it has been a long time since anybody got locked up for degeneracy in this town. The community is very tight, connected to the real world by only four bridges, and is as deeply mistrustful of strangers as any lost tribe in the Amazon.

Some of the first families of Palm Beach society will bear permanent scars from the *Pulitzer vs. Pulitzer* proceedings, a maze of wild charges and countercharges ranging from public incest and orgies to witchcraft, craziness, child abuse and hopeless cocaine addiction.

The Filthy Rich in America were depicted as genuinely *filthy,* a tribe of wild sots and sodomites run amok on their own private island and crazed all day and all night on cocaine. The very name Palm Beach, long synonymous with old wealth and aristocratic style, was coming to be associated with berserk sleaziness, a place where price tags mean nothing and the rich are always in heat, where pampered animals are openly worshipped in church and naked millionaires gnaw brassieres off the chests of their own daughters in public.

Big names in the mud, multiple sodomies, raw treachery, bad craziness — the Pulitzer gig had everything. It was clearly a story that a man in the right mood could have fun with.

And I was *in* that mood. I needed a carnival in my life: whoop it up with the rich for a while, drink gin, drive convertibles, snort cocaine and frolic with beautiful lesbians. Nevermind the story. It would take care of itself. It was ripe in every direction.

LAILA NABULSI

During that first year apart, I met up with him for Thanksgiving in Grenada when he went there to cover the "war" for *Rolling Stone.*

MICHAEL CLEVERLY

Loren Jenkins told me about going to Grenada with Hunter. The two of them were the only journalists that brought dates to the invasion. All the rest of the guys showed up with their bush jackets and their equipment and tons of other stuff. Hunter and Jenkins showed up in Hawaiian shirts, each with a date on his arm.

JANN WENNER

I thought it was certain wo weic going to get the Grenada piece, but the editor who I delegated to hand-hold that one made the mistake of letting Hunter come to New York to write, and then also went along with Hunter's work-avoiding notion that a transcript of this interview he had had with a fucking taxi driver in Grenada was going to be the larger part of the piece. It was another broken play.

It took me a long, long time to give up. For so long it had been, "That would be perfect for Hunter. Let's try it." Finally I had to understand that it was not worth making the phone call. It was frustrating and upsetting. So I stopped.

LAILA NABULSI

We kept having these weird trial reunions — he'd come to New York, or I'd go out there — with the idea that maybe it would be okay this time, or that we'd try again, and then I'd be crawling out of there ten days later.

But by then I had the rights to *Fear and Loathing in Las Vegas* Hunter and I had gone to see a stage play version in England in '82, right before John died.

LOU STEIN *directed the stage play of* Vegas *in London's West End.*

Ralph Steadman, who lived near me in Kent, put me in touch with Hunter. Ralph thought a *Fear and Loathing* play was a great idea. When I first called, Laila answered the phone, and she was fairly hostile: "Who gave you permission to do this?" and "We're not letting you do this" et cetera, et cetera, and then said, "Hunter wants to see your work."

By the time I finally spoke to Hunter on the phone, his only comment to me was "We're coming out to see the play, and if we don't like it we're going to wreck your theater."

He came to the opening night, and of course all of the actors wanted to meet him, so he went backstage about a half hour before curtain and basically said, "Does anybody have some hash?" Some of the actors lit up with him backstage, and he then went out and sat in the absolute back row. He was slapping his knee with his hand and saying things like "Oh man!" throughout the show. And when he first saw Dr. Gonzo — the guy playing Gonzo — he howled and said, "That's him, that's him — I remember that." He didn't see it as fiction. I saw it as a play based on his book; he saw it as meeting people from his life. I'll never forget. At the intermission, he said, "I lived that! I lived that! That was *him*."

LAILA NABULSI

Hunter and I had a great time in London. We had all these scams going on from *Time Out* and some other magazines to pay for the trip. Hunter was supposed to give one of them X amount of words and somebody else some other story, but when we had to check out of our hotel, we didn't have any money. Hunter had written pages — I don't even remember what the hell they were about — and I had all the people who were going to pay for them waiting in the lobby of Claridge's. I would say, "Okay, give me the check, here's the pages; give me the check, here's the pages; give me the check . . ." Then I had to add it all up to make sure we had enough money to pay the bill. I don't think Hunter ever went back to Europe after that.

Because of the play, I saw how the book could work dramatically. Hunter had sold the movie rights in perpetuity to this guy who was the heir to the Jergens hand lotion fortune, for twenty-five grand, in 1972 or '73. He had tried to make a movie at one point — and at another point Scorsese was thinking of doing the movie, and he wanted John and Danny to play Gonzo and Hunter, but some weird guy was attached as the producer, and it fell apart.

Hunter didn't really know about any of this. He'd just taken the money. But I renegotiated so that the rights reverted back to Hunter in seven years. It ended up taking way longer.

+ 🐃 + 🐃

DEBORAH FULLER

After Hunter and Laila separated, he called me and asked if I would help him. I had my own glass-blowing studio at the time, but he would call from time to time, and I would go out.

Usually I had just gone to bed, and he'd call and say, "Get over here, Goddamn it! We've got a deadline." So I started working with him in '82 or '83, eventually helping him run his life and Owl Farm. We established an early mutual trust — he trained me to his ways — and that lasted more than twenty years.

At that time he had an assistant, Maria, and we became good friends during the three years we worked together. We're still very good friends.

JUAN THOMPSON

There was a little testing period with Hunter's relationships. It was just wait and see how long they were around. Laila, Maria — they were around for a long time, and I got along very well with them. Others came and went. Some of them, it was strange: I didn't even meet them. I only heard about them.

BOB BRAUDIS

The girlfriends all blend into one. When I became sheriff, Maria Khan, a beautiful Pakistani lady from Phoenix, was his squeeze. She eventually went back to Phoenix, but Hunter lured her back to Colorado for Juan's graduation and sort of held her prisoner. I rescued her.

DOUG CARPENTER *was Hunter's neighbor in Woody Creek.*

Hunter did have a tendency to suddenly drop the guillotine and just snap, and that would be it. This time it ended with Maria moving from Hunter's house into the house of a friend of mine. My friend called me up one day and said, "I think Hunter's gonna shoot me." I said, "Jesus Christ! You know you've taken a little risk." Hunter was walking around with a gun in his belt. That kind of turned ugly.

DEBORAH FULLER

Hunter and I were involved at the beginning, but very briefly. You can't work with him in the capacity that I did and do that. I loved Hunter very much, but I didn't fall in love with him. I also wasn't in awe of him or his work, because when I met him I hadn't read most of what he had written. He was a very powerful man, as well as charming — that Kentucky charm.

Working on pieces with Hunter was really our fun time. He wrote, I facilitated, and then I took care of everything else — joyfully. I'm good at it, so it was easy. We cursed each other from time to time, and I would quit, and he'd fire me, though we were usually back working together within a few months.

He'd pay me when he could, and I had another job at a gallery in Aspen to support myself. When Hunter had money, he was one of the most generous people I knew, and not just to me. To many. But money was tight in those early years. He wrote, and he lectured to make extra money.

BILL STANKEY *was Hunter's lecture agent for thirteen years.*

In 1983, some kid from the University of North Dakota called me because he wanted Hunter to come out and give a speech. No one could get hold of him, so I started sending Mailgrams to the Woody Creek Tavern. Months went by with no answer, and then one day my assistant said, "There's a Dr. Thompson on the phone." North Dakota was the first gig. He got $5,000, and in what would become a typical event, he was about an hour and a half late, insisted on drinking Chivas onstage — and drew a huge sold out crowd.

The next gigs were UCLA and then Berkeley, back-to-back. I flew out to meet Hunter for the first time with about $200 for five days and stayed at a Travelodge. Hunter was staying in the Lauren Bacall Suite at the Westwood Marquis Hotel and had brought one of the Hells Angels, Tiny, with him as a security guard. In the front row at the show, there were ten kids who'd dyed their arms blue, and when he came out onstage, people were running up to the stage bringing him joints and little envelopes with drugs in them. After the gig, he had a party for some students in his hotel room, and after about an hour, Tiny came up to me and said, "Hunter wants you to leave. You're making him nervous." I went down to the bar and started ordering drinks on Hunter's tab, and an hour and a half later, Tiny came down and gave me $500 in cash and said, "Hunter knows you don't have any money."

The next day we had two sold-out shows at Berkeley, and some corporate gig for a computer guy there. I was supposed to meet Hunter at ten a.m. for breakfast, but he didn't show, and I couldn't get hold of him all day. Finally I flew to Berkeley on my own and got to the show at eight o'clock . . . no Hunter. Twenty-five hundred kids were howling and barking at the moon, so I walked out and said, "I just got a call from Dr. Thompson, and he'll be here momentarily" — and then walked backstage thinking, "Where is he?" A few minutes later he showed up and yelled at me. "Never lie for me, goddamn it."

ALAN RINZLER

He got on the stage and was incoherent, just fall-down drunk. It was sort of what everyone expected — that he would show up and be so drunk, or so fucked up in some other way, that he couldn't speak.

BILL STANKEY

For the corporate gig, Hunter showed up late, told a couple stories, and then left — $10,000.

A couple years later, he did a show at Brown University with G. Gordon Liddy. Hunter decided he was going to sit at the airport bar and drink and wait for Liddy to arrive. Liddy landed, and Hunter went wandering out onto the tarmac with a handgun, yelling, "Gordo! Gordo, it's good to see you! We're going to have a lotta fun tonight, Gordo!" Liddy wanted nothing to do with him.

Hunter was a wreck that night. Liddy was articulate and sober, and the comparison between the two was not in Hunter's favor. Afterward he held some students hostage in a room, screaming and yelling at them that he needed drugs immediately and demanding that they drive him to find acid.

BOB BRAUDIS

Over the years, when he was flush, Hunter would give me nice collectibles. He was very generous. He could spend $5,000 at a truck stop when he had a pocketful. Then there were times between royalties, or when he owed the publishers a book and they wouldn't give him any money, when he would borrow from a few of us. In my case it was very little money because I don't have a lot, but other generous patrons like George Stranahan and a few other guys, when Hunter had an IRS bill with penalties and interest mounting, they'd bail him out.

DEBORAH FULLER

I lived at Owl Farm, in the cabin about a hundred feet from his house. Living that close was both a curse and a blessing. I was on call twenty-four hours, but it was essential. The cabin was small and very old. It had huge windows and it was a place to sit and watch the deer and elk and the occasional marmot or skunk or porcupine or bobcat or fox or coyote pass by. And the peacocks, of course. We added another cage on to the cabin, so that there was one at Hunter's house and another at the cabin.

There were eight to fifteen [peacocks] at any time. It was really important to Hunter to be able to watch the birds, just their sheer beauty. Hunter called it "living art." The kings always had them, he said. They were watch-birds, and we always knew when anything or anyone approached the house.

JUAN THOMPSON

I've always been very, very private about acknowledging that I was Hunter Thompson's son. I wouldn't volunteer that. But when people did find out — yes, inevitably the first questions would be "What was it like?" "Was he really that crazy?" I might tell a story about him, but I didn't like answering those types of questions, partially because from as early as I can remember, protecting privacy was paramount. The idea of sitting down with a stranger and giving them the "inside dope" was unthinkable. That was one of Hunter's prime directives: Maintain the privacy. It was not specific, and it was not talked about. It was implied. Every time I picked up the phone — this was before answering machines — I had to get enough information to find out who it was, but without disclosing anything, and then find out if Hunter wanted to talk to them or not. Physical privacy as well — people were not welcome to just drive up to the door and knock. It was strictly forbidden.

DEBORAH FULLER

The kitchen was the center of everything, and if Hunter didn't know you well or didn't trust you completely, the kitchen was just off the list. And whatever happened in the kitchen was to be kept private.

There were always notes tacked up to that effect: "What happens in the kitchen stays in the kitchen," or "Never call 911. Ever. This means you."

BILL DIXON

You had to be polite in the kitchen and you had to be on your best behavior — not to bow down to him, but you had to say something on point. Hunter was a lover of great conversation, and he did not dominate conversations. He was a great listener. You wouldn't know that from his public persona.

DEBORAH FULLER

There was a certain organization to Owl Farm that had to be kept. From Hunter's perspective sitting in his chair in the kitchen, there was the typewriter right in front of him, and to the right and left of Hunter's typewriter were two phones that he would often talk on simultaneously. Straight across from Hunter was a big TV in the corner, and to the left of that was the piano, and on the piano there were always books that he wanted access to.

I always kept an edition of each one of his books there in case we needed to do any research, as well as any other books that he wanted to be able to see: *The Reluctant Surgeon,* which was about one of his ancestors, along with reference books related to the project of the moment. There was always a storyboard of the working manuscript hanging over the piano. To the right of his typewriter was a window through which he could see out to the bird feeders, or he could look out and see a car come around the circular driveway.

All the daily newspapers and the latest magazines would be to his right, and the coffeepot was on the counter behind him. Just under that window were various books of his in which he made many corrections over the years.

The living room had large windows and a door to the front porch. Hunter used to like to have his late-afternoon breakfast on the porch and sit outside in the morning before he went to bed. At the far end was a built on birdcage. Hunter would lock the peacocks in every night, and there were lights inside the cages for heat and viewing. The birds were active at night, especially when Hunter cranked up the music.

At the far end of the living room was a large fireplace, which was going most of the time during the winter, and a window to the right of the fireplace that looked out onto the firing range and to the back and the side of the property. To the left inside the room was another story-board — we always had two storyboards going — and there was a big round table with a marble center that had a lazy Susan on which we could lay out material when we were working. That table was in front of the chair that Hunter always wrote in before he ended up at the counter in the kitchen.

As you walked into the living room, to your left were all book-shelves — that's also where the taxidermied owl of Owl Farm was perched, right above the master dictionary — and as you turned right to go out to the porch, there were more floor-to-ceiling bookshelves with a rack of hats hanging over them. Hunter could go straight to where he had put books thirty years ago.

Downstairs was the War Room, another place where Hunter used to write. This room had all sorts of memorabilia on the walls from as far back as when he was in South America and Puerto Rico, along with things that Ralph Steadman had done. There was another large fire-place right under the living-room fireplace. When Hunter started writ-ing upstairs, this room turned into archival storage and is where a lot of first editions were kept, as well as collected artwork, guns and am-munition, original manuscripts and their backup materials, all communication . . . It was a large, locked, private room with everything from Hunter's early days as a writer. And he kept everything.

I'm not sure why, but there were bullet holes through the window in the Red Room, or the mud room, upstairs, and instead of just replacing the window, Hunter chose to sandwich it in glass. It became another piece of Hunter's art — as well as a warning to those who came to the door.

Owl Farm had rules. Various people broke those rules, and those people weren't invited back. There were a number of people who came for an interview and then decided to just drink with Hunter; they'd think that they had become such good buddies that they would just get their story the next day. And Hunter would say, "Sorry, you had your chance."

I dealt with a lot of "pilgrims" over the years. They wanted to pay homage, and they came from all over the world, usually bearing gifts. Many sat across the road taking pictures, and some walked up the driveway. Usually I had very little trouble with them. People liked to eat acid and come by the house. Some people would leave notes under rocks or taped to the gate. Some people would stay down at the tavern, eating and drinking for four days just in the hope of seeing him.

TEX WEAVER *was a neighbor of Hunter's in Woody Creek.*

Sometimes I'd get a call from Owl Farm about somebody bothering them, so I'd go up there and try to convince whoever it was that they were lost, maybe by pulling a gun and sticking it in their face and saying, "Get the fuck out of here" or something like that. Let's just say I shooed people away.

DEBORAH FULLER

Tex would do anything for Hunter. Hunter wrote about Tex once in a while; he would use him as a character. He was a friend and a wild boy in the neighborhood. He lived with a guy named Tom, another friend, who fixed Hunter's cars and motorcycles. I could call on either of them in a second for any kind of help. You wanted Tex on your side — let's put it that way. You didn't want to fuck with Tex.

TEX WEAVER

I first met Hunter when I was visiting my sister-in-law in San Francisco in the late sixties, and I used to go out to Golden Gate Park on my motorcycle at two or three a.m. and ride through the park as fast as I could possibly fucking go. I was always watching, because if you see some headlights coming, maybe it's the police, you know. But I see headlights coming at me and I realize it's a motorcycle, and I realize the son of a bitch is going as fast as I am. So I go to the right, and this guy mirrors it. I go to the left; he mirrors it. All of a sudden I'm thinking, "Oh my — this is a game of chicken." So I just aim for him and he aims for me, and we barely missed each other; I mean, we could almost smell each other's breath as we went by each other. I got pissed and wheeled around, thinking I was going to get this son of a bitch, and I chased him down and asked him, "Who the fuck are you?" And he says, "Who the hell are you? I thought I killed you back there." I started laughing, and he was laughing, and I took out my medicine bottle and dumped a whole bunch of it in his hand, and we ended up in a bar that evening. And that's how we met.

I didn't see him again until three or four years later, when I came out to Aspen and ended up on a bar stool next to him. I said, "Golden Gate Park," and he looked at me. "Motorcycle." He said, "Yeah."

Both of us were kind of recluses, but we ended up spending more and more time together. We played softball. Jimmy Buffet had a softball team, which was interesting, because I think you had to be a felon to be on it or something. We called ourselves the Down-Valley Dough-boys. In those days Hunter still was quite mobile.

We did all the drugs and the ether and dah-dah-dah. On ether you slobber; you're a fucking piece of shit. One time we were driving, and I had a tank of it. We were doing acid at the time and drinking and you name it. I had a mask, so you just turn the tank on and you go. You can get that in a liquid form also. One of the things he said in *Vegas* was that you might as well pour it all over a towel and stick it down by the floorboards and turn the fan on so the fumes would come up. This was us.

He used to call me the Princess of Darkness because I would dress up in drag. The first time I did it with him was in San Francisco in '84 or '85. Hunter had driven his car down one of the main drags there and rammed into the back of a carload of colored people. I got this call from him — "Come get me out of jail. . . ." I put on an old Mexican dress like you might see in a cowboy movie — the ones you can pull down over the shoulder — and I put lipstick on and a little wig and went and bailed him out. He was just in because of a small accident or something, but Hunter's approach to all that stuff was lots of yelling — you know, he was trying to pull off this weird demeanor — and they sent an 800-pound pacifier into the cell with him. They have guys that do things if someone is unruly.

I got him out of there, and after that he kept calling me the Princess of Darkness.

DEBORAH FULLER

When friends would come over, Hunter would make Biffs, which were a mix of Bailey's Irish Cream and Irish whiskey, or put out shots of tequila — Hunter loved good tequila. In general, he drank Chivas and Grolsch or Molson and an occasional Bloody Mary or margarita. Later, after he'd been to Cuba, he liked mojitos.

There were always gatherings at Owl Farm for ball games and for the Kentucky Derby.

JACK NICHOLSON

He loved gambling on football. One of the times I definitely impressed him was when he came up to visit when Rafelson and I were shooting *The Postman Always Rings Twice* in Santa Barbara. The weekend we finished was the Super Bowl. I was a child gambler, but I don't much care anymore. It's one of the few vices that I've definitely completely defeated. But they started off trying to get me involved until eventually I'd just say, "Well, okay, what about this?" And just by manipulating the room with little tiny dollar bets and so forth all I was doing was trimming them with the numbers and the spread and preying on their excitements and misunderstandings of the moment — I think I made out of this room with a couple hundred bucks. This was totally impressive to Hunter. He couldn't believe that I'd hustled everybody in the room with numbers, getting them to bet both ways and back and forth.

DEBORAH FULLER

He didn't like going to big gatherings or big dinners. He preferred one-on-one or small groups. If one of his good friends had a birthday party, it was still a big thing to get Hunter to go. He was notorious for accepting dinner invitations and not going, or showing up late. He'd pop in and out, eat oysters and drink and talk and smoke, but it was hard for him to just sit and eat. There were a few places that he would go regularly: to the Goldsteins', the Rafelsons', dinner at Ed Bradley's over the holidays, and to Jack's — small gatherings. And he'd throw a few of his own parties: for the Derby, or the Super Bowl, or the Fourth of July; for the lawyers in town for the National Association of Criminal Defense Lawyers conference or the NORML conference.

People would often ask Hunter if they could bring a friend, or a few friends, with them when they came out. Once in a while Hunter would say okay to this, but sometimes people would just show up with other people, and that was unacceptable. Eventually he put a sign on his fridge that said, "Guests of Guests Are Not Allowed to Invite Guests."

BOB BRAUDIS

Those of us in town recognized that the weeks before and after Christmas we wouldn't see Hunter much. That was the celebrity period, when all of the high rollers, the Jack Nicholsons, et cetera, would come to Aspen for the Christmas holidays, and Hunter was hanging with them, not with us. But as soon as the Rose Bowl was over, he was back to his local crowd.

JACK NICHOLSON

He always liked reading things that he thought might be shocking to me — and almost everything he brought to me was shocking, really. He was always socially pyrotechnical when he talked about things, and he could turn on a dime. I remember a line he gave me, a fragment of something he'd written that ended with the character contemplating how this dry French kiss that he was getting from his cat was making him feel. The image stuck with me as much as anything he ever wrote. It was spectacular — just three or four words could suddenly stun you.

He always came over like he was carrying stolen goods when he had these things. There was a lot of paper fumbling, and he was always saying things like, "I don't know if you're ready for this."

He told me about how this girl had sent him some of her poetry — which I read, and we both agreed that this girl, who was very young, had shocking talent. Apparently this group of young people had taken to breaking into morgues somewhere in Colorado and having parties with dead bodies, and this girl wrote poetry about it. What delighted Hunter in some way was that they called the body of the night "the bride," for instance.

Before that he had turned me on to a book called *The Hellfire Club*, by Daniel Mannix, which was about this secret club that existed when Benjamin Franklin was in England. This one guy, Sir Francis Dashwood, had gone through a lot of different kinds of religious conversion and was apparently a very brilliant man, and at one point he swung back and forth from extreme piety to being insane — things such as this always appealed to Hunter, this kind of behavior. One night Dashwood was fallen upon by demons in the form of two cats fucking that fell through the skylight and this four-eyed glaring monster hurling around his bed. He wound up forming this thing called the Hellfire Club. Sir Francis was the [club's] pope, and he commissioned a lot of pornographic statues. The members would sail down the Thames wrapped in robes, and the people would line the shoreline to see them going up to this crazy place where they just debauched beyond belief. You kind of get the picture.

Those kinds of literary evenings were always pretty much just him and me up at my house, and we'd have a ball. I kept what he liked to drink in the shed, and we'd sit there and tune up for the night. I'd ask him things I wouldn't know about — what's happening here or there politically — and he was always very informed about that. His contacts were very impressive.

DEBORAH FULLER

One reason he lived as long as he did was that he held the least amount of anger inside himself that he could. He vented at anyone around him. He could be quite cruel, and you had to learn how to stand up to him and know how much of it you would take, and let him know. One thing that was very important was that you held no grudges. There wasn't time for that; we had way too much to do. We might be yelling at one moment, and then I'd say, "All right, do you need another drink? Let's get back to the page you're writing." But he would get into his dark moods. You didn't always know where they came from; any number of things could cause them.

The world definitely revolved around him — that's just the way it was. He had to make those choices, and so did I, and I was able to do it longer than a lot of people. But yes, it took its toll. There's not much that he didn't say to you if he felt like it.

It was my life. You either did it full-bore or you didn't, and I accepted that. Any assistant knew that you didn't have time for another life. I helped train the new ones the best I could and helped them get through some of the rough times. Hunter would have them call me and talk to me about the reality of what the job entailed. Just honest stuff, really: Yes, it really does mean working nights, and some days. It's a lot of intense work. Are you nervous driving fast in a car? Do you like birds? Can you type? All of the assistants were extremely bright, and they were all women, basically. He wanted a woman to flirt with while working, and he liked younger women to be there because they had the energy to keep up with him. It was a very difficult job to walk into cold. They either had the spirit and the fortitude, or they left.

TIM FERRIS

Hunter would travel sometimes with assistants, and often it never came up whether they were girlfriends or not. It was this endless parade. They all tended to be good conversationalists.

JACK NICHOLSON

Those migrations from assistant to girlfriend — it was pretty consistent behavior, but I never quite really knew when the transition had occurred. It would just eventually become apparent.

DEBORAH FULLER

He would find them in different ways. He would meet people at the tavern or at a lecture. He had *Rolling Stone* put something in the magazine saying that he was looking for an assistant, or he would have people connected to the literary world looking for him; people would write offering to work for him.

DOUG BRINKLEY

The ones that were successful knew when to back away from Hunter — when the going gets weird, get the hell out of there — but a wayward personality could get psychologically trapped in the spider-web of Owl Farm. In your twenties, you're vulnerable to things. In that way, Hunter had a very unfair advantage in those relationships. On the other hand, you have to be responsible for your own life — to know whether to get away from Hunter or not. Hunter was going to be Hunter. If you're the moth coming into the flame, and you get burned by the flame, and then you complain, "Oh my God, I got burned" — well, what did you expect? He's an inferno. Did you think you were special?

A dynamic got created, and it usually crashed because it wasn't a dynamic based on deep love — it was based on a kind of convenience and expediency, on loneliness and friendship. He had some bad crack-ups in those regards.

DEBORAH FULLER

All assistants were taught to shoot. Most seemed to enjoy it. I certainly did, and became a good shot. Hunter was a good teacher. He had a shooting range, and there would be things like old water heaters he'd have placed around for targets. He'd teach you to shoot in different ways — up close and at a distance, as well as with different kinds of guns — handguns, rifles, shotguns. We used to put out beer kegs he had found behind the tavern. Hunter felt there was a reward in hearing each shot hit the target, so the metal targets were perfect. He liked using exploding targets attached to small propane canisters, like the ones used for camping stoves. Now, those were fun for everyone — a big bang.

MARY HARRIS *was a neighbor of Hunter's in Woody Creek.*

I used to live just up from Owl Farm in a little cabin, and I woke up a couple of times at three in the morning with a machine gun going off so loud that it sounded like it was under my window. I'd fly out of bed screaming, but then I'd remember that I lived next door to Hunter.

PATTI STRANAHAN *is George Stranahan's wife.*

Every now and then some windows would get blasted out when George and Hunter were making bombs. That was always a big occasion: "Oh boy, let's get together and blow something up."

GEORGE STRANAHAN

We did some pretty good bombs. I was always the supplier. Hunter would go buy the gunpowder, but I always got the gel, the dynamite. It was easy. And I'm no expert on this stuff, but that's the way it was, from the seventies on up until 9/11. Out of politeness we would call the sheriff if we were going to do something, and tell him that if somebody calls in with a report of an explosion in Woody Creek, you don't need to send a deputy. The sheriff understood.

BOB BRAUDIS

Most of Hunter's dynamite came from George Stranahan, who actually was raising cattle and had ditches and stumps. George and Hunter liked to blow up shit as a recreation. They blew up an old Jeep Wagoneer. The hood was blasted three hundred feet up in the air. Hunter told me they used a half a case of Dupont 80 percent, twenty-five pounds of black powder, and five gallons of gasoline. Often they would blow stuff up before George would go in for surgery. He had an awful lot of spinal surgery, and he was warned that he might come out of one of them in a wheelchair forever. So it boosted his spirits to blow something up beforehand.

GEORGE STRANAHAN

Hunter felt that there was ceremony around the bomb, and that it was important. I guess he knew that I was a rancher and enjoyed dynamite — I mean, I'd like a "boom" right now! — and because I had the shit, I could.

PAUL PASCARELLA

He appreciated sheer firepower — explosions, huge weapons.

GEORGE STRANAHAN

Soldier of Fortune, of course, was fascinated with Hunter and with guns and explosives in general, so some of their staffers came out to Owl Farm with a .50-caliber single-shot assassination rifle. Now with .50 caliber, you could be three miles away and with a good sight still kill a guy. The cops aren't going to get you; you'll make your escape. So the magazine called Hunter and said, "We want to get a picture of you shooting this thing at dusk, and we need to have an explosion where the bullet hits so that we can get a picture of you and the muzzle blast, and then whatever you're hitting exploding." And these assholes came out, and I was called in as the munitions expert, and we got everything all set up with this big rifle and the explosion waiting to happen.

We put a car up the hill, and I put a whole bunch of dynamite in the cylinder block, figuring that if they hit it, it would be enough impact, as well as enough flames. But I also thought that we might have trouble actually hitting the dynamite precisely — it was Hunter shooting, after all. Hunter was in the kitchen drinking while we were doing all of this stuff, and so I put a can of gasoline in the front seat and a fuse leading from the dynamite to the can of gasoline, with the idea that in the worst case, we miss the dynamite and we'll hit the gas can with a tracer, the gas will burst into flames, it will light the fuse, the fuse will go, and we'll get an explosion and we'll get good pictures. Finally they got Hunter to come out, and he was pretty drunk. *Soldier of Fortune* snapped him as he pulled the trigger, and we saw the tracer go fifty feet above the goddamn car. Not even close.

JEANETTE ETHERIDGE *is the owner of Tosca, a bar in San Francisco.*

I met Hunter in San Francisco in the late sixties, but we got to be good friends when he was working as the night manager of the O'Farrell Theater — which was run by the Mitchell brothers, who had made the classic porno film *Behind the Green Door*. Hunter was also writing a weekly column for the *San Francisco Examiner,* and became a regular at my bar in North Beach.

JEFF ARMSTRONG *is a manager of the O'Farrell Theatre.*

In 1984, he accepted an assignment from *Playboy* for a story he called "The Night Manager." Which led to *The Night Manager* by Ralph Steadman, which we have on our wall. It shows all these naked, writhing women at the bottom, and in the middle of it all, Hunter sitting on what looks like a lifeguard chair. He's looking down at all these women writhing about underneath him, nude and screaming. Hugh Hefner paid for it and he gave it to us.

We had yellow business cards made: "The O'Farrell Theatre — Night Manager, Hunter S. Thompson," which I thought was kind of cute. He would pass those out and tell people, "Come down and see us. I'll be down there. I'm workin'." He actually did *some* sort of work; he talked to the DJ and he made recommendations. He didn't sweep up or anything, or count money.

At any rate, the piece never came out.

DAVID MCCUMBER *was Hunter's editor at the* San Francisco Examiner.

Word came down that the owner of the *Examiner,* Will Hearst, had hired Hunter as a columnist. His very first column came in — "Buffalo

Gores a Visitor" — and Hunter and his editor immediately got into a violent disagreement.

I got a call from Will at ten in the morning. He invited me to his office and said, "I've got a new job for you. How would you like to be Hunter's control?" At that moment Hunter burst out of Will's bathroom, where he'd been listening to the conversation, poured me a drink and handed it to me, did ten push-ups, got up, shook my hand, and said, "Hi." We hit it off immediately and somehow rocked into this weekly motion.

We used to go to the O'Farrell together. The Mitchell brothers loved him, but he didn't really do anything there. Hunter just liked the sort of thumb-in-your-eye approach that they took. When the mayor tried cracking down on the O'Farrell, they put his home phone number on their marquee. Things like that appealed to Hunter. He just hung out and absorbed the culture.

JEFF ARMSTRONG

People have said that he didn't write much about sex or women, and that bothered him. People threw that in his face and said that even the few scenes when he did, like with the maid in *Fear and Loathing in Las Vegas,* were abrasive and offensive. We talked about that a couple times.

When Hunter was the night manager, he interacted freely with the women. It was very cordial and open and funny; he never looked down on them. In fact, he admired the strippers. He thought that their strength and uniqueness were laudable qualities. These girls put on skits — they dressed up like gorillas and wore dildos.

He was interested in the business of sex and fascinated by the customers. I wouldn't say Hunter was promiscuous. He loved to flirt, and he loved the attention of women.

MARGOT KIDDER

In '84, I arrived at the Sir Francis Drake, this big, wonderful hotel in San Francisco. Pat Caddell was already there, and these gay friends of mine had arranged for me to have this wonderful driver, this muscle-bound drag queen in heavy makeup, ferry me around in this gold fifties Cadillac. We got an emergency call from Hunter — he was at Ann Getty's house and he had just slammed his fist through the wall and called Linda Ellerbee a fascist dyke or something, and we had to go and rescue him. We jumped in the gold Cadillac with the driver and raced over to the house and had to run in and grab Hunter from the kitchen with everybody yelling and screaming and haul him out and throw him in the back of the car and whisk him away.

JEANETTE ETHERIDGE

Everyone hung out at my bar, and it was Hunter and Ed Bradley who made that happen. Those two guys made it their headquarters. Hunter was writing a piece for *Playboy* about the Democratic National Convention, which was in town in July, called "While the Delegates Slept." It was about all the shit that was going on in my bar at night. Bill Dixon and Pat Caddell were writing Gary Hart's speeches on the pool table in the back room.

I remember wanting to hear Mario Cuomo speak, and Robin Williams offered to take care of the bar. So I called in to Robin later that night — "Everything's fine; don't worry about anything." Well, he had Ron Reagan Jr. telling him to come to the back room, and he had Hunter and all the Kennedy kids mixing it up.

MARGOT KIDDER

Then Hunter started his adventures with Ron Reagan Jr. Ron was ga-ga, just starstruck with Hunter. That was also the period when Hunter fell in love with a porn queen. He'd be sobbing on my bed about her, telling me how his heart was being broken and how he couldn't quite get the girl. This was supposed to be the Democratic convention, but I suppose Hunter was the sideshow.

DAVID MCCUMBER

Hunter and I were sitting in Will Hearst's office about eight o'clock one night, waiting for Will to show up, and Hunter was getting increasingly agitated. He'd been traveling, and I don't think he had his normal supply of drugs, and he was not in a good mood. He just sat there drinking scotch and really getting pissed off because Will wasn't there.

Will's office was on the second floor, right above Fifth Street. We heard some noise out on the street — just a couple of pressmen out on the street, horsing around. Hunter threw open the window and stuck his head out and screamed, "You pigfuckers! Shut up down there! Don't you know we have a newspaper to put out?!" What he didn't know was that the pressmen were in the middle of an intense labor negotiation at the time — and having some freak scream and shake his fist at them from the publisher's window didn't do much to help this. They started flipping him off and screaming back, and then Hunter shouted back, "You bastards!! I'll teach you some manners," and whirled around, picked up a wastebasket, ran into Will's bathroom and turned the shower on full hot, and started ferrying bucketfuls of hot water and throwing them out the window onto these guys. They were screaming — and then Hunter turned around just cool as a cucumber and picked up the telephone, hit 0, and said, "Operator, this is Dr. Thompson in the publisher's office. There seems to be some sort of riffraff down on the street. Would you get security to deal with it, please?"

It shifted his mood completely. He was feeling fine the rest of the night. Sometimes he just needed some fun, a sense of mischief, to pull himself out of the black moods.

WAYNE EWING *was living next door to Hunter and working as an independent documentary filmmaker in the early eighties.*

I had just produced a couple of pieces for a PBS series called *Frontline* and was looking for a new subject. Hunter was doing his night manager thing, and I had this notion that the reason why Hunter was interested in the O'Farrell Theatre was political. Perhaps he saw in pornography and sexual liberation the same elements that the anarchists in America at the turn of the century did — that it was just breaking that final bond with society.

He was with Maria Khan at the time. They had an apartment in Sausalito, so Deborah and I flew out to San Francisco and met him for dinner in this country club setting — the oddest place you could imagine in Marin County, right across the Golden Gate Bridge — and then retired to the O'Farrell Theatre for the weekend.

They had a big pool table, and one wall was almost completely shot away from a pellet gun that they had given Hunter, which he would use constantly. At the same time, there were naked or almost completely naked women just walking around casually, and he would supervise the proceedings from a big high chair above the New York Stage, as they called it, and would choreograph various things for the girls to do — acts.

JEANETTE ETHERIDGE

We were at the Mitchell brothers' one night, and I got kind of excited that these girls were dancing and people were throwing money at them. I thought I could do that, so I got up on the pool table in the office upstairs and started dancing, and the next thing I knew, Hunter was shooting a pistol off into the wall between my legs. To this day I don't know if it was live ammunition or not. There were boxes of Ivory Snow detergent all around the room because Marilyn Chambers, who the theater was associated with, was an Ivory Snow girl before she got into porn, and Hunter was using them as targets.

WAYNE EWING

Hunter and Jeff Armstrong, who was the real night manager for the Mitchell brothers, would talk about the best way to go up before a grand jury — the best frame of mind or, actually, the best chemical mix. Hunter had a glass in his hand and was leaning up against the pool table, and he would bend over so his nose was almost down on the green felt while he was listening to Jeff, and suddenly he would have something to say and would lurch back up, and the glass in his hand would stand straight up; it was an exclamation mark. He would say, "No, no, no. The way to go before a grand jury is you take acid the night before, so that when you go in and they ask you the very first question, you immediately start crying and slobbering on the stand, helpless in fear."

It took me a number of years to really get enough trust to be able to film Hunter, all the time, and then he started to ask me to shoot things more and more. He put me through an early test. Once I got a new video camera flown up from Denver for him, and I called him up and said, "It's at the airport — I'll bring it out." He was very excited, and said, "Come right on out. I might be in the bathtub, so just come on in." I would never have gone into the kitchen without announcing myself and being invited in, and when I got out to Owl Farm, I went up on the porch and made a bunch of noise, purposefully. I thought I heard a grunt inside, so I walked in, saying the whole time, "It's Wayne, it's Wayne, Hunter, I've got the camera." I thought I heard another grunt, so I stepped into the kitchen doorway, and there was Hunter about six feet in front of me, dripping wet in a bathrobe, with a twelve gauge shotgun in his hand and this wicked smile on his face that told me, "I could kill you right now and no court in the land would ever convict me. You are an intruder." And damn if he didn't raise the gun and fire from the hip and blow the door frame out that I was standing in, about six inches from my side. I had never been shot at before, and my voice went up three octaves, and I screamed, "Hunter, you motherfucker!" and ran out of the house. He was laughing his ass off, and eventually I ended up laughing too. I had to just take it as a hug from Hunter — and, I think, a test that I wouldn't call 911.

MICHAEL SOLHEIM

Hunter and I got into a beef with two guys at the J-Bar one evening. It was New Year's Day — I think 1985 — and we'd been in there all day watching football; we were into our fourth game, and Hunter said, "There's two guys back there by that table, and they've been watching us — I think they're up to something." He could see them in the mirror. He said, "I'll let you know if they come over." I said "Good idea. Then what do we do?" He said, "We'll drop the fuckers." I said, "That's a great idea." Sure enough, the two guys get out of their seats and walk over, and just when they get close, Hunter says, "Now!" and spins around in his seat and punches one of the guys. I spun around and got the other guy, and then all four of us are rolling around.

KALLEN VON RENKL

Michael and Hunter beat the absolute crap out of them and threw them out the front door. That was the first time I saw the other side of Hunter. The Jerome was crowded, and it was pretty bloody.

MICHAEL SOLHEIM

All four of us wound up having to go to the hospital for stitches, because we'd gotten little nicks in our hands — and at the hospital, one of the other guys walks over to us and says, "All we wanted was your autograph." We felt like the biggest assholes in the world. We felt terrible, so we brought them back to the bar and bought them a bunch of drinks. It was the least we could do.

SHELBY SADLER *began working as an editor and researcher for Hunter in 1986.*

Hunter would come to Washington quite frequently, and we'd hole up for two or three weeks at the Embassy Row or the Ritz-Carlton and do a lot of writing. That's when we began working on a new novel called *Polo Is My Life*. It's unclear exactly how it started.

Very early in our relationship, Hunter had been flirting with a polo player from California named Paula Baxt, who rode at the Empire Polo Club in Indio, California. Her husband had some connection to Aspen, and she was spending time out there when Hunter met and became desperately enamored of her for a week or so. He kept asking her to run away with him and all this, and Paula is the one who said, "I can't go with you, Hunter. Polo is my life." When Paula said that phrase, it all came together for him. He was crazy about it. It struck him like thunder that all the elusive women in the world, in the end, would tell him essentially the same thing in different words: "Sorry, but polo is my life." It all led into class and money and all of that. Paula Baxt was Hunter's Daisy Buchanan.

I've talked to her about it since, and she finds the whole story to be hilarious, because it was just a throwaway line for her. She had no interest in Hunter. He was just a strange, crazy guy who was fun to hang out with. But Hunter took this all very seriously — he was infatuated with her, and her husband became Tom Buchanan in his mind, and it just went on from there. I don't think he ever saw her again.

DEBORAH FULLER

The visual progress of each book was very important to him. There were two storyboards, each made of cork. Each was marked off in sections by colored tape to denote the beginning, middle, and end of the book, and beyond that by chapter. As he wrote pages, they would be tacked up, along with headlines and subheds and any pictures. If there was a character named Jilly, Jilly's picture went up. The *Polo Is My Life* board had a road map, polo mallets, two belts of machine gun bullets, and a five-foot-long rusty two-handed saw with "Confessions of the Best Piece of Ass in the World" written on it.

Hunter made up a lot of his own letterheads for writing faxes on.

These were mostly handwritten, often accompanied by some strange picture, and they'd often be headlined with things like "The Horrible Cokie Monster," "Rich, Drunk Teen Seized in Shootout at Bogus Animal Shelter," "Woman Seized by Game Wardens: 'I don't know what's wrong with me, doctor — I keep waking up naked in the woods. Do you think I'm sick?'"

SHELBY SADLER

He always intended *Polo* to be his story of lost love, the green light at the end of the dock — not so much in the way Fitzgerald presented it, but more from Samuel Taylor Coleridge's original use of the term "green light" in "Dejection: An Ode:"

> Though I should gaze for ever
> On that green light that lingers in the west:
> I may not hope from outward forms to win
> The passion and the life, whose fountains are within.

It's the only time Hunter has ever truly written about a female character — usually they're just throwaways, as are most of his characters other than the Hunter alter ego, which is also fractured in two in *Polo:* There's Hunter and there's Raoul Duke, and they're two very distinctly different people in the book.

When Hunter found out that I lived a fifteen-minute walk from Fitzgerald's grave in Rockville, Maryland, he was astonished. One time when he visited, we walked to the grave. We stopped and bought a white rose to leave on the grave, where the last line of *Gatsby* is inscribed on the headstone: "And so we beat on, boats against the current, borne back ceaselessly into the past." I will never forget Hunter gently laying the white rose down across the words and peering up and being absolutely silent the whole walk back.

The thing is, *Polo Is My Life* had nothing to do with polo —

absolutely nothing. Polo is in *The Great Gatsby* as well, and Hunter saw it as being in *Polo Is My Life* to the same extent. Hunter went to the polo matches because Jann paid for it, and because he wanted to be able to watch the polo society, but with some distance. He wanted a reason to be there and meet these people so that he could get a sense of the ethos and write characters from that.

DEBORAH FULLER

Hunter worked on *Polo* — the novel — for twelve to fifteen years, I'd guess. His work habits stayed the same as long as I knew him. People tried to get him to use a computer, and he would get them and hate them and never use them. He often wrote notes by hand and then typed a page and then hand-corrected. He could cut and paste.

SEMMES LUCKETT

We started the Woody Creek Rod & Gun Club because Hunter and some of us thought that Colorado might pass a restrictive gun-ownership law. I was the first president, Paul Pascarella did the logo, and Joe Edwards was a counselor. That was so important to Hunter. He wrote about the club in a wonderful piece, "Turbo Must Die," from *Songs of the Doomed*. In the story, Stranahan has a prize bull, Turbo, and we're going to blow him up after selling 1,000 vials of the bull's semen at $10,000 apiece. We got this charter from the NRA without having to deal with a lot of the normal requirements. Hunter also used me as the "spokesman" for the club, and we had everything set so that if they did pass a gun law, we'd all be able to keep our weapons.

PATTI STRANAHAN

Hunter would come over to our house for Thanksgiving dinner, and we used to let him swim in our pool every night. He was quiet, and he could do whatever he needed to. He would drive up and make sure that all the lights were out, or that everyone was asleep. He never came in when he thought he would be disruptive. He'd sneak in with a flashlight through a side door.

GEORGE STRANAHAN

He felt safe here. He trusted me and I trusted him. Absolutely. And if he had a loaded gun and was messing with it, I trusted him not to hit me.

PATTI STRANAHAN

Our kids always felt safe with him. They would go down and talk to him late at night, and he would often drop little presents off, whether it was on Christmas Eve or on any random night.

GEORGE STRANAHAN

He left a lot of presents, usually high-powered flashlights or some sort of gadgets. He'd come up for his swim, and we'd get up in the morning and say, "Wow."

PATTI STRANAHAN

Sometimes there would be roses for me, or I'd be getting up to get the kids ready for school and he'd still be here swimming, and we'd sit and have grapefruit. That was his favorite thing. One Christmas morning we came out, and there was this taxidermied raccoon holding Hunter's expired American Express card in his paw. There was a sign on it that said, "To Ben."

GEORGE STRANAHAN

When our son Ben was about seven, we had a tarantula in a glass cage. One night at maybe nine o'clock, Hunter dropped in with a great big athletic bag full of toys — he had a new gun to show me, and he had his whiskey, and a bunch of other things. He dropped the bag, and we started having a political talk, when Ben woke up and came out and sat down with the guys. Talk then turned to the tarantula, and the fact that we had read that it was perfectly safe to let a tarantula walk right across your hand. We had never actually done it, but I had been drinking with Hunter, and so somehow we decided that this was the night when we would do what needed to be done, and bravely. So Wilky was brought out in his cage, and he was sitting in front of us. Hunter poured another glass of whiskey and then reached down into his big sports bag and said, "Wait a minute. We're not ready for this yet." And he pulled out some lipstick from his bag and said, "Lipstick is important."

Hunter put the lipstick on himself, on me, and on Ben, and we got the tarantula out of the cage with considerable care and were letting it crawl on the palms of our hands. That was the moment when Ben's mother came out to see what was going on, and that's what she saw: two drunks and her son wearing lipstick and playing with a tarantula.

TERRY SABONIS-CHAFEE *was working at an energy policy think tank outside of Aspen in July 1989.*

One night I was going out to dinner with an old friend of Hunter's who wanted to introduce me to him. Shortly after we sat down at the Woody Creek Tavern, Hunter pulled up on a motorcycle. The three of us went up to Owl Farm and spent the evening bullshitting and drinking, and then I went off to my conference. When I got back, the secretary at work said I had five phone messages from Hunter Thompson. His writing assistant was off that week, and he asked me to come out to help him with a column. It seemed like a good idea at the time, and it would have been just a hell of a lot of fun, except that I fell madly in love with him.

We were only about a month into the whole mad romance when I had to go to grad school. I was twenty-seven — old by Hunter's standards — and I had finally gotten into Princeton and wasn't about to blow off graduate school for this lunatic I had just met, a fact that just filled him with rage.

He took me to the Aspen airport to fly to Denver and then Princeton, and when I was in the Denver airport, I got paged. It was Hunter. In his marvelous, growly voice he said, "Goddamn it, I love you and I want to marry you — will you marry me?" and went on about how much he missed me, even though I'd only been gone two hours. I said, "I will marry you, but I've got to do this thing first" — which was very much not the answer that he was expecting. I didn't realize the extent to which this was an effort to get me on the next plane back to Woody Creek, and from the time I left to the time I finally came back to stay in June, Hunter flew me back to Colorado every other weekend.

Hunter had a box of loose gemstones that he enigmatically said were from Africa and had been given to him by somebody to settle a debt. We sat down with the box, and Hunter told me to pick out whatever stone was my favorite. I picked an implausibly huge rectangular aquamarine, and he picked out a beautiful uncut green emerald, and he gave the two gemstones to a local artist friend to make jewelry for the two of us. The aquamarine was placed in a beautiful white gold setting on a ring, and the emerald was made into a necklace — that's the one that Hunter wore for the rest of forever.

Hunter really needed someone to be an assistant, and I told him to interview my younger sister.

CATHERINE SABONIS-BRADLEY *was about to start her last semester at the University of Florida in the winter of 1990.*

Hunter flew me out to Owl Farm while I was still on Christmas break. David McCumber was out working with Hunter on *Songs of the Doomed,* and the two of them got in a fight over some insanely minor point. He went ballistic in the middle of the night and destroyed a typewriter — just beat it to death with a phone. I was trying to stay awake on coffee, but I fell asleep on the couch just a few feet away from Hunter while these bits of typewriter were flying by my head.

DAVID MCCUMBER

There was metal Selectric shrapnel flying all over the kitchen. I said, "Goddamn it, Hunter, this shit gets old." He picked up a piece of something and brought it back behind him and took a step toward me like he was going to hit me with it, and I grabbed a beer bottle in my hand — and then we both started laughing at the same time, and he just said, "I think it's time we took a little break." And then he was fine. Everything dissipated. Sometimes he would just have to shoot something or break something, and then he'd be okay.

CATHERINE SABONIS-BRADLEY

Earlier I was taking reams of notes on everything he and McCumber were saying, and when the smoke cleared, Hunter told me that I understood him and what needed to be done, and that since I wasn't freaked out by the flying pieces of typewriter, I was hired.

Deborah left not too long after I'd gotten there. McCumber had left, and Hunter had told me and Deborah that we shouldn't be talking to him. For several days he had been saying that he wouldn't have him out and would never talk to him again, and McCumber was calling to try to find out what was going on. Eventually I called him back from the cabin to tell him, and somehow Hunter found out. Since Deborah was in the cabin with me, we were both implicated. Hunter went after the cabin's electrical box with a hatchet and cut the phone line and the power. That was when Deborah decided that enough was enough, and she and I were driving down the driveway, trying to figure out where we were going to stay, when Hunter came at the car with a very large rock and threw it at the windshield and shattered it.

We left and stayed the night with another assistant who now lived in town. She had worked for Hunter for a short time earlier and had left in fairly short order, not pleased, and concerned for her mental health — literally.

TERRY SABONIS-CHAFEE

Everybody knew that Hunter was a very tough beat no matter how much you loved him. Hunter's friend Tim Ferris had just done a documentary on the nature of genius, and he looked at me and said, "You know, there's a kind of genius that consumes everyone around them to keep from consuming itself, and Hunter is like that. You'll stay with it for as long as you can, and someday you will leave, and it'll be okay." It was such a bizarre thing to hear from someone I didn't even know that well, but the image of that vortex consuming everything but Hunter himself resonates with me.

When Hunter failed at things, he made you feel like you had failed. He could make you feel like the world hung on making him smile, and when he did, he convinced you that the world did hang on this. It was a hillbilly laziness. He could be brilliant, or he could have these quirky ideas that he thought would make lots of money — and he liked the quirky ideas that he thought would make a lot of money.

CATHERINE SABONIS-BRADLEY

A lot of time was wasted on this "gonzo bikini" he was trying to have made. The bikini top was women's blow-up hands, and he wanted them very realistic-looking, with long nails, and he wanted drawings done. The bottoms would be gonzo bikini bottoms. He had a book that was overdue, and he was trying to get bikini sketches made and get me to research a prototype.

CHAPTER NINE

Circling the Wagons at Owl Farm

—ᴗᎪᏔᎶᏁ—

Hunter's defense on the LSD charge, which he was quite proud of, was to say that you can't get good acid anymore — if he'd known it was there, he would have eaten it a long time ago.

HAL HADDON *is a former McGovern staffer, now a prominent criminal-defense attorney in Denver.*

The Roaring Fork Valley consists of three somewhat-defined communities: There's Aspen, which is considered ultraliberal in terms of the toleration of lifestyle issues and people have lots of money; there's Basalt, which has changed a lot, sort of in the middle of the valley at the head of the Frying Pan River; and then there's Glenwood Springs — all part of the same judicial district. Glenwood Springs, at least at that time, was predominantly rural, very conservative.

The city district attorney for the whole judicial district was from Glenwood Springs, and he was active in the war on drugs — a very conservative, hard-right guy. Hunter was a beacon of what he viewed as an intolerable kind of lifestyle — a bad example — so they set out to get him.

I had known Hunter for about fourteen years, and he hired me as his lawyer. Hunter had a great need for lawyers. He was committing felonies every day. He needed to appreciate criminal defense, and he would not infrequently get busted in small ways. His writing is replete with a lot of the problems he had earlier in San Francisco. It was all small stuff — DUIs, disorderly conduct. Gerry Goldstein and Michael Stepanian, his San Francisco lawyer, were constantly on retainer, and Hunter would always plead to something. But this one was really serious.

Gail Palmer-Slater was a producer of pornographic movies. She was living in Michigan and kept sending Hunter letters saying she wanted to meet him, and suggesting she wanted to talk to him about taking one of his books and turning it into a high-art porn movie. At some point she sent him a card, and the front of it read, "Sex is a dirty business," and the inside read, "But somebody has to do it." And she enclosed a note saying she was going to be in Aspen on such-and-such date.

Hunter never responded, but he kept the card — because he kept everything; he was a pack rat — along with a sample of one of her porn movies. And she showed up at his house in 1990 to talk to Hunter about letting her do one of his books. It was a typical raucous night.

CATHERINE SABONIS-BRADLEY

Gail Palmer-Slater hung out flirting and partying. Various friends who had been hanging out started to leave because she was so boring, and then Hunter said, "I'm going into the Water Room," and said to her, "You need to leave." She started begging and whimpering and saying "No, no . . . the fun's just started; I can't leave yet."

She started getting in Hunter's space and leaning in toward him and begging him and whining and touching him. He picked up the phone to call a cab, and she hung it up. He didn't like that, and he pushed her away, knocking over a glass gallon jug of cranberry juice, which broke. She slipped on it and fell on her ass and was weeping hysterically. There was lots of yelling and weeping, and then I called a cab and waited outside with her for the cab to come. She was still weeping and saying, "Why won't he talk to me? I'll stay, I'll be good. . . . What did I do?" And then she left.

A couple days later, Hunter called me at the cabin and told me to come over and make him breakfast because he had to go down to the police station. There was a warning of some sort prior to him going down, but while he was down there, six cops showed up and handed me a search warrant.

HAL HADDON

Gail Palmer-Slater claimed that at some point she was offered cocaine, and that Hunter then lured her to his hot tub and viciously twisted her breast, attempted to assault her sexually, and then threw her out in the snow and called a cab for her. The last part of it is true. He did throw her out in the snow and call a cab. He claimed she was obnoxious and disruptive. But there was a search warrant executed.

BOB BRAUDIS

That case came into my office early in the morning by way of her husband, who was an optometrist from Minneapolis. He dropped the dime on Hunter, and my guys launched the investigation, and they were waiting for me at eight in the morning when I came in. They gave me a briefing, and I said, "I'm handing this over to an outside agency." Hunter got really pissed at me for giving it to the DA, but that's when I said, "I can be your friend or your sheriff, but not both."

The DA was looking to bust Hunter for anything. I told the deputy DA, Chip McCrory, that there were several witnesses at this get-together who hadn't been interviewed, and that the search warrant was perhaps prematurely applied for and signed by the judge. The DA's investigator, Mike Kelly, agreed with me, but the deputy DA said, "No. We want to toss his house, and I'd like a couple of deputies to help us."

I had no involvement with it other than to lend two deputies to the DA to conduct the search. They didn't want to have anything to do with it, but they helped.

GEORGE STRANAHAN

Actually, the sheriff called me. We knew that somebody was trying to get a search warrant. None of the local judges would sign one, but in any case, Braudis, of course, would know whether or not there was a search warrant. Finally they got one about five days after the event, and Braudis gave a call and said, "You should get our friend out of the house and clean it up." Which was the code that there was going to be a search. I had about an hour. We got bags of shit out on the lawn, we looked under the couch, and we brought a big grocery bag of crap out of there and up to my house to hide.

SEMMES LUCKETT

We hid everything we could find — and the thing Hunter got busted for was the shit he couldn't find! He just couldn't believe they found some acid he'd be looking for for years.

GEORGE STRANAHAN

I was down at Owl Farm fourteen hours altogether while they searched it. They literally took every book out, one at a time, thinking that there had to be something in there. The event had happened between the kitchen and the garage, and presumably the search warrant was to be the location of the crime, but they went down into the wardrobe, where they discovered a shotgun that was approximately twelve inches long. And they're on the phone about it — is it exactly twelve, or twelve and under? They took apart the dryers, thinking that he had something hidden up in the little holes. Eventually they slammed the refrigerator door and something toppled out behind the refrigerator, and they found a mason jar of pot — and when Hunter found out about this, he said, "Oh, I lost that twelve years ago."

In his bedroom they found a Bic pen with the works taken out. Maybe there was a little white powder in it. They took that, and they found a film canister with a blue pill.

They also went through a filing cabinet and found a little file called "Juan." And they realized that in this file were letters to a young person. So they asked me, "Do you know this person? Do you know what their age is?" And I said, "Fucking assholes! You're trying to interpret letters to his own son as child pornography?!"

Now, to be honest, Hunter would sometimes take Polaroids of the sorts of things he did with women, and he would pull these pictures out sometimes and show his friends. But now they decided that they were going to go after him for child porn.

HAL HADDON

Bob Braudis and I videotaped the search. They went through every inch of that house, searching for "evidence," and they found two tabs of LSD in an old suitcase that said Juan Thompson on the outside — the LSD was probably twenty years old — and they found traces of cocaine on a dish — not usable traces — and some dynamite in Hunter's garage.

They charged him with sexual assault, possession of explosives — a felony, unless you have a legitimate agricultural business — and possession of a trace of cocaine, along with the LSD. That was essentially the case.

TERRY SABONIS-CHAFEE

I'm at Princeton trying to get some kind of clue as to what the fuck just happened, reading the front-page story in the *New York Times* that my fiancée is wanted for assaulting a porn star — and that a search of his home revealed a machine gun, child pornography, and a pound of magic mushrooms. And I can't reach him.

By the time I got out there, he was having such a violent reaction to everything that I figured probably more of it was true than wasn't. He wouldn't even let my sister talk to me. Cat stayed in the guesthouse, and he would literally give her the "Cross the threshold of the front door and you die" order. My only role was to never be forgiven for not having been there. He'd say, "You weren't here, goddamn it. If you had been here, I wouldn't have been in this bad crazy mood, and none of this would have happened. And if you weren't trying to do this loveless, passionless long-distance relationship I wouldn't be in this situation." If I had been there he wouldn't be depending on a twenty-one-year-old material witness — my younger sister — who might hate him. He seemed to think that he'd been really, really wronged.

CATHERINE SABONIS-BRADLEY

He went straight into anger and then paranoia. Hunter became convinced that Bobby Braudis wanted to arrest him and had planted the whole thing to get him into rehab, and Bobby was in for two years of pure hell.

I was not prepared for Hunter's many definitions of truth. I kept feeling that the actual truth was going to clear everything, and I kept being told that it wasn't about that — it was about loyalty. All of a sudden, everything about Hunter seemed to be more about loyalty than about truth.

HAL HADDON

In the courtroom, Hunter sat in the middle of the defendant's table with lawyers on both sides of him, and a bunch of water glasses in front of him. He had one glass that was all tequila. We had a visiting judge from Glenwood Springs who presided over the whole thing. He had a very good time.

The way the courtroom was set up, the witness box was no more than six feet from where the defense table was. So here's Hunter, drinking his tequila, and he's being braced by his lawyers to pull him down if something weird should happen, because he had a tendency to try to stand up. He did that a couple of times. Gail Palmer-Slater testified, and because the witness box and the defense table were so close, it was almost as if she and Hunter could have a dialogue if they wanted. She's sitting there, a huge woman — six-two, six-three — and just after she's sworn in as a witness, she looks over at him and says, "Hi, Hunter." She was making eyes at him during the whole hearing.

GERRY GOLDSTEIN *is a criminal-defense attorney who was a longtime friend of Hunter's.*

At first when Hunter ranted and raved, you always had a tendency to write off about 20 percent of it, but damned if he wasn't always right. It was part of the way he hooked you, and he liked that. It not only made him look better in the long run, but it made you a true believer. This woman was out to get him, she was up to no good, and the authorities played right into her hands, and ultimately right into his. Hollywood couldn't have sent you a better prosecution witness. She was made to order — a treacherous heat-seeking missile who was focused and determined to get her prey. It became so obvious that Hunter was the victim here.

HAL HADDON

Hunter's defense on the LSD charge, which he was quite proud of, was to say that you can't get good acid anymore — if he'd known it was there, he would have eaten it a long time ago.

In the end, the judge threw it all out, including the drug possession. He felt there wasn't a usable quantity of cocaine. They had also charged Hunter with use — which is a felony in this state — but they didn't prove. She claimed that this plate of cocaine got passed around, but since she didn't take any, she didn't know what it really was, and she claimed she really didn't know what cocaine was anyway.

We stepped outside at about five o'clock in the afternoon on a nice summer day, and the Mitchell brothers from San Francisco had brought in eight strippers, who were all walking around the courthouse with placards saying, "Free Hunter! Save the First Amendment." Hunter came out and saw all this, walked down the steps, gave them the victory sign, and then rolled somersaults on the grass.

We repaired to the Jerome hotel, to the J-Bar, and started drinking. Hunter went across the street to a hardware store and bought this enormous pair of bolt cutters and came back and snipped every lawyer's tie off, and then put them on his wall later as a souvenir of due process.

After the bust, Hunter became obsessed with the Fourth Amendment and created his own Fourth Amendment Foundation as a kind of bully pulpit. He had a letterhead and put a bunch of people's names on it, including mine and George McGovern's, without asking. Whenever Hunter would see something that he thought was a particularly egregious violation of the Fourth Amendment, he'd send out a bunch of faxes with the letterhead. It was never a real foundation — he didn't have any money. It was crazy.

He would always pay me something for my services, but it wouldn't be a lot. More often, he would give me art or some sort of trinket. He gave me a painting for my work on the Gail Palmer-Slater case. Hunter and a local artist, Earl Biss, had stayed up one night and done this painting together. It was a double-breasted horse with a woman's head, this big long thing. My partner sold it for five grand — it was probably worth fifty.

BOB BRAUDIS

My role as sheriff and my role as friend never caused me an awful lot of anguish or conflict. I was criticized by a very small minority of Pitkin County residents for associating with a self-proclaimed dope fiend.

But his chemical use really didn't contribute to anything that was a real threat to the social fabric here. In order to be discreet, I didn't witness Hunter's drug use. And of course there was the rule of the kitchen: What goes on in the kitchen stays in the kitchen. I knew Hunter wasn't going to compromise me, and I was not going to do anything to compromise him or his friends in the kitchen.

TOM BENTON

For the last fourteen years, I've been a sheriff's deputy in Aspen, and Bob Braudis was Hunter's best friend and had to walk that fine line. I don't know whether Bob learned from Hunter or what, but Bob was very, very good. He managed to use the friendship in a way that worked. A lot of people would say, "One day we'll get that fucking Hunter." Well, they never got him, did they?

TERRY SABONIS-CHAFEE

I moved back out to Owl Farm in May, right after the court case, and lived there until January '91. But by the time I got back, there was a real edge on everything. He wasn't ever going to forgive me for being gone, and I wasn't ever going to get over the fact that simply being there was something that Hunter valued more than almost anything else. It was impossible to conceive of a life with him in which I had any kind of agenda.

Hunter used to say from time to time that nothing was more fun than being in love with someone who on any given day might be smarter than you. The thing that was so incredibly attractive about him was partly that extraordinary charisma and power that he had over everybody. But if he loved you, If you were part of that very small community of two and Hunter was in a space where he just was focused on you, there was just really nothing else like it in the world. For all his effort to be savage and ridiculous, he was also an absolutely incurable romantic.

It was your job to make him feel successful enough that he could pull it all off. And I was not good at that. Something that Hunter really wanted was the same woman to love him and to manage him. I loved him enormously, but I had very limited patience for trying to be his manager or his editor.

CATHERINE SABONIS-BRADLEY

Hunter's interest in being a celebrity was exhausting. He was so willing to turn off things that were brilliant and interesting and likeable to be a parody of himself if he felt the people surrounding him needed to see that. And there were those that he kept on payroll who he just wanted around so he could play that side instead of working too hard or thinking too hard.

JANN WENNER

For Hunter to travel at this point was getting to be a major and problematic undertaking because of the drugs and the paraphernalia he needed. He could only work certain hours, and now the story had to come to him — he was too famous, and he couldn't easily go on the road and report. I'd give him another and another assignment, until it finally just got too frustrating and upsetting. In the meantime, he was making some money doing college lectures.

BILL STANKEY

In addition to his college gigs, clubs had started booking him. He did a gig at the Ritz in New York and was staying at the Essex House on Central Park South. The balcony of his suite overlooked the Wollman ice-skating rink in the park, and someone saw him pointing a rifle he'd brought with him out toward the rink. The next thing you know, the cops were beating on the door, Hunter was hiding the gun, and people were running around the room because there were obviously all kinds of drugs in there — and then Hunter simply convinced the police that nothing had happened and that someone must have been seeing things.

I had a secretary named Brenda who I put in charge of watching Hunter that night, and when I came in the next morning, she was covered in Magic Marker — there were circles drawn around her eyes, and triangles on her cheek, and a lot of other stuff. I said, "What happened to you?!" and she said, "Uh, I was out with Hunter last night. . . ."

That was a fairly memorable gig.

LYNN NESBIT

He could have gotten big money, but if he didn't show up — which he didn't for a lot of them — that market dries up. It's very lucrative if you just show up. Hunter could have been top dollar.

BILL STANKEY

I probably booked 100 dates for him between '83 and '96, and each time one of two things happened: He would show up late, or at the eleventh hour of the day that he was supposed to be leaving Aspen, I'd get a call because "something happened." I got tired of dealing with the insanity, and we got into a verbal altercation over him not showing up and being unreliable. I was exhausted by the process. If I tried to send him on his own, he'd never make it, so I learned that I had to send somebody with him — somebody who was reasonably uncorruptible. There were times I'd realize too late, "Oh God . . . I sent the wrong guy. They're supposed to be at the gig, and they're snorting coke in the bathroom."

He didn't have a "rider" per se; he just required a bottle of Chivas and an open tab with room service and the bar — though I can remember a few instances when he was getting $5,000 for his lecture and the room service was $1,700 for one night. The top money he made was fifteen to twenty grand per gig. Had he been reliable, he could have made a million dollars a year, because he drew a huge crowd. I don't think we ever did a gig that wasn't sold out. As it happened, he probably made a couple hundred thousand dollars in a good year.

He was funny and always entertaining, but at the end of the day, when you're trying to run a business built on relationships, relationships got burned. Club promoters were out thousands of dollars when Hunter didn't show up. It would be one thing if he was calling a month in advance to cancel. He was calling *four hours before the gig*. "Funny" just goes away, and it becomes "Why can't you get it together?" He was just debilitated by drugs and the alcohol.

TERRY SABONIS-CHAFEE

He always had that lazy-ass way out. If he could traffic in his own name instead of actually doing something, he would. There was a BBC documentary that had been made about him some years earlier, and one night we watched it. He had this enormous fascination with watching himself — he would often say that he wanted to "Write the movie, direct the movie, and star in the movie," but the movie he was talking about was his own life. He was constantly caught up in this tension between doing what he wanted to do and doing what he felt would make a good story. It makes me think of John le Carré in *Tinker, Tailor, Soldier, Spy*, when he writes, "The best spies build a mythology about themselves. The worst spies come to believe it, and they have to be destroyed." That's exactly what Hunter did — he almost would ask himself, "What would Hunter do?" He was driven by that.

I was working at the Rocky Mountain Institute. Hunter knew I had a meeting early on every Wednesday morning, and he would always go on a total bender on Tuesday nights, and I'd be up all night. One night he went through one of his bouts of paranoia and bolted the gate shut with all these extra chains, and in the morning I was dressed for work and trying to leave, and Hunter was in his bathrobe and couldn't find the key for the gate. He had to get the bolt cutters and was in his bath-

robe trying to cut the bolts to open the gate so I could go to my respectable job, and one of our neighbors drove by and looked at us
standing there and said, "Ah! Another day of domestic bliss at Owl
Farm. . . ."

He absolutely despised any friends I had that weren't his friends, any
work I had that wasn't related to him. You staked a really tiny piece of
turf and said, "This is mine," and that was not acceptable. He wanted
all of it, all the time.

The problem with living with Hunter was when your primary job is
padding the walls, you don't get to bounce off of them yourself. From
the time I moved back to Owl Farm in June to January of the following
year, we had a sort of deteriorating dance of love and hate and anger
and all sorts of other stuff. In August, we had a big fight, and Hunter
lapsed into one of his long unconsciousnesses that he did from time to
time. I had been trying and trying to wake him up because I was livid
about something, and I couldn't. I went into the kitchen and loaded a
pistol and stood at the foot of the bed and shot the window out. When
he woke, he said, "If you're shooting for me, I'm down here." And I
said, "If I was shooting for you, I'd shoot you in the balls, and you'd
live. I don't want to be the woman who killed Hunter Thompson."

I had been offered a job in Moscow, and in January I left him and
moved there. I was in this country that was collapsing, trying to learn
Russian and work and survive, and Hunter decided that it was in my
best interest to make me come home. He started sending me really
raunchy, obscene faxes with naked bodies and swastikas, warning me
that I'd fallen in with the wrong crowd and that violent overthrow of
the Soviet government was a bad idea. He sent them to the central
telegraph, which was like the post office. Central telegraph would read
them first, and then they'd deliver them. Then Hunter got the number
of my office, which was at the Soviet Academy of Sciences, and sent a
fax there. I got pulled in for questioning by the KGB.

CATHERINE SABONIS-BRADLEY

One night after I had finally left Owl Farm, Hunter called me and told me he needed my help for a speaking engagement in West Palm Beach. I laid down a few conditions before I agreed, but as soon as we got down to the Breakers, where we were staying, he was sparring with me, saying, "Oh, okay . . . you say you're not going to do any drugs, you're not going to put up with any of my shit. . . . How exactly are you going to pull that off?" And then he dosed me — a large dose of acid in something I was drinking. I went very far over the edge, and he started the "Ho ho — isn't this great acid?" I was pretty pissed off — and then he passed out in the bedroom of the suite. I spent over twelve hours tripping out of my mind by myself in the hotel room, including about seven hours of crying hysterically, having wallpaper talk to me and all that, and finally calmed myself by watching palm fronds, because they sway. Someone from the hotel came around because the phones were off the hook and someone had been trying to call the room, and Hunter woke up. It was just after six p.m., and the speaking engagement was at ten, and he told me that he wouldn't go anywhere unless he had a "Haspel cord sport coat" — he insisted it was the only thing to wear in Palm Beach — and then went right back to sleep. I was still tripping, but I called a local Brooks Brothers, which was closed, and somehow begged an elderly sales guy into essentially stealing one of these and bringing it to the hotel by cab. I tipped him $200, and Hunter got his goddamned Haspel cord sport coat.

TERRY SABONIS-CHAFEE

Two weeks after my KGB interrogation in August of 1991, the coup happened in Moscow — the Committee on Emergency Situations overthrew Gorbachev and took control of the government — and I ended up in the middle of that in a barricaded building. The coup failed, and I went back to the Rocky Mountain Institute to write an account of it, and when I finished it, I went to see Hunter.

He loved the article, and we had this absolutely gorgeous long couple of days where we stayed up straight through and he told me about the riots of Chicago in '68 and why he never wrote about them. What bothered him was that this was such a huge turning point in history, so central to his mythology about what bothered him about America and what was wrong with America. He had all these stories, but they were fragmented and very personal, and he felt that he had to write something that was big, that really told why it was important, and he couldn't do it. He talked about some times in life when things around you are profoundly personal but too big to be about what you saw. It was one of the most amazing conversations I ever had with him. It was extraordinary to listen to a story that Hunter told where he didn't even really try to make it about him.

And then I left Colorado. I went out maybe three times over the next couple of years, but it was already too late for poetry, as they say. The last letter I have from him is from 1994.

I think there are really only three ways, if you loved Hunter, that you could leave him, three states you could be in: homicidal, suicidal, or determined to get into rehab. He demanded such an extraordinary amount of loyalty, commitment, and energy, and although he paid back a lot of that, he just sucked people dry. And I think I left him because I was homicidal.

Bobby Braudis thanked me once for being the first woman to leave Hunter who didn't require police action to get her extricated.

GERRY GOLDSTEIN

One night he took me out driving from Owl Farm in the convertible. The first thing we did was try to drive up the levee to the racetrack by the rock quarry, but we missed it twice. Finally we got to the top, and Hunter started gathering these smooth stones. We then drove to the house of a nice lawyer here in town, John Van Ness, who did some work for Hunter. I've forgotten whether Hunter was angry or happy with John, or what exactly had happened that week. First Hunter placed these defrosted elk hearts on John's front doorstep, and then he started throwing these stones he'd collected onto the tin roof of John's house and just listened as they rolled down. Then he shot off a couple of rounds from a 9 mm and started playing a continuous looped tape of pigs or rabbits being slaughtered — a godforsaken screeching, curdling sound. This poor little girl came to the window screaming. Apparently Van Ness was out of town and this teenage girl was housesitting for them.

From there, he proceeded to Nicholson's house, where he engaged in the same folly.

ANJELICA HUSTON

He had a loudspeaker on top of his truck and drove to the top of Maroon Creek and started to play these tapes of terrible dying-animal cries. Jack was in his house with two small children and the nanny. Hunter proceeds to fire off a few rounds for good measure, and the animals are screaming, and Jack is horrified and locks all the doors and takes the children down to the basement in a state of panic and calls 911 and asks to talk to the FBI and has the sheriff on the phone, and this thing is a nightmare. Animal death cries are going out all over the valley.

At which point Hunter drives down to the house, takes the frozen elk heart, and places it directly in front of Jack's front door, where the blood seeps into the living room, and then drives back home to Owl Farm before the arrival of the police and the FBI and everybody else on the scene.

GERRY GOLDSTEIN

Apparently some of Jack's neighbors were in the process of digging fence poles and had somehow severed the telephone lines of Jack's place so that when all this shit happened and the security people tried to use the phone, the lines were all dead. They were convinced there was about to be another Mansonesque slaughter, so an all-points bulletin went out.

Hunter and I were back at his house when the sheriff's deputies called him to ask where he'd been for the past two hours. I advised Hunter — as his counsel, of course — that he couldn't answer that question

JACK NICHOLSON

I didn't put two and two together because I didn't see the elk heart until the following day. But the animal noises and the screaming and the beating — I had people in the house who were petrified, and so was I.

ANJELICA HUSTON

Hunter got away with this completely scot-free.

CHAPTER TEN

A Writer Resurgent

"Polo Is My Life" is where Hunter tried most consciously to evoke the spirit and style of his hero, F. Scott Fitzgerald, and it was set on Gatsby's turf. But "Fear and Loathing in Elko" was so dark, it made Vegas look like a tale of innocence — and it was as funny as anything he had ever written.

COREY SEYMOUR *was an editorial assistant at* Rolling Stone *in 1992.*

Nobody told me what to expect, or what was required of me, when Hunter came to town. Jann told me, "Just meet him at the airport and see what happens." I had no idea what he looked like — I actually seemed to believe that some sort of Ralph Steadman caricature was going to walk off the plane. Hunter walked right past me, and I had to scramble to meet him down at baggage claim. He looked pretty tired and pissed off — he was sitting on the floor surrounded by a half-dozen pieces of his Halliburton metal luggage — and he stuck his hand out, and as I went to shake it, he almost yanked me to the ground and barked, "No, goddamn it!! Help me up!!"

When we walked into the Carlyle, I guess I was a little paranoid. I thought that the people behind the front desk might run screaming from the concept of Hunter checking into their beautiful, elegant hotel, but he was greeted like a returning hero. When we got upstairs to his suite, Hunter started railing about "this fucking dump" and calling the concierge to get the temperature adjusted — he was demanding a bigger suite and basically telling this guy he was lied to — but somehow he calmed down and we hit it off well and had a few drinks, and the phone in his suite started ringing almost immediately. Jann was on his way over. Terry McDonell was on his way over. Ed Bradley was on his way over with Kathleen Battle, the opera singer.

It was the night before *Rolling Stone*'s twenty-fifth-anniversary party at the Four Seasons restaurant, and Hunter wanted to surprise Jann with this shotgun-art portrait he'd made of Jann with a bullet hole through his heart and blood-red paint exploding all around it. Hunter was in a great mood, and all the men except Jann got summoned into Hunter's bedroom for the unveiling of the portrait. He had a shroud over it, and he whisked it off in this grand manner — he was so proud of it — and everyone sort of universally agreed, "It's beautiful, Hunter, but you can't give that to him tomorrow night. He's going to be sitting at the front table next to Yoko Ono. You can't unveil a picture of Jann with a bullet through his heart." Hunter looked abjectly demoralized, but he kept a brave face while everyone was still there.

At the end of the night, though, when it was just him and me left in his suite — well, let's just say his mood fell. Everything turned black. Almost as soon as the door shut when Jann left, Hunter started cursing and going on about how the art was stupid, he shouldn't have brought it, the trip was a failure, he wasn't going to the party, he wanted to leave. And then he hit on the solution, or at least a partial solution. He said, "Well, fuck. Help me throw this fucking thing out the window," and started dragging this large framed portrait over toward the window. He started screaming at me, "C'mon, goddamn it! Help me!" but somehow I was able to convince him that that wouldn't be a good idea.

TERRY MCDONELL

Every time he was in New York was like showtime.

COREY SEYMOUR

The next day I brought over an Armani tux that the *Rolling Stone* fashion department had arranged for Hunter to wear, and he had to try it on so I could see how it fit and check the hem on the pants. But Hunter's interest at this point was in two things — or three, if you count cocaine — CNN and room service. As I would soon learn, he went large on breakfast. The first time he told me his order, I cracked up laughing, which seemed to make him angry. He gave me this stern look and said, "Do you think I'm fucking *joking?!*" I remember him sitting on the sofa in his robe, grinding up coke and mumbling, "Uh-hh . . . ahhh . . . two pots of coffee . . . uhhh . . . six-pack of Heineken, uhh . . . two pitchers of Bloody Marys, corned beef hash . . . white toast . . . better make that four orders of white toast . . . uhhh . . . large basket of fresh grapefruit . . . lemons, yeah . . . better get some limes too . . . couple jars of peanuts . . . uhhh . . . and get something for yourself too." But beyond that, I never saw him eat much.

DEBORAH FULLER

When he woke up, he liked eating a really big breakfast — always with fresh fruit and usually eggs and sausage or bacon. He'd usually start out with orange juice, coffee, and whiskey — Chivas, snow cone-style with a lot of ice — and a Molson or a Grolsch beer. He liked the big bottles of Grolsch because he could recap them.

COREY SEYMOUR

After Hunter ate and drank his breakfast, he muttered something about taking a bath. He ambled into the bathroom, shut the door, and I heard the sound of gigantic amounts of rushing water. Almost an hour later, I started to worry and knocked on the bathroom door and called his name and finally cracked the door open — and saw Hunter, naked and completely submerged beneath a full-throttle Jacuzzi. He was doing some weird Axl Rose–like underwater horizontal serpentine dance with his arms going crazy like he was trying to fly. I shut the door.

Eventually he got himself dressed, and we were now late for meeting Lynn Nesbit downstairs for drinks before the party. Hunter was smoking dope out of his skull pipe, and refused to leave his suite until he'd thrown a piece of crumpled paper into the wastebasket from across the room. And it needed to be a clean bucket too — no off-the-rims and no off-the-wall rebounds. But he kept missing, and he was getting angrier and angrier. Then he made one clean, stood up, pumped his fist, and let out a roaring "WHOOOP!" Between that exact moment and the moment he kissed Lynn's hand downstairs, he'd somehow transformed himself from unhinged child-like maniac to Hunter S. Thompson, southern gentleman and man of letters.

As our car pulled up to the Four Seasons on Park Avenue, Hunter became very jittery and nervous about his appearance and his entrance — there were paparazzi waiting, but with Lynn and me in tow, he made his way inside to an adoring and celebrity-laden crowd, where he was besieged by people wanting their picture taken with him. The only problem was the speech he was scheduled to give — he hadn't written it yet, of course, so midway through the cocktail hour in the Grill Room, I tried to keep his audience away from him while he jotted some things down at the bar.

A few minutes later, as Hunter was being introduced, he plopped down on the floor of the Pool Room, Indian-style, took his coke grinder out of his sock, and leaned forward with a hollowed-out Bic pen up his nose. This was right in front of the dais and right next to several tables of guests — including the head table with Jann and Yoko Ono and David Bowie, among others — who were now looking at me strangely, as if they were waiting for me to explain what was going on. I was trying to very consciously act normal — "Nothing weird happening here, folks" — and Hunter cracked me hard on my shin with his knuckle and barked quietly, "Shield me, goddamn it!!!" When he stood up, his glasses were sideways on his head, so I straightened them out and reminded him to wipe his nose.

He gave a long speech with a number of detours in it that I thought was pretty good, but Ed Bradley, who was the MC, had to gently give him the hook to keep things moving. As Hunter made his move to leave the podium, he took a wrong step and hit the ground, spilling someone else's drink but, incredibly, not his own. After the speech a lot of people came up to me and said, basically, "What the fuck?" They couldn't understand a word of what Hunter had said.

I passed by a hallway a little later during the party and saw him talking alone with Keith Richards, which was absolutely amazing to hear. It sounded like two dogs barking at one another, or the secret language of dolphins. It was almost nonverbal, but they both seemed to understand what the other one was saying.

Later, as we were walking out with Jann, Hunter took great glee in bursting the helium party balloons that people were carrying out by burning them with his lit cigarette. He progressed from popping nearby balloons to actually lobbing his lit cigarettes across the Pool Room of the Four Seasons to try to hit faraway balloons until Jann told him, basically, to cut it the fuck out. We went back to Jann's house, where the first thing Hunter did when he walked in the door was grab a tangerine out of a bowl and throw it through the only open pane in Jann's window from about fifteen feet away.

On the day Hunter was supposed to fly back to Colorado, I had a fax waiting for me when I got to the office from his girlfriend-assistant Nicole out in Woody Creek:

To: Corey
URGENT!!!

Hunter has just gone down for some desperately needed sleep. How-ever, we need your help this morning to wake him.

Faxes and phone calls will not suffice — Hunter would like you to make sure he gets up by 10·30 a.m. (best achieved by pounding on door w/ rm service coffee/fruit/pastries in hand).

Corey, this has to be done, in person, if Hunter is to wake.

I will do what I can from this end, i.e. continual phone calls.

Please call when you get this — I will be by the phone, just SCREAM into it . . . I too, may fall asleep — please scream —

This is very important. Call ASAP.

When I finally got in the room, Hunter was completely comatose on the bed. For a while I thought he might be dead, but I got Deborah on the phone and told her what was going on, and she said, "Go into Hunter's shaving kit in the bathroom — you'll find some big Black Beauties down toward the bottom. Take one and put it in his mouth and massage it down his throat; make sure he gets some water with it." I think Deborah could sense the desperation in my voice, so she told me a secret: "Don't use this too often, because if Hunter catches on, you're a dead man, but use the word 'professional' around him — just say things like, 'Well, I guess we've got to be professionals about this' or something like that. That'll usually help."

I did the business with the pill and the water, and Hunter eventually stumbled out in his robe and sat down and started grinding up some coke. We ordered breakfast, and a couple of hours later we were in the cab going to the airport, and by that point everything was kicking in. His whole face was twitching and sort of jumping, and I asked him some simple question, but he wasn't really quite speaking English — he clearly knew what I was saying, but he was just making these strange squeaking sounds, and he was pouring sweat.

He had taught me how to pack up his carry-on briefcase with his coke in it — in two double-sealed Ziploc bags. I'd dump two room service jars of peanuts all over the inside of his briefcase and then squeeze lemons over everything, then seal it tight, and then give it to him. He'd have his plastic grinder in his sock for the flight.

When we got to the airport he handed me his wallet and told me to check him in and headed straight for the bar. I've never seen anyone more completely blasé about the prospect of missing their flight. He just sat down on a bar stool and casually ordered us up a couple Heinekens. And he handed me a $100 bill and said, "You did a good job. Oh, and if anyone asks you if you saw me do drugs, tell them no. For that matter, you didn't even see me drinking — okay?" Then he ordered another round.

BOB BRAUDIS

Hunter called me one night and said that Nicole was unconscious on the kitchen floor and unresponsive. I called Hunter's next-door neighbor and told him to grab another neighbor and go down to Hunter's to help. On the way to the hospital she stopped breathing, but they got her to the hospital, they treated her, and then she moved into my guesthouse and got healthy. Hunter was not insensitive to her medical condition, but he had that rule — Never Call 911. He called me instead. Nine-one-one wasn't necessary. There weren't people bleeding with gunshot wounds.

Hunter was real pissed at me that I was housing his gal — who refused to communicate with him — but I said, "Hey, Hunter, don't give me any attitude. She wants to be here. She's a friend too." Eventually she packed up and went back to Cincinnati or wherever she came from.

+ 🐃 + 🐃

JAMES CARVILLE *was chief strategist for Bill Clinton's campaign in 1992.*
We used to drink a lot. He hung out at the Capitol Hotel in Little Rock, where I lived, and we always hit it off. I mean, we weren't that far apart in age — he was seven years older than me. He grew up in Louisville; I grew up in Louisiana. And Hunter did something that none of us had the guts to do — he led the kind of life that secretly all of us would like to have had the guts to lead. To hell with the whole thing, just stay drunk and high and smoke and hang out and write outrageous things. He'd never lived his life on anybody else's terms.

He had a way of describing Clinton attacking a plate of french fries that was just the funniest thing ever. We all couldn't stop laughing. His powers of observation were only exceeded by his powers of exaggeration. I remember that he had this crazed story in his head with about 5 percent of truth to it about how I stole his jacket. And what Hunter would do is find something with the slightest grain of something to it and make it into this hilarious thing. He had this whole thing he'd written about this kind of death struggle that we were in and so forth. We were mightily entertained by this kind of story, and in the midst of being entertained there were a bunch of insights.

JANN WENNER

It was Hunter's idea that the political wizards of *Rolling Stone* should go down to Little Rock as a group to meet this new person that had just become the Democratic nominee — actually, by that point it was pretty clear that he was going to be the next president. So Bill Greider, P. J. O'Rourke, Hunter, and I flew down on my plane. Mark Seliger, our photographer, was also with us. Hunter brought along some high-end super–video camera to record the encounter — the assembled wisdom of *Rolling Stone* on the road. It was quite a team, and Hunter was at the center of it.

WILLIAM GREIDER *was the national-affairs editor at* Rolling Stone *in 1992.*

My knee went out just as we were getting on the airplane at Teterboro, and Hunter helped me onto the plane. He was quite solicitous and so forth. Usually when that happened with my knee, the pain would come back in a hour or so and then go away, but this time it didn't. We got off the plane in Little Rock and I was in serious agony — although we'd had a lot to drink by that time. But I got into a wheelchair, and we went to this famous Little Rock political hotel. Hunter wheeled me into this lobby crowded with people, shouting, "I want the best sports doctor in Little Rock — immediately!"

Everybody else in our party headed off to the bar or to their rooms, but Hunter took care to get me up to my hotel room, and I was lying on the bed while he literally called every hospital in Little Rock demanding that they send over an orthopedist or a sports doctor immediately, and he couldn't understand why these hospitals wouldn't comply. Finally he called the Clinton campaign and got hold of Carville or somebody. I remember Hunter saying, "What?! I wanna know the doctor, the candidate's doctor. Get him over here." Finally I said, "Hunter, I really appreciate it . . . but why are you doing this?" He said, "I can't stand to be around pain."

JAMES CARVILLE

I was in the middle of a presidential campaign, so the last thing I was doing was staying out drinking at night, but I remember that we were all having dinner, and the *Rolling Stone* people would disappear for five minutes and come back kind of refreshed. I said, "Gee, it's been a long time since I've seen people do that."

WILLIAM GREIDER

When we did the Clinton interview, Hunter, as he often did, had constructed a sort of dramatic arc to this event that he was living out and that we were all invited to live with him. The narrative for that event was that Jann and P.J. and Hunter and I were all flying down to Little Rock to "deliver the *Rolling Stone* vote" to Clinton for that election. That was kind of his running gag. On another level, he really did seem to think that there was something momentous happening in this event. He had packed up a photograph, which he entitled "Politics Is a Dirty Business," which was a picture of him in Woody Creek, sitting on his haunches with a rifle he had just fired at a big drum of gasoline. This huge burst of flame was flying toward him. It's quite dramatic. Hunter had a three-by-four-foot framed blowup of this photo shipped down from Colorado to give to Clinton. Hunter brought it to the interview at Doe's Eat Place, and we were all pretty primed. We were also all hung over.

JANN WENNER

Everyone on our team had their own agenda. P.J.'s was to throw these very arcane intellectual curveball questions at Clinton. He was going to trap him in some dilemma based on some idea from a conservative think tank that he had come up with. But while he was quizzing Clinton, P.J. was also trying to eat a tamale. He was trying to cut it with a knife and fork without unwrapping it and was about to eat the paper. Clinton calmly leaned toward P.J. and said, "Here's how you eat that." That sort of took the wind out of P.J.'s sails.

Hunter wanted to ask about the Fourth Amendment and drug searches. He leaned back and did one of these long windup Hunter kind of things where everybody is supposed to be amused by it all, and Clinton wasn't going to have any of it. Hunter was pouring sweat at this point, and his question was way off the point of what we needed to talk about with the soon-to-be president. Search and seizure was not really an issue in the campaign, but it gave Clinton an opening to talk about drugs, and he whacked Hunter. I'm pretty sure that Stephanopoulos set him up. He was trying to insulate Clinton from being too associated with someone like Hunter, and I think Stephanopoulos had warned Clinton about what to expect. Clinton came back with this really tough, aggressive answer involving his brother Roger's cocaine problem and how he had seen the horrors and destruction of drugs.

We were all unprepared for the intensity of his response, and Hunter was especially taken aback. The interview then went back and forth between Greider and myself and Clinton. Hunter essentially withdrew. There was no "ho-ho" component, which Hunter had hoped to establish. Carville understood Hunter and appreciated him, but George was way too serious an operator to let his need to protect Clinton every second be overrun by Hunter's charm and fun, or as a little favor to Hunter. Forget it. George was cold.

WILLIAM GREIDER

Hunter wilted. It was almost poignant because as much as he wanted us to think he was running a gag, he was also quite sincere about the Fourth Amendment. He had a kind of little-boy's innocence sometimes, and then Clinton, for his own purposes, just smacked him down verbally.

I think that innocence is what kept Hunter going for so long. I feel like that's the core of who he was, and also why he was such a great writer — so expressive and so real and all the other things he was. That innocence and sweetness were driving him. He knew the world was big and bad and ugly, and he would take it on the way a little boy takes on a demon. And sometimes he'd get smacked.

Hunter got up from the table right after Clinton's response. He just stopped asking questions. He wandered back after a while with a drink in his hand and sat down, and I suppose he said a few other things, but it was like the dream had been smashed, and what was the point of going on with this? I think after you saw that sort of thing about Hunter up close, you felt a sort of protectiveness and forgivingness toward him.

JANN WENNER

When it came time to publish the interview, I wanted to endorse Clinton, and I wanted each of us to write his own statement. I wrestled back and forth with Hunter. He had these deep reservations about him based on something — either that incident turned him off, or he had something intuitive he knew about a type of southerner that we just didn't get. Ultimately Hunter came around, though somewhat tepidly.

The Clinton candidacy was frustrating for him. By that time the politics of the country had kind of passed him by — it wasn't clear-cut good-versus-evil as Nixon seemed then to have been. Clinton was a centrist, but more than that, I think we were now dealing with what was now such a technological and complex society that decisions couldn't really be deeply ideological anymore.

DOUG BRINKLEY

In 1993, I had done my doctorate in history at Georgetown and was teaching at Hofstra University on Long Island. I was talking with my students about Harry Truman's Independence as different from Dwight Eisenhower's Abilene, but without going there and seeing it for ourselves, it all seemed stilted and remote. So I created a class called "The Majic Bus" with the insight that instead of students going to Europe for a semester, they would stay in America, get on a bus, and live for a semester on the road. Our bus driver looked like Buffalo Bill, and he called his bus the Highway Hotel. We read Whitman's *Leaves of Grass* and then visited Whitman's grave in Camden, New Jersey; we read Willa Cather and then went to her home in Nebraska; we read John Steinbeck and toured his museum in Salinas.

But I also wanted to bring in living writers. My students were reading *Fear and Loathing in Las Vegas* as we were coming through Colorado, and I had sent Hunter a couple of books I had just done with a note to him saying we had mutual friends in George McGovern and Doris Kearns Goodwin, and Hunter's then-assistant Nicole Meyer called and said that Hunter really liked the idea of the bus thing we were doing and would like to meet me and my students. She told me that Hunter's hours were erratic, and that we should just show up at the Woody Creek Tavern with the bus.

I had two busloads — twenty-seven students. We pulled in to the tavern and waited, shot pool, hung around. Nicole had come down and checked me out on a reconnaissance mission, and we talked for a while, and then sure enough Hunter came rolling in with a very expensive video recorder and started taping the students instead of them taping him, or he'd grab their video recorders and film himself. He was being very playful and was in a good mood, and the students were asking good questions. He had dressed to be the Hunter Thompson that the students were looking to see, with the Tilley hat, smoking a Dunhill with the holder and eating a snow cone margarita. Then he said, "I don't know who really wants to come up to Owl Farm, but I'll put some food on. We've got some beer if you want to come up." So one group stayed and slept in the Woody Creek Tavern parking lot, and a second group came up to Owl Farm.

Instead of autographing the students' books, he made them queue up and then took his gun and shot a hole in each of their copies.

Hunter had asked us to report back to him about the rest of our road trip after we'd left Colorado, and on one of our phone calls he said to me, "Look, Nicole and I were wondering if you would help me pull together this book I'm working on, *Better Than Sex*. It's a disaster zone. It's a lot of writing about Clinton. You're a political historian. You know a lot about politics. Maybe you could come out for a week and help us." *Better Than Sex,* at that point, was like a deck of cards in disarray; the writing was all there, but it needed to be shuffled in some direction or repackaged, fast. Hunter was in a jam.

I ended up going up there and doing my thing, and it worked, because Hunter and I had certain things in common. We both loved politics and literature. He loved talking to me about where he was at in the pecking order of journalism and literature — about David Halberstam, Maureen Dowd, Seymour Hersh, Scotty Reston, and Walter Isaacson, and others. I think Nicole liked having me around because she didn't want any more female assistants for Hunter. Apparently they'd had some bad experience as a couple, and I came in as a kind of straight man to help them pull it together. It was a productive week. We got a result, which always meant a lot to Hunter. We didn't waste time.

One of the other things we shared were the hours we kept, which was rare for Hunter. My most productive hours are from about ten p.m. until three or four in the morning, so when he called me at two-thirty or three, I was guaranteed to be up. That window of friends for Hunter was limited. And we both had the habit of writing or working with CNN on, so if there was a news flash, we'd call each other up. That became a big part of the relationship — our schedules.

JAMES CARVILLE

He used to send these faxes on this weird letterhead that said "Forget the Shrimp Honey — I'm Coming Home with the Crabs." He'd write me these crazy memos — at three o'clock in the morning he'd fax me, and I'd come to work in the morning and there'd be three or four faxes waiting for me. And like an idiot, I didn't keep them, but he published them anyway in *Better Than Sex*.

STACEY HADASH *met Hunter in 1992 when she was working in the so-called War Room of the Clinton campaign.*

After the campaign was over, Hunter was working on *Better Than Sex,* and he called me up and said, "Why don't you come out to Woody Creek to help with the book?" I had been helping him out with stuff over the phone — questions about who ended up where and how the whole transition was working — and now he wasn't meeting his deadline.

First I called Carville: "Hunter's just asked me out to his place. I like

Hunter a lot, but I've heard all these things about him attacking women and the guns and the explosives and the drugs and the knives. Do you really think that it's safe for me to go out there?" James said, "Oh yeah, you'll be fine."

Owl Farm was bizarre. The first weekend I went there, sitting at the end of the table in the kitchen was Ed Bradley, smoking a pipe and reading the paper. The next time I went out there, Don Johnson was in the kitchen with a whole bunch of people, and everybody was fooling around and putting lipstick on — you know how Hunter loved lipstick. I was taking pictures — Hunter loved pictures — and naturally, D.J. did not really want to have pictures of him with lipstick on floating around. We ended up fighting, with D.J. trying to wrestle my camera out of my hand. Hunter was watching the whole thing — people were spread out through the room, tossing the camera around; it was this whole fight scene. It was bizarre. Everything around there was bizarre.

One night we went out for a drive on McClain Flats, which was his first test for me. We were heading back to Hunter's house, going straight toward this hairpin turn. Of course Hunter was driving the Red Shark with his Chivas on ice and his sunglasses on and stepped it up to about a hundred miles an hour, heading straight for this curve in the road. All I saw was a mountain-face wall coming at me fast. I really did think I was going to die.

Before too long, I was riding on the back of Hunter's motorcycle at a hundred miles an hour down to Basalt for lunch and then sitting there for four hours drinking margaritas before getting back on the bike and riding home.

We talked a lot about politics. Hunter was able to get to the heart of things, to simplify things, really quickly. He'd make these weird predictions that you'd say were totally crazy, but they'd turn out to be true. Hunter was disappointed in Clinton — really disappointed. He thought that Clinton had a position of power to do a lot of things and he let the Democrats down. Hunter thought that Bill Clinton didn't fulfill his promises, basically.

SANDY THOMPSON

Hunter's younger brother Jim was gay. I took care of Jim in San Francisco when he was dying in 1994. I begged Hunter to come out to see him, and he finally did.

PETE PETERS *was Jim Thompson's best friend growing up in Louisville.*

Jim and I met each other in the eighth grade, but the first time I ever heard anything about Hunter wasn't until years later, in 1967, right after he'd written *Hell's Angels.* He told me that Hunter was going to be on *To Tell the Truth,* this prime-time game show on TV.

Jim always said the hitchhiker in *Fear and Loathing in Las Vegas* was him. He had taken the train out to Colorado to visit Hunter in the very early seventies. While he was away, I got an envelope in the mail from him, and on the back of the envelope was written "cunnilingus." The only thing he wrote was "Just wanted to see if this would make it through the mail." A couple of days later, I got a phone call from Jim. I said, "What the hell are you doing back home so early?" He said, "Hunter would get up and start smoking hash and drinking wine, and then his buddies would come over at night and they'd just get crazy. They'd drink and do acid — the only thing I could do was go sit on the porch, because it was sheer insanity."

SANDY THOMPSON

We went to Jim's when he was dying, and I think Hunter spent two days with him. Jim was very grateful. Hunter gave him a thousand dollars or something. Hunter did leave at one point, and he came back drunk and coked up. But Jim was just really, really glad that Hunter came to see him. They didn't speak much. I'm sure that Hunter was embarrassed by Jim's gayness earlier in his life. I don't know if that was true later on. He might not have been. But they were real different people.

Hunter didn't talk to his other brother, Davison, very much either. And he didn't talk to Paul Semonin or a lot of other old friends. A lot of them just went by the wayside as his whole world changed.

PETE PETERS

I never actually met Hunter until Jim's wake. It was a bizarre day. As I understand it, their mother hadn't had a drink for eighteen years until the day Jim was buried. At the burial at Cave Hill Cemetery, when the car showed up with Davison, Mrs. Thompson, and Hunter, Davison got out, and then Hunter got out and was trying to help his mom. And I'll never forget this: I didn't know if I felt worse for Mrs. Thompson because she was burying her youngest son, or if I felt worse for her because of the shape Hunter was in. It was just god-awful. He was like a six-year-old kid. It was pitiful. It wasn't because he was drunk or drugged. I was just looking at a guy who was adult in body only. He didn't know what to do. He didn't know how to take care of her, how to help her. He looked like he was looking to her for guidance. He looked lost.

DOUG BRINKLEY

Hunter came down to New Orleans in April of '94 for an event for one of his books, and I put him in touch with Stephen Ambrose, the late historian who wrote the three-volume biography of Nixon. They got along famously, but while Hunter was here, Nixon died. Hunter was staying at the Pontchartrain Hotel and wrote his obituary for *Rolling Stone* from New Orleans. He would go into the St. Charles Tavern, a twenty-four-hour bar-and-grill, and would sit and eat gumbo and watch CNN and write notes. He liked watching the trolley car go by. He said, "If I don't write the obituary on Nixon and make it tougher on him than Mencken was on William Jennings Bryan, I will have utterly failed in my career." He was obsessed with Nixon's death. He felt he had spent all of his life going after him, and now he had to summarize it all. He felt that pressure to publish just the right statement intensely.

GEORGE MCGOVERN

It's not any secret that Hunter had total contempt for Nixon. He just couldn't handle him. When Nixon died, I went to his funeral. I figured that as he was a former president of the United States, and was my opponent, that that was the proper thing to do. I said a couple of words to his family and friends. That was the one exception Hunter drew to my honesty. He said, "Yeah, you went in the tank; you went in the tank." He never forgave me for that.

COREY SEYMOUR

Most of my time with Hunter was spent in hotel rooms, just the two of us, or with a few of his friends over. But in 1994, I was with him at the Beat Generation Conference that Doug Brinkley had organized at NYU.

The conference was my first real experience of seeing what kind of an insane following he had. We were late, of course — I had my usual ordeal trying to get Hunter up. That day's random time-stop was Hunter's obsessive attention to a fax he was making to send Jack Nicholson, who had been in the news for bashing somebody's car in with a golf club on a highway in California. Out came about seven of his thirty or so different-colored markers and pens that he always traveled with, and he started hand-detailing this note to Jack that said something like "Ho ho, bubba — you do know that if you would have come to New

York with me like I'd told you to that none of this would have happened, right? Oh well — never mind. Selah, HST."

When we finally got to the conference, Hunter was sitting up on the stage as part of a panel, and as soon as he sat down, he called up some student in the first row and gave him some cash and had him run out to buy him some beer. Hunter and I had a plan to watch a basketball play-off game afterward — we wouldn't have time to get up to his hotel room, because we were all the way downtown — and we ran into some poor young NYU student who eagerly offered up the only set of keys to her apartment, which was a block away, for us to watch the game. We were all set to head over after Hunter's talk, and then he got mobbed — really mobbed — by a couple hundred people. It didn't get really ugly, but it was on the way to that. We had to rush him into a car, and people were jumping on top of the car and sticking their hands in through the windows to try to get him to sign things. He had to speed off with this poor girl's only set of keys in his pocket. We never saw her again.

Hunter had told me some stories about Allen Ginsberg intervening with the Hells Angels during protests in San Francisco in the sixties. Hunter had actually been trying to reach Ginsberg since he arrived in New York — they hadn't spoken in quite some time — and by coincidence, while I was walking home from the conference I stopped in a bookstore and sat down to read something. When I looked up, Ginsberg was standing almost directly in front of me, packing up his stuff after giving some kind of reading there. I introduced myself and mentioned that Hunter was trying to get hold of him. "I've been trying to call him at the Four Seasons," Ginsberg said, "but they said there's no Hunter Thompson staying there." I told him to try again — "Hunter's there, but he checked in under the name Ben Franklin."

Ginsberg thanked me, asked me to help him finish the rest of his soy milk, and left. When I told Hunter about this, he mumbled something about Ginsberg being too embarrassed to see him ever since some weird time in the late sixties when the two of them spent a lost weekend together — something about running around in the woods together in California. "It's a little-known fact, Corey, that Ginsberg was a horrible drunkard." They ended up having dinner that night.

DEBORAH FULLER

Hunter hated Christmas. One year it was just the two of us at Owl Farm, and we were in heaven — not having to go out to any of these big events. Hunter canceled everything and we drank, caught up, played loud music, watched TV — just "whooped it up," as Hunter would say — and then he decided to call up everybody he knew, and in a very weird voice left his "Christmas greeting": "This is Santa Claus — ho, ho, ho — I shit down your chimney." He called Jann; he called everybody he could find in his Rolodex at all hours of the morning — waking some people up, of course. "Ho, ho, ho — I shit down your chimney." We taped them all and would laugh hysterically in between each call. We had such fun — and remember: Hunter was a fun hog.

JANE WENNER

One Christmas when the kids were small, Jann and I went to Aspen and rented a house on Red Mountain. Hunter and Deborah came over with Juan and brought presents for all the kids — he bought one a black plastic rat and one a wig. But the big thing was the Bedazzler, which was a small machine that you could order on late-night TV, and you could fasten bits of colored plastic, like jewels, to your T-shirts or jeans or whatever. Hunter had this Bedazzler, and he let the kids play with it, but he wouldn't give it to them. And I couldn't believe he wouldn't give it to them. They Bedazzled all day, and then he took it away. But they were happy with the plastic rat and the other things, and we had a lot of fun. Juan used to stay with us on summer visits, so for all of us, it was a mellow family Christmas.

Years later, right after Jann and I were separated, out of the blue Hunter sent them the Bedazzler. Around this time I was tussling around with my son Theo, and I sort of absentmindedly said to him, "How did I get such a crazy kid?" and he said, "Well, you know, I'm not as crazy as Uncle Hunter." I said, "Really, Theo? What do you think it is that we do with Uncle Hunter?" He said, "I think you stay up late, you eat fire, and you Bedazzle all night." And I looked at Theo and I said, "Yeah, that's about right." Hunter loved that.

JANN WENNER

After Hunter stopped writing big pieces for us, he struggled with his craft, essentially doing a lot of ephemeral writing in tiny bursts, nothing inspired or meaningful. Then suddenly came what were his two last major pieces, which I thought were two of his best — "Fear and Loathing in Elko" and "Polo Is My Life." They were really different: not reportorially based but just great, flat-out pieces of expansive, elaborate, swinging writing.

"Elko" was one of my favorites, and it came out of nowhere. It was hysterical, but it was also dark and evil. He made me reread *Vegas* and compare it to that, which at the time we thought was dark. Well, "Elko" makes *Vegas* look like a tale of innocence — which in fact it was. "Elko" was a nightmarish piece about sex and torture. It's also as funny as anything he's ever written.

From "Fear and Loathing in Elko"
Rolling Stone *622; January 23, 1992*

On my way to the kitchen I was jolted by the sight of a naked woman slumped awkwardly in the corner with a desperate look on her face, as if she'd been shot. Her eyes bulged and her mouth was wide open and she appeared to be reaching out for me.

I leapt back and heard laughter behind me. My first thought was that Leach, unhinged by his gambling disaster, had finally gone over the line with his wife-beating habit and shot her in the mouth just before we knocked. She appeared to be crying out for help, but there was no voice.

I ran into the kitchen to look for a knife, thinking that if Leach had gone crazy enough to kill his wife, now he would have to kill me, too, since I was the only witness. Except for the Judge, who had locked himself in the bathroom.

Leach appeared in the doorway holding the naked woman by the neck and hurled her across the room at me. . . .

Time stood still for an instant. The woman seemed to hover in the air, coming at me in the darkness like a body in slow motion. I went into a stance with the bread knife and braced for a fight to the death.

Then the thing hit me and bounced softly down to the floor. It was a rubber blowup doll: one of those things with five orifices that young stockbrokers buy in adult bookstores after the singles bars close.

"Meet Jennifer," he said. "She's my punching bag." He picked it up by the hair and slammed it across the room.

"Ho, ho," he chuckled, "no more wife beating. I'm cured, thanks to Jennifer." He smiled sheepishly. "It's almost like a miracle. These dolls saved my marriage. They're a lot smarter than you think." He nodded gravely. "Sometimes I have to beat *two at once*. But it always calms me down, you know what I mean?"

Whoops, I thought. Welcome to the night train. "Oh, *hell yes,*" I said quickly. "How do the neighbors handle it?"

"No problem," he said. "They love me."

Sure, I thought. I tried to imagine the horror of living in a muddy industrial slum full of tin-walled trailers and trying to protect your family against brain damage from knowing that every night when you look out your kitchen window there will be a man in a leather bathrobe flogging two naked women around the room with a quart bottle of Wild Turkey. Sometimes for two or three hours . . . It was horrible.

He reached into a nearby broom closet and pulled out another one — a half-inflated Chinese-looking woman with rings in her nipples and two electric cords attached to her head. "This is Ling-Ling," he said. "She screams when I hit her." He whacked the doll's head and it squawked stupidly.

TOBIAS PERSE *was an editorial assistant at* Rolling Stone *in 1993.*

Somehow it was decided that the U.S. Open of polo, which was being held at Bethpage on Long Island, would be the beginning of this whole gear-up for "Polo Is My Life." At the time — or, I should say, in Hunter Time — it was like the whole world revolved around this tournament. There were four or five people in the galaxy of this story, and Hunter was at the center, with everyone else moving around him to plan and coordinate and pay for everything. It was a general attitude that pervaded everything: Hunter Is Coming, and Corey would be introducing me to him. I remember this look of relish in Jann's eyes when he knew that I didn't know what I'd be getting into. He said, "Don't forget that you have a job." But I never was sure what the expectations were.

When Hunter had asked for help with the research, I jumped on it because it all somehow felt like journalism to me in some way. It felt like the job. But it wasn't journalism to research luxury hotels in Garden City, Long Island. It wasn't journalism to find out what color Lincoln he'd be getting.

Jann understood that Hunter's expenses had to be contained and what that meant, but I fucked everything up constantly. It was decided that *Rolling Stone* would pay for Hunter's hotel room, but under no circumstances would they pay for any incidentals — or damages. That was part of the deal. Deborah told me all about these special requirements about Hunter's airplane reservations, and there were concerns about Hunter's expenses that I had no idea about. I got Hunter's first-class tickets for him, but then I had to get another set of first-class tickets just in case he didn't make the first flight. Later on, this became a matter of course, but Deborah was very insistent on all this from the beginning.

He FedExed cocaine to me before his trip, and on the phone there was that strange code or etiquette of drug users. It took me years of later experience to really recognize how much cocaine he was sending, but one day I got a package containing a thick pile of *National Geographics* with a hole cut out inside — like the way you'd cut out the inside of a Bible to put a gun in it. It was sealed with tape on every side and sprayed with Right Guard, and it arrived via FedEx. I got a call from Owl Farm: "Did you get the FedEx? Um, I think you'll find one of those *National Geographics* has something in it. Keep that for when Hunter arrives." This was three hundred grams, four hundred grams in two Ziploc bags. It was a huge amount of cocaine, and it was sent using Jann's FedEx account, which we were never supposed to use, of course. We had an Airborne account for normal use, one FedEx account that we could use if we got permission, and then Jann's FedEx account. Hunter just sent the coke on Jann's FedEx to "Tobias Perse" with no return address.

In addition, Deborah had given Corey strict instructions to buy blow-up sex dolls for the hotel room.

DEBORAH FULLER

Hunter thought blow-up sex dolls were fun, mostly just for the reactions he could get. He would always think of something new to do with them — throw them off balconies, down into the lobbies of hotels. He threw one out on the street into traffic once, and this guy thought he was running over a real woman. Mona was always his favorite name for them. When a reporter was on camera interviewing Hunter at home, or just when he was expecting people, Hunter would sometimes take the lid off the hot tub in the Water Room and throw a bunch of sex dolls in there, and he would take these unsuspecting people around the house and he'd remove the top of the hot tub, and there'd be all these dolls floating inside.

TOBIAS PERSE

All in all, he was on Long Island for two weeks, and we didn't go to more than four matches. I remember them distinctly, though, because everyone there was looking at us. Hunter had . . . not exactly a diaper, but this weird thing on his head. He looked bizarre. He was enjoying himself thoroughly, but part of the enjoyment was in shocking the people there. When Jann and his wife got there, they didn't seem embarrassed by it, but I was.

Hunter was really interested in the polo equipment, and after the matches, we'd go around to the vendors' tents and look at things like high-end Argentinean leather saddles. Hunter was really serious about it and was asking people questions. A lot of this detail showed up in the story, which at the time I didn't understand at all. He wasn't taking notes.

The low point was probably when Hunter interviewed a dentist by mistake. We were out at the polo fields, and Hunter was supposed to have interviewed one of the Gracida brothers, Carlos and Memo — or Hector and Homo, in Hunter's coinage — the premier polo players in the world, or their team owner. But Hunter either mistook the meeting place or mistook a random man for being the owner of their team and was interviewing this completely normal-looking guy for about fifteen minutes. At some point it became apparent that this guy wasn't a player or an owner, but just a local dentist who liked to watch polo now and then. But it had taken Hunter a long time to uncover that — long enough that he was really angry. That turned out to be the beginning of the end of the trip. It started to get ugly.

COREY SEYMOUR

Later that night, Hunter was late to meet Ginger Baker and some of the other polo crowd at the Huntington Hilton. I'm not sure if we knew if Hunter really wanted to go out or not, but at the same time he seemed furious that he was late. When we got downstairs, the car was taking a few minutes longer than expected to arrive from the valet — he was barking that it had taken "forty-five fucking minutes!" when it really had only been maybe ten minutes, and then yelled to anyone within earshot, "I'M BEN FRANKLIN, AND I WANT MY FUCKING CAR NOW, GODDAMN IT!!! THIS IS FUCKING BULLSHIT!!!"

When the car finally showed, I made a move to drive it myself. "Fuck that!" was Hunter's response. Inside the car were broken wineglasses and empty wine bottles; in the backseat, empty Chivas bottles and liquor stains on the white leather seats; on the dashboard, smudged streaks of a white powdery substance. I really think the whole thing was just too much to comprehend for the valets to really do or say anything about anything. We were supposed to wait for Tobias to lead us to the next hotel, as he had directions or a map, but when I mentioned this to Hunter, I got another, "Fuck that!!" He gunned the car over a couple of speed bumps in front of the hotel and then hit both the front and rear bumpers of the car squealing out onto the road. We were going sixty-five or so in a twenty-five zone, but we had no idea which direction we should be going. Hunter was seething with rage, and I wasn't sure where it was directed. He seemed really angry at me for not knowing how to get where we were going, and he seemed furious at not being able to find his radar detector, which he blamed on "that fucking cunt Shelby!! Bitch!!" whom he had been driving around with the previous night. I asked him to pull over to a gas station so I could ask for directions, which he did, but when I got back in the car after talking with an attendant for maybe eight seconds, he gave me a cold stare and seemed to accuse me of being some kind of traitor. "What the fuck *took* you so long? What the fuck were you talking to *him* about?"

He gunned it down the Long Island Expressway at a little over a hundred miles an hour with complete nonchalance: He held the steering wheel with only his thumb and his two smallest fingers; between the two other fingers on that hand was his cigarette, in his other hand was his tumbler of Chivas — rotated on some sort of unconscious axis to counterbalance the g-forces when the car cornered sharply — and, at Hunter's request, I'd light up his skull-shaped hash pipe and hold it to his lips as he turned sideways to toke.

Then he turned off the lights. At this point, I went from thinking I might die to knowing that I was gonna die. We were floating back and forth from lane to lane, I had a shaving kit full of enough drugs to put one or both of us in prison for the rest of our lives, and Hunter was driving drunk and enraged. And the dome light was on. I was half into the backseat, rooting around double-dong dildos and beer bottles and wineglasses and oddball porno magazines trying to find the goddamned Fuzzbuster, when Hunter found it on his own — in the glove compartment. Again, my fault.

TOBIAS PERSE

The thing about those unpleasant nights is that they didn't really end. The unpleasantness wasn't a quick outburst.

At some point a couple of days later, he turned the wheel over to me. He just said, "You drive." Hunter was a great driver, and more than that was a *confident* driver, so this was saying a lot. And then I hit a bump, and he spilled a drink on himself. Then it happened again, and he said, "If I spill one more drop of whiskey on myself, I'm going home tonight." Well, I wanted him to go home more than anything in the world, so I sped up suddenly and then braked suddenly to go over a speed bump — on purpose. Hunter spilled his drink everywhere and just started beating the dashboard — "That's it. I'm going home."

I went upstairs and booked the first flight I could. I arranged for a limo with the concierge — who hated us — and then at seven a.m., a *van* arrived. Hunter had no baggage except for his leather satchel with the Chivas and the bucket of ice and the Heinekens in his pockets, and he got on with a beer in his hand. What we didn't know, but what we learned quite quickly, was that we were in a van that was making multiple stops to pick up business types in these upper-middle-class suburbs of Long Island.

By this point there was no way Hunter had slept in two or three days, and he kept lighting cigarettes, and each time the driver got angrier and angrier. Hunter just kept putting his cigarettes out on the floor of the van. He was talking to himself and making these weird sounds, and everyone else in the van was completely silent.

We finally got to the airport, and Hunter stepped out right in front of two cops, drinking his beer and carrying the bucket of ice. As he lit a cigarette, the cops told him that he couldn't drink beer, and I stepped in and said, "That's Hunter S. Thompson — believe me, it's not a problem. He's in and out of this airport all the time — they all know him." Hunter kept walking a straight line. The cops were kind of bewildered because Hunter didn't even look at them. I checked him in. Walking toward the metal detector, he set the ice bucket down on the floor and kept going — smoking, of course. Security was getting into it, but he didn't interact with anyone. I got to the metal detector with him and explained that I was his assistant and I'd be checking him onto the flight, and he walked through. At this point we were not talking at all. I got on the fucking plane with him, and Hunter sat and leaned his head to one side and looked like he was going to go to sleep, but just before I left him, he raised his fist and just said, "Take no shit."

And he went home and "went down," as Deborah always called it when Hunter slept. That in itself was a great thing: If you worked for Hunter and he went down, that was thirty-six hours that school was out. You may be back to answering the phone at work, but you've had this amazing experience.

I think I spent a year working on that piece. It was always an interesting give and take with Jann. He kind of disapproved and approved of it at the same time. He disapproved that Hunter required that, but approved of doing it if that's what it took, and if I was willing to do it.

The writing part of it was torturous. I went out to Owl Farm twice specifically for that reason. I took a week off work, and Hunter put my flights on Michael Stepanian's credit card, but by the end of the trip, things had turned sour between us or I'd just really want to go home. Hunter would always rally for a strong good-bye, though. Sometimes it would involve an act of contrition — I'd admired the white dinner jacket and white pants that he was wearing earlier, and now he was saying that he wanted me to have something, which in a certain sense seemed to mean, "I'm sorry for everything that went bad," and all of a sudden I now had this white alcohol-soaked tuxedo. I tried it on for him, and he was straightening it out and manhandling me as if he was a professional tailor, turning me around and telling me where to take it in a bit and checking to see if there was enough fabric in the sleeve. He said, "You look really handsome in that."

He had been writing me into the "Polo" story as a character, and that character went from being kind of fierce — beating people with golf clubs and that sort of thing — to being introduced like this: "The magazine sent me an assistant, a tall, jittery young man. He said, 'My name is Tobias, but my friends call me Queerbait.'" Over four months, I cut "Queerbait" every time I sent it back to him, and every time he'd change it back. I finally had it cut in the copy department just before we closed the issue.

From "Polo Is My Life: Fear and Loathing in Horse Country"
Rolling Stone *697; December 15, 1994*

Polo meant nothing to me when I was young. It was just another sport for the idle rich — golf on horseback — and on most days I had better things to do than hang around in a flimsy blue-striped tent on a soggy field far out on the River Road and drink gin with teen-age girls. But that was still the old days, and I have learned a lot since then. I still like to drink gin with teen-age girls on a Sunday afternoon in horse country, and I have developed a natural, friendly feeling for the game.

Which is odd because I don't play polo, and I hate horses. They are dangerously stupid beasts with brains the size of cue balls and hoofs that can crush your whole foot into bone splinters just by accidentally stepping on your toe. Some will do it on purpose. I have been on extremely mean and stupid horses that clearly wanted to hurt me. I have been run against trees by the bastards, I have been scraped against barbed-wire fences and bitten on the back of the head for no reason. . . .

At the age of 5, I got trapped in a stall for 45 minutes with a huge horse named Buddy, who went suddenly crazy and kicked himself to death with terrible shrieking noises while I huddled in the urine-soaked straw right under his hoofs.

My uncle Lawless, a kindly dairy farmer, was flogging the brute across the eyes with a 2-by-4 and trying to get a strangle rope around his neck, but the horse was too crazy to deal with. Finally, in desperation, he ran back to the house and got a double-barreled 10-gauge shotgun — which he jammed repeatedly against the horse's lips and teeth until the beast angrily bit down on the weapon and caused both barrels to fire at once.

"So much for that one," he said as he dragged me out from under the dead animal's body. I was covered with blood and hot, steaming excrement. The brute had evacuated its bowels at the moment of death. . . .

No one seemed to know why it happened. "It was a suicide," the vet said later, but nobody believed him. Uncle Lawless loved animals, and he was never able to reconcile murdering that horse with his basic Christian beliefs. He sold his farm and went into the real-estate business in southern Indiana, and finally he went insane.

The main problem with horses is that they are too big to argue with when they're angry — or even bitchy, for that matter, and highbred horses are notorious for their bitchiness. Which might be cute or fey in a smaller animal, but when a beast that weighs 1,200 pounds goes crazy with some kind of stupid pique or jealousy in a room not much bigger than the handicapped stall in the Denver airport men's room, bad things will happen to anybody who tries to argue with it: fractured skulls, broken legs, split kidneys, spine damage and permanent paralysis. The kick of a horse at close range, a hoof flicked out in anger, is like being whacked in the shins with a baseball bat. It rips flesh and shatters human bones. You will go straight to some rural Emergency Room, and you will be in a cast by nightfall . . . if you're lucky. The unlucky will limp for the rest of their lives.

TOBIAS PERSE

Once all that was finally finished, it was time for him to start reporting the second installment of the story down in Palm Beach. By the time I got to the Breakers, where he was staying, it looked like he'd been up for a long time. He was wearing pajama bottoms — or maybe wrestling pants. Hunter normally put so much time and preparation into how he looked, but this was the opposite. Maybe he'd put that time in three days ago, but this was day three, and people were staring.

I'd lie to Jann. He'd ask me how the writing was going, or how many matches Hunter had been to. The answer was usually none, but I'd brazenly say, "I think he went to a few chukkers," because I felt it reflected on me — as if I had any bearing on what he would do.

Jann would ask, "Has he been doing a lot of cocaine?" What was I going to tell him? "Uh, yeah, he's doing more cocaine than any person that I'll ever see in my entire lifetime — in fact, he's gone through almost all the stuff he FedExed to me at the office on your personal account?" I would be kind of low-key: "Uh, I don't think a *lot . . .*"

He never finished part 2. Unfortunately, it took about a year and a half to figure out he wasn't going to do it.

While I was down there, somebody had found Hunter's Lincoln Town Car on an abandoned polo field that had been absolutely ripped to shreds. The car had been sitting there for two or three days; Hunter had apparently just abandoned it and seemed to have no memory of it. I remember the detail that he loved: The keys were still in the ignition, and the door was ajar and still pinging.

I didn't say anything to Jann about it; I just rented another Lincoln Town Car. When the expenses came in, they were sent to me — on top of all my other jobs, I was the accounting liaison for the trip. I'd try to trickle the bills through the finance department instead of submitting them all at once, and Hunter would say things like, "Good boy." There were things on the Breakers receipt like a $7,500 charge for "incinerated sofa." The expenses on that were enormous — maybe $25,000 or so — and he wasn't there for more than a week.

Hunter could be incredibly vicious. His voice could be so fraught with what seemed like an unreasonable anger, an illogical anger at some perceived incompetency or fuckup. And the allegation that you could be ineffectual would be the gravest offense — that Hunter seemed to imply that you weren't an expert in what you did, that you weren't professional, or that you, in Hunter-speak, "went sideways" on him. The pressure was extreme but intelligent in a particular way. He used to say things to me like, "By the time I was your age I'd written *Hell's Angels;* what have *you* done today?"

Jann was the only person in Hunter's life who would tell him no. I was always really impressed at Jann's confidence, and at the way Hunter would accord him respect. Hunter could be excoriating toward Jann — he was always talking of this hidden stash of first editions; he had calculated the cost on a piece of paper with amounts written down, like $1.2 million, $900,000. But Hunter would get people riled up about Jann and then as soon as somebody else said something bad about him, he'd turn on them. Ultimately, Jann was sacrosanct.

CHAPTER ELEVEN

Vegas Goes to Hollywood

✝

Johnny would jump into his Hunter character at any given second. He is a brilliant actor, and the way he held a cigarette or picked up Hunter's walk would give us the creeps. Hunter was always screaming, "Stop that!" Johnny would turn it on and off just to fuck with him.

DOUG BRINKLEY

Hunter was about making money, and there was money to be made in Hollywood. You only get paid so much for book advances and writing for *Rolling Stone*.

LYNN NESBIT

He said to me, "If you don't get me more than $300,000 for *Rum Diary,* I'm not going to give you the commission." And I didn't, so he took the contract but didn't pay my agent's commission. It wasn't a pleasant result, even for Hunter's sake, but he was getting more and more desperate. I don't think it was just that the bills were piling up. I think that somewhere in there, he knew he couldn't keep doing it that much longer. He wasn't happy with the way his work was going, and there's always somebody who's going to get kicked — either the wife or the agent or somebody. So I took it philosophically. Hunter knew I cared for him; it wasn't just about the money.

He had a generous heart, which gave him so much conflict, and that led to, I think, so many kinds of abuse — self-abuse and abuse of others. He couldn't deal with that part of himself consistently. What a great, great writer he would've been — to have been able to bring that into his prose. I had really interesting conversations with him about life and love, and he never touched on that in his writing. They weren't really about his personal life, just sort of philosophical talks about "What is love?" It was more abstract but more interesting. He needed that in *Polo Is My Life,* and he really needed it in *The Rum Diary.* That experience was painful because he was so smart about his own work. *The Rum Diary* came out when it did because he needed money, absolutely. He never would've published that twenty years before.

WILLIAM KENNEDY

It's very hard to become a novelist unless you give it your full time. You are not necessarily going to create a valid work of fiction by desiring it. You have to go through all the failures of the work to know what fiction is all about. But if Hunter left the traditional fictional form, he created a new one, a fictional hybrid with his persona dominant; and he produced these incomparable pieces of work, some of which stand, for me, as works of art. Most people still think of him as a journalist, but I think the form, as it exists in some of his work, has serious validity as a variant of fiction. And I think that was willful on his part. He had put in the time as an apprentice in fiction, but then he stopped and did other things.

DOUG BRINKLEY

There was money to be made selling movie rights, and he sold successfully. He liked showbiz folks. He gravitated to Jack Nicholson, Dennis Hopper, Harry Dean Stanton, Johnny Depp, and Sean

Penn — i.e., the Hollywood rebel continuum. He saw himself as an extended member of that group.

He was the same way with rock & roll. He was not interested in rock bands per se. Before he died, Korn was trying to pay him a ton of money to just quote something from him, and he rejected it completely. The same with Garbage. He didn't like their music, and he would be specific about it.

He would do anything for the music he liked — people like Warren Zevon, Willie Nelson, Bob Dylan, Lyle Lovett, Townes Van Zandt, Jerry Jeff Walker; old Kentucky bluegrass masters like the Stanley Brothers, Bill Monroe, Earl Scruggs and Lester Flatt; and some blues people like Howlin' Wolf and Willie Dixon. Those were gods to him, and a lot of them were friends. He would do anything to promote their CDs, to go to their concerts, to talk them up. But his interest in rock music was not as deep as people think. Because he wrote for *Rolling Stone,* people sometimes think he was a big music guy. Hunter was not up on current music and didn't really care to be. He knew what he liked: some Bruce Springsteen; Van Morrison could really get him writing. He knew Leonard Cohen songs by heart. But it was Dylan first and foremost. Any of the Dylan live bootlegs he thought was the greatest thing of all time.

JOHNNY DEPP *was on vacation in Aspen in December 1995 when he met Hunter.*

I had read the old standards — *Fear and Loathing in Las Vegas, Fear and Loathing on the Campaign Trail* — and then moved on to the books of essays like *Better Than Sex.* His writing was a presence in my life and an important one long before I ever met him.

I happened to be in Aspen around Christmastime and really couldn't stand the whole celebrity jet-set ski thing. I thought I'd ended up in the wrong place — I felt like I was in someone else's Christmas. But I saw this guy Alan Finkelstein, who I'd known on and off in Hollywood, and he told me that Hunter was in town and would I like to go out to Woody Creek and meet him?

We arrived at the Woody Creek Tavern and were having a drink, and suddenly there's this big commotion at the front of the bar, where it kind of twisted back. The doors open, and I see this kind of force, this brute force, making his way through the place with a giant electric cattle prod in one hand and a Taser gun in the other and cursing, "Out of the way, you swine!" It was like time stood still; I was thinking, "Holy God . . . it's all real."

He made his way to the table, and we were introduced and shook hands. I'll never forget that: It was the handshake of my grandfather or my father; it was a man's handshake. In the first thirty seconds we discovered that we're both from Kentucky, which was something that was important to him. We had a couple of drinks, and he invited us up to his house. I was admiring some of the weapons that were around — handguns, shotguns, rifles, and things of that nature — and I made a comment about this beautiful nickel-plated twelve gauge. He said, "Oooh yeah, Christ!" and got it down off the wall and said, "Yeah, let's take this out back and fire it off. We need a target. We'll make a target." He had these propane tanks, and he handed me some duct tape and these things that were a little bit bigger than a matchbook and started showing me how to tape these things to a propane canister. I had a cigarette dangling out of my mouth. We were in his kitchen, the command center. I said, "What are these things?" He said, "Oh that . . . yeah, that's nitroglycerin." I immediately heaved my cigarette into his kitchen sink, finished the job, and then we went outside, set one up, and he loaded a shell into the shotgun and handed it over.

His eyes were telling me, "This is a test. This is a test." Because we weren't all that far from the propane tank, and we had a twelve-gauge shotgun loaded with double-ought buck, which is a pretty powerful little combination. I pumped the gun and leveled off on it and KABOOM!! — this enormous fireball went shooting in the air, and

Hunter started whooping and screaming, "Hot damn! Good shooting, man!" And that was it — from that moment on we were pals, and stayed in almost constant touch.

DEBORAH FULLER

Sometimes he would say, "Get the Colonel on the phone!" — he called Johnny "the Colonel" — so he could bounce around a few ideas and try to get some questions answered.

JOHNNY DEPP

I'd get these weird calls — in retrospect they were super-weird, but from Hunter they were normal, an everyday thing. I got a phone call one time where he said, "Where are you?" I said, "I'm in the car; I just got off work and I'm heading home." With Hunter, very rarely would I say, "I'll call you right back" or "I can't talk now," and it was never a five-minute call. It was at least an hour, more like three. But this time he said, "What do you know about hairy black tongue?" And I said, "Uhhh . . . hairy . . . what is hairy black tongue?" He said, "Oh fuck! You don't know anything about it?" I said, "No, I don't. What is it?" He started going into this huge and very knowledgeable speech about this disease known as hairy black tongue. What it all boiled down to was Hunter had been to the dentist, and he'd read some pamphlet on hairy black tongue, and it concerned him gravely. This turned into a three-hour conversation about hairy black tongue and how we could avoid getting it. There were certain guidelines and rules that were set up: Peroxide was out. You could never brush your teeth with baking soda or peroxide or any such thing; it got into that weirdly specific realm. As weird as it was, that sort of thing became normal.

GEORGE TOBIA *is a lawyer and trustee of Hunter's estate.*

One of the great joys in Hunter's life was a place in Boston, where I live, called Jack's Joke Shop. It's the oldest continually operating joke shop in America. It sold everything that Hunter loved, so it became a running thing over the years where he'd call and say, "I need a care package." I'd get some stuff from the store together and write him a letter listing everything in this big box — maybe two and a half pages of an "exhibit listing": "hideous squirming rubber rat caught in trap," "fake dog doo," "fake vomit," "blue-mouth gum," "black-mouth gum," "gelatinous tablets" you're having a drink with someone, and you slip this little tablet into their drink, and it slowly turns to gelatin — "Richard Nixon mask," "infected thumb." Hunter would be talking to someone for a half hour with it on, and they wouldn't notice it, and then he'd pass them something, to make it more obvious.

I bought him a life-size guardian raven with infrared eyes and fake feathers. Hunter put it on a perch in the kitchen; the infrared eyes acted as a motion detector. If you were creeping through the kitchen in the middle of the night, as soon as you crossed the motion sensor, the wings would go up and the raven would go nuts. Absolute heart attack material.

Another one of his favorites was fake scratch lottery tickets. You run into a gas station — say there's four people in the car — and you buy three real scratch tickets and slip this one in. Everyone's got one, everyone's scratching one, and one guy scratches off an "Instant $50,000 Winner." It's a heart-wrenching experience to watch the victim try to redeem it.

But the exotic stuff was what he really liked, and the most noteworthy was the "shocking beer can." It became a trademark of Hunter's. In the United States of America, where ladders have a warning not to fall off them and hair dryers have warnings not to put them in the bathtub, this beer can would be the least likely thing that you could ever imagine getting approved for sale. It's a severe shock. Not a jolt but a continual current. As long as you're holding the can, it delivers. You'd look like one of those lit-up cartoon figures — and you can't let go of it because you're caught in the current. Once I showed Hunter that thing, I think it was his favorite toy of anything he ever had in his life, and he's had many.

BOB BRAUDIS

He was a kid in an adult's body. He handed me a ballpoint pen once and said, "Here, give this a test drive. It's one of the best pens I've ever used." And when I pressed the button, I got this huge shock. He would spend hours poring over catalogs of practical-joke products and then get on the phone and order thousands of dollars' worth of them.

DEBORAH FULLER

Hunter's friend Dan Dibble built a potato gun for him. You shoved potatoes in it, and then it was just another gun that the two of them would shoot off the porch. I was buying boxes of potatoes for a while. . . .

There were always Chinese firecrackers, usually a whole line of them, each one going off like a gunshot. Hunter would throw those around and scare the living shit out of people in the living room or the kitchen or a hotel room. And he always had these toy hammers that sounded like a screaming woman or like breaking glass when you smacked them against somebody's head. He would call somebody up on the phone and leave a "hammer message," and he enjoyed giving people this pen that would shock them when they took the top off. That was always fun — "Ho ho." I hated that one.

WILLIAM KENNEDY

When my wife and I went to see him at the Four Seasons Hotel in New York once, he had a rubber rat on the floor. He could squeeze a ball on a tube, and the rat would run around. It was a four-second joke, but he kept doing it. At his Lotos Club party for the *Fear and Loathing in Las Vegas* Modern Library edition, he had a hammer, and he hit people on the head with it. It made a sound like glass breaking, and it was funny one time, but he hit Tom Wolfe with it at least twice, and I remember Tom not thinking it was terribly funny.

TOM WOLFE

The Lotos Club has a rule that men have to wear a jacket and tie, and so somehow Hunter was forced to do this — but he got even. When each person came through the door, he hit them over the head with a mallet made of rubber. It wasn't a heavy thing like a truncheon, but it did something odd, and he loved that. And when somebody is having as much fun as Hunter could, even if it's not funny, it just sweeps everybody else up in his mood. He was just bopping people on the head left and right.

WILLIAM KENNEDY

In the later years, when his substance intake got more intense, it was hard to get serious with him. When he was sober in the early part of his waking day — the afternoon or early evening — you could get something reasonably lucid out of him. One night we had a conversation for about an hour, and I said, "Hunter, this is unbelievable. You're really cogent." He was so clear I thought he'd stopped drinking. I was wrong.

RALPH STEADMAN

I think that by the end of the nineties he had gotten a bit bored with the whole thing. He didn't want to do it. We tried to do a few things together, but . . .

WILLIAM KENNEDY

Life ganged up on him in the late years, and he ganged up on himself. By this time he was repeating himself, and some of the work became a self-parody. That is not uncommon with writers. But Hunter continued to think of his fictional icons from the past, talking about them, quoting them — Faulkner and Conrad and Fitzgerald and Hemingway, none of whom he resembled in the work. But he still looked to them as shaping influences on his writing life.

MICHAEL CLEVERLY

To change his lifestyle was such a flat-out, unthinkable impossibility that wasting more than a minute of fretting about it was an utter waste of time.

KALLEN VON RENKL

He could recognize that some other people needed to change their lifestyle. When a group of us in Aspen thought a friend of ours might need an intervention, Hunter was part of that conversation.

MICHAEL CLEVERLY

I was there too — Don Johnson, the sheriff, Hunter, me, and a couple of others. A friend of ours was in the business, and for decades he maintained it, but at some point he crossed the line into cocaine psychosis the likes of which I have never seen. He thought everything was covered in slime. The sheriff had actually thrown him out of town at one point. He basically said, "Listen, pal — you get out of town or get out of the business, or you're going to end up getting caught." A lot of our friends over the years did a stretch.

Hunter would always be behind you if you had a drug problem. If you wanted to clean up, he would be behind that. If you got busted, he would find you the best lawyer to try to cut you deals. He would do all the weird backroom stuff, moving the pieces. He would always rise to the occasion. He was all for people improving themselves — as long as they didn't try to improve him.

Let's face it — Hunter was an alcoholic. He was a drug addict. People had tried to do an intervention on Hunter too, but you can write your own script to that one. Ask Bob about it.

BOB BRAUDIS

Some of his friends did an intervention in the mid-nineties, and he said to me and some other friends, "If you ever try that again, I'll never speak to you."

TOM BENTON

This was the dumbest thing I've ever done, but some of us were convinced that Hunter was running amok and his health was going to crack and he was getting a little out of control and his mind was going. Well, that was just crap, but we convinced ourselves. So we got some of Hunter's friends lined up and talked to a lawyer and a doctor about an intervention — it has to be done a certain way — and we called Hunter to this confab. Hunter came in and listened to us for a little bit and then just muttered something or other and left.

The next time I talked to him, he said, "Listen, we won't talk about it again . . . the inquisition . . . we won't talk about it. We'll never mention this again." And he meant it. I said, "I apologize. It was stupid for me to think that I could assess you in any way, and my God, as you've always said, everybody should be allowed to go to hell in their own manner. Even if we were right, we were wrong." That was about as serious as he ever got with me.

He never brought it up again — though once in a while he'd utter the phrase "the inquisition" and look around the room.

COREY SEYMOUR

One day in 1995, we were at the Four Seasons Hotel in New York getting ready to go to the *Rolling Stone* office. We were already hours late, and we were just about ready to walk out the door, when Hunter decided he wanted to change his blazer. For anybody else that might be a thirty-second operation, but Hunter had to take out his grinder, the hollowed-out Bic pen, the skull-shaped hash pipe, cigarettes, lighters, pens, notepads — and a lot more stuff — and transfer it all from one jacket to another. It was taking him forever, and at one point he let out one of his shrieks — "Aiiiggghhh!" and looked over at me and said, "You know, Corey — it's a lot of goddamn work being a drug addict." He didn't seem like he was looking for a laugh, and I was young and naive enough to actually think, "This is my chance." I said, "Do you ever wonder if it's worth it?"

He sat down and was silent for what seemed like five minutes straight. Finally he looked up at me calmly and said, "You know, I've seen a lot of friends over the years go straight and clean up their act. But you know what? They're just not having as much fucking fun as I'm having." And that was that. He put on the new jacket, grabbed his tumbler of Chivas, and off we went.

We had people waiting for us on the street outside of the office, and there were staffers gawking at us through the windows as we pulled up in the car. Hunter did the long walk down the hallway, and he had his skull-shaped pipe filled with hash. Jann was with him and introduced him to every editor down the hallway, and Hunter made a point of offering his pipe to each of them. They'd all laugh nervously and say, "No, thank you." But there was this woman, the editor of Australian *Rolling Stone,* who said, "Sure," and went for it. She told me later that she literally thought this happened every day at *Rolling Stone.* She took this huge hit off this thing and seemed to think, "Wow — these guys are still keeping it real."

JANN WENNER

He'd come to town as the conquering hero and set up shop at the Pierre or the Carlyle or the Four Seasons. He'd pay a royal visit to the office, always two hours late. Everybody wanted to see the legendary Hunter S. Thompson. The ice machines were working overtime, and we'd have plenty of Wild Turkey in stock, and he'd make the ambling entrance trailed by a couple of people. He'd have his satchel and he'd be smoking with that cigarette holder. It would take him forty-five minutes to get down the hall to my office.

It was great. I was always so happy to see him.

TOM BENTON

Around this same time, Hunter and I left his house one day to head down to the Woody Creek Tavern. I noticed that he grabbed a twelve-gauge shotgun as we left the house and put it in his backseat. We parked at the tavern, and just then, George Stranahan was walking in front of the car, and Hunter gets out and reaches in the back and pulls out the shotgun and says, "George, I've had as much as I can fucking take of this!" and puts the shotgun to his shoulder and points it right at him and pulls the trigger from less than ten feet away. He had these twelve-gauge shells that were loaded with confetti, but the sound and the smoke and everything else were like a twelve-gauge going off in your face. I mean, fuck — poor George thought he'd been killed.

GAYLORD GUENIN

George Stranahan probably did more for Hunter Thompson — in terms of renting him and then selling him the property he lived on, and then buying the property back during the divorce so he could protect the property, and buying part of it back again to help Hunter with the IRS — but then again, that's Hunter.

GEORGE STRANAHAN

I don't care who it is or how well you know them. When you see a stainless-steel sawed-off shotgun pointed at you and then see the blast, there's that instant of absolute terror. Then there's the next instant when you realize you're not dead, that it's just Hunter, and it's a joke. I just said, "Fuck, Hunter, why'd you do that? I nearly shit my pants."

ANN OWLSLEY *was Hunter's neighbor and worked at the Woody Creek General Store.*

Hunter was very dear friends with the Stranahans, and the Woody Creek General Store, next door to the tavern, was the Stranahans' store. We've always carried the Gonzo stuff here — the T-shirts and books and everything — and Hunter would get a percentage of all the sales. He'd come in now and again and count how many T-shirts were left and how many we must have sold and wonder if he was really getting his fair share of the profits. Of course he ran up an enormous tab here as well, so I don't think anybody felt they had to cut him a check.

GEORGE STRANAHAN

Hunter and Ralph always had this not-so-funny competition. Ralph would always say, "I'm as good a writer as Hunter — maybe even better." And of course Hunter would give it right back to him: "I'm as good an artist as Ralph — maybe better." Well, Hunter could shoot, but you know the motherfucker couldn't draw. So Hunter would put ink bottles in front of posters of some kind and then blast it all up with pistols and shotguns to create his art.

DEBORAH FULLER

Mary Grasso, who had an art gallery in Aspen, offered to help. She got posters and supplies and came out regularly to assist. We would be out there at the house setting up the firing range, and then we'd set up the table. It was always a big thing to set up the table so that everything was there. All the ammunition and food and liquor — he loved to create a party and dictate how he wanted it to look. Of course, a lot of the people who came out for interviews wanted him to shoot.

We would fill little hotel room jelly jars with different colors of paint and hang them down in front of the poster or the picture as Hunter directed. He chose different guns depending on what effect he wanted. Sometimes he would lay the poster on the ground and stand on the picnic table and shoot down to get a certain splatter effect, or he'd shoot the poster upright for a splatter-drip effect. It was usually at night; that was the only way to do it for maximum effect. We had firing-range lights, and we'd crank up the stereo in the living room so you could hear it outside.

JACK NICHOLSON

He was printing images of people and then putting targets on them and shooting them. A splatter job. He thought this was going to be a marketing coup for him, but it seemed to me to be just a reason to go out back and fire away, more or less. He always needed something like that. Some people might have tried collecting them. I just remember that Hunter kept saying, "It's not art until it's sold."

GEORGE STRANAHAN

He sold one in a local gallery for $10,000, and that really wound him up. I don't think he produced more than a handful of pieces. He tried to price his Mickey Mouse portrait at thirty-five grand. That's in the archives now — where it will stay.

BARNEY WYCOFF *is an Aspen art dealer.*

I really respected Hunter as a fine artist, not just as a journalist and a writer. I thought he created a new way of producing a kind of artwork that was legitimate. Hunter shooting up posters of J. Edgar Hoover or Mickey Mouse with his guns was a real statement of who he was. It brought his guns, his writing, and his philosophy all together in a piece of art. I found it very original and bold and brilliant, and I wish he had more time and energy to take that another couple of steps further.

✛ 🦬 ✛ 🦬

DOUG BRINKLEY

Hunter was hugely interested in the academic world — he wanted to be taken seriously by English professors, PhD students, people doing master's theses — and I became his broker for that. There was never once, if somebody was working on a PhD and wanted to talk to Hunter, that he would not talk to them. He wanted to be part of the canon of American literature; he didn't want to be fringed off as some hillbilly buffoon or as the *Doonesbury* cartoon or the guy that frat guys liked because he drank so much booze. He wanted to be taken as a serious American writer whose named was uttered in the same breath as Mark Twain or Ambrose Bierce or H. L. Mencken — an equal to Jack Kerouac or William Burroughs or Norman Mailer or Tom Wolfe. I'd say, "Well, I don't think you're as great as Twain, but certainly you're in the Ambrose Bierce category." He wanted to be in the Twain category. He loved the sport of literary salon talk — whose poem was influential or what book was the hot book of the moment. It was as deep a passion for him as watching the NFL or the NBA.

I had asked him about his unpublished work and his letters, and he told me that he'd kept his correspondence from way back. Eventually he said, "Look — I don't like people in my papers, but I will trust you. Come on out, and you can spend a week in my basement going through the boxes. See if there's something we can do with all that." I went down there and I was stunned. There were hundreds of boxes of stuff. He saved any article he did as a journalist, and he saved the scraps — whether it was the rent-a-car bill or the hotel receipt or the program from a show he saw. There was the manuscript of *The Rum Diary* and reams of correspondence that had never been published. Hunter had included a couple of letters in *Songs of the Doomed* or *Generation of Swine,* but I had thought that was just filler, and now I realized that those couple of letters were only the tip of the iceberg.

Hunter was very much influenced by Winston Churchill and Franklin Roosevelt. He picked up the idea of the cigarette holder from FDR, who used to do his radio addresses with a cigarette holder in his mouth. He loved Churchill's history of the Second World War and he started envisioning *The Gonzo Papers,* which he wanted to be like a warped multivolume Churchill work, maybe six volumes of material on Hunter's life. He didn't have it in him anymore to write those six volumes, but through correspondence and other collected writings, he started seeing that he was going to have a great body of work.

My relationship with Hunter was mostly on a scholarly basis. I didn't really party with him. The last thing he wanted was somebody drunk or stoned or in a stupor dealing with his sacred archive. He was very conservative in that way. He used to say that alcoholics or junkies were untrustworthy because their addiction was always put far ahead of their sound judgment.

He was looking for clear judgment. He was the junkie. He was the alcoholic. He was the bad boy. He didn't need another bad boy. He did that schtick with Oscar Acosta or others in his writing, but in real life he did not want outlaw competition. He was the number one gunslinger. He was Billy the Kid with a brilliant mind and an incredible intuitive genius. He was a criminal by nature who essentially cased every room he walked into and saw things that nobody else saw. If you went to get gas with Hunter and you were buying a soda at the counter, when you got back in the car he would have an elaborate story about what was occurring in there. "Did you notice that the man working was from El Salvador and that his girlfriend was standing in the back? That kid pumping the air into the tires — why do you think he was in such a hurry?" His observations about the behavior of people were stunning. Sometimes he would freeze-frame something on CNN and say, "Look at that face. You can tell that he's lying."

Another amazing quality of Hunter's — largely unheralded — was the keen, accurate advice he could give you. He was a total disaster on himself, but his ability, if you were in a bind, to solve problems for you was amazing. His advice was always so good — which sounds nutty because he seems like the last person you'd want to take advice from.

Hunter didn't hide from much of his past when we were choosing letters for the first book. His big concern was how his first wife, Sandy, would be perceived. He didn't want her to be embarrassed or humiliated, so of the great writing that did not make *The Proud Highway*, the majority of it pertained to Sandy — letters to her when he was traveling, letters he would write at night at the typewriter when they were fighting about their marriage, or letters alluding to the fact that they had struggled with some miscarriages and what that entailed.

Secondly, old girlfriends — if it was something that was a little risqué, or he knew that this woman was now married and had a family, he didn't want to embarrass her by publishing some old love letter. When he excised material, it was usually to protect the women in his life, or who used to be in his life.

I pushed very hard to publish his letters from the Louisville jail to his mother, but Hunter completely nixed it. There was a box full of them — handwritten, extraordinarily heartfelt — but he said, "No way."

CURTIS ROBINSON *is a former editor of the* Aspen Daily News.

For those of us who worked with him, it was essentially a really abusive relationship. I'd walk away from Hunter's place telling my wife, "God, I'm never doing this again. If I ever bring up doing this again, just shoot me." And you'd be back the next day.

TERRY SABONIS-CHAFEE

If you were having an argument with Hunter about something else — not about writing, but about something more substantive — if either one of you said something that was a particularly lovely turn of phrase, it would immediately be the end of the argument. He would just stop to admire it: "God damn — that was a good insult!" It was regardless of what you had said to him, and it didn't matter if it had been you or him. Everything stopped.

CURTIS ROBINSON

You might come up with the idea of saying that someone had "the loyalty of a snake," but Hunter would come back with "the loyalty of a rented snake." Sometimes we'd have a four-hour search for a word that's like *posh* but not *posh*.

SHELBY SADLER

Hunter loved the Mark Twain quote "The difference between the almost-right word and the right word is really a large matter — 'tis the difference between the lightning bug and the lightning." He knew that better than anyone I've ever met. I think that's what he appreciated so much about Coleridge. I remember the first time I explained to Hunter the literary term *scansion* and how to figure out prosody and feet and meter. I taught him Coleridge's little doggerel about it — "Iambics march from short to long; / With a leap and a bound the swift Anapests throng" — and Hunter became obsessed with anapests for about two weeks. He would say, "Now tell me again: When I want to speed it up, I use an anapest, and it's got that dot."

He was so appreciative of learning all the little technical details. He knew how to write beautifully, but he didn't know why it was beautiful. He liked being taught the names of things — that this is an anapest, this is a spondee, this is a dactyl trisyllable. We worked on dactyl trisyllables for a week so he could learn what he was doing in his sentences to make them faster or slower, to put the poetry in and know what it was. He was almost childlike when I'd teach him something. That was when the innocence came out, and the sweetness.

CURTIS ROBINSON

When he would get cranked up, he would get that look and start laughing while he was writing. "Hot damn — I have it now!" Sometimes he'd take hundred-dollar bills and put them around the typewriter because he just liked to have money around. He'd get into it, and you'd see the look of a small child on his face. It was euphoric. He looked like the Dalai Lama when he was like that. Then the phone could ring, or a GM commercial would come on and he'd just start talking about '66 Chevy Impalas. You'd be thinking, "You were so close. *So* close."

DOUG BRINKLEY

When the first volume of letters, *The Proud Highway,* came out in 1997, it got rave reviews. And whatever we published, both then and later, in the second volume of letters, *Fear and Loathing in America,* was just a hint of Hunter's total correspondence.

Those books, plus the Modern Library publishing the twenty-fifth-anniversary edition of *Fear and Loathing in Las Vegas* as a classic, would bring Hunter into the category where he wanted to be — a serious American writer. At the same time, Johnny Depp was coming into the picture. Laila Nabulsi had been working for a long while to get *Fear and Loathing in Las Vegas* made into a movie, and Hunter wanted to determine who the actor was who was going to play him, and he was looking in particular at Depp and Matt Dillon. But once Hunter met Depp, the deal was done. Johnny was from Kentucky, which meant a lot to Hunter, and Johnny came from humble roots like Hunter. Johnny was very much into Baudelaire, Rimbaud, Genet, Breton, Artaud, and a perverse sort of French literature which Hunter always admired. They had a real and immediate bond.

JOHNNY DEPP

It wasn't until 1996, when I was almost done with *Donnie Brasco* in New York, that I got this phone call from Hunter asking me if I would be interested in playing him in the film of the Vegas book. He always referred to *Fear and Loathing* as "the Vegas book." I said, "Of course I would." We talked that night over the phone, and that was the last I heard of it for quite a long while.

LAILA NABULSI

It was basically thanks to Johnny that the movie got made at all. In Johnny, I finally had somebody who matched my passion. I knew he'd stay the course even though he shouldn't. It wasn't like everybody in his camp was jumping up and down saying, "Make this movie!" His agent and lawyers didn't want him to do it.

JOHNNY DEPP

I was in New York, I think for the twenty-fifth-anniversary party for *Fear and Loathing,* and I cornered Hunter and asked him if he really wanted me, if he really felt I was the guy to do that, because I knew he had other friends who were actors, and I would have been more than happy to back out. It was Hunter's book, and if it was going to be me, I needed to have his blessing. And he said, "No, of course you're wanted. You have my blessing." I said, "If I do a remotely decent job of portraying you, you know there's a very good chance you'll hate me for the rest of your life," and he said, "Well then, let's hope for your sake that I don't, ho, ho."

WAYNE EWING

One January Sunday during the play-offs, Hunter called me up and said, "You've got to come up with your camera. The writer-director of *Fear and Loathing in Las Vegas* is coming up to have a script conference, and we'll watch football and talk about the movie." Hunter was in a great mood. He was really looking forward to meeting Alex Cox and his partner. He put a naked blow-up doll out in the snow as a signpost for them to know they were at Owl Farm.

He cooked them sausages — I had never seen him cook breakfast for anybody before — but unfortunately, they were vegetarians. It was my first clue that things were going to go a bit awry. We all began to watch the football game, but they weren't into gambling, which I could see was perhaps another problem, but Hunter was hanging in there. I spent a couple of hours trying to copy the only copy of the script they had brought with them so there could be a decent script conference after the game was over. Immediately, Hunter — who had been saying repeatedly throughout the afternoon that he had not read the script — asked the most pertinent question of all. It was about a structural problem that had always existed in *Fear and Loathing in Las Vegas*, because it's a combination of two trips that he actually took: the first one to cover the Mint 400 and the second one for the DAs' drug conference. They were totally separated in time, and Hunter's question was, essentially, about how you put those two trips together in one film.

They said, "Well, you get swept back to Vegas on this tidal wave." Hunter said, "Tidal wave? What do you mean, tidal wave?" They replied, "You know, like what you wrote about in the book." The "wave speech" is one of the highlights of the book: He talks about how, in 1970 or '71, you could go outside of Las Vegas, and with the right kind of eyes, look up at the mountains and see this high-water mark, this place where this wave that represented the energy of the 1960s broke and rolled back. Alex and his partner had come up with this idea to have him surf this wave back to Las Vegas.

Hunter asked, "It's a wave? How are you going to show that? Some kind of animation?" They said, "Yes, animation!" Hunter began to refer to that as a "cartoon." They wouldn't back down on the idea, and this went on for about two hours. It was excruciating to watch. Alex and his partner thought that they were fulfilling "the Steadman vision," as they referred to it, and then Alex made the mistake of saying, "What people remember about *Fear and Loathing in Las Vegas,* most notably, are the drawings of Ralph Steadman."

I really thought he was going to get hurt. Alex then said something to the effect of, "You probably didn't even like cartoons as a child," and Hunter's response was, "Do I look like I suffered for it? You've had one and you're already at two. You don't want to get to three or you're out of here." They threw their coats on and ran out of the kitchen, and that was the end of *Fear and Loathing in Las Vegas* for them.

JOHNNY DEPP

So Alex Cox split, and we got Terry Gilliam to direct.

DOUG BRINKLEY

Around this time I organized — with Ron Whitehead, a Louisville poet — a retrospective on Hunter in Louisville. And we called Jann Wenner about throwing Hunter a party, and Jann, without hesitation, said yes, he'd throw Hunter a huge party for the anniversary of *Vegas*. I was MC of the event in Louisville, and we got all of Hunter's childhood friends together, and Virginia, his mother, came and sat in the front row. We pulled together this great event, and Hunter's son, Juan, wrote a beautiful tribute to his dad's outlaw legacy.

JOHNNY DEPP

When we did Hunter S. Thompson Day in Louisville — he was very proud of this — at the end of the night it was Hunter and me onstage taking questions from the audience. I was the interpreter. His mother, Virginia, was right there in the front row, and it was wonderful.

Hunter decided that since we were both brothers from "the dark and bloody ground," as Kentucky is known, there were several fish to fry in Louisville. We were going back there to clear his name — they were going to celebrate him, and his mother was going to be there, and she would be proud. He said he wanted to make me a Kentucky Colonel — which almost anyone can be. There's a society of Kentucky Colonels. Hunter was one and he made me one. You don't need to do anything — you just write in and ask for it, and they give it to you. From then on, he always referred to me as the Colonel.

WAYNE EWING

All Hunter's childhood friends were at the event. It was a sold-out crowd, and as it came to a close, there were people all over the stage. It ended with David Amram leading Johnny Depp and a lot of good local musicians in "My Old Kentucky Home." Just as it was ending, Hunter beckoned me over and said, "You've got to help me get out of here. That man is after me" — and he pointed to someone backstage.

BOB BRAUDIS

I had a walkie-talkie, and Hunter was yelling at me through it to grab his bag, run out the back door, and dive into the stretch limo because fans were attacking him. All of a sudden flames were flying. Some rednecks set fire to the backstage of the theater. This is the kind of shit you worry about. If Hunter had come back in, who knows? He might have started throwing punches and gotten the shit kicked out of him.

WAYNE EWING

Later, when we looked at the footage, Hunter showed me who the guy was — it was one of his boyhood friends who had been arrested with him when he went to jail when he was seventeen. I can't say that the person was a threat or not. It's probably more likely that Hunter just didn't want to have to see him, but he built it up, as Hunter would, into a huge drama.

BOB BRAUDIS

The day after the event in Louisville, Juan wanted Hunter to go see his mother, who I think was eighty-nine. They didn't have any time together the previous night — she got to the show late and left. But Hunter was waffling on it, and we had this stripper hanging out with us that we had picked up — a cute little thing wearing a micro-miniskirt — and I said to Hunter, "Here's the deal. I will drive you and Juan out to the nursing home. I'll kill an hour with whatever her name is — Bambi — at a bar and then come pick you up. Hunter said, "You promise? An hour? No longer?" I said, "Yeah." So I dropped Juan and Hunter off at this nursing home out in the boondocks, and Bambi and I took off looking for a bar. When we got back to the nursing home, there were Hunter and Virginia and about eight relatives. Virginia wanted all of her relatives to see her son, the famous writer. Everybody was smoking and drinking, and the nurses were very upset.

The next day we were taking off out of Louisville on a forty-five-degree climb toward the sun, and the seatbelt sign was still on. We were in the first row of first class, and Hunter claws himself into the bathroom. We leveled off, and the next thing I knew there was a long line in front of the door, and he'd been in there for forty-five minutes. The flight attendant came to me and said, "Exactly what is your friend doing in the restroom?" I said, "He's had hideous diarrhea for the last twelve hours." She said, "Oh, okay. Thank you. No problem." So Hunter finally came out and sat down, and I said, "What the fuck were you doing in there?" He said, "I took a bath, I shaved my head, I brushed my teeth, I meditated." Then he reached into his carry-on and pulled out a liter of fucking Chivas and started chugging. The flight attendant said, "Hey, we'll give you all of that you want for free, but you're breaking the law." Hunter said, "Well, bring it."

That's when I decided it was easier for me to decline invitations to travel with him.

WAYNE EWING

Any time with Hunter on the road was like dog years. It was always a production, and it got to be more and more of one as time went on. He was not an easy guy to travel with by any means. It wasn't just the traveling, but checking into the hotel, getting the right suite. That could be two hours of excruciating agony — just getting the right suite. The climate had to just be right. The view had to be right. The furniture had to be just the way he liked it. And very often the finest hotel you could imagine — the Four Seasons in New York or the Brown Palace in Denver — would never have a suite that was good enough for him. He could always find something wrong with a suite, although there were a couple he liked at the Chateau Marmont in Hollywood — either suite 59 or 69, one on top of the other. Those had been road tested.

Before I left Hunter's room at night, I would say, "Hunter, whatever you do — do not double-lock the door, because I can't get back in. I've got a key, but if you double-lock it, the key doesn't work anymore, and you can't hear me banging on the door. He would say, "Yes, yes, I understand, I understand." More than once I had to get security to take the door off its hinges because he would double-lock the door. He was dead asleep, and of course he'd have some twelve o'clock appointment he'd made with a film executive who was already waiting in the lobby.

CURTIS ROBINSON

If you were working as his road manager, when you got in the car with him, you would make sure the jimson weed and bowl were easily available, because that's one of the things he would go searching for at ninety miles an hour — a smart person would have those in his hand. I always said that advancing Hunter was always about the next fifteen minutes. You really couldn't plan beyond that.

When you tried to get him to events — and I had a great record of getting him to events pretty much on time — you'd lose him. If you were able to get him out of his house or his hotel room or wherever he was holed up, you wanted to move him like a candidate. You didn't want any hang-up. If the elevator wasn't there — "It's a sign; I'm going home." If there was no parking spot in front of the venue — "It's a sign; I'm going home." Town Car instead of a limo . . . anything. I developed a rule: Anyone you send in to bring him out of someplace — if they're not out with him in twenty minutes, you write them off. They're part of the problem.

With Hunter, there were no days off. He got up and went through first gear with breakfast: read the papers, have a beer. Second gear: scotch, phone. Third gear: the boomer gear. That was the fun gear. Fourth gear could be free fall.

WAYNE EWING

There was a lot of fun on the road, but we didn't do the road so much toward the end. It became more and more difficult for Hunter to travel, and when he did, he really needed to go on a private plane. That was a sad thing to watch. It was just the physicality of being in small tight spaces as much as anything. There were some security concerns as well after 9/11, but security was always there. And once you've flown private, you can't go back. Once you've been in a Gulfstream, it's hard to go back to the friendly skies of United. So that was always part of it — the search for a private plane that somebody might come up with.

He'd call his famous friends, and very often they would come through, but sometimes they wouldn't. So he traveled less and less. I think it was really a testament to Hunter's writing ability and his perceptual abilities that he could sit in his kitchen and watch a thirty-six-inch TV and talk on the telephone and know as much as he needed to know about the world and be able to synthesize it and comment on it as well as he did. That's primarily how he worked the last decade of his life. The forays into Hollywood or New York or anywhere else were rare.

DOUG BRINKLEY

After the Louisville event, Depp came out to Woody Creek and lived in Hunter's basement, which Hunter forever after called Johnny's Room. I came out and stayed in the cabin, so it was really Deborah, Colonel Depp, myself, and Hunter for a week. I was going through Hunter's files and finding things related to *Vegas* for the second volume of letters, *Fear and Loathing in America,* so Johnny could read some of that stuff. We dug up clothes from the basement so Depp could dress just as Hunter did.

DEBORAH FULLER

Johnny was a great guest; he never missed a thing and would help with anything. I would retrieve things for Hunter, and Johnny would see where I had gotten something, and after Hunter was done with it, he would put it away. He would be the first one to take the dishes out of the dishwasher. Watching him study Hunter was hysterical. I would get Johnny the same hats and jackets, and of course he used Hunter's cigarette filters. I found all the original clothes that Hunter wore in *Vegas* — they fit Johnny to a tee — and he had copies made of everything.

They would stay up until all hours. Johnny quickly became a trusted friend who could roll with Hunter and keep the same schedule. They had the best time talking, calling people, drinking, going to the tavern, going for wild drives, buying matching guns, shooting on the range, plotting scenes for the movie — you name it and they covered it. They would be up for as long as it took. Hunter had found "a bright boy and a gentleman," as he put it, a Kentucky Colonel that he could play with, one that he respected. Hunter also loved to have Johnny read his work. Johnny knew all of Hunter's writing and had a true feel for it; he also had a beautiful voice and understood how to read Hunter's work. Of course, Hunter trained him — "Slower, slower, goddamn it! Emphasize that this is *music . . .*"

JOHNNY DEPP

I knew then how special every second of that time was. You can make more room in your body and in your brain and in your heart to store that stuff, and I did. I never got sick of it. Even talking about things that I wasn't particularly interested in — point spreads or various sporting events and things like that. You'd be talking about Michael Jordan and his brilliance or his athletic abilities one second, and the next thing you know you've made some turn and you're talking about moonshine running.

The only thing that I knew that I wanted, that I needed, was the years of 1970 and '71, the *Vegas* time, and Hunter's relationship with Oscar Acosta, the model for Dr. Gonzo. That was really the main focus, but then it just went everywhere. We talked about everything, from his earliest memories, his youth in Louisville and beaning people's mailboxes and petty thievery, and his air force days. I asked him if it was okay to videotape. I said, "I'm not going to interview you, but if you don't mind, I'll set a camera down on the counter, click it on, and then we'll just be. We'll just talk." He said, "Yeah, that's fine." And neither one of us, by the way, looked at the camera after that. We just sat and talked for hours and hours and days. I have endless amounts of footage of that, which was very, very helpful.

He spoke a lot about Oscar. He basically said that he had great respect for him and thought he was brilliant, but the one thing that he always stressed about Oscar was that he was scary. Hunter never knew what to expect of him — he could snap at any moment, and things could go ugly. He said that he'd never been with anyone in his life who could make things uglier and darker and more dangerous in such a short period of time — like seconds. He loved Oscar, obviously. I think he really believed that there was a chance that Oscar was still around, that he was too large a force to have been taken out so easily.

TERRY GILLIAM *directed* Fear and Loathing in Las Vegas.

It's a very important thing to have chaos as part of the world order. I was only up to Woody Creek once, and it was a very funny evening. Hunter was writing the introduction to Ralph Steadman's gonzo art book, and he read it out loud to me — "Hitler took the high road and you, Ralph, took the low road." I was in tears. But even on an evening like that, the video camera was recording him the whole time. It was like observing the *Queen Mary,* with a lot of tugboats servicing him, recording his moments, making him an utterly historical figure. Every moment became a little bit of history. And that's a lot of work.

CURTIS ROBINSON

I think Hunter had an intuitive understanding of the brand of "Hunter Thompson." He knew to wear the same kinds of things when he went out. He was aware of things like entrances and exits.

How much of Hunter was spontaneous and how much was arranged was always one of those questions that people would kick around. I found that he was like jazz. The piece was arranged. It was disciplined. But within that, he was the free instrument and he would go off. Nobody else went off because we were just trying to get through the piece, but he would go off. I always found his writing to be a lot like that. He needed a story. He needed a surprising amount of structure in his head, but within that structure he would go crazy.

JOHNNY DEPP

I started to get fascinated with the way that he would approach a meal. It was incredible to watch, because if Hunter had a plate of crab cakes, oysters, and some rice or something, the meal would arrive, and he would then sort of study it. "Yeahhh . . ." It seemed that aesthetically, it needed to be at the right kind of angle, and then he would take the salt and pepper and kind of hover over the dish — and he would salt and pepper his food for fucking twenty minutes. For me, it became an obsession. And then the lemon. He'd squeeze a lemon over everything — the whole fucking lemon. I started really getting into these odd details.

He got a little freaked out when I started to act like him. You had to learn to be as quick as Hunter. There was a borrowing it for a period of time — sponging to a degree that went beyond mimicry. But it used to freak him out.

DEBORAH FULLER

Johnny would jump into his Hunter character at any given second. The way he held a cigarette and the way he picked up Hunter's walk — it would give us the creeps. Hunter was always screaming, "Stop that!" Johnny would turn it on and off just to fuck with him. Hunter shaved Johnny's head again after he arrived so it was just right, and he had me trim the sides because I always cut Hunter's hair.

JOHNNY DEPP

I'd been staying there for weeks, and my nightstand was this barrel. It was where the lamp was and it was where my ashtray was. I was in there doing my homework at night before I'd fall off to bed, and I had stacks of photos of Hunter and Oscar and all the bits and pieces from the manuscript of *Fear and Loathing,* Hunter's early works, tons of reading materials — important stuff. I'd be going through that, and at a certain point, as I was putting a cigarette out, I thought, "Fuck, man — that's a keg. There's no way in hell this thing can be, like, *live,* can there be?" It's where my ashtray was and the whole bit — matches and lighters. I went upstairs and said to Hunter, "I need you to come downstairs for a minute, man; you've got to check this out." He said, "What's the problem?" He came downstairs, and I said, "Come in my room. What the fuck is that?" I pointed to the keg. "Is that what I think it is?" He looked at it and he goes, "Oh fuck — *that's* where it is!" I said, "Is it gunpowder?" He said, "Oh yeah . . ."

By the time I had to go back to L.A., I had amassed a collection of copies of stuff and photographs and bits of his notes from the *Vegas* years — a lot of stuff. I had a bunch of his clothes from that period, and not only that, but I was getting ready to drive the Red Shark to L.A. from Colorado. It was cute in a way, because I guess some part of it had to do with the fact that I was leaving, but he got a little like, "Fuck you — you come here, you sponge off me and move into my house, and now you're leaving and taking all of my clothes and all of my shit with you." We sort of battled and verbally challenged one another to outdo the other. I'd say, "Yes, Hunter, that's true. But it's for the greater good now, isn't it? You want to be represented well, don't you?"

TIM FERRIS

Johnny was completely earnest. The first time we ever hung out together, Hunter had left the room, and Johnny, with this tremendous sincerity, said, "He really is quite remarkable, don't you think?" I was really touched by it. This was a guy who was putting himself on the line for Hunter. I mean, it was a lot of time, a lot of work, and a lot of abuse to make a film that nobody expected was going to make any money or advance anybody's career.

JOHNNY DEPP

When it was just Hunter and me in our relationship, I was the Colonel. In other instances, such as out on the road, he would refer to me as Ray. It was always, "Well, go talk to Ray. He's got the music set up." I'd made these CDs for Hunter — there would be the CD that we would listen to in the motel before we split, and there'd be the CD we'd listen to in the car on the way to an event, and then I would go in and set up the blaster and put the CD on for the event itself. It was "Spirit in the Sky" and "Mr. Tambourine Man" and "One Toke Over the Line," "Sympathy for the Devil," "White Rabbit" — all that stuff. And he fucking loved it — we'd drive down the street, and he'd be whooping. He had a polo shirt made for me that said, "Just Call Me Ray," and when he introduced me to people as Ray and they said, "Well, but that's Johnny . . . ," he'd go, "No! His fucking name is Ray."

We were on the road on a book tour for *The Proud Highway*, and Hunter's back went out on him — sciatica. He was in a lot of pain. His back had been acting up before that, but now we were locked in his hotel room in San Francisco together, just the two of us, for about five days.

One night the phone rang. I picked it up, and the guy on the other end said, "Dr. Thompson?" I said, "No, this is not Dr. Thompson. This is Ray. What can I do for you?" He said, "My name is Ramundo. I can do things." I was dead sober, thinking, "What the fuck?" But again, when you were in those situations with Hunter, nothing was bizarre anymore. I guess I sounded confused, because he said again, "Yes, my name is Ramundo — I can do things." I said, "Excuse me?" He said, "I can do things." I said, "All right . . . uh, we don't need anything right now, but thank you very much for your call, and take it easy." Click.

Maybe forty-five minutes later, Hunter and I were sitting there still talking, and Hunter flinched and suddenly said, "What the fuck . . . Did you hear that?" I said, "No, I didn't hear anything." He said, "That sound — I heard a dog; fuck, it's a mastiff; I heard a mastiff." For him to be that specific — I was laughing my guts out. I said, "Hunter, c'mon." He said, "No, no — we've got to check this out." So we got up — and Hunter was hobbling because of his back — and we were trying to look out the peephole head-to-head, and there was nothing in the hallway. Then we looked down, and there was a black business card that had been stuck under the door. It had gold lettering, and it said, "Ramundo: I can do things," with a phone number below.

Hunter started walking back to the living room, and suddenly I heard a dog, a big dog, way down the hall. I called the number on the card, and it's this fucking guy Ramundo. I said, "Were you just in the hallway?" He said, "Yes — I left my card, which is how you are calling." I said, "Do you have a dog?" He said, "Yes, I do." I said, "Do you have a dog *with* you?" He said, "Yes, I do. A bullmastiff." I said, "Where are you now?" He said, "I'm across the street" at such-and-such a bar, "and I just want you to know that if you need me, I can do things."

Hunter and I fucking howled. We had no fucking idea who "Ramundo" was.

When Allen Ginsberg's memorial was being held in Los Angeles, Hunter couldn't come down for it. But since we'd both known Ginsberg, Hunter and I talked and he said, "Listen — I'm going to write this piece, and you're going to be at this deal anyway, and I'd like you to read it." Ten days later, nothing. I called and said, "Hunter, the thing's tomorrow, man." He said, "Yeah, yeah — it's coming. I'll get it to you; it'll be there tomorrow morning." I wake up in the morning, and it's not there. The thing was at eight p.m., and I talked to Hunter in the afternoon at three or four, and he said, "I can't do it. I can't do it. I don't like anything that I've written, and fuck it — I'm just not going to do it. I'm abandoning the piece." I jumped all over him and said, "Fuck you, man — you can't do that. These people are expecting me to be there to read your words."

I had to leave the house at 7:30. At 7:29, it came in on the fax machine, and I read the piece in the car on my way to this memorial, howling with laughter. He called Allen "a dangerous bull-fruit with the brain of an open sore and the conscience of a virus." It was unbelievable. He wrote, "He was crazy, queer, and small," and said that Allen was happy, that he was looking forward to meeting the grim reaper "because he knew he could get into his pants."

TERRY GILLIAM

We had this fairly scratchy relationship. I was a huge fan, but we always seemed to be circling each other the whole time during the film, which was interesting. When you make a film of somebody else's book, you're so wanting to impress him and so wanting to make him feel good about the way you're interpreting his work, and at a certain point you learn to hate him because it's causing you so much anguish trying to live up to — or down to — the standards that he's set. It was a strange experience. I had to be cut off from him. I didn't want to have to be beholden to him.

JOHNNY DEPP

He only came to the set of the film toward the end — only when we were in L.A. I had wanted to get him back to Vegas, but I think Gilliam was probably a little frightened of the idea of Hunter being on set in Vegas. I kept him well informed, that's for sure. I talked to him every day and every night to tell him what we did, and I would also call him if I was unsure about the context of the book versus the screenplay and the situation we were working on.

TERRY GILLIAM

It was always a wary dance that we performed, and it was good fun. But I could only take a certain amount of Hunter on the phone with his long ramblings, because I had work to do. He was happy with the script and he was happy with what we were doing. That was the important thing. He dredged up extra bits and pieces, which were very nice.

The only real time during the shooting that we had to deal with Hunter was the day he turned up to be in the film. He was like a child, with this great big ego that demanded immediate attention. We were in the middle of shooting, and suddenly bread rolls were bouncing off the back of my head. But at the end of the day, we had to do the scene where Hunter actually appears for the one and only time. He dressed exactly like Johnny, or Johnny was dressed exactly like him, with the corduroy patch jacket and the hat with the green visor and things like that. It was just a funny idea — that Johnny, playing Hunter, would have a weird flashback to himself. We had all these extras and we were running into overtime, and suddenly Hunter decided that he didn't want to do it.

Laila and Johnny and I were doing everything to convince him, and finally he walked on and looked at the set and where we'd positioned him and said, "No. I wouldn't have been in the middle of things. I would have been an observer over on the edge. I would be watching. I'm a journalist." So we rearranged the whole fucking set, and then he found another reason to stall.

There were probably a hundred and fifty people waiting around to make this happen. It might have been Laila who was the clever one who lured him out on the floor by introducing him to the best-looking girl extra on the set, whom we then sat opposite him at a table in the club. He actually seemed quite happy, and he settled in and was chatting her up. While this was going on, we came shooting through there with a camera — and Johnny was doing all this very complicated stuff, and all these extras, a hundred people, were singing and dancing — and when we came by, Hunter paid no attention whatsoever because he was too busy charming the girl as best he could. He had completely forgotten about the film.

So okay — take one was fucked, and on take two he was still not paying attention, so Johnny actually went over, while staying in character, and gave him a nudge. Hunter spouted one of his trademark "huh?"'s and sort of woke up, and we moved on. We did one take which wasn't particularly great but was passable. On the next take, Johnny was walking by the table, and Hunter jumped out and did something really stupid. I mean, once we actually got him on the set, it was like, "Why did we do this?" In fact, the one we used works very well in the film, but at the time, everything felt like we had just brought this two-year-old onto the set and given him a house to play with.

When we finally finished it and felt really good about it, we had to show it to him. Both Johnny and I were terrified of what he might think. We'd arranged these screenings, and Hunter, at the last minute, kept failing to make them. It turned out he was as terrified as we were about seeing the film because he didn't want to be disappointed. But he finally saw it, and I've seen a tape of him from the end of that screening, and he's so happy — it's one of the moments that made it all worthwhile.

JOHNNY DEPP

It was the moment that in Kentucky they'd refer to as the "come to the quiltin' " — the moment of truth. They flew the film up to Aspen for Hunter to see, and I was scared to death because I really did believe that he would potentially hate me for the rest of his life. After he'd seen the film, I got him on the phone, 'cause I had to know. I said, "Okay, do you hate me? Was I right?" And he said, "Oh, fuck no, man. Christ — it was like an eerie trumpet call over a lost battlefield." Those words just came out of his mouth. I thought, "Well, okay. We're solid."

TERRY GILLIAM

On the other hand, when it came to the premiere, I was very nervous. Hunter turned up in one of those strange public moods that he was into — which usually meant making an ass of himself — and he had this giganzo bag of popcorn that stood about five feet tall. Whether it was the result of his own nervousness or what I don't know, but he ended up making me so pissed off at him that I couldn't even sit and watch the film. I went to a bar and got drunk.

JOHNNY DEPP

There was a photo op, and they wanted a few of us from the movie to line up — myself, Benicio [Del Toro], maybe Gilliam, and Hunter. As we were about to do it, Hunter grabbed this massive bag of popcorn and started whaling on us. Popcorn flew everywhere, of course. I think that was just Hunter staking his territory — and he was right to do it, because those kind of movie premieres, with the hullabaloo and the actors and filmmakers and celebrities or whatever — I think Hunter just felt, "Well, hey man, let's not forget why we're all here in the first place."

TERRY GILLIAM

It was wonderful, and I'm glad we did it, but at the end of the day you just wanted to go home and lie down and be very quiet.

CHAPTER TWELVE

Where Were You When the Fun Stopped?

They put him in the ICU unit, which was insulated from the general patients, because he was screaming and acting out. They had him on an IV for hydration and alcohol. At one point he whispered in my ear, "Get me out of here." I said, "You want me to spring you?" And he goes, "No, take me to the bar."

DEBORAH FULLER

One of Hunter's legs was shorter than the other by a small distance, and he wore Converse tennis shoes for so many years, which were not good for his back. He had also spent years, before he moved into the kitchen, sitting in an Adirondack-style chair in the living room, where he leaned forward over a typewriter for hours at a time writing, which didn't help. On top of that, he had sciatica. Starting around '98, the pain was getting excruciating. He never liked going to the doctor, but when things got that bad, he had to have something done about it.

JUAN THOMPSON

The more the pain in his hip progressed, the less he would move. He spent more time sitting at his kitchen counter. He had an extremely

high tolerance for pain, and he wouldn't carry on about it, but sometimes I could see: He just didn't move around much. He was on pain-
killers to help manage it, but he was mostly quiet about it.

DEBORAH FULLER

The doctors in Glenwood Springs discovered that his hip was in
worse shape than his back, though, and it was time for surgery. Juan
and his wife Jennifer and their young son, Will, were there, along with
myself and Hunter's assistant at the time, Heidi. We'd take turns staying up — we never left him alone for a minute.

JACK NICHOLSON

He made me feel his displaced hip one night. That was so shocking
to me, just to feel it. It was not a displaced hip. This thing was practically loose. It was insane.

DEBORAH FULLER

The staff at the hospital had to know exactly what his toler-
ances were, and Hunter was tested for it just like anybody else. But
he also happened to have this amazing constitution and will, and
those things make a difference when you go into surgery. I was never
worried that he was going to die, but everything had to be well researched. Hunter knew damn well who the anesthesiologist was and
who everybody else in attendance was, but it was still tough on everybody.

JUAN THOMPSON

They had everything scheduled, and he canceled it; it was a huge
production, but he finally agreed, I'm sure just because it was becoming so painful. But the bigger issue was the gradual degeneration of
his body.

DR. STEVE AYERS *is an emergency room doctor and the Pitkin County coroner.*

There's a medical term for Hunter's special needs for medications: tachyphylaxis. You develop a tolerance to a medication — like opiates, for example — and you need more of it. Hunter had some horrible pain. His back and some of his other orthopedic injuries hurt. He might have needed a lot more than the average person because he had so much pain and he'd been taking stuff for several years. That's not uncommon, but at the same time, I don't know how Hunter could tolerate some of the stuff he did. He had a phenomenal constitution when it came to medication or drug use. He was able to function and perform and do things that most people can't.

DEBORAH FULLER

Eventually, Hunter called a few good friends, and they came and sprung him out of the hospital — much to my dismay at the time, but it all worked out. Hunter did physical therapy afterward — he'd go into town to see somebody, and a therapist came out two or three times a week to take him to Stranahan's pool for exercises in the water.

TIM FERRIS

I was after him for a while, particularly when he was rehabbing from his various injuries, to be more healthy or more active. But it's very difficult to influence a person's behavior, even your own, and there's no point in nagging at people beyond the suggestion. I'd send him a case of grapefruit, or I'd advise him not to drink so many of these dark liquors because of all the conjoiners in them. Conjoiners are the non-alcoholic components of booze other than water, and they typically consist of various wood poisons from the oak barrels in which things are aged, and sugars. A lot of what messes up heavy drinkers is not just the alcohol but the conjoiners. A professional drinker will lower their conjoiner level and just deal with the alcohol, because that's the only thing they really want anyway, so I used to talk to him about that stuff. But he was not getting enough exercise. He would swim a bit at night, but it wasn't enough to come anywhere near a proper rehab from the sorts of physical problems he was starting to have.

JUAN THOMPSON

The hip replacement made such a difference in his mood. He was just a much nicer, happier guy. It's all relative, but he was calmer, less likely to have outbursts, more patient; a lot more pleasant to be around. I don't think he realized how much that chronic pain had dominated his life and his mood until it was removed. He put up with it for a long time, and he didn't realize how painful it had been until he replaced it. The top of his femur had worn away.

BOB BRAUDIS

Juan spent a lot of time with his dad in the hospital when Hunter had the hip replacement down in Glenwood. I think Hunter was asking Juan to give him the paternal assistance that he needed, you know? It was a role reversal. And Juan stepped up.

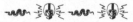

JUAN THOMPSON

I gave my wife, Jennifer, a little speech before she met Hunter for the first time. She'd been an admirer of his for a long time. I think Hunter was sizing her up. If he'd decided he didn't like her, I don't think he would have said anything, but luckily he approved. He would sometimes judge someone by how they reacted to certain things to determine if they were trustworthy — or if they were fun. He'd do something that would throw someone off — throw something at them, maybe — and then, depending on how they reacted to it and how they handled it, they'd go up or down in his estimation. But she passed, and then they became very close.

ANNA STEADMAN *is Ralph Steadman's wife.*

Getting Hunter to Juan's wedding was interesting. We had to hire an airplane to get him there, but he was very good when the time came. He looked lovely in his white jacket.

JUAN THOMPSON

He got there — almost on time. He was not known for his attendance. And, yeah, it was a memorable day. He could be very elegant when he wanted to be. And later, when we had our son, Will — once Hunter adjusted to the idea that he was a grandfather, he liked that role. He liked Christmas. He liked buying toys for Will, and they could play for a while, but he's not someone you'd want as a babysitter. I'd always want to be close by, just because he might not understand the limitations of a very small baby.

DEBORAH FULLER

After Juan and Jennifer were married, they started coming for long weekends on a regular basis. That's when the relationship between Hunter and Juan — and now Jennifer — developed even more. Hunter loved it. It was a very special time, and they became close.

DOUG BRINKLEY

One night I was out at Owl Farm working with him and called it a night around four a.m. and walked out the door, then realized I had left my address book in his kitchen and went back to get it. I didn't knock, and when I walked in, Hunter had the laptop computer — which he hated — and was sitting by himself looking at all the photographs of his grandson that Juan had put up. When Hunter saw me, he tried to cover up the screen. I said, "Hunter, are you a computer guy now?

What are you looking at?" He said, "Oh, I was just looking at Will." It was heart wrenching, but it was sweet — here was a grandfather who didn't want people to know that he was staring at photos of his grandson. He was actually blushing.

BOB BRAUDIS

Hunter was much more generous with some of his friends than with his own son, but in the last handful of years, they really connected. Juan would come up, and Hunter would pay him to clean all of his guns. I think it was five bucks or ten bucks a gun. You'd walk in there to watch a football game, and the house reeked of solvents. Juan would be buffing and oiling guns, and Hunter would inspect them and say, "Good job."

JUAN THOMPSON

The change in our relationship was very gradual. It took decades, but it started with my actually going up to Owl Farm again. I'd take little visits on weekends when I was back from boarding school or when I was living in Aspen, and that was a whole different kind of relationship. It was more intentional. But mostly we just hung out.

Hunter wasn't one to sit down and talk about all the details of life. He had a different lifestyle. He did not relish sitting around and talking about a relationship. It had to be translated.

It's been a long process of first, acceptance — that there was no way to change who he was — and then second, a kind of understanding that just because the way he was able to express his love didn't take the form that I would have preferred or expected didn't make it any less real or powerful.

On top of everything else, he was also born in the late thirties. He wasn't a New Age dad. And his father died when he was a teenager, and I don't imagine they were a real demonstrative pair.

His way wasn't my way, but the important thing was to understand that he had his way and try to learn how to translate that and see it so I could understand it. I started reading his books when I was a teenager. The first one was *Hell's Angels*. That's still one of my favorites. And *Fear and Loathing in Las Vegas* — as a teenager it didn't make a lot of sense to me at first, but those books both helped me to learn more about who my dad was, really. He didn't talk a lot about his past, especially the time when he was in his twenties.

Hunter had a coherent and meaningful philosophy. Individual freedom — that's a core part of Hunter. It could be the freedom to shoot guns on your property or just to own a gun, or the freedom to do the drug of your choice, as long as you're not doing harm to other people. It could have been part of his campaign platform in the sheriff's race — to legalize all drugs but punish dishonest drug dealers. And he really believed in the possibility of change for the better — socially or through politics. He was an idealist about what was possible for this country.

✝ 🐃 ✝ 🐃

ANNA STEADMAN

Being around Hunter, I stuck to the same approach as when I was with animals and children: I don't approach them and stick my head in their faces. I never ventured into that area of the kitchen where he was, and I spent most of the time on the deck outside because I loved the view and I used to read and write in my diaries. He was always quite nice. I think he appreciated the fact that I was slightly scared of him and wanted to keep my distance — and I think he appreciated my relationship with Ralph, because probably he couldn't manage that sort of relationship himself. That's all I can say.

I found that kitchen very claustrophobic. I mean, it suited him, I suppose. He had everything 'round him, you know: a button for this, a button for that, click this, click that, move the channels, where's the football game, quick, get this on. And he had the television set going on, phone calls going off. And he liked people to read his words. Everybody read his words.

GERRY GOLDSTEIN

It could be something twenty years old, and he would correct you and direct you: "Faster!" "Slower!" He would scream at you if you stumbled, if you mispronounced a word, if you didn't stop at the end of the sentence, and he meant it all. He knew every speck of ink that he ever dropped on paper, and he cared desperately about the language.

BOB BRAUDIS

Some of the best readers were guys like Don Johnson. He could really get into the drama of it — until he came upon a polysyllabic word. Don Johnson read the Woody Creek Manifesto for the first time at a party at Ed Bastian's house, and when he got to the word *logarithmic,* he stumbled about six times. I busted his balls and we all laughed. But for the most part, guys like him and Depp — actors — could add to what Hunter had written with emotions and inflections and timing and tempo.

DON JOHNSON *was a Woody Creek neighbor of Hunter's for years.*

Fortunately for me, I traveled in and out of Aspen a lot, so I had built-in breaks from Hunter. I never really got burned out with him. I always looked forward to time together with him. He was an elegant gentleman.

I could talk to Hunter about any subject on the face of the planet, and if he didn't already have some common knowledge of it, he would be extraordinarily astute about it. He cocreated or was the coprogenitor of *Nash Bridges* along with me. It just came out of our friendship, and I had a commitment that I had to fulfill at one of the networks. We were goofing off. We weren't really doing anything; we were sitting around shooting the breeze and watching sports, and it just came up. It started off as something we called "Off-Duty Cops," and then eventually it morphed into *Nash Bridges*. Every year I would take two weeks off to set the story lines for the next season, and I would always go to Hunter and kick around ideas. Those were some of the funniest times — we'd come up with outrageous story lines.

He never quite made it to the set while we were filming, though. I mean, there's real time, there's media time, and then there was Hunter time. But he loved the show, and he would send me faxes in my dressing room, sometimes six a day. He would critique the characters for us, and he would always be dead-on and painfully funny.

He really embodied that feeling of the constant neighbor to me, in an old-fashioned sense. When I was living in Woody Creek, I traveled a lot, and if I had a sick animal or a sick horse, Hunter would get up and go visit the animal and check in on my wife, ask her if she wanted to go get a bite to eat. He was always bringing her orchids or something like that. Every Thanksgiving I would either have him over, or if he was otherwise engaged, I would always make a plate for him and whoever was around, and we'd take it over to his house. We would always exchange gifts. Hunter never came to my house without bringing me something — it could be weapons or books, but he would always bring something. The last Thanksgiving, he brought Kelly an amaryllis plant, and when he came over at Christmas, he was happy to see that it was blooming.

I mean, Hunter helped and watched me raise my children. All of my kids were dearly fond of Hunter, and he of them. He never forgot their birthdays or any of that. He was a brother.

JANN WENNER

Don was a buddy of Hunter's, and they had similar appetites and backgrounds. I went up to a couple of Thanksgivings at Don's with

Hunter, and there was madness in the air. Hunter's name for Don was Boris.

One time in New York, we went to visit Don in some lavish, three-bedroom penthouse suite Don was given at the Four Seasons, and after Don left, quite drunk, for some party, Hunter recruited me to help him cut down the very prickly branches from the potted trees, stuff them into every bed in the suite, and leave some Manson-esque messages soaped on the mirrors so that when Don came to the next day, he would be terrified about what he had done the night before.

DEBORAH FULLER

A woman named Anita Bejmuk was hanging out with Don Dixon, a friend of Hunter's, and one night Don brought her out to the house for a football game. Hunter often told his friends, "You can't come out unless you bring two beautiful women." Sometimes he'd demand that because he was bored, and sometimes he was looking for assistants. Something clicked, and she stayed later and later on some other nights, and then Hunter said, "Oh — I need someone to type some things." He always could run his number on women. He was quite good at it, and it was a great thing to watch — he was a master.

I don't think it took too long. He was in need of an assistant.

MICHAEL CLEVERLY

Don Dixon was a big mover and a major player. He was in Hunter's circle, and then he brought Anita up to see the great man, and next thing you know, Hunter stole Dixon's girlfriend. That's not reputable behavior in a lot of circles, but Dixon told me that he was willing to let bygones be bygones.

JUAN THOMPSON

Hunter was a huge flirt. He loved women — beautiful women, intelligent women, preferably both at once. That was just a basic part of his nature. I'm sure he was that way from whenever he first realized there was such a thing as girls. With guys he was often a charmer, but with women there was always a sexual overtone, and he was totally unapologetic about it. I don't think there was one second that he felt guilty about flirting. I think he looked at it as, "Hey — it's a woman's choice. If she's interested, I'm interested, and if her guy has a problem with it, well, too bad." Though he would have been a fearsome adversary.

SHELBY SADLER

Hunter enjoyed romancing women whom he shouldn't have. He used to make a point of being friendly with certain women in front of their husbands or boyfriends just for laughs. One time when he was at my apartment, my boyfriend Tom was present, and Hunter made a great show of grabbing me and necking with me in front of Tom, who handled it beautifully.

Hunter treated romance as a job — not as a conquest, but as a process. The reason that every woman who ever met him fell in love with him — and I've never met one who didn't — is because he put so much effort into it. Any woman who came to Owl Farm would be wined and dined. Hunter would prepare elaborate meals with oysters, chocolate, strawberries, champagne — drugs, if that's what they were into. He had a magical ability to make a woman feel as though she was the only one who ever existed — he actually used to laugh at other men because he knew how good he was. I think he was prouder of that than anything — his ability to sway any female he met not with his writing, not with his brilliance, but with his ability to focus on whoever "her" was at the moment. You would get phone calls, presents, elaborately thought out gifts, love letters. He would make himself the sun, the moon, and the stars. And in most cases, it never turned tragic.

JUAN THOMPSON

After Hunter and Sandy got divorced, there were a lot of women in Hunter's life. There were the major women like Laila, Maria, Nicole, Terry — those were the big ones — and there were countless other women in between them that I never met, or met briefly. So for me, meeting Anita was "All right — here's the next woman. Let's see what she's like." I took a cautious attitude and got to know her a bit. She struck me as sort of nervous, obviously intelligent, and as with so many women, it was like "Let's see if she's here next time." Because you didn't know.

As with all of Hunter's women, it was very dramatic. That's how Hunter did his relationships — there was lots of drama: big fights, arguments, and then reconciliation, romance, all sort of alternating. It was very intense, and that seemed to be the pattern.

DOUG BRINKLEY

One night when he was down in New Orleans staying at the Pontchartrain, he turned the bathwater on but then fell asleep. We were going to go to Jazz Fest together to see Jimmy Buffett perform and then do something with Buffett afterwards, and I walked into the Pontchartrain in the morning with coffee in my hand, just waking up. This SWAT team was in the building, and I heard them say, "Water keeps pouring down from the top floor." They were having some sort of negotiation at the front desk about how to go knock the door down, because they had been banging on it, but there wasn't an answer.

I immediately thought, "Oh God — Hunter's room." Lord knows what he had lying around, and these guys were going to come bust in on him. I got up to his floor and started kicking the door and pounding and screaming, "Hunter! Get up!" I thought maybe something had happened. Maybe he had a heart attack or a stroke. The whole floor was squishy.

Suddenly I heard this weird moaning wail on the other side of the door, and I yelled, "Hunter! It's Doug. You're flooded in there." I could hear him say, "Oh my God!" He opened the door and I walked in, and there was water maybe four inches deep, and it was leaking down to the other rooms. I said, "Hunter, there's a fire department SWAT team down there. They're coming up for you right now. Now. We've got to get you out of here." We walked down a stairwell to a different floor and got down to the lobby to the breakfast room and got him a seat and some coffee. Only after the fact did I realize that he had cut his whole hand up and needed stitches. He had slipped on the bath tiles when he got up to shut the water off in the middle of the night, and his whole hand was like a huge, bloody slab of meat. The fire guys saw him, and the owner of the hotel knew who Hunter was and explained what had happened, and everybody was apologetic. They got him a new suite on a dry floor, but all day they had to deal with what happened. They had to kick people out of rooms because of the water problems that Hunter had created. But around Hunter they just wanted to know, "Are you okay, Dr. Thompson? Is your hand okay?"

DEBORAH FULLER

He liked to always have a tube of bright red lipstick, for the shock factor. He'd pull it out and put it on when people weren't looking, all nonchalant, just to freak people out.

JUAN THOMPSON

He was very conscious of how he appeared. He would choose things to project a certain image, even if that image was "I don't care what you think." There was a quote he kept pinned up on the lamp in the kitchen next to his typewriter: "What is the desired effect?"

He was an exhibitionist; he liked to shock people. And sometimes he liked to wear lipstick. Whether it was to shock me or my girlfriend or my son — he just liked to get a reaction. It was a social thing. I think there's some truth in one of his favorite descriptions of himself as "the soul of a teenage girl trapped in the body of an aging dope fiend."

ED BRADLEY

Once at Owl Farm he was trying to get some stuff out of the refrigerator, and a bunch of things fell out. Hunter just sat down on the floor like a little boy and started banging on the floor and screaming. I said, "What the fuck is wrong with you, man? Pick it up." He looked at me and said, "I pay them a lot of money." Sure enough, his assistants came running in to take care of it all. "Oh God, Hunter, what did you do? Hunter, let us pick it up, just stay there."

DOUG BRINKLEY

When it came to national politics, his basic feeling was that politicians were whores. He didn't like them unless he befriended them — and then he would stand by them. He would exaggerate the qualities of the few people that he decided were good; George McGovern and Jimmy Carter were possessed of a Gandhi-like saintly nature in his mind. They were pulling for the underdogs of the world. There were others — Gary Hart and John Kerry were friends of his, and he would go to the mat for them. He believed that they were statespersons, and there was a small handful of others, but beyond that, whether it was Reagan or Bush or Clinton, he was bipartisan in his disdain for presidential power.

He was a libertarian. He preferred to vote for a third-party candidate as a throwaway vote — he voted for Dick Gregory in '68 and Ralph Nader in 2000. He felt that the politics of both the Republican Party and the Democratic Party were worthless. He formed a friendship late in his life with Jesse Ventura when he was running for governor of Minnesota, and he liked the idea of Kinky Friedman running for governor of Texas. He would always be behind outsider candidates.

When it came to understanding grand geopolitical strategy, Hunter was no good. He did not understand why we had to go fight in Afghanistan or why we needed to put pressure on the Soviet Union. He was much more about the town that he lived in — whether an airport gets expanded or a smoking ordinance introduced — than he was able to grapple with big cold war issues.

Hunter was never an egalitarian. He believed that the people who are good at what they do in any profession would rise to the top, that that was the natural order of selection. He would say, "There are people who are snow leopards, and there are people who aren't." Snow leopards are the rarest animals, the species wandering around at the top of the mountain in all their beauty. They were the animal he loved the most. If Hunter was talking about the CEO of a company or a county sheriff or the head of a political party or a top Hollywood actor or a big rock & roll star, he would say that they were a snow leopard. And it wasn't just famous people — so was the man who ran the biggest construction company in Colorado, so was the best trial attorney in the Texas Hill Country, so was the owner of an NFL club. Even though he didn't like some of the snow leopards, Hunter thought that the art of achieving put them into a society above the rest. It was a kind of elitist, Darwinian way of looking at success, and he held to it very firmly — though sometimes he would parody Hemingway and say, "Don't forget — the scum also rises."

BOB BRAUDIS

There was a bully component to his personality. He was rational most of the time — he wanted to create humor; he liked to have fun with a capital *F*. He'd get that boyish grin, and you knew that he was going to put on a show for you. But if someone was annoying him, he could turn on them like a pit bull and literally cripple them. He did that to some very close friends of his. Hunter always had an explanation, and it was usually a chickenshit reason: "He was too loud during the football game. I wanted to watch the game, not listen to him." Or "He drank too much."

Most of the people Hunter kicked out of his kitchen were just thrown out temporarily, but some of them were long-term eighty-sixed. Some of them asked me to broker reconciliations, and I would agree and make a phone call: "Hunter, so-and-so just called and is really suffering because of you shunning him. Are you ready to talk?" "No, not yet. Maybe someday." Or, "Sure, why don't you bring them down?" It depended on his assessment of the situation, his mood at the time, and the person.

TOM WOLFE

George Plimpton threw a party for Hunter in New York at his apartment on East 72nd Street. Before I came to the party, I had watched Hunter interviewed by Charlie Rose, who had to ask the questions *and* answer them because Hunter couldn't. He would start to speak and just slur. It's possible he could have been nervous because there was no way he was going to be as funny in person as he was on the page. You read Hunter and you think, "Well, boy! This stuff is just pouring out of his head as fast as he can write it down!" — as if he were Jack Kerouac, who was supposedly doing automatic writing. But he worked at it. Those funny lines were not instantaneous, and in a way, somebody that funny shouldn't even expose himself on camera.

He was pretty far gone when he got to Plimpton's. He was doing a mock stagger up the stairs — but it was only partly mock. He wasn't so stoned that he was going to fall down — he was just staggering around. We had a little conversation in Hunterese, and that's actually the last time I saw him.

DOUG BRINKLEY

Hunter thought that things were going to go haywire starting in the year 2000. He was extremely paranoid about Y2K. He had decided that this was the year the fun stopped — no more good times, good-bye Strawberry Fields forever. Part of this was natural aging and looking back at his life and realizing that being in San Francisco in the sixties was not an experience to be replicated. It was the holy apex. He would look back at that era with such longing — riding his motorcycle across the Golden Gate Bridge, being ensconsed at La Honda with Kesey, getting to know Neal Cassady and Allen Ginsberg, killing wild boar in Big Sur, living in the Haight. Hunter lived right there in the middle of all of it.

With his health deteriorating, the things in his life that meant a lot to him were Anita; his son, Juan; and his grandson, Will. Hunter kind of got in a groove when he met Anita; he thought that he maybe had this gonzo elder-statesman-like thing to look forward to, but his body just didn't cooperate. His mind was ready to go on to be a hundred, but his body wasn't.

JOHN WALSH

In 2000, I asked Hunter to write a sports column for the ESPN Web site I was overseeing. He loved the idea of doing it — he thought it would be a great arc for his career, because he had started off doing sports, and he loved sports, and we got along well. He really had no concept of the Internet or what it was.

At this point, Hunter was in pretty good decline physically and intellectually. Not spiritually or emotionally — he had a great relationship with Anita — but you could see the decline in so many ways, and it was sad. It was clear that he didn't have his A game, and especially on a weekly basis, he couldn't focus enough to pay enough attention. We would give him stories and tips and clues, but it rarely registered. He would frequently be distracted and go in another direction — a direction that sometimes led to not such a good place. The story didn't hang together. There wasn't enough there to make a piece out of it. Sometimes it would take days.

But he got paid by the piece — and we paid him a handsome price by Internet standards — and he came to rely on the income. It became his economic heroin; he had to have it. I told him, "Hunter — this is the Internet. You get paid when we publish. When you send it in, we'll get it up in two hours. You want to write Sunday night for Monday morning? We'll have it up Monday afternoon. If you miss it Monday, it'll come Tuesday. But if you don't write at all, we're not gonna send you a paycheck." He loved the immediacy, but the procrastination and the writer's block and the deadline pressure and everything else were debilitating to him.

JANN WENNER

It must have been a little humiliating doing that ESPN column for the money — like the earlier work for the *Examiner*. But I just couldn't get him back writing strong or sustained pieces, long or short, for *Rolling Stone*. He was no longer in shape. He knew it and didn't want to try. He proposed something about health and fitness for *Men's Journal,* which, although it made no sense, I agreed to publish if he wrote it.

I made several serious attempts to get him to write a 1,500-word column once a month. I offered him quite a bit of money to do it — anything to get Hunter back in the paper — even if for purely mercenary purposes on my part, just to have that byline back and some of that energy. How difficult can that have fucking been? Fifteen hundred words for $10,000. Write that once a month. Just sit there and closely consider any subject. Watch television and write about some outrage you saw. But he couldn't do it.

WAYNE EWING

He would get an idea on Saturday night, just a thesis for a potential column, and he'd write down a sentence or two in his little spiral notebook. Then we would watch a couple of football games — the middle game and the evening game. There might be a half-dozen people around for that, and we'd gamble a lot, and money would fly around. But then as people were leaving, he'd always say, "Now, you're going to stay, Wayne, aren't you?" Then it would generally be me and Hunter and Anita and maybe one other assistant, and it would be time to write. I would talk out ideas with him. The other way to get him to write would be for him to listen to the things he had written before that might be similar — he just liked to hear the music of his words, and so Anita or I would read to him for a half hour or so.

It was always a matter of getting him to pull that typewriter about six inches closer to him and put a blank piece of paper in it. You could usually get that accomplished by about eleven or eleven-thirty — about an hour and a half or two hours. If we were lucky, we could get him to type out a lead by midnight. If I saw him get down a lead on paper, or even two sentences, and if he was still typing, then I would leave, and he would generally finish with Anita by five or six in the morning. Anita was invaluable in getting the real work done in the end.

JOHN WALSH

There were some good columns, and then there were some that the editors had to try to save. There were times when the budgets were strained, and people asked, "Should we keep paying Hunter?" As the years went on to 2002 and 2003 and we kept doing it, I kept saying, "You know, Hunter, you've got to get these better." He was always so proud of his work that I think it hurt him that I had to say that. But he knew it had to be said.

JANN WENNER

The columns that I saw were not very memorable. By this time his writing consisted of disjointed fragments of larger thoughts and fairly lifeless repetitions of his brilliant phrasemaking and descriptions of people and places. Hunter could still write those jagged bursts in letters — though even those were deteriorating — in which he would reuse his colorful, original outbursts, but it was the same bag of tricks you'd seen many, many times, and it made me very, very sad.

BOB BRAUDIS

The fact that most of Hunter's recent books were letters and reprints of columns, like *Hey Rube,* caused a lot of people to comment that he couldn't write anything new anymore. But that was bullshit. If he had the time and the muse visited him, and he had the assistance and the help, he could write.

He explained to me once that drugs didn't make him creative. I asked him, "Do you write better or more when you're fucked up, or not fucked up?" He said, "No. It all depends on the whole team working together." He had a lot of volunteer help. His publishers would often send out editors to help him make the deadline — or the fifth deadline. They had to go to the lip with him at times, and it was hard work with no compensation other than bragging rights.

JANN WENNER

He was an alcoholic. That was his real problem. It worked together with the drugs, of course, but with either one, you can't sustain the attention to structure, flow, and coherence that you need. The problem with the proposed *Rolling Stone* column was that it was going to have to be 1,500 *good* words. He was going to be putting his name on it for his audience — not in the local San Francisco paper and not on a Web site, but in front of the people who knew and cherished his work. And he couldn't sustain even that because of the damage of the alcohol and drugs.

Hunter didn't want to do bad work for us, and I didn't want to publish his bad work, so we fell out of regular contact with each other during those last five years. We had once had something extraordinary by any measure. Why deprecate it with a bunch of whining between the two of us like some old couple that doesn't get along anymore? We were still devoted to each other, but "Why don't we just not do that" became our general unspoken agreement.

✝ 🐃 ✝ 🐃

PAUL OAKENFOLD *is an internationally known club DJ and producer.*
Hunter wasn't aware of it until I told him, but for some reason — probably because of the *Vegas* movie — his name had become very trendy among those in the club movement. I was recording an album in 2000 and had been working with different artists on collaborations. I told him I wanted to spend a couple days and nights with him working on something that was relative to the generation of today — something to pass on his work. Not long afterward he was in L.A. and rang me up and said, basically, "Show up at my hotel at midnight."

I brought him a bottle of absinthe, and he unscrewed the top — glug-glug-glug — passed it around the room, and we began. The surrealness had started almost as soon as we began: Fifteen minutes in, there's a bang-bang-bang on the door and in walks Sean Penn, and Sean and I started talking a bit, and then Hunter just said, "Shut up. We're gonna get on with what we're doing." Sean left, and this other actor, this really old chap shows up — Harry Dean Stanton.

We rolled on from midnight till sunrise, and we did it again the next night, ending up with this idea of the American dream. He touched on Kurt Cobain. He touched on Richard Nixon and how he ruined the

American dream. He talked with me about a lot of things he had done in his life where he was just chasing a dream, and that's what we were trying to get. I came up with this idea for a track called "Nixon's Spirit."

Some time afterward, my lawyer quite rightly did what any lawyer would do — she took the responsibility on herself for offering a contract for the deal to use Hunter's voice, for the deal that she felt was right — but she did this without speaking to me and knowing that I'd already worked out a sort of "gentleman's agreement" with Hunter.

Pretty soon he's on the phone screaming at her, and he's writing a letter saying that you're this and you're that.

Dear Sonia,

    I'm in receipt of your second (or third) letter in 5 (five) days, in re: the mess you have made of my very private and personal relationship with Paul Oakenfold, perhaps the finest and most nakedly original musical talent of our generation.

    What the fuck is wrong with you? Are you one of these socio-legal Perverts who get their jollies by fucking with other people's lives because you don't have one of your own? Is that how you like to introduce yourself, Sonia — like a teenage slut with an anal compulsion? Is Money all that matters to you, or do you crave the thrill of cheating, too? In any case, get out of my fucking life or I will do what you suggested in your earlier message — slice off your nipples and suck out the blood while you dance and scream in my lap. The image horrified me, of course. Paul never mentioned anything like this.

    How old are you? Who gave you a goddamned Job? And why?

    Not me, Sonia. Never in hell. I would hire a mutated giant Pack-rat before I would ever hire you. . . . But who am I to jeer at Paul's corruptive decisions? I am not that sane, myself, in this regard. We all make mistakes.

    So here is where we're at, Sonia: If you (and my friend Paul) don't want to pay me even a cheap fee of 10,000 Pounds and fifty per-cent, (50%) of all royalties, earnings and all other monies for the right to publish/record/ sell/share and otherwise earn in re: my Song/lyrics for Nixon's Spirit, (currently on Paul's new CD BUNKKA) — you can jam that song up your ass and I will record it with some other contemporary Musician with his tongue on the pulse of Youth Music.

I don't like your attitude, Sonia. And it was worth a few stupid little pence or shillings or shiny new dimes in order to shit on the chest of your Ftkiss. You represent all that is venal and cheap and mendacious in the Human Race.

NIXON'S SPIRIT is already a copy-righted monument to the bed-rock ability of the American Dream to recognize itself, even in the breach, and heal itself smartly without unseemly delay. It is people like you who depress and degrade our collective future.

As always,
Hunter S. Thompson

He CC'd George Tobia, Walter Isaacson, Graden [sic] Carter, Sean Penn, Greg Shapiro/Nick Nolte, Ralph Steadman, [Indianapolis Colts owner and longtime HST friend] James Irsay, Johnny Depp, [Depp friend and former Viper Room manager] Sal Jenco, Don Johnson, Jann Wenner, David Letterman, Charlie Rose, Ed Bradley, Jeanette Etheridge, and [ABC News correspondent] Jake Tapper.

He made her cry. I had to send her flowers.

JEFF KASS *is a journalist who covered the story of Lisl Auman, a twenty-one-year-old Colorado girl who in 1997 was riding in a car driven by a skinhead with a rap sheet who later killed a policeman and then himself after a brief chase. Though already in police custody before the cop was shot, Auman was later found guilty of felony murder due to her association with the skinhead — whom she had just met that night — and was sentenced to life without parole.*

I wrote a profile of Hunter that appeared in the *Rocky Mountain News* on December 31, 2000. And I didn't know it at the time, but Lisl Auman read that article when she was in prison in Canyon City, Colorado. Hunter Thompson seemed like an interesting character, and she decided to write him a letter just to say hi. She explained her situation and thought Hunter may have remembered her case, but she wasn't asking him to do anything for her.

Hunter did remember the case. He had been horrified by it. He wrote her back saying, "I've got this column on ESPN.com. Let's see if I can stir up any trouble." One of Hunter's driving quotes at this time was Edmund Burke: "All that is necessary for the triumph of evil is that good men do nothing." This was his battle cry for the Lisl Auman case. And Curtis Robinson said, "You know Hunter's on a tear when he starts quoting Burke." Hunter started to get his friends on board.

Hunter was facing long odds. He was often saying things like "This could always blow sideways." But this was already sideways. This was upside down. Now, the facts of her case alone convinced a lot of people she got a raw deal, but trying to take on the cause of a woman who's technically a convicted cop killer is not an easy thing to do. It's felony murder. But Hunter's level of interest was always high and always genuine. He was very savvy with politicking and campaigning and PR.

HAL HADDON

He dove into the case. He correctly figured out that this was a monstrous injustice and rallied support and brought attention to it. He got lawyers involved in helping with her appeal. In the last couple of years of his life, that was his big cause — and it was a great example of Hunter's organizational skills.

MICHAEL STEPANIAN *is an attorney who had become close to Hunter in San Francisco in the sixties.*

Hunter and Gerry Goldstein and Hal Haddon and I talked for

twenty-five and thirty hours, easily. Hunter was a great, great cross-examiner. I've been a criminal lawyer for thirty-five years, and whenever I related a set of facts to him, he would get into the nuances of the facts, the weaknesses in the arguments, and the concepts of what the facts were driving toward as very, very few men could do. He was incisive, and he was deep in the sense that he could analyze facts. He played with facts, he slept with facts, and he bathed with facts. They warmed him like a blanket. Facts were key, and they weren't arbitrary or ambiguous. They were precise. And he was very, very precise.

Hunter got Hal Haddon's office to write the brief that took Lisl's case to the appellate court for nothing, and Hunter organized some demonstrations on her behalf. He got his friend Warren Zevon to come out for a rally on the steps of the capital in Denver and sing "Lawyers, Guns and Money."

JEFF KASS

There were appeals and more appeals, and it took years, but Lisl was transferred from prison to a halfway house in October 2006. In March of 2007, she was released from the halfway house to serve out the rest of her probation.

Some people might say that he just took on this cause because of his distrust of authority — and I do think that psychologically it helped him to have a cause; it almost seemed like a muse to him at times. But his relationship with and interest in Lisl simply as a person was always genuine. They never met, but Hunter would send her books and talk with her on the phone.

MICHAEL STEPANIAN

Hunter Thompson saved her life. The felony murder law as it was applied to her was wrong. The public defender who did the case tried their best. But if it wasn't for Hunter Thompson, she would not have gotten the kind of appellate work that she did.

JUAN THOMPSON

He called me up in 2003 and told me he was thinking about getting married and wanted to know what I thought. I said, "Well, if that's gonna make you happy, go ahead." They were married April 23, 2003.

There were times over the years when he proposed marriage to different women. He and Maria came really close to getting married, but again it would have been a deal down in front of the judge in Glenwood Springs. For him, getting married was not a public act. It was something between two people, and he would not have had any patience for all the bullshit that goes into a wedding. So he and Anita just went down to the courthouse and signed the papers.

Hunter was a romantic at heart, and I think he liked the idea of getting married, but if he had been ten years younger he wouldn't have done it. There had been many women he was in love with that he didn't marry, because he didn't want to restrict himself. It's no secret that Hunter was not the soul of monogamy. He valued his personal freedom very highly, and I don't think he was interested in compromising that until he had to.

WILLIAM KENNEDY

When *Kingdom of Fear* was published a thousand people came out to see him do a book signing, and he loved that. But he was an unbelievable mess. Anita was there — this was right before they were married — and my wife, Dana, and I went up to their suite at the Carlyle. He was being interviewed by a reporter, and Hunter was dying for him to leave — he kept calling him a geek — so he could bring out his coke grinder. He was in an ultimate condition — a constant movement of hands to smoke with the cigarette holder, or tip the glass of Chivas, or pack the pipe with dope, or pop the pills, grind the coke, sniff it, smoke it, drink it, eat it, inhale it, hand-to-mouth, hand-to-hand; he had turned himself into a perpetual-motion machine, a perpetual intoxicating device. I said, "Jesus, you keep busy."

He said to us, "I'm an addict." Hardly big news, but I'd never heard him say it. We were there a couple of hours, and at least twice he went in and out of focus, almost to sleep after the dope, then he'd do the coke and straighten up and we could talk again. He was in severe pain, but he wouldn't talk about it. He was truly far gone, but in the lucid streaks very funny and sharp. I never saw him fall-down drunk, and he wasn't that on this night. But I never saw him this bad, ever.

JUAN THOMPSON

He didn't want to go into surgery for his back. He really wanted to stay out of the hospital, for a lot of reasons. I could tell that Hunter was nervous about the surgery, but then he'd say things like, "This is just like taking the car in for some service. Just gotta do some work on the mechanics." I think it was the easiest way to make himself more comfortable with the idea. But he knew what was at stake. I think he finalized his will before the surgery. He was aware that there was a possibility that he might not survive.

Alcohol dependence was a factor in both the hip-replacement and the back operations. At first the doctors said, "You'll have to stop drinking so many hours before the surgery." And then they'd say something like, "This would be a perfect opportunity for you to stop drinking; you might take that opportunity." Hunter would answer, "I have no interest in that. I intend to start drinking the moment I wake up. Don't ever mention that again." And in both cases they accepted that. Hunter was such a longtime and consistent drinker, he couldn't go very long without it before his body would start to react, and it's a very dangerous condition. For someone like Hunter, to suddenly stop drinking cold turkey can kill you.

Dr. Corenman at the Steadman-Hawkins Clinic in Vail basically scooped out and fused Hunter's L4 and L5 vertebrae. One of them had flipped forward, pinching the spinal cord, so he pulled that back and fixed it. The spinal cord had become compressed by material that built up in there, and that was what caused a lot of pain.

DR. STEVE AYERS

There's acute withdrawal, which lasts up to seventy-two hours, and that's seizures and tremors and elevated blood pressure and sweating and vomiting and all sorts of things. Delirium tremens starts at about the third day, at about seventy-two hours. That's where you can develop a true delirium or confusion and your brain gets out of whack, and the part of the brain regulating the other body functions like temperature, heart, and breathing gets all out of whack. And it carries about a 30 percent mortality rate. You go into true DT's and about 30 percent of those people die. It's very dangerous. You don't want to let that happen.

JUAN THOMPSON

They spent another week or two nursing him through the detox process. Once it starts, you have to ride it out. They couldn't get him awake and drinking alcohol quickly enough after his surgery, so then his body started to detox, and they put him into a drug-induced coma using IV drugs and very gradually, with a combination of drugs, helped the body transition.

The idea for both surgeries was to get him drinking as soon as possible so that we didn't have to go through that, but both times we had to go through it. No one expected it to actually happen, so when it started to happen it was scary — scary and risky.

He was delusional; he remembered nothing about either one of his stays, even though he was there for two weeks, awake and carrying on for much of the time. In both cases he had to be restrained; he would wake up and not know where he was; he'd get angry. It was scary for him, and scary for us to see him restrained and getting very angry about things. Just the fact that he was *there* — he didn't like hospitals and wanted to go home as quickly as possible, and we had to tell him that he couldn't go home. Someone would watch him all the time, and there were all sorts of approvals needed and rules about what you could and couldn't do. There was no privacy.

Deborah was there for both surgeries, as were Jennifer and I; Hunter's assistant Heidi was at the hip surgery; Anita was at the back surgery, along with a college student that helped out with Hunter a bit on and off. But for the bulk of it, it was Deborah, Anita, and me doing a rotation. Braudis came down a couple days before Hunter got out.

BOB BRAUDIS

They wound up putting him in the ICU unit, which was insulated from the general patients by two or three doors, because he was screaming and acting out. They were worried because he wasn't eating or drinking anything. They had him on an IV for hydration and alcohol.

At one point when I was there, he asked Juan, Anita, and Deborah to leave, and he whispered in my ear, "Get me out of here." I said, "You want me to spring you?" And he goes, "No, take me to the bar." I said to the nurse, "He wants to go to a bar," and she said, "Well, it's against doctor's orders, but I think it would be a great idea." So I wheeled him through the fucking streets of Vail over potholes and gravel, and I get him to this bar. Just before I took him out out of the hospital, the nurse gave him a shot in the thigh. I said, "What's that?" And she said, "Haldol. It's an antipsychotic." We use it in the jail as a chemical restraint for crazy motherfuckers, and it works. But I said, "You're giving him Haldol and asking me to take him for a wheelchair ride?" She said, "It's a very low dosage." Well, we got to the bar and Hunter was nodding off. He said, "Okay — you better take me back."

DR. STEVE AYERS

I think Hunter had a superhuman liver. I don't know how you could have that much alcohol for that long and not have liver failure. Hunter apparently tolerated it well. I have no idea how. Just different physiology, I guess. If you want to figure that one out, you'll have to ask God someday.

TIM FERRIS

After both the hip replacement and the back surgery were the only times since I've known him that I can think of that he went days without a drink. He came back home and was recovering in his bedroom, where no drugs or alcohol were ever permitted. He always observed this interesting scrupulosity.

He was in there for a couple of days and was still kind of dried out, and we would talk, and he was the most tender, sweetest guy, just charming. When people drink all their lives, part of them stays emotionally at whatever age they were when they started. And suddenly it was as if I was talking to Hunter as a teenager — he had these wonderful dreams that he would tell me about. It was this little window, but pretty soon, once he was up and about, he was out of the drug-and-booze-free zone and was back on everything.

The key to Hunter's personality is the question of why he had to be so deeply involved with intoxicants from such an early age and never found his way out. That's sort of the Rosebud of this story. It's not that he didn't think about it. He certainly thought about it. There's never been any shortage of answers, but the question is, are any of them actually illuminating?

JANN WENNER

Hunter always told me that without the drugs, he would have had the mind of an accountant.

JUAN THOMPSON

For Anita and Deborah both, once they got home, things were far more difficult because there was no nurse, no one else on duty. It was just the two of them, and I'm sure it was a real shock, especially since Anita was a young woman, thirty-one at the time.

At first, the physical therapist would come out to Owl Farm and work with him there; later he'd go into town to do it. I think he actually enjoyed it; he got a sense of accomplishment from it, and it was very important for him to recover from this and to be mobile again, so he could go where he wanted to go when he wanted to go and not depend on someone to get him there. He had a lot of motivation to do it.

DEBORAH FULLER

I did a great deal facilitating Hunter's life the best I could for twenty-five years, and then in the fall of 2003, it was time for me to take a break and have my own time. I never saw Hunter after I left. We spoke often, but we never got together again.

DOUG BRINKLEY

Hunter cared about Deborah dearly. She is one of the four or five most important people to ever be in his life. He considered her family — but of course, families have disputes too. Deborah had a saintly tolerance for Hunter's indiscretions and went through a lot with him, but then Hunter met Anita and fell head-over-heels in love with her. He did not want Deborah to go, but it was a question of whether he could get Anita and Deborah to work together so there was some kind of harmony at Owl Farm. It's very hard when you have a bride and another woman in the same house. That's not an easy prescription. Hunter cared deeply and dearly about Deborah right up to the very end, but he thought he needed a time-out to get his marriage jump-started properly for a few years, to get a new high-octane rhythm going in a new direction.

Marriage was a big deal for Hunter. He had a lot of different girlfriends, but after Sandy he never went as far as to get married. This was a big move that said, "I want to make this marriage work. I really want to do this." He bought Anita a huge diamond ring in New Orleans. That was hard not just on Deborah but on some of Hunter's previous girlfriends, who would sometimes come and visit him for a week.

Suddenly he was a married man. He was trying to get a good rhythm going with Anita and get working with her on the ESPN column, and they had an incredible groove going — romantically, professionally. Anita magically transformed him into a boy again. But then Hunter's health started going sideways on him, and what he thought was going to be a decade of fun with Anita started looking more like two years.

BOB BRAUDIS

For years, Deborah was the Girl Friday — if the phone rang at three in the morning and it was someone that wanted to see Hunter, she knew whether this person should see Hunter or not. And that historical knowledge disappeared when she disappeared.

Hunter needed Deborah, and Hunter's theory was that Anita ran Deborah off. Deborah was the most loyal, hardworking, qualified assistant that anyone could have, and when she moved out, Hunter told me that his production, his literary factory, had ground to a halt. Anita tried very hard to fill that role as well as all the others, and she was exhausted herself. My sympathy for Anita is sincere and intense. She was working five jobs: wife, cook, cleaning woman, editorial assistant, groundskeeper. She was running the whole farm.

JOHN WILBUR, *a former guard for the Washington Redskins, had been a friend of Hunter's since 1972.*

The Honolulu Marathon organizers considered Hunter a director of some sort because of *The Curse of Lono.* He had put their marathon on the map. He went to the dinner, and people would come to see him at the Kahala Mandarin. He was kind of an offbeat mascot. The directors invited him back year after year — he didn't come in 2004 because he had caused so much trouble in 2003 that they needed a year off. But they invited him back for the 2005 race, and that was when he broke his leg.

The night it happened we'd had a nice dinner — Michael Stepanian and Brooke Hart, Anita and Hunter. I left their suite at eleven-thirty or twelve and got a call from Anita about four-thirty. He had been heating up some saimin soup, spilled some on this very slick marble floor, slipped on it, and broke his left tibia and fibula. He was in the hospital getting the leg set, and it was very, very painful,

We couldn't get him on a regular airplane because his leg was immobile. A physician friend of mine told me about a flying ambulance service, but the cheapest one was thirty thousand, and Hunter didn't have that kind of money.

We called Jeanette at Tosca in San Francisco, and Sean Penn was there and volunteered to put his credit card down to take care of the flight. And for that, he got the option for *The Curse of Lono* for a certain time. They tried to boot Hunter off the plane in L.A. because he was so disruptive, but somehow he made it all the way to the Steadman-Hawkins Clinic in Vail, and after a week or so he was able to go home.

BOB BRAUDIS

Anita had been up for five nights, and she checked into a lodge. Juan was there, but he had a day job. I said, "I'll sit here until he's stabilized, and I'll get him home. It was a Sunday. There was a TV in the lobby of the hospital, and I was watching football games, and finally it was time to take Hunter home. We got him into a van. His cast went from his balls to his ankle, and it was heavy, and it had a bend in it. I called a deputy of mine, Joey DiSalva, and told him to go up to the hospital and borrow a wheelchair. Joey met us at Owl Farm, and the driver, Anita, Michael Cleverly, and I lifted Hunter by the ass, put him in the wheelchair, and carried him up the stairs and into the kitchen. The Denver Broncos were playing on *Sunday Night Football*. Hunter said, "Hot damn, the Broncos are playing — you wanna bet?"

Joey and I bet him twenty bucks. He didn't even remember it. I stayed there for five days and nights and gave Anita a break, and I saw him go through the worst psychosis I've ever seen. He was really pissed that he was once again infirm, but I kept saying, "It's just a broken leg, Hunter. We have three or four of them every day on the mountain. It's just a broken leg. Get over it."

STACEY HADASH

The last time that I spent real time with Hunter was when I think he knew he was going to kill himself. He called up and said he had broken his leg in Hawaii, and Anita had about had it, and he had fired every nurse that came near him. He said, "I'm really desperate — please come out and help me." It was right after Christmas. He had hired some kid, somebody's relative from down the road, to come at noon and wake him up and help him with things.

BEN FEE *started work as an assistant at Owl Farm in January 2004.*

My mom was looking after some of Hunter's animals when he was away, and she mentioned that Hunter might be looking for someone to document the behind-the-scenes preparations for the movie version of *The Rum Diary,* so I talked to Anita, and she set up a meeting later that night with Hunter. She warned me — "Hunter doesn't really take well to males." Hunter told me that they were planning on going into production with the movie but that the script sucked and they couldn't do anything until they got a good script, and he didn't know when he was going to approve one. We hung out and talked, and he asked me to stay up and help him work on the ESPN column. I was there until about six a.m., and then he said, "Can you come back tomorrow?" Eventually he and Anita hired me full-time and I moved into the cabin. I had my video camera and my still camera, and whenever anything picked up, I'd document the experience. Hunter was really excited about having a camera looming around in the background. It was another way for him to be immortalized.

STACEY HADASH

That time was the most fun that I ever had with Hunter. We would stay up late talking politics and all sorts of things in the kitchen. We'd always tried to make weekends like that happen, because a lot of Hunter's assistant-girlfriends would get jealous. They'd kind of get over it when they'd figure out that I was just a friend who'd been around for a long time who was not going to become — and had not been — his girlfriend.

On one of my final nights there he left a note for me when I woke up that said, "Fuck everybody — lock up the gates. These are the final nights that we'll ever get to spend time together. We'll build a big fire in the kitchen — no guests, nobody coming over for football. I'm firing Tobia. I'm firing Juan as my son." But during my final day there he became so ugly — he started screaming at me, for *hours,* because he didn't have some medication. He was getting incredibly vicious. I couldn't figure it out, but finally Anita told me, after Hunter was dead, "You know what? He was mad at you because you were leaving. He didn't want you to go."

Part of the problem was that he had no mobility at all, and he would not be able to bathe for days. Carl Bernstein was coming by the house and called from the bottom of the hill, and I'm like, "Jesus God Almighty! I need to help him get dressed!" He smelled like a homeless person. I was going to help him take a bath, but he just never really got there.

He had this portable toilet, and one day he said, "All right, you have no choice, you have to join the club." I'm like, "What club is that?" and he said, "I've got to shit, and you've just got to help me. Bring that thing over here." He had no control over his bodily functions at all.

During that December we talked a lot about his relationship with Anita, and he said that he wrote a lot about it and that there were always letters in his kitchen drawer right underneath his typewriter. There are things he kept very, very private, and there's a lot more of that in terms of the letters that he didn't want seen. But these notes to Anita — obviously she must have read them; they were sitting right in his drawer.

He completely loved her — he really did — and he said she was a lover but a fighter, and that it was an incredibly volatile mix — it was like a tinderbox. There was an enormous amount of passion, but an enormous amount of fire.

SARI TUSCHMAN *began working as an assistant to Hunter in June 2004.*
Anita was trying to get out of harping on Hunter to write. She wanted to be more of a wife, so I ended up working with him until January of the next year.

His ESPN column was due every Tuesday, and at first I'd just come down on Monday night and help him put together the column — oftentimes it was just writing down things he said. Sometimes he just wanted someone to come down and read. We'd read some of his unpublished work; sometimes we'd read old stuff from *Campaign Trail '72*. Sometimes I'd be down there three nights a week; other times I wouldn't go at all.

Sometimes he'd be in a funk, and hearing his stories read aloud would cheer him up. I think he just wanted to be reminded of how much he'd done and how brilliant so much of it was. At times, it was impossible to get him to write, and he'd get really upset with himself. Whenever he wasn't producing, he'd get angry and yell and get upset about ridiculous things. He'd throw things; he'd scream, he'd give up. He went through a stage where if I spoke I got yelled at — I couldn't breathe without getting yelled at. And I just had to weather it. He knew how to shut you up and put you in your place and make you feel very small. I saw him do that to pretty much everybody. On the other hand, sometimes he was really fatherly and downright sweet. When I arrived on one Friday night, Hunter said, "Sari, the sheriff just called, and *Fear and Loathing*'s on TV." And we watched *Fear and Loathing* together, and he told me how every single thing in the movie actually happened, and how if anything Hollywood downplayed it.

We watched his A&E biography with his arm around me — it was one of those days he was being fatherly and adorable, and he told me these unbelievable stories. He loved talking about how incredible his life had been and where he'd come from. He had so much to tell — and I don't think enough people were asking anymore.

✝ 🐃 ✝ 🐃

SHELBY SADLER

The last piece that Hunter and I worked on together was *Rolling Stone*'s John Kerry story. Hunter asked me, "How can we get Nixon into this piece? I want this to be about Nixon. Find me a quote from Nixon that will explain this election." I finally came up with one from Nixon's book *Real Peace*. Hunter had originally wanted a very negative quote, and I said, "I'm not doing that. We're going to make Nixon look smart here, because you know that's what you really think." In the end, when he read the quote, he said, "Okay, go for it. Write a paragraph to go with it and you can say it. You can say Nixon was the last liberal president." And he let me do it. In retrospect, I think he meant it as his parting gift to me.

JANN WENNER

In the summer of 2004, Hunter wanted to cover the John Kerry presidential campaign. He couldn't go on the road anymore, so he was set up to ride with Kerry in his car when he came to Aspen for a fundraiser and spend the day following him and hanging out. He had wanted to do a big story, and I told him that we'd set up phone interviews with some key players, and that he should get at least one scene, even if he couldn't attend the convention, and write about the TV coverage. We'd make it as easy as possible.

Hunter wanted very much to again be a part of the national political story — to maybe return to that time and era in his life — especially with the war, when the stakes were very high. He'd want to do the piece, but he kept failing at it. He failed to take the first step, or the second step; he didn't make that phone call. By that time it was too late, or there were too many drugs or too many people in the house.

I give credit to Anita. Hunter turned some stuff in, and it was okay. A few pages were nice. I sat down with one of my editors and said, "This works, this doesn't work . . . Write a memo to Hunter explaining what we need. Put it in writing and send it off to him." I would encourage him and encourage him, and then nothing would happen. We'd talk on the phone. I'd say, "Let's set a deadline for Monday for you to turn in at least a section on this," and nothing would happen. He'd written a few more pages. He had about half of a short piece. I had to cut all the Nazi stuff out of it, because at this point it was too old-fashioned, and it didn't work anymore. But he had some nice snappy paragraphs in there. Anita finally called me — I didn't really know her at this point — and said, "He really needs your help. Please, please call him and encourage him. You've got to do this." It was that appeal that got me back into it.

I guess it was just enough to push Hunter to write a small but righteous piece that we'd publish with his byline on the cover. He was thrilled. He was so proud to be back in the game.

Of course, then there was some haggling over the price, just for old time's sake; and of course he got top dollar. He was happy. But it was the end of the road.

DOUG BRINKLEY

Hunter got very motivated that Kerry could beat Bush. He thought, "You know what? Maybe I shouldn't throw in the towel. Maybe with Kerry — a guy that I knew back in the seventies — maybe we can roll these bastards back." He got very animated about the Kerry campaign going into September '04, and even in October and November he really thought that Bush was going to be tossed out and that there would be a president in the White House whom he could probably get on the phone when he needed to. He was feeling really up — and then he was devastated by Bush's win. He felt that the election was fixed, that democracy truly had become a sham, that two elections in a row were rigged.

All the things that he had championed in the cultural wars of the sixties were now not just being pushed back — they were being destroyed by the radical right. Team Hunter was losing, and it was heartbreaking to him. He thought Reagan was the worst of it, and now Reagan was like a genial way station in the conservative movement. Hunter was very hard on his generation; he thought a lot of them had just sold out. He felt the press corps was being bitch-slapped by the Rove White House, that the media were losing their nerve.

RICH COHEN *is a contributing editor at* Rolling Stone.

I went to Owl Farm in October 2004 to interview Hunter. Jann had commissioned me to write a profile of him for *Rolling Stone*. Anita wasn't there. She would call me from her mother's to make sure that I was going to be there.

From the first moment I saw Hunter, he was losing it. He entered the room cursing and kicking a chair, and then he sat down and opened a drawer full of pills and took some pills and started drinking. After that you could talk to him for a while, and then as the night went on, he started smoking pot and drinking more, and suddenly he actually became more and more normal. Most people start out on the first floor and take drugs to take them to the second floor. He started out in the basement and took drugs to take him back up to the first floor.

He was frail. He would line up his movements like a pool shot — I'm going to go from this doorway to that stool — and if anything was in his path, something you'd just normally step around, it might pose a real problem, and when he came in contact with it, he would have a fucking shit fit. He'd toss shit and scream.

Hunter was really paranoid, and we got in a couple of arguments because he was saying things that I thought were crazy. At the time, it seemed like Bush might not win the election, which was in a week or two, and Hunter said, "Oh, they'll find a way for him to win. He'll win." His theory was that if it looked at the very end like Dubya wasn't going to win, suddenly we'd see that George Bush the elder would die, and that would swing the election to the son. I said, "How's that gonna happen?" He said, "They'd just tell him, 'Look, old-timer. You've had your shot; your time is up. You'll have to do this for your son.'"

He wanted me to stay longer and do a lot of shit for him. I thought I was going there as a reporter to write a story, and he wanted me to become an assistant. At one point I was there all night and got back to my hotel at seven in the morning, and there was a message from him — he wanted me to come back to Owl Farm. He had a story about John Kerry due for *Rolling Stone,* and every night I was there he got a call at two in the morning from their national affairs editor, Eric Bates, and every night he would blow it off. All Hunter had to do was write a couple of sentences; the story was basically done. But he couldn't do it. He wanted *me* to do it. He wanted me to come back, type up the whole story, write his additional sentences, read him the whole thing, and then fax it back, because he couldn't work the fax machine. I pretended I didn't get the message.

He had also wanted me to sleep in the cabin next door to his house — he wanted someone to be with him all the time — and I couldn't do that. Every night I had to try to get out of there, and I'd be waiting for a natural pause in his conversation to make a move, and he'd know that's what I was waiting for — so he wouldn't pause.

MARILYN MANSON *met Hunter in 2000 when Johnny Depp called him one night from the Viper Room and said, "Get down here. You've got to meet this guy."*

A few days before the election, he was in L.A. doing a book signing and he invited me up to the Chateau. He was always in some kind of amazingly cinematic predicament of some sort, and this time he had a pair of handcuffs around his neck — I think this symbolized a moment in his life, or in his marriage, because he really, really wanted to come to my house to get in my swimming pool, which I had told him was as hot as a Jacuzzi. He said that his "chrysalis muscle" really needed to be soaked. I said, "Will it bloom into a butterfly of some sort?" and he laughed. He had a duffel bag full of things that only bad people wish for on Christmas — it was like if Al Capone and William Burroughs and Sam Peckinpah directed *Candyman.* But I think he really wanted to swim with some of the women that I keep around the house. This was because of no lack of love for his companion, but at the same time I think he felt imprisoned. He talked to me about this when we went back to his bedroom to try to figure out an escape plan for him to get to my house.

I told Hunter I was ready to go back into journalism, and we were talking about going on a college speaking tour as a team. It was a really exciting idea — he of course wanted to make sure that we'd be going only to girls' schools — but we were talking a lot about art and politics and society and how they affect one another.

One thing I always liked about him was that his drug use was shameless. I once made the mistake of letting someone drag me along to an Alcoholics Anonymous meeting — I got asked for autographs, and then they started talking about God too much, and I just left and called Hunter immediately. He told me that he would be my sponsor and get me back on my road to recovery — to drug use and alcohol use again.

ANJELICA HUSTON

The last time I saw him was at the Taschen bookstore party in L.A. for the special edition of *The Curse of Lono*. I had gotten a call from Laila because Benicio Del Toro and Harry Dean Stanton were doing readings from *Lono* and Sean Penn had dropped out at the last minute, and Laila said, "Would you come read one of the stories? Hunter wants you to." Taschen is a very select bookstore in Beverly Hills, and when I walked in, Hunter's influence was immediately felt — the room was thick with smoke, and champagne was being poured in more than liberal amounts, and Hugh Hefner was there with four of his blondes in gonzo thongs — it had all of the earmarks of a "Hunter situation." It immediately felt like the old days in Aspen when the mad magician was at the helm.

Hunter was rubbing my knee throughout. He could barely walk. He was obviously in a lot of pain and was medicated — but then again, I don't know that I've ever seen Hunter unmedicated. Somehow I did the reading, and he was very happy about it, which was good, and it got some laughs from the crowd. Then we all went to the Chateau Marmont, and Laila came over and said, "He wants you to go sit with him." I went and sat on Hunter's lap for a while, and he ordered a variety of drinks, and then he said, "Mai tais!"

Hunter didn't really eat much, but the variety of the drinks that he consumed was another thing — the actual scope of his drinking. Hunter could go from bourbon to crème de menthe back to fruity tropical drinks like *that,* or he'd order these horrible sticky drinks — Bailey's cream with a little champagne. And he always encouraged you to order alongside him, and of course you could see a reason not to order mai tais or horrible sticky drinks, but the next thing you know your eyes are rolling in your head. That was a sign that I had to get out of there.

I said, "Hunter, I think I'm going to go" — and he took off his amulet from around his neck and put it around my neck and said, "Here — take this." I knew the importance of this thing — he'd had it for decades and wore it constantly — and I was taken aback. I left with it around my neck, and the next day I woke up with a bad feeling about it. It was weird. I sent it back.

MITCH GLAZER

When we all ended up at the Chateau after the book signing, I left feeling kind of sad. I didn't think I'd see him again, truthfully, and I didn't. It was a shitty night, a rainy night; the reading went well, and the whole feeling was nice. But afterward the lobby got separated into a sort of hierarchy of who was closest to Hunter; it had a very stratified feel to it that wasn't really him. I passed along a message from Billy Murray — an edited version of it. He looked up from where he was sitting and said, "How is Mr. Murray? Is he okay? What's going on with the family?" He kind of engaged for a second. But the rest of that night felt unsatisfying to visit. It didn't feel completely right.

Sometimes you don't realize how old people really are. He was so iconic when I met him in '77. The guy was a specimen. He was just — even at rest, even sitting in a chair — he was a physical presence. So to see him kind of broken like that was maybe inevitable, but still hard to handle.

BEN FEE

People came over less and less toward the end. Hunter would just tell guests straight up that they had to go, or "Get the fuck out." If he wanted to be alone, he would make it known pretty abruptly, and everyone who was over at that point knew how to take it, so they wouldn't get sore about it. They'd just go.

MICHAEL SOLHEIM

Braudis was on me a lot about going out to visit Hunter in the last couple of years. He'd call me up and say, "He really needs some of the old friends more — he's getting really tired of everybody else." Hunter was hanging out with guys from around the tavern and younger guys from town who had no experience and who were a bother. I'd say, "Bob, it's the same deal. I'm not too interested in hanging around with a bunch of sycophants. The people who are out there these days bore the shit out of me."

JANN WENNER

I'd speak to him on the phone every few months and say, "I'm going to be in Idaho this summer, and I'm going to come down and visit for a day." How difficult would that have been? But then I questioned if I really wanted to go down there, stay up till three a.m., and take drugs. We'd sit there and laugh and then come up with some scheme to do something, an article to write, some political move, knowing it would fall apart, and I'd see him aging. I didn't want to do that. Maybe I was lazy or just neglectful, but I just wanted to remember Hunter in his glory. And I was angry that I couldn't help him.

SEMMES LUCKETT

There were times when I didn't go out to see him as much as I should have. Physically, I just wasn't up to it anymore — all the substances involved at the time. And if you were there for a specific purpose, it could be two or three in the morning before you got to it.

BEN FEE

Having his work read to him would always make him feel better, and shooting guns on his range rejuvenated him whenever we did it. We usually shot in the afternoon because he had some cleaning ladies come, and *God* — he would lash out at them so hard. So I'd try to get him in a different place so they could do their job without getting harassed.

I was never frightened of Hunter physically, but one time he was smoking a bunch of weed and then pulled out a shotgun. He was kind of weak, so the gun would just fall low and he'd pick it up high and wave it around. Things like that happened a couple of times.

Whenever Hunter and Anita got in a fight, she would leave. Their relationship was so up and so down. Hunter was paranoid — he had all these scenarios concocted in his head about Anita taking his money. He hated that feeling. It was usually when the fumes of an argument were still in the air.

He and Anita could be all lovey-dovey, and she would always go and give him hugs, and twenty minutes later they could be yelling at each other. It could go for a few minutes or a couple sentences back and forth, or for ten minutes — if it ever escalated to that point, I would leave.

CHAPTER THIRTEEN

The End of the Road

The hardest part of creative writing is finding your own voice — an authentic, original voice that can translate into a culture. Only a handful of writers in a generation can pull that off, and Hunter transcended his competition.

JUAN THOMPSON

I never had any doubt that at some point he was going to commit suicide. That's how he was going to die, barring some strange illness or a car crash or something like that. As long as it was in his control, I knew that he was going to kill himself. I would guess that if he hadn't broken his leg, he would have lived longer, but it would have just been a matter of time — months, a year or two.

It's not something he talked about — the practical details of dying. He never told me anything to the effect of, "Here's what I'm going to do," or "This is how it's going to happen." It's more a sense that I had.

BEN FEE

He never talked to me about the act of suicide itself — doing it — he just talked about the control of doing it. He said he never wanted to be an old fart, or wither away, or become crippled, and he *was* becoming crippled. That's just the way it happened. He *saw* it happening, and the closer it got to the end, the less he brought it up.

JUAN THOMPSON

When he finally did choose to kill himself, he was very careful not to let on. I think he'd made a decision and he didn't want to put me or anyone in a position of trying to stop him. It would have put a horrible burden on somebody.

There was trouble between him and Anita, sure. But after a certain number of months, there was always trouble with Hunter and his women. He was a very difficult guy to live with — very charming and extremely loveable, but very difficult too. So the difficulty now was no surprise. Just as every other woman had finally decided to leave, I assumed she would come to that point too.

SARAH MURRAY *worked as an assistant to Hunter starting in November 2004.*

I was looking in the local paper and saw a job advertised as a sort of errand girl. I called and talked to Anita, and realized very quickly that I wasn't going to be an errand person. Anita wanted me to hang out with Hunter — maybe that wasn't a conscious decision on her part, but I could tell that she was overwhelmed and that she had things she needed to do out of town. I spent one evening at Owl Farm from seven until three, and then shifted into this new job as assistant. It was often full-time.

Hunter didn't do much writing. He seemed to be entering a reflective period. We did other things. We did a lot of reading — that actually felt like an accomplishment — and he was trying to be very diligent about swimming. We would go to George Stranahan's pool, which was something that brought him great joy — whenever we could finally get everything we needed together, that is, which would take a while.

Swimming with Hunter was a beautiful experience. Hunter made me aware pretty quickly that it was a privilege to go swimming with him, which is not how I saw it at first. I dreaded it; I was uncomfortable with it, but I came to see that it *was* a privilege. It was very peaceful, very calm, and I loved it because I knew that it made Hunter feel so good physically. He would just be in total ecstasy when he was in the water; for once he was not in pain. He did need some assistance.

It was just a very quiet time. We didn't talk much. I was one of the few people who refused to be naked in the pool with Hunter, and that was frustrating for him for a while. Anita had told me that this was what all the assistants had done in the past, but I chose not to. We came to a kind of compromise — I would float on an inflatable raft, and Hunter would spin me around. It was amazing — I would be looking up at this amazing Colorado sky filled with stars. It was a bonding experience without words. It was special. That's about all I can say.

We talked a lot about future projects that we would work on together in April. We always talked about "in April," like it was going to be this new chapter of our time and our relationship together and my job with him. I would take on more of — I don't know how to put this — an official role come April. I would work with him full-time at the house and with writing. We talked about working on a new book that would be called *Dr. Thompson's Guide to Physical Fitness*. It was going to be something really light and fun for him, more of an adventure.

ED BRADLEY

I had gotten pissed at Hunter because he was supposed to make a toast at my wedding that summer, and he left. I was angry, and I didn't talk to him for a while. He came to the party the night before the wedding and stayed for the whole thing, and he came to the wedding and stayed through the wedding — and he left before the reception, for whatever reason. My wife, Patricia, said, "You can't carry a grudge like that." Eventually I called Hunter and said, "You know, I'm not pissed at you anymore, but I want you to know I was pissed. But I'm not pissed anymore. I let it go." We had a nice talk and put it behind us, and then I saw him at Christmas. He came to Jack's annual Christmas Eve party, and he was in great form. He was handing out gonzo paraphernalia — T-shirts for the men, thongs for the women — and he was chuckling and having a great time. That was the last time I saw him.

JACK NICHOLSON

He had missed my Christmas party for a year or two — he always said he was coming and then, for one reason or another, couldn't make it because he wasn't well or ambulatory in the same way. But he sounded good that night. He had such a good time. He gave me a copy from a privately published edition of one of his books. It was called *Fire in the Nuts*.

CURTIS ROBINSON

Fire in the Nuts has some of the stories he wrote about being in New York, including one where things aren't going well for the guy and he starts to beat women pretty indiscriminately. It's not a happy story. He did several books like this that he published as very limited-edition art books.

JIMMY BUFFETT

That Christmas he was in pretty damn good shape. We had a great visit at Jack's party. He was laughing. I'm glad I got to go out on that one, but then when I look back on it, you know . . . I got it.

SEAN PENN *had formed a friendship with Hunter at Tosca in San Francisco in 1988.*

Things were very, very clearly not good. I saw it when I went to pick him up at the New Orleans airport. This incredibly physical guy could barely walk. The first night we got in, I had arranged a dinner, and he was having a tough time moving around. It ended up being mostly wheelchairs the rest of the time. I could see, and I know that Brinkley could too, that this was different. What it was doing to him emotionally was different.

DOUG BRINKLEY

Hunter was going to do a piece for *Playboy* on the remaking of the movie of *All the King's Men* with James Carville as the producer and Sean Penn playing Willie Stark. The climate in January was warm, and they were offering him a lot of money, and Sean sent a private plane to pick him up.

When he got into town with Sean, he was very tired; he couldn't walk ten yards without people holding him up. He had lost weight, and he didn't look good. It was heartbreaking. At one point, he was in a wheelchair getting pushed over to the set, and he fell out of the wheelchair onto the street. He was really upset — he felt like a gutter person, and he couldn't get himself off Esplanade Avenue.

Hunter had always talked about suicide, but it was very, very low in his playing deck. But when he came to New Orleans, and even in the whole year before, it was an option he would verbalize. He'd say things like, "Well, I may have to do myself in soon." I would naturally say, "Hunter, stop it. Don't talk like that." He would say, "What — I can't talk real with you now? I don't want to hear your fake shit. Of course it's a fucking option of mine. Who the fuck do you think I am? Do you think I'm gonna go in to live with a goddamn Nurse Ratched in the hospital and be put through some detox thing? Fuck that."

The question became "What kinds of therapies could work?" He had tried to work on his knee, his hip, his head, his back, his blood pressure. He had to use an oxygen tank. He was monitoring his blood pressure every day and writing it down and taking medication for all these ailments. He had no real exercise, yet he was putting a lot of alcohol and drugs into his body.

He felt his entire life would have been a failure if he went out institutionalized. To be a man, in his view, was to live. You light out after the territories, like Mark Twain said, and you carry a big club with you wherever you go, like Jack London said. He had lit out for the territories, and he had carried the club wherever he went, but he had hit a point, at age sixty-seven, where his body was not cooperating. He felt that he had lived too long, and he was hugely conscious of his image. He was a persona writer — it helps sell books — and Hunter realized that if the headline "Thompson Put in Detox Hospital" was written, all of his macho drugging and drinking and tough-guy anarchy would go down the tubes, and suddenly he would be just another frail old man.

Sometimes he'd be screaming, but there were also these mournful, sad, quiet outrages. When he was screaming, you felt that at least there was some life going on there, but he'd get these faraway teary stares. . . . I saw him three or four times with tears in his eyes for no reason. Suddenly the mission became "How do we cheer him up?" We had only limited success, but there were moments. We went to the Circle Bar in Lee Circle. There was a bluegrass fusion band there, and Hunter loved them. He would sit at the bar, and the bartender knew Hunter's work and was giving him free drinks and the VIP treatment. We had a wonderful night. He couldn't walk, but he was dancing in his seat and whooping and doing his Iroquois war cheers in the air.

He was connecting with Sean Penn and Jude Law and James Carville; some of the actors and actresses would come around him and read some of his works in his hotel suite. He didn't do well on the set, though. One time they were filming and Hunter screamed in the middle of a take. But Sean kept a real attentive eye on him, and at night when he was done shooting he would go visit him.

JEFF KASS

My last conversation with him was about a month before he killed himself. I called him to talk about Lisl, and Anita said, "He's in New Orleans. He's staying at the Ritz-Carlton, but I'm sure he'd like to hear from you. He originally checked in under 'Richard Nixon,' but now you can reach him just as 'Hunter Thompson'."

DOUG BRINKLEY

When he was alone at the hotel, I would let myself in and he would be sitting by himself, and you could see that he had been crying. But when a crowd would come, he would try to put on a happy face. People wanted to see the legendary Hunter Thompson, and he tried hard to be upbeat and be Hunter, but he only had so much energy. When those people would leave, the real him emerged.

He said, "You know, I don't think I can take it anymore. I'm making a fool out of myself." I'd try to be booster-like, as anybody would: "Hunter, you're doing great. So what if you don't write this thing? Don't be so hard on yourself." And he said, "What kind of friend are you? Don't do that. Don't start telling me how great things are. Let's be honest. My whole body is gone. I'm in great pain. Don't cheapen our friendship by telling me how rosy things are."

He was starting to lose interest in sports, even, which was pretty much his last thing. What he was interested in in New Orleans was his catalogue of works and hearing people read some of them out loud. It was like he was hearing the music of his own prose for the last time.

SEAN PENN

Warren Beatty once said about Jack Nicholson that he was "a man who goes to great lengths to get into a good mood." Hunter would do that. Out of nowhere, he could go on a genius riff. And there were several nights of the genius riff, but something was very troubling; he was going inside himself, and you could feel it. That period was unlike the rest of the time that I knew him, where he was all the colors of the rainbow. It was all forward motion, and now I felt that the forward motion had stopped.

JUAN THOMPSON

I think he realized that his physical condition was not something he was going to recover from. And I think that realization was a big part of his decision to kill himself. New Orleans really brought it home to him that he was very dependent on people for almost everything, and that this was a situation that was not likely to change.

SEAN PENN

The last morning I saw him, Brinkley and I were heading off to Atlanta. Hunter and Anita were flying back to Woody Creek, so we'd said our good-byes the night before. Then Brinkley and I went to a Wendy's on the way to the airport, and as I walked in I saw Anita there. They were on their way to this other airport in New Orleans, so we walked out to the car, and Hunter was sitting there — again visibly emotional but very tender and very kind.

DOUG BRINKLEY

We thought we'd surprise Hunter. Sean and I ran over to his car, and he was sitting in the front seat crying.

ED BRADLEY

He was an incredibly talented, smart, caring man, and I don't think he could live with what he had become. I don't think that he could live with the deterioration of his physical self and the continuing deterioration of his creative self. Most of what Hunter was doing in his last years, except for the ESPN column, was old work. His letters books, *The Gonzo Papers* — that's stuff that was written years ago, and yes there was some writing involved in putting it together, but it didn't come from the same wellspring of creativity. I think he recognized that.

DOUG BRINKLEY

Once he got back to Colorado, I talked to him nightly. His spirits stayed down, but in the last week of his life, he developed a kind of businesslike clarity that frightened me. Instead of our usual meandering conversations about things, he was coldly efficient, telling me things like, "Always remember that the basement room in the house is called Johnny's Room," or "You have to make sure that Owl Farm is always preserved, because developers are going to try to bulldoze it, and I'm counting on you to make sure it's a historic place."

WILLIAM KENNEDY

About two weeks before he died, he called and said he wanted to find a way to hang out and talk. He liked my introduction to *The Proud Highway* and said he'd just reread it for the eighty-fifth time. I think he was saying good-bye, calling people when he was on the way out.

LAILA NABULSI

Hunter started saying good-bye to people differently when they'd visit him or when he talked to them on the phone. I talked to Hunter a week before he died. There was definitely a good-bye about it.

Hunter was never one to look back, and now he was talking about what happened with us and asking me why, and what did I feel. I was really honest with him, and I said, "It was because I loved you so much that I was so worried, because of John. And I didn't understand." There were so many things that went with that, but he apologized: "I'm sorry I put you through that."

BEN FEE

One night in mid-February, Hunter and I were going to go down to the tavern. He just couldn't get motivated, and then finally he came out of his bedroom ready to go — with no pants or underwear on. He'd forgotten to put them on. Then something snapped, and he was back to being Hunter, and he laughed and said, "Oh, Jesus Christ," and turned heel and put on some pants and we drove like madmen down to the tavern. We threw back some shots and had dinner.

PATTI STRANAHAN

The last two weeks before Hunter died, he couldn't really walk on his own anymore, and one of his assistants came up with him almost every night. He was in good spirits. We would sit in the kitchen at about five o'clock in the morning, and he would raid my refrigerator. I think he knew he was getting ready to go, but he wasn't sad. He'd just peel a grapefruit and sit. At his Super Bowl party, he told me a million things. I was just laughing at him and slapping him and stuff, but he hugged me. I know now that he was saying good-bye.

TEX WEAVER

"Chance favors the prepared mind" was one of Hunter's favorite quotes for the last couple of years. Looking back, he was getting everything lined up. Anita kept saying to me, "I'm worried that Hunter is going to shoot himself." I pooh-poohed it at the Super Bowl party with her — "What are you talking about? He's not going to do this."

SARAH MURRAY

Hunter's Super Bowl party was a wonderful gathering. Hunter wanted me next to him the entire night. My husband was so understanding and so impressed by that. Hunter and I had a wonderful conversation that night. He actually called the next day because he was concerned that maybe he had freaked me out or was too weird, but I reassured him that it just made me feel good. We were alone. I decided to spend the night in the cabin, and Hunter had Ben help him over to the cabin. We were in a room together and it was just very, very touching and very, very soulful and sweet. I know I was truly loved by him.

BEN FEE

Hunter was in a jovial mood — there was a big bonfire in the backyard, and the night seemed to go on forever. One of his friends had brought a random large-busted girl by, and girls always brought out a side of Hunter that a man couldn't. He loved entertaining women, and he pulled out a tube of lipstick and had a lipstick-pressing contest to see who had the best lips. We took turns passing *Screwjack* and *Kingdom of Fear* around and reading different passages.

Anita retired early that night, but everyone else was up super-late. I went to bed around seven a.m. Hunter really took to Sarah that night, and she had imbibed quite a bit and was staying in the other bedroom of the guest cabin, and Hunter kept wanting to go over to visit her.

At four or five in the morning, he asked me if I wanted to take a ride, but he just drove us back and forth from his garage to the guesthouse, which is maybe a hundred feet. He was kind of fucked up — not kind of fucked up, he was *really* fucked up — health-wise, plus he had eaten some brownies. He kept saying that he heard people breaking into his house, and that's one of the reasons he wanted to go visit Sarah — he wanted to make sure she was okay — so we drove over. He couldn't walk on his own, so I gave him a hand, and then he peed on the door of the cabin. I think he just realized that he had to go, and he always liked doing whatever he wanted whenever he wanted, so he just went. Once he was inside, he used everything to put his weight onto.

He was sort of speaking in tongues. He did that a couple nights I was there; this was one of them, and February 19 was the other night.

BEN FEE

That week, Hunter had finished an ESPN column, which was his first in a long time. We had started to read *Fear and Loathing in Las Vegas* as a kind of celebration — he wanted to hear the book again — and we probably got about three-quarters of the way through it.

Juan and Jennifer and Will showed up early on Saturday, and Hunter asked to be alone with Juan, so I let them have their family day and just hung out here and there. There was a basketball game on, and Hunter was teaching Will how to gamble. I think he was five or six.

Things were tense between Hunter and Anita. I only saw her once, and then she went out.

JUAN THOMPSON

He told me to take some family mementos — some silver julep cups that are traditional in Kentucky, engraved with his name and some names of his family members; a clock that had belonged to his mother. He also pointed to the medallion that Oscar Acosta had given him and told me, "When I die, I want you to have this."

He was wearing the emerald pendant that he wore pretty much all the time, and he told me that when he died, if he and Anita were on good terms he wanted her to have the emerald.

BEN FEE

I went over to the cabin for a while, and then Juan came over with Will — really late, around two-thirty a.m. Juan said Anita was back, and there'd been a terrible fight. Hunter had pulled out a gun and was waving it around, and Anita freaked out.

JUAN THOMPSON

Hunter was sitting at his typewriter goofing around and showing off with a pellet gun he kept around, and he wanted to shoot a gong that was across into the next room, the living room. He was in a good mood; he might have been stoned, but he just wanted to show off and shoot the gong. The pellet would have had to pass within a foot or so of where Anita was sitting, which would have been a little scary, but he wasn't in a malicious mood.

Anita was very upset, and they got into a big fight.

BEN FEE

While Juan and I were talking in the cabin, my phone rang, and it was Hunter, saying that Anita was trying to kill him and kick him out of his house. He said he wanted help and a witness. Juan and I went over, and we calmed Anita down and separated them. They were throwing shit. Hunter was yelling. He was saying he was sick of people, that he was scared that his life was going to be taken away, that she was going to go tell the cops that he was pointing guns, and then he wouldn't be able to have any guns and he'd get thrown in jail and she'd get everything he owned. He said that there was no point being in this place if he couldn't live how he wanted.

Anita was in hysterics. She was probably still in shock from having a gun pointed at her. She finally went downstairs into Johnny's room and stayed there, and we read a little bit from *Kingdom of Fear,* and that soothed him for a while, and then it got into talking about guns and he got ranting again, so we put on the original *Cape Fear* in black and white and watched that. Hunter felt like shit. Closer to five-thirty or six a.m., he was sort of speaking, mumbling, still sitting in his chair, and we helped him into his room. He had another temper tantrum about his remote control, saying that the cleaning lady fucked up and was out to get him, but he found the remote and then asked Juan and me, "Do you mind just waiting until I'm asleep, just to make sure I'm okay?"

JUAN THOMPSON

The next morning, Hunter was up pretty early — before noon, which was unusual.

Anita went into town to her health club. The argument from the previous night was not resolved, and it was tense between them. After she left, Hunter and I talked further, for three or four hours, about some business matters that he wanted my help with, acting as a messenger for him to some people. It was about how he wanted to move forward and that he wanted me to convey some information to his lawyer. He was pretty calm, which is why what happened came as a surprise, because he was talking about this business, and how he wanted to deal with it, and what he wanted to do depending on the outcome. There wouldn't have been a reason to discuss this stuff if he wasn't going to be around.

He very deliberately did not have a final good-bye. He didn't want to let on. It was a really nice afternoon. He was reading the paper, and me and Jen were reading, and I was taking a picture of something for Jen, and I think he just decided that that was the moment. I think he'd been hanging in there for a long time and just got tired of it.

I was in the back office when he pulled the trigger. Jennifer and Will were in the living room. I ran into the living room to get Jennifer, and we left Will in the living room. We were trying to find the sheriff's phone number. It was terrifying.

BOB BRAUDIS

Afterward I asked Juan, "What did you think happened?" He said, "It sounded like a book falling from the counter and slamming onto the floor."

Everyone was wondering why the hell Juan and Jennifer were summoned that weekend. Why did he do it while they were there? What if Anita had gotten pissed with him and taken off for the weekend to

Fort Collins? I believe he wanted to be found quickly by people that he knew loved him.

JUAN THOMPSON

I knew immediately what had happened, but I couldn't quite believe it. I don't think it even occurred to us to call 911. I called the sheriff.

I went outside and loaded a gun — what Hunter called his "working gun," the twelve-gauge Winchester Marine — with five or six shells, and then fired them up in the air as a tribute. It just seemed really important to mark that moment. A deputy pulled up, and he was a little freaked out when he heard a shotgun blast.

BOB BRAUDIS

I got a phone call from Juan saying, "You gotta get down here right away." I didn't know what was wrong, but I called 911. The ambulance got there before I did, and they had connected the leads to the EKG, the heart monitor, but there were no vital signs. I had to comfort Juan, Jennifer, and Will, and find Anita. She was at the Aspen Club. I spent about an hour in the cabin and called in a child psychologist to talk to Will. I finally got Anita on the phone and said, "I'm going to send a police car to get you." I explained to her what happened. She was hysterical.

After Hunter died, Anita found a page from this spiral notebook where Hunter used to start his writing. This was titled "Football season is over." It read, "No More Games. No More Bombs. No More Walking. No More Fun. No More Swimming. 67. That is 17 years past 50. 17 more than I needed or wanted. Boring. I am always bitchy. No Fun — for anybody. You are getting Greedy. Act your old age. Relax — This won't hurt."

It was dated the last night I was with him, four nights prior.

DR. STEVE AYERS

Hunter's body was still sitting in the chair. The .45 was on the floor. There was blood and stuff around from the gunshot wound. The sheriff's guys had already done most of their photography, and we got some extra photographs and looked closer at the position of the hand and the gun and the gun case. This is all pretty much done before you disturb anything. We checked things like body temperature and the degree of rigor mortis to see if the time of death was consistent with what we'd been told or when the gunshot went off, and everything was kosher. As far as the position of the gun, it looked like after he fired it, it just fell down to the floor.

Normally, for a suicide with a gunshot wound, I don't get an autopsy. You don't need one. You know what killed him. If it was a celebrity, I usually do get a full autopsy because of the questions that come up, but in Hunter's case, he had had so many medical things and CAT scans and MRIs that we knew what his insides — his heart and liver and everything — were like.

The bullet went basically right in the back of the throat, the palate, and right out the lower part of the head — right through the brain stem, which is instant death. He couldn't have placed it better.

I made the decision as coroner when I worked that night that I wasn't going to do a drug screen on him. I knew his health status enough to know that it probably didn't have any acute influence on his decision. The cause of death was gunshot wound. The manner of death was suicide.

JUAN THOMPSON

CNN was on, as it almost always was, in the kitchen, and a few hours later I remember seeing the ticker scrolling across the bottom of the screen: "Author Hunter S. Thompson is dead at 67."

LYNN NESBIT

I think he was quite a good father, in his own bizarre way. And Juan loved him. I think Hunter was embarrassed when he felt too much. I think he was almost embarrassed about how much he cared about Juan. His whole life was making show-business out of everything, and when you got down to real feelings for people close to him, he was awkward. If only he hadn't been as awkward, I feel that would've helped him get his life more under control as he matured — or grew older. Because at the end . . . well, at some point or other, the irregular lifestyle was going to catch up with him.

I remember Hunter saying he didn't expect to live past forty. I'm surprised he never had a heart attack. He must have had the heart and liver and kidneys of a master race. Who could survive what he put his body through for as many years as he lived? What's interesting is that the physical structure of his body is what broke down, but it was the organs that were really getting the abuse.

There was part of him that was always slightly embarrassed by his extremist behavior. So this was the dichotomy that he, as a human being, had to deal with within himself. And those of us who knew about him and cared for him had to deal with that too. Of course, there were times when he would go into ranting and rages, but for the many, many, many years that we were together, it just bounced off of me. I knew this was a part of Hunter, and I accepted his behavior.

I think every writer writes out of some schism in their personality, and I do think Hunter was underneath quite lonely, and the drugs and the alcohol helped mask that. Hunter is also the one writer I know of where everything he wrote would be more or less true but he would pretend it wasn't, whereas others would try to say it was true when it wasn't. He threw caution to the winds early on, and that became part of his persona, and he thought he had to keep doing it. He had to live out who he was.

JOHNNY DEPP

About a week before it happened, he left me a message that once again promised to be one of those long, drawn-out Hunter experiences. I listened to about half of it, and then the clock was ticking and I had to run. The part of it I did hear was so sweet, and up, and light. I saved the message and went on to do my stuff, and by the time I got the news that Hunter had made his exit, that message was gone — it just evaporated. I never heard the end, and that will fuck with me forever.

JANN WENNER

I got back from Christmas break in mid-January and picked up a New Year's Eve message from Hunter on the machine. It was not the typical crazed ramble or rant — this was just to say he was thinking of me, and all our times together, how good they had been, how much they meant to him . . . and it was just going through his mind and he wanted me to know. It was out of the blue. He had said this to me before, in person and in letters. But this time it was a little more personal, a little more tender . . .

PORTER BIBB

In retrospect, his bitterness at being hung out to dry when he was in jail in high school stayed with him for a long, long time — forty or fifty years. Up until a month or two before he died, he started calling me again, after years of not having any regular communication, every night at two, three, four o'clock in the morning. He kept talking about Louisville and how mean-spirited it was. One night, in one of these conversations, I said, "Well, why the fuck didn't you give somebody a call?"

He could have called me or called Paul Semonin; either one of us could have sprung him from jail in a second. But he wouldn't answer.

Hunter's youngest brother, Jim, who was gay, died of AIDS a few years ago. And Davison, his other brother, is just rock solid — he looks like Mr. Normal Guy out of Normalville, Illinois. I saw him at a memorial service after Hunter died, and he told me, "I don't know where Hunter came from." The whole thing didn't compute to him. Then he asked me, "Why do you think he hated Louisville so much?" I told him I didn't know, except that maybe all these years he resented the fact that nobody had helped him.

MICHAEL STEPANIAN

Keep in mind that he had my American Express card. He didn't have enough credit to get one himself, so he said, "Look — do this for me for a couple of months." And it turned out to be twenty years. The last bill, when he died, was for thirteen thousand bucks, and I picked that up. I didn't mind doing it because he always paid his bills on time. Plane tickets, obscene movies, condoms . . . I mean, I had shit on that card that was unbelievable. It was such a wonderful experience getting those bills every month.

I represented him. I loved him. We loved each other. We both came from the same generation, and we were basically righteous. We don't suffer from schmucks.

He was a great, great man with an amazing sense of the now. He followed the Buddha; he followed the way. He had great wah.

DON JOHNSON

Hunter was incredibly knowledgeable about Buddhism, and I had read pretty much every book ever written on the subject and was meditating three times a day — walking the walk. We were talking and joking around one night, and I said, "Hunter, what is the sound of one hand clapping?" And he reached up and slapped me upside the head.

TOM BENTON

People talk about "closure." I do not want closure. I cannot have closure with this man because for almost forty years, he was my stability. I told that to someone, and he said, "What do you mean? Hunter Thompson couldn't be anybody's stability." But he was my stability. He was the Rock of Gibraltar for me. And his death leaves a hole. I don't want closure — fuck no — I want to curse him and laugh with him.

For me, he's as big as Hemingway. I said to him once, "You know, you really are pretty good." And he said, "You know what? Sometimes I can be the best."

LAILA NABULSI

He had a great sense of knowing when somebody needed attention; he had this unerring instinct to reach out at times and make sure you were okay. I met him when I was twenty-two, and for almost thirty years he was always there. Even as I grew older, he was the person who got me. Even if it had to change form, the love never ended, and the connection never ended.

GEORGE STRANAHAN

I will say one thing about the man: It was always clear in my mind that if I got in a situation where I was down at the cop shop and had one phone call, it was absolutely clear to me that that call would be to Hunter.

CURTIS ROBINSON

Spending time with "Hunter people" is like being with other addicts. If there's three of us at a party, we're going to go stand by ourselves and tell Hunter stories. For a long time after being with Hunter, for weeks afterward, it was like that scene from *Trainspotting* where a heroin addict says to another addict, "The problem with being off is you know you've had your best day." For weeks after being in the trenches with Hunter, I would wonder, "Will it ever be that kind of fun again?"

JACK NICHOLSON

He was a very, very gentle guy with a lot of problems, and I guess he never found the right way to share them. He kept his own counsel, and when he did say things, it was often to provoke. To many people, he was the Good Doctor in this area, and as long as Hunter was around, somebody was watching certain things that the rest of us might be too complacent to start jerking the alarm bell on.

DEBORAH FULLER

Hunter shooting himself did not surprise me. I always felt that he was in charge of his life and knew that he would be in charge of his death if and when he chose that path. He would say so, and I believe he was preparing me for the possibility that he would go out that way. So I accepted it from the beginning — you had to, if you were his true friend. I am honored that I was an important part of his life.

I guess I was always an action junkie, but I didn't know the true meaning of that until I met Hunter.

RICHARD GOODWIN

He was as close to being a truly liberated intellectual and individual in today's society as anyone I've ever known. It might have taken strange forms, but what did I care about that? He had an inner integrity that was distinct from anything else he did in literature.

DOUG BRINKLEY

He did not commit suicide in a burst of irrational anger or because he was having a bad day or because his karma was off-kilter or just because he was in chronic pain or because he was feuding with family. This was an intellectual, pragmatic decision that he had contemplated for all of his life, that was becoming his favorite focal point of conversation and thought in his last six months of life. This was an act of no regret.

SANDY THOMPSON

I've thought a lot since Hunter's death about his ability to seduce. It's an energy — and yeah, you use people here and there. It's not all bad, and it's not all good. I just think people like him were born with something, and then they worked on it a little bit, honed it a little bit finer.

For so many people — and for me for years, even though I had this angst, and I was scared — being around Hunter was exciting. It was exciting and it was very dramatic. I was madly in love with this person, and I was terrified always that he would leave me. I came to find out years later that Hunter was also terrified that I would leave him. But he was a scary guy. Even some of his best friends, who were big, substantial, successful people, could feel that.

I think that underneath all of that bravado and violence and anger and fear, though, was an understanding that he was not living the right life — that he was hurting people. He knew he could get what he wanted and that he could make people feel really, really scared and make them tremble. It was like being in a cult. He knew all of this, I believe, at the very core, and that was unbearable for him. I understand now, as of course I did not when we were together, that someone who suffers truly unmanageable energies and such dark mood swings will inevitably attack his external world in a desperate attempt to relieve his internal world. Hunter — Hunter's life — was tragic.

Hunter was not a man to reveal his true self. He was not a man to reveal his fears. It was the opposite. It was about the power and the magic and the charisma and the wisdom — and the intelligence and the creativity and the imagination. But all of us have fears, and Hunter had great fears. Hence the life that he lived.

When I asked him once, long after our divorce, if things had turned out like he had wanted, he said, "Well, of course not" — and he paused and then gave me that look — "but it's been glamorous."

DOUG BRINKLEY

Hunter is going to be read and read and read, and in that sense he is never going to go away. His books will be a part of people's lives; his voice is so unique and powerful and funny. Just rip any page out of any Hunter book and read it and you will immediately know that it's Hunter. There is nothing he did that didn't have his own stamp on it. The hardest part of creative writing is finding your own voice — an authentic, original voice that can translate into the culture. Only a handful of writers in a generation can pull that off, and Hunter, in that regard, transcended his competition. *Gonzo* is now in the dictionaries. There are a lot of people who write beautiful *New Yorker* essays and craft elegant novels, but they don't have an authentic voice. Hunter's voice is going to echo the longest of any writer of his generation.

DAVID HALBERSTAM *wrote the introduction to* Fear and Loathing in America, *Hunter's second volume of letters.*

Much more than most, the best of his work stands up and endures because there's such a strong viewpoint. The further you are from the event, the more important the chronicler becomes — in this particular case, Hunter's writing becomes twenty-five and thirty years later often more important that the events themselves. The events shrink, but Hunter's performing and reinterpreting them is enhanced.

He was magical, and I think that anybody who starts pigeonholing or categorizing him is going to get his fingers burned. I think there was always going to be one more book, one more terrific piece. He really had a long span for someone so original — and one who was leading a Hunter-esque life.

The great thing about Hunter is that when he heard that voice saying, "This is the way to do it," he listened to it.

NORMAN MAILER

Las Vegas is a helluva book. Everything he did, in a way, is a helluva book. He broke so many rules that I would get dizzy trying to evaluate him. I didn't always approve of the rules he was breaking, since I was much more of an established writer than he was, but his daring always appealed to me. He's one of those people who you could read a *page* of his work and be turned on by it, and you can't say that about too many writers.

I found him immensely stimulating, but for that reason alone I very often didn't read much of him — I didn't want to get *over*stimulated. We're very competitive, we writers. I felt if I read too much Hunter I was going to start saying, "What can I do that's in a vein like Hunter Thompson?" And I didn't want to get into that. If you're dealing with someone who's the absolute best at something, I wouldn't necessarily try to ace them.

DOUG BRINKLEY

Everybody always talks about Hunter being influenced by Hemingway and Fitzgerald — and of course they loomed very large on the literary landscape of his time — but it was Norman Mailer that Hunter really gravitated toward. *Advertisements for Myself* was his bible. Mailer concocted a character called General Marijuana, which knocked Hunter out. He later modeled *The Great Shark Hunt* on that weird anthology. And it was Mailer's book *Cannibals and Christians* — with the detailed reportage on the 1964 Republican Convention — which would lead to *Campaign Trail '72*. Mailer is also where Hunter picked up some of his odd salutations and verbal tics like "Selah" and "Hot Damn" — "Hot Damn" came from Mailer's *Why Are We in Vietnam?* Even as late as 2001, when Mailer was raising questions about the 9/11 attack, Hunter burst out in cheer. "Thank Jesus for Norman," he'd say. He felt Mailer was the only contemporary writer he still had something to learn from, and he loved the fact that he took risks.

TOM WOLFE

Hunter was the only twentieth-century equivalent of Mark Twain or Josh Billings or Petroleum V. Nasby. These were all people who were part journalist and part people having fun with the truth. If you read something like *Innocents Abroad,* it's a travel book, but everything is stretched to the nth degree. You're learning things, but you're also watching acrobatics done with the information. That's what *Fear and Loathing in Las Vegas* is — it's a different mind-set from Mark Twain because Twain would take dignified things and show their idiocy with a few changes. It was very subtle compared to Hunter. Instead of saying, "Let's put this thing up against the wall," Hunter would say, "Let's just go *through* the wall." He was just brilliant — there are very few writers who could top him. I can't think of any humorist in the whole century who could touch him.

DAVID HALBERSTAM

Certainly anybody who tries to imitate him falls on his face because he was such an American original — and in an odd way, very much in control of what he was doing on the page, and many people don't know this. The impression is that he's wild and out of control, but if you're a fellow writer watching him, you're watching someone who's very much in control, knows how to approach things, how to turn the normal prism upside down. He was almost cold-blooded in knowing how to do the Hunter Thompson take on something. It's a very strong, focused mechanism.

RALPH STEADMAN

I think he should be lying in state next to the Lincoln Memorial, myself. That's how they should have done it. They should have embalmed him properly. He was a genuine son of the Kentucky pioneers.

He was a shy guy, but he overcame that by being full of bravado. He was humble, but then he'd come out with an outrage of some kind against somebody that triggered another deeper spirit within that would not show itself unless somebody provoked it. Of course he had to be a tyrant too. He had to be tireless all the way down the line. He took it seriously — being a decent human, seriously caring about the rights of man — and I'm afraid that a lot of people in the last thirty years have corroded that whole idea.

I know that inside he felt this deep outrage because people were fucking with his beloved Constitution. That was the most important thing for him. He was still fighting to the end.

I tried to become an American citizen once, and Hunter said, "I will do everything in my power, Ralph, to prevent you from becoming a member of the United States. You don't deserve it."

BOB BRAUDIS

From now on when the phone rings at four a.m., it's just bad news.

JEFF ARMSTRONG is a manager of the O'Farrell Theatre, an adult-film house in San Francisco.

DR. STEVE AYERS is the coroner of Pitkin County, Colorado.

SONNY BARGER is a founding member of the Hells Angels.

ED BASTIAN helped manage Hunter's campaign for sheriff and later became his neighbor in Woody Creek, Colorado.

JUDY BELUSHI is the widow of John Belushi.

TOM BENTON was an Aspen architect and artist who designed the posters for Hunter's campaign for sheriff.

SANDY BERGER was a speechwriter for George McGovern in 1972. Berger later became President Clinton's national security adviser.

PORTER BIBB grew up with Hunter in Louisville, Kentucky, and became *Newsweek*'s White House correspondent and later served as the publisher of *Rolling Stone*.

NEVILLE BLAKEMORE grew up in Louisville with Hunter.

BOB BONE was a writer at the Middletown, New York, *Daily Record* when Hunter joined the paper's staff in 1959.

ED BRADLEY was a correspondent for *60 Minutes*. He met Hunter while covering Jimmy Carter's 1976 presidential campaign.

BOB BRAUDIS has been the sheriff of Pitkin County since 1986.

DOUG BRINKLEY, a professor of history at Tulane University, is the editor of Hunter's letters and the literary executor of Hunter's estate.

PAT BUCHANAN was an adviser to the Nixon campaign in 1968 and later served in that capacity in the White House.

JIMMY BUFFETT, the singer, moved to the Aspen area in the early seventies.

PAT CADDELL was the chief pollster for the McGovern campaign in 1972.

TIM CAHILL was an associate editor and writer at *Rolling Stone* in the seventies.

DOUG CARPENTER was a Woody Creek neighbor of Hunter's.

JIMMY CARTER is the thirty-ninth president of the United States.

JAMES CARVILLE was the chief strategist for Bill Clinton's presidential campaign in 1992.

JOHN CLANCY was a Columbia University law student and Hunter's roommate in 1958.

MICHAEL CLEVERLY is an Aspen artist and writer.

RICH COHEN is a contributing editor at *Rolling Stone*.

TIM CROUSE was a *Rolling Stone* reporter who covered the 1972 presidential campaign with Hunter. He is the author of *The Boys on the Bus*.

JOHNNY DEPP, the actor, portrayed Hunter in the movie *Fear and Loathing in Las Vegas*.

BILL DIXON managed the 1972 McGovern campaign in five states.

JOE EDWARDS is an Aspen lawyer who helped manage Hunter's sheriff's campaign in 1970.

AL EISELE was a Washington correspondent for Knight Ridder newspapers during the 1972 campaign.

JOE ESZTERHAS is a former writer for *Rolling Stone* and the author of several screenplays.

JEANETTE ETHERIDGE is the owner of Tosca, a bar in San Francisco.

WAYNE EWING produced and directed three documentary films about Hunter.

BEN FEE began working as an assistant to Hunter at Owl Farm in January 2004.

DAVID FELTON was a *Rolling Stone* editor in the seventies.

TIM FERRIS was the New York bureau chief of *Rolling Stone* and is the author of numerous books on astronomy.

DEBORAH FULLER was Hunter's assistant from 1982 to 2003, living in the cabin adjacent to Hunter's house at Owl Farm.

DR. BOB GEIGER, an orthopedic surgeon and novelist in Sonoma, California, met Hunter in 1964.

JACK GERMOND was a national political reporter covering the 1972 presidential campaign for the Gannett papers.

TERRY GILLIAM directed *Fear and Loathing in Las Vegas,* as well as other films, including *Brazil, Twelve Monkeys,* and *The Fisher King.*

MITCH GLAZER is a screenwriter and producer in Los Angeles.

GERRY GOLDSTEIN is a board member of the National Organization to Reform Marijuana Laws and a past president of the National Association of Criminal Defense Lawyers.

MIRIAM GOOD and her husband, Lloyd, own Sugarloaf Lodge on Sugarloaf Key, Florida.

RICHARD GOODWIN is a former speechwriter and adviser to John F. Kennedy, Robert Kennedy, and Lyndon Johnson, and a former contributing editor of *Rolling Stone.*

WILLIAM GREIDER, a former *Washington Post* assistant managing editor, replaced Hunter as national affairs editor of *Rolling Stone* in 1982.

GAYLORD GUENIN is an Aspen writer and editor.

STACEY HADASH was a member of the Clinton campaign "War Room" staff during the 1992 presidential campaign.

HAL HADDON, formerly a campaign manager for Gary Hart, is a criminal-defense attorney in Denver.

DAVID HALBERSTAM was a Pulitzer Prize–winning journalist and the author of numerous books, including *The Best and the Brightest*.

MARY HARRIS and her husband, Shep, own the Woody Creek Tavern.

JOHN D. (JERRY) HAWKE served in the air force with Hunter and was his roommate in New York while attending Columbia University.

ROGER HAWKE roomed with his brother Jerry and Hunter while attending law school at Columbia.

WARREN HINCKLE was the editor of *Ramparts* and *Scanlan's* magazines in San Francisco.

ANJELICA HUSTON, the actress, visited Aspen regularly in the seventies and eighties.

LOU ANN ILER was a childhood sweetheart of Hunter's.

LOREN JENKINS moved to Aspen in the sixties and was the Saigon bureau chief for *Newsweek* during the Vietnam War.

DON JOHNSON, the actor (*Miami Vice*, *Nash Bridges*), was Hunter's neighbor in Woody Creek.

JEFF KASS is a reporter for the *Rocky Mountain News*.

WILLIAM KENNEDY was the managing editor of Puerto Rico's *San Juan Star* in 1959. Kennedy has published many novels, including *Ironweed*, which won the Pulitzer Prize.

MARGOT KIDDER, the actress, met Hunter in the mid-seventies in Key West.

SARAH LAZIN joined *Rolling Stone* in 1971 as an editorial assistant.

SEMMES LUCKETT was a law school dropout working at a restaurant in Aspen in the seventies.

NORMAN MAILER has twice won the Pulitzer Prize — for *Armies of the Night* and *The Executioner's Song.*

FRANK MANKIEWICZ was George McGovern's campaign manager.

MARILYN MANSON is a musical artist.

DAVID MCCUMBER was Hunter's editor at the *San Francisco Examiner* in the mid-eighties.

TERRY MCDONELL is a former managing editor of *Rolling Stone.*

GENE MCGARR was a copyboy at *Time* magazine in New York in 1958, and Hunter's roommate.

GEORGE MCGOVERN, a former U.S. senator, was the Democratic candidate for president in 1972.

SARAH MURRAY began working as an assistant to Hunter in November 2004.

LAILA NABULSI met Hunter in 1977 while she was working at *Saturday Night Live* and later produced the movie *Fear and Loathing in Las Vegas.*

LYNN NESBIT was Hunter's literary agent for more than thirty years.

JACK NICHOLSON, the actor, has a home in Aspen.

PAUL OAKENFOLD is a British DJ and producer.

ANN OWLSLEY was a Woody Creek neighbor of Hunter's.

PAUL PASCARELLA, an artist, moved to Aspen in 1968. He helped create the "gonzo fist" logo.

SEAN PENN, the actor, was in talks with Hunter regarding a film of *The Rum Diary*.

CHARLES PERRY was *Rolling Stone*'s first copy chief. He is the author of *The Haight-Ashbury: A History*.

TOBIAS PERSE was an editorial assistant at *Rolling Stone* in 1994.

PETE PETERS was a friend of Hunter's younger brother Jim.

ROXANNE PULITZER met Hunter while he was covering her 1983 divorce trial in Palm Beach.

SALLY QUINN, formerly a reporter for the *Washington Post,* is an author and hostess in Washington, D.C.

CLIFFORD RIDLEY was Hunter's editor at the *National Observer* from 1962 to 1965.

ALAN RINZLER is a book editor who worked with Hunter on several projects.

CURTIS ROBINSON is a former editor of the *Aspen Daily News.*

CATHERINE SABONIS-BRADLEY began working as an assistant to Hunter in 1990.

TERRY SABONIS-CHAFEE was working at an Aspen-area energy think tank when she met Hunter in 1989.

SHELBY SADLER began working for Hunter as an editor and researcher in 1986.

PAUL SCANLON is a former managing editor of *Rolling Stone.*

PAUL SEMONIN was a childhood friend of Hunter's in Louisville.

COREY SEYMOUR was an editorial assistant at *Rolling Stone* in 1992.

JAMES SILBERMAN assigned Hunter his first book, *Hell's Angels,* when Silberman was editor in chief of Random House.

MICHAEL SOLHEIM managed the Jerome Bar in Aspen in the seventies.

BILL STANKEY was Hunter's lecture agent for thirteen years, starting in 1983.

ANNA STEADMAN is the wife of Ralph Steadman.

RALPH STEADMAN, the illustrator, began a long collaboration with Hunter in 1970 while on assignment to cover the Kentucky Derby.

LOU STEIN is a theater director who staged *Fear and Loathing in Las Vegas* at the Gate Theatre in London in 1982.

MICHAEL STEPANIAN is on the board of the National Organization to Reform Marijuana Laws and is a member of the National Association of Criminal Defense Lawyers.

GEORGE STRANAHAN is a founder of the Aspen Center for Physics, the former owner of the Woody Creek Tavern, and the former landlord of Owl Farm.

PATTI STRANAHAN is the wife of George Stranahan.

JACK THIBEAU, an actor and writer, met Hunter in San Francisco in 1964.

JUAN THOMPSON, Hunter and Sandy's son, was born in 1964.

SANDY THOMPSON (now Sondi Wright) married Hunter in 1963. They divorced in 1980.

GEORGE TOBIA was Hunter's literary lawyer and is now an executor of his estate.

SARI TUSCHMAN began working as an assistant to Hunter in June 2004.

GERALD TYRRELL was an early childhood friend of Hunter's in Louisville.

KALLEN VON RENKL was a cocktail waitress at the Jerome Bar in Aspen.

JOHN WALSH, a former managing editor of *Rolling Stone,* is now a senior vice president and executive editor of ESPN, Inc.

TEX WEAVER was a Woody Creek neighbor of Hunter's.

JANE WENNER is the wife of Jann Wenner and a vice president of Wenner Media.

JANN WENNER is the founder, editor, and publisher of *Rolling Stone*.

JOHN WILBUR is a former guard for the Washington Redskins.

TOM WOLFE is the author of *The Electric Kool-Aid Acid Test, The Right Stuff,* and *Bonfire of the Vanities,* among many other titles.

BARNEY WYCOFF is an Aspen gallery owner.

ACKNOWLEDGMENTS

Fifteen years ago, Jann charged me with being Hunter's aide-de-camp in New York. Two and a half years ago, he directed me to compile Hunter's life story. I'm grateful to him for the opportunity, direction, leadership, advice, wisdom, and the many good times along the way.

Paul Scanlon, a *Rolling Stone* veteran who helped edit and shape this book into its present form from an unwieldy manuscript more than three times this size, provided genius edits and institutional knowledge, esprit de corps, and a necessary dose of sanity. The trustees of Hunter's estate — Hal Haddon, George Tobia, and especially Doug Brinkley — were invaluable allies, and my heartfelt thanks goes out to Hunter's family and closest friends, both current and former. It was one of the privileges of my life to meet each and every one of them to talk about my old hero. Some couldn't wait to pass on the rich tales they'd been storing up for decades; others enjoyed my interviews with them as much as oral surgery without Novocain — or laughing gas. I'm grateful to both camps, and especially to Tobias Perse for the comradeship on the Hunter beat at *Rolling Stone*. A number of people close to

Hunter—Ed Bradley, Tom Benton, John Clancy, David Halberstam, and Gene McGarr—have also died since work on this book began. So did one person very close to me—my mother, Betty Seymour, to whose memory my work on this book is dedicated.

Corey Seymour

INDEX

Acosta, Oscar Zeta ("Brown
Buffalo"), 104, 128–31, 144,
202, 218, 345, 359
as "Dr. Gonzo," xiii, 109
Hunter talks about, 145–46, 227,
357
Adventures of Augie March, The
(Bellow), 45
Adventures of Huckleberry Finn, The
(Twain), 45
Advertisements for Myself (Mailer), 45,
435
Agee, James, 45
Akroyd, Dan, 216, 249
Alcohol, Tobacco and Firearms
(ATF) division of the Treasury
Department, 108–9
Alcoholics Anonymous (AA), 241,
408
Algren, Nelson, 45
Ali, Muhammad (Cassius Clay), xx
fights Foreman, 190, 191, 208
Allott, Gordon, 189

All the King's Men (movie), 416
Amazing Rhythm Aces, 226
Ambrose, Stephen, 314
America's Cup race, 124
Amram, David, 352
Angelou, Maya, 71
Animal House (movie), 218, 225
Apple, R. W. "Johnny," 161, 163
Armstrong, Jeff, 266, 267, 270–71
"Ask Not for Whom the Bell Tolls"
(Thompson), 170–71
Aspen, Colorado, 101–4, 118–19,
213–14, 281
Hunter's ideas for changing,
111–12, 114
Aspen Daily News, 346
Aspen Illustrated News, 100, 118
Athenaeum Literary Association, 8,
11–13, 15, 17–19
Hunter barred from, 18
Auman, Lisl, 389–91, 418
Ayers, Dr. Steve, 369, 394, 396,
427

Baez, Joan, 54
Baker, Ginger, 322
Baldwin, James, 44–45
Ballantine, Ian, 75
"Banshee Screams for Buffalo Meat,
    The" (Thompson), 145–46
Bantam Books, 233
Barger, Sonny, 80, 83–86, 88, 108
Baskin, Alan, 104
Bastian, Ed, 105–10, 113, 114, 374
Bates, Eric, 407
Battle, Kathleen, 299
"Battle of Aspen, The"
    (Thompson), xiii, 111–12
Baxt, Paula, 273
Baxter, Tiny, 81, 83
BBC documentary about Hunter,
    292
Beat Generation Conference,
    315–16
Beatty, Warren, 172, 418
Behind the Green Door (movie), 266
Bejmuk, Anita. See Thompson, Anita
Bell, Joe, 5
Bellow, Saul, 45
Belushi, John, 216–17, 227–28,
    238–39, 241, 247, 420
Belushi, Judy, 218, 224–25, 238, 242
Benton, Tom, 104–7, 113–14, 118,
    223, 230–31, 289, 339, 341, 431
    political poster by, 106, 170
Bergen, Candace, 228
Berger, Sandy, 171, 186–88, 198–99
Bermuda Gazette, 50
Bernstein, Carl, 402
Bernstein, Leonard, 56
Better Than Sex (Thompson), 310,
    311, 332

Bibb, Porter, 6, 8, 11–20, 22–23,
    429
Bierce, Ambrose, 344
Billings, Josh, 436
Biss, Earl, 288
Blakemore, Neville, 3–5, 12, 15–19
Bone, Bob, 38–39, 42, 44, 47,
    56–60
Booker, James, 126
Boston Globe Magazine, 126
Bowie, David, 173, 302
"Boys on the Bus, The" (Crouse),
    174
Bradley, Ed, 240, 259, 299, 302, 389,
    414–15, 419–20
    at Owl Farm, 312, 380
    and politics, 268; Carter
    campaign, 212–13, 440
Bradley, Patricia, 414
Brando, Marlon, xxiv, 16
Braudis, Bob, 264, 338, 372,
    398–400
    appointed sheriff, 115; and drug
    search, 283–86
    and Hunter's girlfriends, 220,
    249–50, 295, 304
    Hunter's relationship with,
    183, 239, 252, 260, 288–89,
    336, 381–82, 395, 410, 437;
    intervention, 339; travel,
    352–53
    and Hunter's suicide, 425–26
    and Hunter's writing, 374, 386
Brenda (secretary), 291
Brinkley, Doug, 123, 314–15,
    330–32, 348, 351, 378–79
    on Hunter's personality, 9–11,
    19–20, 22–25, 263, 344–46,

383, 397–98; politics, 380–81,
405; suicide, 416–20, 432–33
on Hunter's writings, 434–35
Majic Bus, The, 309–11
and origin of "gonzo," "fear and
loathing," 125–26, 128–29
works with Hunter, 356, 371–72
Brodie, John, 78
Brokaw, Tom, 244
Bromley, Chuck, 108
Brown, Lee and Martin, 17
Brown-Forman distillery, 16–17
Bryan, William Jennings, 315
Buchanan, Pat, 126–27, 184
Buckley, William, 198
Buddhism, 53, 110, 430
"Buffalo Gores a Visitor"
(Thompson), 266–67
Buffett, Jane, 219
Buffett, Jimmy, 219, 222, 224, 243,
257, 378
talks about Hunter, 193–94,
225–26, 415
Burke, Dave, 186, 187
Burke, Edmund, 390
Burroughs, William, 344
Bush, George H. W., 380, 406
Bush, George W., 405, 406

Caddell, Pat, 172, 186, 199, 245,
268
in political campaigns, 163–64,
170, 188–89, 211–12
Cahill, Tim, 139, 140–41
Campbell, Frank and Pauline, 23
Camus, Albert, 45
Cannibals and Christians (Mailer),
435

Cape Fear (movie), 424
Captain Steve, 231–32
Cardozo, Bill, 126, 190
Carpenter, Doug, 250
Carter, Graydon, 389
Carter, Jimmy, 188, 209–12, 380
Carville, James, 305, 306, 308,
311–12, 416
Cassady, Neal, 11, 81, 383
Castro, Fidel, 235–36
Cather, Willa, 309
Chambers, Marilyn, 270
Cheech and Chong's Up in Smoke
(movie), 225
Chitti, Monte ("Boohoo"), 163, 164,
181
Churchill, Winston, 344–45
CIA (Central Intelligence Agency),
202
"Cigarette Key" (Thompson and
Corcoran), 225
Clancy, John, 27–30, 52–54, 72–73,
77, 79, 83–84, 93–94, 104,
198
Clay, Cassius. *See* Ali, Muhammad
Cleveland Plain Dealer, 131
Cleverly, Michael, 213, 15, 246–47,
338, 376, 400
Clifford, Peggy, 66
Clinton, Bill, 186, 305–13, 380,
439
Clinton, Roger, 308
Club Wow, 70
CNN (Cable News Network), 300,
311, 315, 345, 427
Cobain, Kurt, 387
Cohen, Leonard, 332
Cohen, Rich, 406–7

Coleridge, Samuel Taylor, 274, 347
Colorado, first civil rights suit in,
    101
Colorado Bureau of Investigation,
    109
Colson, Charles "Chuck," 184
Command Courier (air force base
    newspaper), 23–25
Conklin, Sandy. *See* Thompson,
    Sandy
Conrad, Joseph, 88, 338
Cook, Captain James, 231, 233
Corcoran, Tom, 225
Corenman, Dr. (at Vail clinic),
    393
Cox, Alex, 349–51
Craig, Bob, 94, 103
Crawdaddy magazine, 227
Crouse, Tim, 156–60, 174
Cuomo, Mario, 268
Curse of Lono, The (Thompson),
    233–35, 399, 408
Cusack, John, xxi

Dalai Lama, the, 110
Daly, John, 191
DAs' (district attorneys')
    convention, 130, 137, 350
Death in the Family, A (Agee), 45
*Death of the American Dream,
    The* (imaginary title), 99
Decameron, The (Boccaccio), 45
de la Valdene, Guy, 243
Del Toro, Benicio, 365, 408
Democratic National Conventions,
    99, 100, 268
Democratic Party, 186, 380
Denver Broncos, 400

Depp, Johnny, xix–xxiv, 331–34,
    356, 374, 389, 407, 429
    assumes Hunter's persona for
    film, 348–49, 357–59, 363–66
    as "the Colonel" or "Ray," xxii,
    xxiv, 334, 351–52, 360–62
Dibble, Dan, 129, 336
Dillon, Matt, 348
Dinesen, Isak, 45
DiSalva, Joey, 400
Dixon, Bill, 183–84, 209, 212, 254,
    268
Dixon, Don, 376
Dixon, Willie, 332
Doctorow, E. L., 215
"Dog Took My Place, A"
    (Thompson), xvi, 245–46
Donleavy, J. P., 45
Donnie Brasco (movie), xxi, 348
Don Quixote (Cervantes), 45
Doonesbury (comic strip), 198, 344
Dos Passos, John, 45
Dowd, Maureen, 311
Duke, Raoul (pseudonym), 133, 136,
    179, 274
Dylan, Bob, xxiv, 332

Editor & Publisher (periodical), 25
Edwards, Joe, 101–5, 108, 109,
    112–15, 129, 275
Eisele, Al, 160–61
Eisenhower, Dwight, 309
Electric Kool-Aid Acid Test, The
    (Wolfe), 142
Elko conference, 185–88
Ellerbee, Linda, 268
Ellison, Ralph, 45
Esalen Institute, 52, 54, 149

ESPN columns, 383–84, 390, 398, 401, 402, 418, 423
Esquire magazine, 236
Eszterhas, Joe, xvii, 131–32, 142, 143
Etheridge, Jeanette, 266, 268, 270, 389, 399
Ewing, Deborah, 270
Ewing, Wayne, 269–71, 349–55, 385

Faulkner, William, 45, 338
"Fear and Loathing" as phrase, 128
"Fear and Loathing at the Super Bowl" (Thompson), 179, 185
Fear and Loathing in America (Thompson), 348, 356, 434
"Fear and Loathing in Elko" (Thompson), xvi, 318–19
"Fear and Loathing in the Eye of the Hurricane" (Thompson), 61–62, 161–62
"Fear and Loathing in Horse Country." *See* "Polo Is My Life"
Fear and Loathing in Las Vegas (Thompson), xiii–xiv, 82, 136–37, 210, 258, 332, 423
characters in, xiii, 109, 202, 313
criticism of, 267
Hunter starts, continues writing, 129, 138, 174; writes memo on, 134–36
movie version of, xxi–xxii, 248–49, 348–51, 362–66, 387; shown on TV, 403
praised, 132–33, 435, 436; "Elko" compared to, 318
publication of, 138, 147; Modern

Library 25th-anniversary edition, 336, 348, 349, 351
sales of, 146–47; unsold copies, xv, 147, 242, 329
stage play version of, 247–48, 447
young people reading, 309, 373
"Fear and Loathing in Saigon" (Thompson), 201
Fear and Loathing on the Campaign Trail '72 (Thompson), 171–74, 185, 233, 332, 402, 435
Hunter's memo about, 166–69
Fear and Trembling (Kierkegaard), 128
Fee, Ben, 400–401, 410–11, 412–13, 421–24
Felton, David, 130–31, 169, 210–11
Ferris, Tim, 132, 173, 262, 280, 360, 369–70, 396
and *Rolling Stone* conference, 148–49
Finkelstein, Alan, 332–33
Fire in the Nuts (Thompson), 415
Fitzgerald, F. Scott, 43, 45, 68, 274, 298
Hunter influenced by, 12, 23, 28, 338, 435
Flat, Lester, 332
Foreman, George, and Ali-Foreman fight, 190–91, 208
Fort Walton Playground News, 23, 24
Forty Niners football team, 78, 79, 83
Fountainhead, The (Rand), 13
Fourth Amendment, 307, 308
Fourth Amendment "Foundation," 288
Franklin, Benjamin, 260

"Freak Power in the Rockies"
(Thompson), 128
Friedman, Kinky, 381
Frontline (TV series), 269
Fuller, Deborah, 4, 222–23
as Hunter's assistant, 249–50,
261–63, 273–75, 334, 398;
leaves, 279
life at Owl Farm, 253–59, 300,
303, 317, 320–21, 325, 336,
342–43, 356, 359; last months,
367–69, 371, 376, 379, 395,
397–98, 432
Fuller, Kristine, 223

Gannett newspapers, 156
Garbage (band), 332
Geiger, Dr. Bob, 70–74, 75–77,
82–83
Geiger, Terri, 76
Generation of Swine (Thompson),
344
Germond, Jack, 156–57, 161, 210
Getty, Ann, 268
Gilliam, Terry, 351, 358, 362–66,
442
Ginger Man, The (Donleavy), 45,
134
Ginsberg, Allen, 32, 81–82, 116–17,
316–17, 362, 383
Glazer, Mitch, 227–28, 409–10
Goddard, Don, 120
Godfrey, Arthur, 25
Goldstein, Gerry, 259, 282, 287,
295–97, 374, 390
"Gonzo"
gonzo paraphernalia, 342, 415;
bikini, 280; logo, 445

Hunter's gonzo behavior, xv, 90,
111, 174, 216, 383; vs. private
persona, 200, 301
instrumental song, 126
origin of, as writing, 125–26
as term, now in dictionaries, 434
"Gonzo, Dr.," xiii, 248, 357
Gonzo Papers, The (Thompson), 345,
419
Good, Miriam and Lloyd, 235–38
Goodwin, Doris Kearns, 186, 309
Goodwin, Richard "Dick," 186,
189–90, 432
Gorbachev, Mikhail, 294
Gothic Tales (Dinesen), 45
Graciela, Carlos and Memo, 322
Grasso, Mary, 342
Great Gatsby, The (Fitzgerald), 12, 45,
73, 99, 245, 274–75, 298
Great Shark Hunt, The (Thompson),
195, 237, 435
Green, Norvin, 16
Green Bay Packers, 25, 83
Greene, Graham, 203
Gregory, Dick, 380
Grenada, U.S. invasion of, 208,
246–47
Grieder, William "Bill," 305–8
Guenin, Gaylord, 100, 118, 341

Hadash, Stacey, 311–13, 400,
401–2
Hadden, Briton, 179
Haddon, Hal, 281–83, 285, 286–87,
390–91
Haight-Ashbury scene, 75, 101
Halberstam, David, 142, 311, 434,
436, 443

"Half Moon Tapes, The" (cassettes recorded at Elko), 188
Harris, Mary, 264
Harrison, Jim, 226, 243
Hart, Brooke, 399
Hart, Gary, 188–89, 268, 380
Hawke, John D. "Jerry," 23, 27, 29, 72–73
Hawke, Roger, 27, 28, 73
Hearst, Will, 266–67, 269
Hearst, William Randolph, 186
Heart of Darkness (Conrad), 88
Hefner, Hugh, 266, 408
Heidi (assistant), 368, 395
Hellfire Club, The (Mannix), 260
Hells Angels, 75, 77–82, 86, 120, 129, 142, 208, 316
    Hunter beaten up, threatened by, 84–85, 108
    photographs of, 95
    "Tiny," security guard for Hunter, 251
Hell's Angels (Thompson), 74, 75, 77, 82, 142, 174, 179, 313
    admiration/success of, 88–90, 97, 110, 116, 131, 373
    excerpt from, 86–88
Hemingway, Ernest, 23, 42, 45, 69, 194, 233, 381, 431
    Hunter influenced by, 12, 28, 338, 435
Henley, Don, 118
Hersh, Seymour, 311
Hess, Rudolf, 100
Hey Rube (Thompson), 386
Highway 61 (record album), 134
Hitler, Adolf, 100, 124, 358
Honolulu Marathon, 230, 399

Hopper, Dennis, 331
Howlin' Wolf, 332
Hudson, Jo, 54
Humphrey, Hubert, 157, 158, 164, 167–68
Hunter S. Thompson Day, 351–52
Huston, Anjelica, 181–83, 227, 229, 240–41, 296–97, 408–9

Iler, Lou Ann, 6–8, 10, 20–21, 24
Inferno, The (Dante), 45
Ink Truck, The (Kennedy), 63
Innocents Abroad (Twain), 436
Intel corporation, 128
"Interdicted Dispatch from the Global Affairs Desk" (Thompson), 204–5
Irsay, James, 389
Isaacson, Walter, 311, 389

Jack Daniel's company, 17
Jack's Joke Shop, 334–35
Jarvis, Birney, 80
Jefferson Airplane, 76
Jenco, Sal, 389
Jenkins, Loren, 93, 104, 215–16, 223, 246, 47
    Hunter's advice to, 66–67
    in Vietnam, 201–4, 206, 207–8
Jenkins, Nancy, 223
Jerome Bar, 98, 109, 116, 118, 213–14
Jerry's bar, 133, 179
Johnson, Don, 312, 338, 374–76, 389, 430–31, 443
Johnson, Kelly, 375
Johnson, Lyndon, 189
Junkie George, 84–85

Kass, Jeff, 389–90, 391, 418
Kearns, Doris. *See* Goodwin, Doris
  Kearns
Kelly, Mike, 283
Kennedy, Bobby, 99, 154, 186, 189
Kennedy, Dana, 43, 392
Kennedy, Ethel, 189–90
Kennedy, Jackie, 189
Kennedy, John F., 68, 151, 186, 189
Kennedy, Ted, 186, 187, 188, 209
Kennedy, William "Bill," 42–50, 68,
  90, 104, 109, 183, 215, 336,
  392–93, 420, 444
  on Hunter's writing, 62–63, 124,
  127, 141–43, 216, 331, 337–38
Kentucky Colonels, 351–52, 356
Kentucky Derby, 120, 258, 259
"Kentucky Derby Is Decadent and
  Depraved, The" (Thompson),
  110, 122–26
Kerouac, Jack, xxiv, 11, 32, 344,
  382
Kerry, John, 380, 403, 404–5, 407
Kesey, Ken, 79–80, 81–82, 142,
  383
KGB (Soviet State Security
  Committee), 293, 294
Khan, Maria, 249–50, 270, 378,
  392
Kidd, Billy, 116
Kidder, Margot, 178–79, 194,
  267–68
Kienast, Dick, 113–14, 115
Kierkegaard, Søren, 128
Kingdom of Fear, The (Thompson),
  392, 422, 424
Knight Ridder newspapers, 160
Korn (band), 332

La Raza movement, 128
Law, Jude, 417
Lawrence, D. H., 45
Lazin, Sarah, 165–66
Leary, Timothy, 97, 133
Leaves of Grass (Whitman), 309
le Carré, John, 292
Letterman, David, 389
Lewis, Grover, 132, 133
Liddy, G. Gordon, 252
Lie Down in Darkness (Styron), 45
Linson, Art, 227
Logan, Judge, and son George, 19
London, Jack, 417
Lono (Polynesian god), 230–31,
  233
Los Angeles Free Press, 104
Lotos Club party, 336–37
Louisville, Hunter S. Thompson
  Day in, 351–52
Louisville Courier-Journal, 15, 47
Lovett, Lyle, 332
Luce, Henry, 179
Luckett, Celeste, 196
Luckett, Semmes, 196–97, 222, 275,
  284, 411

MacArthur, General Douglas,
  69–70
McCrory, Chip, 283
McCumber, David, 266–67, 269,
  278–79
McDonell, Terry, 243–44, 299,
  300
McGarr, Eleanor, 35, 37, 39, 40,
  53
McGarr, Gene, 25–40, 47, 49–54,
  72–73, 97–98

McGovern, Eleanor, 159
McGovern, George, 174, 281, 288,
    309, 315, 380
  1972 campaign, xiv, 139, 148,
    153–73, 183, 186–87
McGuane, Tom, 178, 194, 226, 243
McNamara, Robert, 70
Mailer, Norman, 32, 45, 190–92,
    344, 435, 444
Majic Bus, The (Brinkley), 309–11
Malcolm X, 71
Malle, Louis, 228
Mankiewicz, Frank, 154–55, 163,
    173
Mann, Herbie, 126
Mann, Michael, 225
Mannix, Daniel, 260
Manson, Marilyn, 407–8
Man with the Golden Arm, The
    (Algren), 45
Mariel boatlift (Cuba), 235–36
Mayfield, Julian, 71
Meat Possum Press, 104
Mencken, H. L., 315, 344
Men's Journal, 384
Merry Pranksters, 81–82, 142
Meyer, Guido, 101, 103
Meyer, Nicole, 302–3, 304, 309–11,
    378
Miami Herald, 43
Middletown Daily Record, 35, 38, 42,
    43, 50
Midnight Express (movie), 225
Mint 500 motorcycle race, 128, 350
Missionaries of the New Truth, 104
"Mister Tambourine Man" (song),
    134, 360
Mitchell, Joni, 178

Mitchell brothers, 266–67, 270, 288
Mobutu Sese Seko, 191
Monroe, Bill, 332
Morrison, Van, 332
Murphy, Dennis and Mike, 52
Murphy, Vinnie, 53, 55
Murray, Bill, 224, 227–28, 237, 409
Murray, Sarah, 413–14, 421–22
Muskie, Edmund, 158, 163

Nabulsi, Laila, 408–9, 420
  meets, follows Hunter, 216–18,
    224–39, 241, 378, 431; leaves,
    242–43, 246; trial reunions,
    247–49
  and *Vegas* movie, 348, 349, 364
Nader, Ralph, 380
Naked Lunch (Burroughs), 134
Nasby, Petroleum V., 436
Nash Bridges (TV series), 374–75
Nation, The, 75, 86
National Association of Criminal
    Defense Lawyers, 259, 442
National Lampoon's Animal House
    (movie), 218, 225
National Observer, 56, 60–62, 69, 71,
    83
Nelson, Willie, 332
Nesbit, Lynn, 89–90, 202, 291, 301,
    330–31, 428–29
New Journalism, 128–29, 142–43
New Journalism anthology (Wolfe and
    Johnson), 142
Newsweek, 201, 206, 439
New Yorker, The, 434
New York Times, 120, 161, 163, 244,
    285
  Times Tower, 43

Nicholson, Jack, 97, 118, 315, 331, 418
  in Aspen, 181–82, 214, 227, 296–97
  talks about Hunter, 258–62, 343, 368, 415, 432
Night Manager, The (Steadman painting), 266
"Night Manager, The" (Thompson), 266
9/11 attack, 355, 435
Nixon, Richard, 154, 172, 314
  campaigns of: 1968, 126–27; 1972, see McGovern, George
  Hunter's hatred of, 154, 170–71, 179, 188, 309, 387–88
  Hunter's stories on, 166, 184–85, 200, 202, 403–4; obituary, 314–15; quoted, 168–69, 170–71
  impeachment and resignation of, 183–85, 200
"Nixon's Spirit" (CD track), 388–89
Nolte, Nick, 389
Noonan, Jimmy, 65
NORML (National Organization for the Reform of Marijuana Law) conference, 259, 442
NRA (National Rifle Association), 275

Oakenfold, Paul, 387–89
O'Connor, Flannery, 45
O'Farrell Theatre (San Francisco), Hunter as night manager of, 266–67, 269–70
Oliphant, Pat, 120
Ono, Yoko, 299, 302

On the Road (Kerouac), 11
"Open Letter to the Youth of Our Nation" (Thompson), 15–16
O'Rourke, P. J., 305, 307
Owl Farm, life at, 93, 105, 117, 178, 182, 213, 264–66, 271, 312, 377, 380
  early days, 94–98; Sandy leaves, 218–23
  Johnny Depp at, xx, xxii, 333–34, 359–60
  Laila and, 228, 234, 238; leaves, 242, 249
  preservation of, 420
  searched for drugs, 284–86
  See also Fuller, Deborah
Owlsley, Ann, 342

Pageant magazine, 70, 126
Palevsky, Max, 150, 154
Palmer-Slater, Gail, 282–83, 287–88
Paramount Pictures, 225
Parton, Dolly, 222
Pascarella, Paul, 102–3, 114, 117–19, 193, 265, 275
Penn, Sean, 331–32, 387, 389, 399, 408, 415–19
Perry, Charles, 129–30, 132–34, 139–40, 148, 150, 445
  as "El Ropo," 166–69
Perry, Paul, 230
Perse, Tobias, 320–26, 328–29
Peters, Pete, 313, 314
Petitclerc, Denne, 67
Pierce, David, 79, 90
Plague, The (Camus), 45
Playboy magazine, 266, 268, 416
Plimpton, George, 382

Police Chief magazine, 150
"Polo Is My Life: Fear and
    Loathing in Horse Country"
    (Thompson), xvi, 273–75, 298,
    318, 320, 326–27, 331
"Popo the Killer Jap" (Thompson),
    26
Postman Always Rings Twice, The
    (movie), 259
Powell, Jody, 209
Prince Jellyfish (Thompson), 32, 40, 63
Profitt, Nick, 203
Proud Highway, The (Thompson),
    346, 348, 361, 420
Proust, Marcel, 45
Puerto Rico World Journal, 43
Pulitzer, Roxanne, 243, 244–45
Pulitzer vs. Pulitzer, 246

Quiet American, The (Greene), 203
Quinn, Sally, 198–200

Rafelson, Bob, 118, 181, 258, 259
"Ramundo" (mysterious caller),
    361–62
Rand, Ayn, 13
Random House, 86, 89
Reagan, Ronald, 380, 405
Reagan, Ron Jr., 268
Real Peace (Nixon), 403
Redford, Robert, 116
Reluctant Surgeon, The (Kobler), 254
Republican National Convention
    (1964), 435
Republican Party, 380
Reston, James "Scotty," 311
Rice, Duke, 9
Richards, Keith, 302

Ridley, Clifford, 61–62
Rinzler, Alan, 233–35, 252
Robinson, Curtis, 346–47, 354–55,
    358, 390, 415, 431–32
Rockefeller, Nelson, 105
Rocky Mountain News, 389–90
Rodino, Peter, 183
Rogue magazine, 55
Rolling Stone magazine, 144, 150, 233,
    298
    editorial conference at Big Sur,
        148–50, 156
    Hunter's relationship with, xvii,
        179, 210, 243–44; visits,
        132–34, 340–41
    Hunter writes for, xiii–xv, 110–11,
        131–33, 138–39, 141–42, 156,
        185, 196, 212; deadlines,
        129–30, 139, 175–77; excerpts,
        136–37, 245–47; full-time job,
        148, 152; high standards, 230;
        memo about, 134–36; Nixon's
        obituary, 314-15; payment, 153,
        330, 405; on politics, 155-57,
        185; Vietnam War dispatches,
        201, 204–7; work diminishes,
        384–87; writes rejection letter
        for, 140
    and politics, 156, 185, 188, 305–6;
        as Democratic Party "house
        organ," 161; Kerry campaign,
        403–5; McGovern campaign,
        164, 165, 170
    profile of Hunter in, 406
    25th-anniversary party, 299–302
    and Vegas book, 146–47
    See also Wenner, Jann
Rolling Stones, xxiv, 86

Romney, George, 105
Roosevelt, Franklin, 344–45
Rose, Charlie, 382, 389
Rose Bowl game, 260
Rove, Karl, 216, 405
"Rumble in the Jungle," 190–92
Rum Diary, The (Thompson), 46–47,
    48, 62–63, 330–31, 344
  movie version, 401
Running magazine, 230
Ruwe, Nicholas, 127

Sabonis-Bradley, Catherine, 278–80,
    282–83, 286, 290, 294
Sabonis-Chafee, Terry, 277–78,
    280, 285–86, 289–90, 292–95,
    346–47, 378
Sadler, Shelby, 272–75, 347, 377–78,
    403–4
Safire, William, 161
Saigon, fall of, 200–201, 207
Salinger, J. D., 45
Salter, Jim, 116
San Francisco Chronicle, 80
San Francisco Examiner, 266, 384
San Juan Star, 42–44
Saturday Night Live (TV program),
    216, 224, 227–28
Scanlan's magazine, 120, 123–25
Scanlon, Paul, 131, 132–33, 143–44,
    174, 179, 185, 201
  Hunter's Vietnam memo to,
    206–7
Schaffer, Paul, 224
Scorsese, Martin, 249
Screwjack (Thompson), 422
Scrooged (movie), 228
Scruggs, Earl, 332

"Security" (Thompson), 16
Seliger, Mark, 305
Sellers, Peter, 69
Semonin, Paul, 39–40, 79–80,
    99–100
  early days with Hunter, 12–15, 18,
    32–35, 47, 49–50, 66–67, 430;
  breaks with, 71–72, 314
Sergeant, The (Murphy), 52
Seymour, Corey, 298–304, 315–17,
    320–24, 339–40
Shapiro, Greg, 389
Silberman, James, 86, 88–89, 99,
    146–47, 196
Soldier of Fortune magazine, 265
Solheim, Michael, 69–70, 106, 108,
    116–17, 195, 221–22, 272, 410
Songs of the Doomed (Thompson),
    275, 278, 344
Sound and the Fury, The (Faulkner), 45
Soviet Academy of Sciences, 293
Spectator, The (magazine), 12, 15–16,
    17
Spector, Judith, 54
Sports Illustrated, 128
Springsteen, Bruce, 332
Stankey, Bill, 250–52, 290–92
Stanley Brothers, 332
Stanton, Harry Dean, 331, 387, 408
Starr, Bart, 25
Steadman, Anna, 371, 373–74
Steadman, Ralph, 123–25, 141, 146,
    196–97, 230–32, 247, 337, 373,
    389
  first meets Hunter, 120–22
  Hunter in competition with, 342,
    350
  works by, 120, 228, 233, 255,

266, 350; Hunter quoted
on, 134–35; Hunter writes
introduction to book of, 358
tribute to Hunter, 436–37
in Zaire, at Ali-Foreman fight,
190–91
Stearns, Rick, 186
Steadman, Ralston, 17, 18
Steiger, Rod, 52
Stein, Lou, 247–48
Steinbeck, John, 309
Stepanian, Michael, 282, 325,
390–91, 399, 430
Stephanopoulos, George, 307–8
Still Life with Raspberry (Steadman),
120
"Stockton, Thorne" (pseudonym),
24
Stone, Oliver, 225
Stranahan, Ben, 276–77
Stranahan, George, 94–95, 116,
239–40, 264–66, 275, 276–77,
284–85, 341–43, 413
and Hunter's and Sandy's
finances, 94, 138, 223, 252
tribute to Hunter, 431
Stranahan, Patti, 264, 275–76, 277,
421
"Strange and Terrible Saga of the
Outlaw Motorcycle Gangs,
The" (Thompson), 86–88
"Strange Rumblings in Aztlan"
(Thompson), 128, 129
Styron, William, 45
Suarez, J. C., 120
Sun Also Rises, The (Hemingway), 47
Sunday Night Football, 400
Super Bowl, 178–79, 185, 259, 421

Talese, Gay, 142
Tapper, Jake, 389
Terry the Tramp, 87, 88
Thibeau, Jack, 73, 77–78, 85, 90–91,
97–98
Thomas, Dylan, 45
Thompson, Anita (second wife),
376, 378, 383, 385
marriage with Hunter, 392, 395,
397–406, 411, 413–14, 418–19,
421–26
Thompson, Davison (brother), 6, 9,
64, 122, 229, 314, 430
Thompson, Hunter S.
in air force, 19, 21, 22–25
arrested, in jail, 18–21, 48, 60,
258, 346, 352, 429–30; on trial,
case dismissed, 286–88
artwork created by, 288, 299,
342–43
in Aspen, *see* Aspen, Colorado;
Owl Farm, life at
attitude toward blacks or
minorities, 71–72
becomes "doctor," 104–5
day honoring (Hunter S.
Thompson Day), 351–52
deformed leg, 10, 121, 132,
367
documentaries about and
profiles of, 292, 389–90, 403,
406
drug/alcohol addiction of, 96–97,
99, 328, 386; begins, 33, 76;
intervention rejected, 179,
239–42, 338–39, 369–70
and education, 8, 20, 22, 23, 27;
reading, 6, 11, 348

Thompson, Hunter S. (*cont.*)
  and finances, xvii, 46–55, 58, 123,
    148, 173, 226, 243, 330–31,
    384–85; expense account,
    130–31, 137–38, 202–3, 320,
    328–29; speaking gigs, 250–52,
    291–92; Stranahan and, 94,
    138, 341
  "gonzo" behavior of, *see* "Gonzo"
  in Hawaii, 230–33
  jokey questionnaires about, 16
  Key West years, 224–26
  last months of, 367–411; breaks
    leg, 399–400; hip replacement,
    367–70; talent dissipates, 190,
    235, 384 (*see also* suicide, *below*)
  and Lisl Auman case, 389–91,
    418
  method of writing, 158, 175–77;
    saves everything, 15, 344
  as night manager of O'Farrell
    Theatre, 266–67, 269–70
  and politics, 99–100, 102–4,
    380–81; campaigns for office
    of sheriff (Freak Power
    ticket), xiii, 105–16, 129, 155,
    168; Carter campaign (1976),
    208–13; Clinton campaign
    (1992), 305–13; considers
    running for Senate, 188–89;
    Kerry campaign (2004), 403–7;
    McGovern campaign (1972),
    148–49, 153–73 (*see also* Nixon,
    Richard)
  in Puerto Rico, 32, 42, 44–48,
    255; leaves, goes to Bermuda,
    49–52
  in San Francisco, 139, 266; and

  Big Sur, 51–55, 72, 74; Haight-
    Ashbury, 75–88
  sex life, 29–30
  in South America, 56–62, 65, 71,
    255
  speaking gigs, 250–52, 290–92,
    294
  speech (mumbling) of, 183
  suicide, xvi, 412–13, 416–23,
    425–34, 436–37
  and Vietnam War, 200–208
THOMPSON, HUNTER S.,
    writings of
  "Ask Not for Whom the Bell
    Tolls," 170–71
  "The Banshee Screams for
    Buffalo Meat," 145–46
  "The Battle of Aspen," xiii,
    111–12
  Better Than Sex, 310, 311, 332
  "Buffalo Gores a Visitor,"
    266–67
  "Cigarette Key," 225
  The Curse of Lono, 233–35, 399,
    408
  "A Dog Took My Place," xvi,
    245–46
  "Fear and Loathing at the Super
    Bowl," 179, 185
  Fear and Loathing in America, 348,
    356, 434
  "Fear and Loathing in Elko," xvi,
    318–19
  "Fear and Loathing in the Eye of
    the Hurricane," 61–62, 161–62
  "Fear and Loathing in Horse
    Country." *See* "Polo Is My
    Life," *below*

"Fear and Loathing in Saigon," 201

Fear and Loathing on the Campaign Trail '72, 171–74, 185, 233, 332, 402, 435; Hunter's memo about, 166–69

Fire in the Nuts, 415

"Freak Power in the Rockies," 128

Generation of Swine, 344

The Gonzo Papers, 345, 419

The Great Shark Hunt, 195, 237, 435

Hey Rube, 386

"Interdicted Dispatch from the Global Affairs Desk," 204–5

"The Kentucky Derby Is Decadent and Depraved," 110, 122–26

The Kingdom of Fear, 392, 422, 424

memorial piece on Allen Ginsberg, 362

memos to Jann Wenner, 134–36, 166–69

"The Night Manager," 266

Nixon's obituary, 314–15

"Open Letter to the Youth of Our Nation," 15–16

"Polo Is My Life," xvi, 273–75, 298, 318, 320, 326–27, 331

"Popo the Killer Jap," 26

Prince Jellyfish, 32, 40, 63

The Proud Highway, 346, 348, 361, 420

reading aloud from, 374, 385, 402–3, 408, 417, 418, 423

as reporter for *Command Courier* (air force base newspaper),

23–25; ESPN, 383–84, 390, 398, 401, 402, 418, 423; *Fort Walton Playground News,* 23, 24; *Rolling Stone, see Rolling Stone* magazine; *San Francisco Examiner,* 266, 384

The Rum Diary, 16–17, 10, 62–63, 330–31, 344, 401

Screwjack, 422

"Security," 16

The Silk Road planned, 236

Songs of the Doomed, 275, 278, 344; storyboards for, 254, 255, 273–74

"The Strange and Terrible Saga of the Outlaw Motorcycle Gangs," 86–88

"Strange Rumblings in Aztlan," 128, 129

"Turbo Must Die," 275

"Voodoo Country," 47

"While the Delegates Slept," 268

See also Fear and Loathing in Las Vegas; Hell's Angels

Thompson, Jack (father), 4, 10–11, 372

Thompson, Jack Jr. (brother), 4

Thompson, Jennifer (daughter-in-law), 368, 370–71, 395, 423, 425–26

Thompson, Jim (brother), 6, 64, 313–14, 430

Thompson, Juan Fitzgerald (son), 67–69, 70–71, 75–76, 81, 85 childhood of, 117–18, 147, 151, 192, 213, 218–19, 317; in school, 152, 153–54, 222–23

Thompson, Juan Fitzgerald (son)
(cont.)
    Hunter's relationship with, 249–
    50, 253, 352–53, 370–73, 383,
    401, 428; early years, 77, 95–96,
    117, 154, 193–94, 219, 221,
    229; Hunter's letters to, 285;
    Hunter as seen by, 377–80,
    392; last years, 367–73, 393–97;
    tribute to Hunter, 351
    Hunter's suicide, 412–13, 419,
    423–27
Thompson, Sandy (first wife)
    first meets, follows Hunter,
    39–42, 46–61, 63, 433–34
    and Hunter's writing, 123, 125,
    174
    marriage, 3, 64–71, 74, 75–77,
    81–82, 85, 94–100, 147,
    157–58, 207, 213; finances, 52,
    55, 173; Hunter's treatment
    of, 154, 193–95, 219–20;
    pregnancies, birth of son,
    deaths of later babies, 54–55,
    67–69, 151–52, 346; sheriff
    campaign, 108; son in school,
    153; in therapy, 192–93,
    194–95
    marriage ends, 196, 218–23, 378;
    cares for Hunter's brother Jim,
    313–14; Hunter's letters to, 346
Thompson, Sara (infant daughter),
    68–69
Thompson, Virginia Ray (mother),
    3–4, 6, 10–11, 13, 63–65, 123,
    314
    Hunter's letters to, 19–20, 346
    pride of, in son, 351–53

Thompson, Will (grandson), 368,
    371–72, 380, 383, 423, 425–26
Time magazine, 28, 29, 38, 179
Time Out magazine, 248
Tinker, Tailor, Soldier, Spy (le Carré),
    292
Tobia, George, 334–36, 389, 401
"Too Much Fun Club," xxi
Torgrimson, Hank, 135
To Tell the Truth (TV show), 313
Trainspotting (movie), 431
Trudeau, Garry, 198–99
Truman, Harry, 309
"Turbo Must Die" (Thompson), 275
Tuschman, Sari, 402–3
Twain, Mark, 344, 347, 417, 436
Tyrrell, Gerald, 6, 8–10, 18, 28,
    64–65

Ulysses (Joyce), 45
U.S.A. (Dos Passos), 45

Vanderbilt, Gloria, 244
Van Ness, John, 295–96
Van Zandt, Townes, 332
Ventura, Jesse, 381
Vietnam War, 148, 200–202, 203
    Hunter's dispatches on, 204–8
Viking Press, 40, 43, 44
von Renkl, Kallen, 214, 272, 338
"Voodoo Country" (Thompson),
    47

Wagner, Carl, 186, 187
Walinsky, Adam, 186
Walker, Jerry Jeff, 332
Walsh, John, 185, 383, 385
Washington Post, 161, 198–99

Watergate scandal, 138, 179, 188, 200, 208

Watts, Alan, 53

Weaver, Tex, 256–58, 421

Web and the Rock, The (Wolfe), 128

Wenner, Jane, 147, 150–51, 317–18

Wenner, Jann, 132, 146, 150 52, 173, 199, 302, 389

and Elko conference, 185–87, 188

and Hunter's expenses, 130–31, 137–38, 202–3, 275, 320, 328–29

and Hunter's personality, 139, 141, 143–44, 177–78, 197–98, 298, 340–41, 375–76; Hunter's drug addiction, 240–42, 328, 386; Hunter's treatment of Sandy, 154, 195–96

Hunter's relationship with, 127–28, 179–80, 317, 325; contact broken, 243–44, 247, 290, 387; last months, last message, 410, 420; letter from, xvii

Hunter's shotgun-art portrait of, 299

and Hunter's writing, 129, 133–34, 138–39, 169, 208–9, 230, 318; deadlines, 175–77; Hunter's memos about, 134–36, 166–69; movie script, 225; New Journalism, 142–43; political, 161, 179, 185; talent dissipates, 190, 235, 384–87; Vietnam, 200–201

party for anniversary of *Vegas,* 351

and politics: Clinton campaign,

305, 307–8, 309; Hunter's campaign for sheriff, 110–11, 114; Kerry campaign, 404–5; McGovern campaign, 148–49, 154–55, 156, 159, 164–65

West, Jerry, 9

Where the Buffalo Roam (movie), 226, 227, 237

"While the Delegates Slept" (Thompson), 268

Whitehead, Ron, 351

Whitman, Walt, 309

Whitmire, Carrol, 101, 105, 106–7, 115

Why Are We in Vietnam? (Mailer), 435

Wilbur, John, 399

Williams, Robin, 268

Wolfe, Thomas, 128

Wolfe, Tom, 88, 128, 142–43, 337, 344, 382, 436, 448

Woody Creek Manifesto, 374

Woody Creek Rod & Gun Club, 275

Woody Creek Tavern, xx, 251, 277, 310, 341

World Cup soccer tournament, bet on, xxii–xxiii

World War II, 4, 5

Wreckers, the, 17

Wright, Sondi. *See* Thompson, Sandy

Wycoff, Barney, 343

Xerox corporation, 150

Zaire, Ali-Foreman fight in, 190–92, 208

Zevon, Warren, 332, 391

ABOUT THE AUTHORS

✠

Jann S. Wenner is the founder, editor, and publisher of *Rolling Stone*. He was Hunter Thompson's editor for thirty-five years.

Corey Seymour is a writer and editor who worked with Hunter Thompson at *Rolling Stone* in the 1990s.

ALSO LOOK FOR

THE ROLLING STONE INTERVIEWS

Edited by Jann S. Wenner and Joe Levy

Introduction by Jann S. Wenner

Since 1967, the *Rolling Stone* interview has been the centerpiece of the most important American magazine of its generation. It is the imprimatur of cultural significance, the place where our greatest rock stars, movie stars, and icons unveil their true selves as nowhere else. Now, for the first time, forty of the best interviews from the magazine's remarkable forty-year history have been collected in a single volume. Including interviews with:

John Lennon	Spike Lee
Ray Charles	Bruce Springsteen
Truman Capote	David Letterman
Joni Mitchell	Kurt Cobain
Jack Nicholson	Courtney Love
Bill Murray	Mick Jagger
Clint Eastwood	Bill Clinton
Eric Clapton	The Dalai Lama
Tina Turner	Bob Dylan
Robin Williams	Eminem

and twenty others. *The Rolling Stone Interviews* is more than a collection; it's a cultural history, a portrait of the defining figures of our times and of the times themselves.

Back Bay Books • Available wherever paperbacks are sold